MACKENZIE KING

MACKENZIE KING

MACKENZIE KING

The Incredible Canadian

By

BRUCE HUTCHISON

LONGMANS, GREEN AND CO

LONDON ⬦ NEW YORK ⬦ TORONTO

LONGMANS, GREEN AND CO LTD
6 & 7 CLIFFORD STREET LONDON W I
ALSO AT MELBOURNE AND CAPE TOWN

LONGMANS, GREEN AND CO INC
55 FIFTH AVENUE NEW YORK 3

LONGMANS, GREEN AND CO
215 VICTORIA STREET TORONTO I

ORIENT LONGMANS LTD
BOMBAY CALCUTTA MADRAS

First published in Canada 1952 under the title
The Incredible Canadian
This Edition first published 1953

PRINTED IN GREAT BRITAIN BY
LOWE AND BRYDONE (PRINTERS) LIMITED, LONDON, N.W.10

TO

Grant   Dexter

AFTER THIRTY YEARS OF JOINT

LABOR, FRIENDSHIP, AND

UNDERSTANDING

A *

Foreword

THE ORIGIN OF THIS BOOK IS TO BE FOUND ON A FORGOTTEN PAGE OF THE
Canadian parliamentary record for January, 1942, wherein the late
R. B. Hanson, leader of the Opposition, is quoted as discussing, in
a rather homely and gauche fashion (as was that darling old gentleman's habit), the character of W. L. Mackenzie King, Prime Minister of Canada.

A previous book by this writer had said that, on occasion, King
found it necessary to cut the throats of friends and enemies, always
in the interests of the public welfare. Hanson, with comical relish,
asked King if that was an accurate description of his methods. King
replied: "That is the only way to treat certain classes of enemies."
He added that if his honorable friend was going to take this writer
"as authority for my character . . . I am ready to abide by Mr.
Hutchison's decision."

The Prime Minister's careless retort seemed to offer an invitation,
even a challenge, though none, of course, was intended. From that
day forward I planned eventually to write a book on King. It took
longer than I had expected. The work proceeded in fragmentary and
disjointed fashion over the years. I soon found it impossible to separate the individual man from the collective substance of the nation
which he dominated for some three decades. Consequently, this
book is an attempt to study a Canadian era and many of its major
inhabitants—an era of great men, great events, great achievements
in Canada, and bitter disappointments.

From that era we inherit the present. The teeming years of King,
his friends, his enemies, and his people, may be worth examination
if the present is to be understood and mastered.

This book is not an authorized or even a detailed biography. It
does not pretend to be anything like a complete study of King or of

his era and it is solely the writer's interpretation of both. Some of King's friends and many of his enemies will quarrel with the opinions offered here. In a subject so large as King and his times—the man and the myth, two entirely different things—opinions are certain to vary and, in time, to produce a substantial library of contradictory versions.

This version is the work of one not specially equipped by personal knowledge. I knew King, long short of intimacy, throughout the thirty years of his life as a political leader but I have depended far less on my own observations as a working newspaperman than on the help of many persons who were as close to him as any man could be, who knew all the facts but differed sharply in their conclusions. What may possibly prove to be the most controversial passages recorded herein came directly from King himself, as indicated in the text.

After his rash assurance to Hanson, I doubt that King would be satisfied with the resulting portrait. It is candid, as the reader will see, it has no sanction save a casual remark in a parliamentary debate, and perhaps if he were alive King would regret that jest.

I am indebted in what follows to innumerable persons. The evidence, taken over so long a time and in so many places, has been merged so completely in the memory that the individual contribution of each cannot be identified or even remembered. None of the witnesses, I feel sure, will agree wholly with the verdict of the writer and none can be held responsible for that verdict or for the evidence underlying it.

I am also under a heavy obligation to Christine Fox and Hilda Weston, whose assistance in researching written material and preparing the manuscript for publication was invaluable.

B. H.

Victoria, B. C.
June, 1952.

Contents

ix

Illustrations

(*All photographs are by Karsh of Ottawa—Camera Press Ltd.*)

1

The Man and the Land

THE MYSTERY OF WILLIAM LYON MACKENZIE KING IS NOT THE mystery of a man. It is the mystery of a people. We do not understand King because we do not understand ourselves.

The full knowledge of both may be some time off. Meanwhile, it is impossible to know whence we Canadians have come in the last half century, where we are now, or where we are likely to go without grasping King's subtle, all-pervading impact upon the nation's life. The two things, man and nation, are inseparable. And they are equal in their massive contradictions.

This man never truly felt the physical presence, the texture, size, and flavor of Canada as many ordinary men have felt them. The whole sprawling substance, the shattering skies, the cruel winds, the empty earth, the sound of rivers and breaking ice, the chatter of children, the accents of love, the agonies, the triumphs of ordinary men, and all the whisperings of the lonely Canadian life were known to King's mind, for he knew everything. To his inner nature they came as mere facts, relevant to his public career but hardly touching the central fact of his own life, which was concerned with death.

Yet better than any man—by a unique feat of intellect, by a kind of osmosis and guess—this least typical of Canadians summed up by his own contradictions the whole amorphous life stuff of the Canadian creaturehood. With an equipment beyond his own understanding he articulated and then managed the dark, invisible workmanship which holds the nation together. This is the mystery of King and of Canada, in silent compact.

Just as Canada, built against all logic, the laws of geography, the forces of economics, and the accepted theories of politics, became larger than the sum of its parts, so King built a personal achievement incomparably larger than himself. Both the nation and the man who dominated it for nearly thirty decisive years combined the elements of natural weakness into a product of strength. In this chemical process of action and reaction between man and nation it is never clear who led and who followed.

Had he lived in any other place King would have climbed surely to eminence. He was born to climb. While the accident of birth confined him to a nation small in numbers, the history of contemporary politics shows few parallels to his private and public careers, in themselves the greatest contradiction of all. The history of Canada, even the record of Macdonald and Laurier, shows none.

By the public measurement of statesmanship King was the greatest Canadian. By the private measurement of character, by the dimensions of the man himself, his two predecessors tower above him. As a human being he was dwarfed by many other Canadians of the past, even by his grandfather, the broken Rebel, by some men whom he destroyed in his own lifetime, and by millions of others who trod the trails, the furrows, and the back streets of Canada.

However the current riddle of Canada may be dissected in the future, at the core will be found the enigma of King, who was its authentic expression. As Canada is the least understood nation, so King is the least understood statesman of our era. Outwardly the dullest, he was inwardly the most vivid, fascinating, and improbable issue of the Canadian race. The mystery grows, the fascination deepens, and the enigma retreats farther from our clutch when the private man emerges and suddenly is overtopped by the public shadow.

That single fact, more than any other, explains the mystery of King and his Canada—he, like the nation, was bitterly aware of his own stature, he was determined to be larger than his nature ordained, and, in the affairs of this world, he and the nation succeeded.

The affairs of this world were only the visible half of King. The other half of his mind and all his instincts were fixed on a world beyond the grave. Haunted by death, hagridden by a sense of original sin, engulfed in the black tides of time, always hurrying to the end of a brief journey, he erected his public career to vindicate himself to himself, to his rebel grandfather, to his mother, to mankind, and to God, before he moved on.

His reward was not his public achievement, great as that must be counted by any reckoning, but his secret vindication. He was the apotheosis of the self-made man. Considering the materials he had to work with, he was Canada's unequaled success story.

Nevertheless, the savor of worldly triumph, the taste of fame, the sweet tang of power were pleasant in his mouth and his appetite for them was insatiable. He loved the world and he loved King, the corporeal man. Neither fully satisfied him. He seemed to be seeking the welfare of humanity and of King in equal parts; in fact, he was seeking communication with the dead and awaiting the day when he would join them.

He was seismographic in registering every tremor of public opinion, but his real advisers lived on the other side of things. His reliable colleagues and only real friends were all dead.

Beside his intimations of immortality all the uses of this world grew steadily more weary, stale, flat, and unprofitable. Still he clung to them. He grasped greedily for money, creature comforts, and public rewards, never sure that he could grasp anything more. He wanted the best of two possible worlds. Assuredly he got the best of this one.

Here, too, a rough Canadian parallel can be discerned—the half-formed, uncertain nation, like its leader, was yearning for something distant, impalpable, and better than itself. The reach must exceed the grasp or what was a heaven for? King, the individual man, perhaps could find heaven. The nation reaches still, and must always reach, for what it knows not.

Like the people of whom he became the common denominator and mean temperature, King was ambivalent. More than ambivalent, he contained a dozen different characters all in endless struggle, as varied as the races, zones, economic groupings, and local characteristics of Canada.

In the first place, King was a scholar, historian, and philosopher of politics. In factual knowledge he made his friend Roosevelt (a man of nobler mold) appear sadly uneducated and sometimes alarming in his ignorance. Beside King's radicalism, his other friend, Churchill, despite some far superior gifts, became a splendid anachronism.

In his other countless mutations King was also a devious party manager who never missed a trick nor spared an enemy, a wily caucus manipulator, a simple country squire, an attentive host, an implacable hater, and a reckless plunger as the occasion required.

He made himself the supreme court of his Party and administered singlehanded justice without mercy. His allies were rewarded. He extinguished his rivals, wrecked the career of Arthur Meighen, drove the igneous Bennett into the refuge of the Lord, dismissed the great-hearted Ralston in the middle of a cabinet meeting with a stroke peculiarly despicable, and cut the throats of his friends with deft razor strokes whenever necessary, as he once gleefully admitted to Parliament.

Again, with the same sincerity, he was the humble Christian, on barefoot pilgrimage. He was also the paramount egotist of his time. He was the man who loved physical ease, rich food, expensive clothes, and unquestioning service. In public he proclaimed and in private believed the eternal verities, and on the wall of his bathroom he hung a disagreeable placard advising his guests how to keep their bowels in order.

He mourned with genuine sorrow the death of obscure men and women, befriended youngsters, conducted secret charities, and pampered his dogs. He was a passionate social reformer, obsessed with the destitution of mankind. He was so terrified of personal poverty that he piled up a millionaire's fortune, mostly in gifts from his rich friends, while persuading himself that he was too poor to repair the tattered furniture of Laurier House. He was always sending notes and flowers to console the bereaved but he rode his secretaries to nervous breakdowns and, sleeping late himself, would make his ministers sit hungry and exhausted through the lunch hour.

He was modest, boyish, and charming in his home. He was prostrate before the Divinity and the electorate. Before his Cabinet he was a crafty autocrat. A meticulous administrator, he would fuss over the minute details of business and then drop the government of Canada for a week while arranging a banquet and flying into a passion because the menu included beans instead of peas with roast lamb.

Under all this ran a sense of humor too deep for the public to suspect. His public jests were so rare that they became headlines— as when, asked by an indignant back-bencher from the Doukhobor country what he would do if he faced a parade of naked women, he looked over at Bennett, a bachelor and a lady's man, and blandly retorted: "I'd send for the Leader of the Opposition." He was cold, courteous, correct, and diffuse in Parliament, usually tedious and sometimes crudely sentimental on the platform but in his office his eyes sparkled with a cynical wit, he gaily lampooned his colleagues and discussed the sworn secrets of Cabinet with the wildest abandon.

In his final paradox, this the man who understood the social movements of the twentieth century as well as any contemporary statesman remained to his dying day a child of the nineteenth, a gentleman of the old school, and an unconscious snob. The radical, for all his public policies, died a disillusioned conservative in the larger affairs of mankind.

The Canadian people never divined this infinite variety. They saw only his set public act, the round little figure with hunched shoulders, the flat and homely face, the wisp of hair on the bald head, the antique collar and cuffs, the delicate hands, the bouncing, cautious gait of one walking on invisible eggs. Altogether a physical being who, even through the inspired lens of Yousuf Karsh, could never appear more than commonplace because he would never share and finally could not be himself.

As an actor, King was the superior of Roosevelt and Churchill, since he mastered a much more cunning act. Roosevelt's chosen role as the Great Guy and Churchill's as the reincarnated Elizabethan were obvious and relatively easy. King's drab impersonation of the common man—the last thing he ever was—required the highest kind of histrionic genius. It succeeded so well that the people accepted a caricature which he had deliberately contrived for his own purposes. Behind it raged the battle of many different Kings and the two worlds which divided them.

To the end he kept his secret. The caricature already becomes a legend to mislead all future Canadians. A King who never existed is erected as a statue. The man is as unrecognizable in death as in life, precisely as he desired. Through spiritualistic mediums he sought the other world but in this temporary abode he took infinite pains, and even built his own stone ruins at Kingsmere to be remembered for something he was not. The disguise deceived its own creator. He came to believe utterly in a fairy-tale hero of his own imagining.

If the Canadian people also believed in a fictitious King, they never liked him. At times they hated him and often laughed at his diminutive figure in the newsreels. But they came to respect him as they respected no other leader, they relied on him as on the seasons, and when he died they missed him as a comfortable piece of furniture which had long served in every Canadian home.

Grudgingly, in its Arctic fashion, the nation concluded, only when he had gone, that it had lost its indispensable man. This, as it turned out, was not true, but in retrospect no one can deny that he had become the unchallenged master of his times in Canada, the replica of his people. The being nature had writ small defied his dimensions and bestrode the nation like a homemade Colossus.

While the strands of such a tangled personage may never be sorted out, it is relatively simple to fit King into the history of the Canadian era which will be called forever by his name. His works proclaim themselves, but quietly. He wrought them so gradually, he who could move so fast and take so many desperate chances while appearing to stand still, and he could produce such drastic changes with a changeless look, that his revolutionary effect on the nation's life was dimly surmised when his own ended. By now we can see that he was our greatest revolutionary, a wilder heretic than his grandfather, operating on a wider stage.

The factual catalogue of his career is most of the record of Canada through more than three decades. It should be briefly noted before the full portrait of his life and times can be examined.

He found a Liberal Party in opposition and ruin. He gave it a longer term of office under one leader than any party had ever known in any English-speaking state; he created a juggernaut which won seven national elections and lost only one, and it was better lost; he left no other truly national party upon the landscape.

More important, he found a Liberal theory of the nineteenth century—doctrinaire, obsolete, cranky, constipated—and, without altering a label or seeming to shift anything, transformed it into an opposite doctrine for the twentieth. Only when he laid down his tools did Liberalism awake to see that it had been carved into a new shape, painlessly, in the night. Even then it did not realize that this was what King had planned thirty years before.

He found a people divided, quarreling, and weak. He left them reconciled, united, and strong as they had never been before.

He found a nation primitive and depressed. He left it with a living standard never exceeded in all history except by the United States.

He found an economic system called Capitalism. For better or worse, but beyond repeal, he ushered in the Welfare State.

He found a nation of nine provinces and left it with ten. By persuading Newfoundland into Confederation he prevented it from falling ultimately into the hands of the United States and thus, as he believed, saved Canada from such an enfilading pressure of Manifest Destiny across its Atlantic gateway as might well have doomed its future existence.

He found a state which, in spirit, was just emerging from colonialism. He established its autonomy beyond dispute, destroyed the last attempt to reconsolidate the Commonwealth with a single voice in London, and brought Canada closer in solid friendship to Britain and the United States than it had ever been.

He found a people deep in isolationism and he deepened it. Then, lacking a spark of martial fire, detesting physical violence, which he had never experienced, he led Canada through its greatest war, made it a principal among the victors, and, despite this huge dislocation, returned it to peace with hardly a ripple of disturbance. Having embraced internationalism and even world government, having seen a brief vision of humanity set free, he ended his life a convinced pessimist, with no faith in the United Nations, no doubt that men's affairs were ruled by naked power, no confidence of avoiding a final world war, and no assurance that civilization could survive.

As his greatest work, by his own estimate, he found the old racial gulf of Canada newly widened and he bridged it where even Laurier had failed, but only after the most shattering cabinet crisis and the strangest untold tale of our history, after reaching the edge of personal ruin and national chaos, after resisting conscription to the eleventh hour and accepting it in the face of a military uprising which he had invented by self-hypnosis to save his Government, his nation, and himself.

Taken together, these achievements, each enough for one lifetime, will remain as King's monuments long after the synthetic walls of Kingsmere have become the ruin of a ruin. Against his successes must be set his two prodigious failures.

The first and the gravest failure of his life was his misunderstanding of the world's drift to war and anarchy, his refusal to admit Canada's inevitable place in this process or to prepare his people for it, his amazing miscalculation of Hitler, whom he met and described as a harmless and rather stupid peasant. Secondly, as a domestic statesman, while he piled his reforms silently on one another until the total product grew like sedimentary rock, he was never able to breathe the feeling of life into the thing he built. He could lead the nation. He could never voice and perhaps did not feel its dream. It asked for some glint of magic in the darkness of those times. From him it had to be satisfied with a steady candle flame of competence.

Perhaps this was the only kind of leadership which a nation of conflicting interests could endure. Certainly the men of flame and passion, the Meighens and Bennetts, consumed themselves and their governments like suicidal moths and gravely burned the nation's unity in the process. King's candle was safe, but the man who held it must die only as the nation's leader, not as its idol or even as its friend.

Weighing success against failure, one must conclude that for volume and variety our Canadian registry holds no equivalent to his handiwork. There have been only two Canadians who challenge his place as a statesman, but Macdonald and Laurier dealt with problems far simpler than world war and revolution in which King swam blindly, without a chart. They were greater men. He was the greater statesman.

How, history will ask, did such a man achieve something so much larger than himself? To answer that it will be necessary to follow his life in detail. His actual methods of government are clear enough at a glance. Once, in a revealing moment, he described them to a friend as they strolled on the bank of the Ottawa.

"If," said King, pointing to a distant church spire beyond a bend in the river, "I try to reach that point directly I shall drown. I must follow the curves of the bank and ultimately I shall get there, though at times I may seem to be going somewhere else."

In the ceaseless zigzags of his administration he was often and rightly accused of inconsistency, but he always knew where he was going and, above all, he knew how fast he could go. A Prime Minister, as he told his friend that day, must be a sponge, patiently soaking up the diverse trickles of public feeling until the time comes to extrude a policy. Only then, when a majority opinion has clearly formed, can a policy hope to work in this diverse country.

There was the method—the distant objective, the curving course of circumstance, the patient waiting for the tide of fortune to rise and then its sudden taking at the flood.

His art was the calculation of the flood. The oddest legend about King is that he made few mistakes because his judgments were formed deliberately on facts. In his largest verdicts he disregarded facts altogether and resorted to pure instinct.

A few days before his death, he remarked: "The popular theory that I spent immeasurable hours pondering my problems is ridiculous. An issue exists for me by intuition or not at all. I either see it at once or it means nothing to me. I decide my policy right away. I may spend much time planning how to defend it but I know from the start what I want to do and how to do it."

Thus instructed by his daemon, he would retire into the silences of Kingsmere and there drudgingly dredge up facts to support and justify the decision already made. In a few days he would return with a clear policy buttressed by the logic which he had attached to it as an afterthought.

A Prime Minister who rejects the experiment of children's allowances and then, overnight, is converted to it by the moving story of a youth raised on the pension of a dead soldier cannot be called a man of visible facts. He is basically a man of emotion, in his worst moments a mere sentimentalist, in his best a human being who feels the hungry fellowship of his kind.

This method of decision first and factual interpretation later explains King's orotund and tortured speeches. He lacked oratory, that almost essential equipment of statecraft, except in a few inspired moments when he had no time to prepare his words.

His only formidable opponents, Meighen and Bennett, could outshine him in any platform contest and this always hurt his pride. Meighen's frigid pinpricks drove him to anger and then to hatred and at last to an irrational, almost childish horror. Bennett outblustered him in the House, overwhelmed him with a kind of volatile marsh gas, but King never hated Bennett because he knew that when the vapor had ignited and burned out, the ashes would be his enemy's. King would bob up again, incombustible.

He distrusted conventional color either in speech or action, not because he failed to appreciate it in others like Churchill and Roosevelt, or because he would not gladly have used it himself, but because he knew he could never achieve it and would look ridiculous if he tried.

By the usual contradiction he attained an unconventional color of his own, a drab color, a shadowy gray. It took time to acquire but was worth waiting for since it was fast and would not bleach out. The audiences who smirked at his image in the newsreels turned up at the polls next day to vote for the indispensable man.

Besides oratory and flash, King lacked all the physical attributes of leadership except the most vital of all, an iron constitution. While athletic colleagues worried themselves into illness, he, with soft hands and flabby muscles, slept soundly, except for two nights, through the worst years of the war and never lost his appetite. He coddled his health, watched his diet, rationed his exertions, and lived as regularly as a grandfather clock. After its length and unbroken chain of crisis his career was a triumph in body as in mind.

A man so conceived and so completely self-dedicated could not expect or wish to have many friends. Those most familiar with King, the statesman, could hardly name a single person who would call King, the man, a friend. He conducted an endless handwritten correspondence with unknown people all over the nation, he sometimes read poetry to an aged lady beside the brooks of Kingsmere, but it almost seemed that when his first youthful friend drowned he forswore friendship as too painful and distracting. His recipe for safe human association is well known: "I've always found you can control people better if you don't see too much of them."

Still, it was typical of King's perversity that he liked to think he had troops of friends. He exploded with anger when the late Professor E. K. Brown, one of his frustrated speech writers, asserted in a magazine article that King was friendless. Toward the end, King knew it was true. He died a lonely and despondent old man, rebuffing those who came to pay him tribute.

Even the solidarity of his Cabinets was a charade which kept the chief actor perpetually amused. He encouraged the feuds of his Ministers because their divisions strengthened him. Often he disagreed with policies executed in his name, denounced them indignantly in private, and was always chuckling at the Opposition's failure to see his colleagues' obvious blunders.

He never forgave Ralston, whom he apparently had destroyed, because he knew that Ralston was the only man who in fact had defeated him. Crerar, Ilsley, and Angus Macdonald he could hardly tolerate, and they ardently reciprocated his feelings. Gardiner he regarded as an eccentric western comet in constant collision with Liberal principles but uncontrollable. Howe he considered the ablest organizer of his time and a political ignoramus. Dunning, his only serious rival, he engorged at leisure. St. Laurent came to him by accident, grew on him slowly, was once rebuked before the whole Cabinet, threatened to resign, secured an apology, and was chosen as the next Prime Minister by King's skillful management. Only Lapointe could be trusted absolutely and even Lapointe, the single colleague who dared to call him by his boyhood nickname of "Rex," never entered the inner shrine.

These things are understandable. Psychologists will never cease to disagree about what is most obvious in other men, King's relations with women. A woman, his mother, dominated him long after she was dead. But that interesting coterie which has worn itself out hating King and sleuthing the secrets of his life can find no other woman in it, only a few clumsy and boyish flirtations. He remained a bachelor because he considered himself too poor to marry and felt no need for women. Yet he had a woman's mind with all its intuitions. Intellectually he was almost more feminine than masculine, the most successful spinster of his age.

Finally, before it is considered in detail, this solitary pilgrimage must be judged in some substantial part as an exercise in sheer luck. A freak of fortune, a chance in a thousand, saved his career when it appeared finished after a short morning glory. The continuing accident of incompetent opposition followed him faithfully to his last days. If this was luck, he knew how to make it work for him, to exploit every break in the game, to profit by his enemy's smallest mistake.

He believed implicitly in luck and propitiated it with comic zeal. The numeral seven, he said, was favorable to his enterprises. He liked to launch them on the seventh day of the month or in the seventh month of the year. If possible, he would take no decisive step until the hands of the clock were directly opposite each other in a straight line. The Christian was filled with these pagan superstitions.

The combination of genius and chance required time for its consummation. With his equipment King could not hope for quick success. He could not blast the solid substance of Canada as Macdonald and Laurier had blasted it or even make the small dents left by the Meighens and Bennetts before the current swept them down. The rock must be worn away by steady drip, invisibly over the years.

His was a slow, pedestrian odyssey, a foot journey of infinite weariness and perpetual change of direction, toward the distant spire. Did he reach it? No man will ever know the answer. We can be sure, however, that King got exactly what he wanted and planned to get out of this world. He got power, vindication, a sense of divine approval, and an assurance of entry into the world to come.

You could read the log of that journey on his face. The plump, round, and spiritless visage of youth, the almost weak look of his first premiership, gradually took on the veining of granite. His eyes at times acquired the mystic's stare at a far-off horizon line. The man born small had grown large beyond belief. His minute handwriting lay scrawled in black, indelible signature across his native earth. When it reclaimed him an age was ended in Canada. The new age could never escape his legacy or possess his secret.

2

The Rebel's Grandson

THE TWO MEN MOST RESPONSIBLE FOR KING'S PUBLIC CAREER WERE absent at his birth. The woman who would dominate his entire life, public and private, was alone at its beginning—a portent unnoted but notable.

On the snowbound night of December 17, 1874, in Berlin,[1] Ontario, the father had gone to a political meeting when his first son arrived. The grandfather was dead. While the father could give the child from his first hours the surroundings of politics, a good education, the right mixture of gentility and common life in a little Canadian town, it was the dead grandfather, more than anyone else, who, through the sole agency of his daughter, made King into a Prime Minister. The feverish specter of the Canadian Rebel, William Lyon Mackenzie, haunted the infant and dogged the man. The mother made sure of that.

She had been born in the United States, an exile from the Rebellion of '37, the last of five children reared in poverty, hunger, and the disgrace of treason. Isabel Mackenzie had watched her brothers and sisters die. She saw in her first son the chance to redeem the name of her father. That name was given to the child as a title of honor, a challenge, and a sacred trust. It was also, for a politician, a heavy burden.

On King's birthday the Rebellion was behind him only thirty-seven years. His grandfather had been pardoned and re-elected to Parliament but his name still stood for treason. Fortunately, heredity had given King an equal inheritance of loyalty and conservatism. His father, John King, was the son of a professional Scots soldier of the Royal Horse Artillery, who had helped to extinguish the Rebellion. Thus in his parents—the odd combination of the Loyalist's son and the Rebel's daughter—King inherited both sides of the struggle

[1] Later, in 1916, the town's name was changed to Kitchener.

which produced modern Canada. To this long story he was to add his own chapter.

From the beginning he chose the side of his maternal grandfather, the Rebel. He had no option. His mother gave him not only the Rebel's name and blood but a legend of sacrifice, heroism, and reform which must fire the dullest boy. King was not dull. At a time when other boys were absorbed in play, his mind was ignited by his mother's tales of the barricades at York, the exile and the return.

As soon as he could know anything he learned the story of the Family Compact; the embattled Patriots with blunderbuss, home-made pike, and wooden club at Montgomery's Tavern; the Rebel astride a horse in clumsy imitation of George Washington; the absurd skirmish, both rabbles in flight from each other; Mackenzie's retreat through Hogg's Hollow; his escape across the Niagara disguised as an old woman (a disguise which King would often wear himself in times of retreat); the years of exile and foreign jail; the execution and deportation of comrades; the Durham report; the dawn of Responsible Government.

To most Canadians of King's youth these events had a comic or criminal flavor. The Rebel was remembered as an annoying crank, a Tiny Creature, as the fatuous Governor Bond Head had called him, with cadaverous face and burning, fanatic eye, who had caused much unnecessary trouble and the death of better men.

To the boy in Berlin, the Rebel must have loomed gigantic as a native Cromwell. The scared farmers of '37 took on the look of heroes. The blunderbuss, pike, and club were the weapons of freedom in Canada as they had been in England more than two centuries before. Of all this glory King was to be the inheritor, protector, and vindicator. A formidable freight of destiny for one small boy to carry.

Amid all these stirring memories the home life of the Kings in Berlin was simple and, by the standards of those days, well-to-do, cultured, and genteel. Its foundation was an idyllic love affair. In the parents the boy beheld an unbroken affection between man and woman such as he could never experience. Love of this sort was outside his nature but its appearance in his parents helped to shape him.

So did the easy, prosperous, and Victorian rhythm of the home. His father had made himself the leading lawyer of the town, read well, wrote in the newspapers, spoke in public with eloquence and in the home with gentleness, took an active interest in the Liberal Party, but, preferring his profession and a student's life to politics, refused a seat in Parliament. With this kindly and understanding nature he achieved the rare parental triumph of making the son his friend.

The boy adored his mother blindly. To her and only her, King gave his whole self. The study of his life begins and ends in that woman's tender dominion. Isabel King, though jealous of her father's fame, ambitious for her family, and frail from her early privations, was a woman of extraordinary sweetness—saintly, mystical, yet playful, the boisterous companion of the children's games. Probably she alone, among all who knew him, ever understood her son.

The household, including King's elder sister Isabel, his younger sister Janet, and his younger brother Macdougall, showed no signs of distinction. The Kings were small gentry when gentility still counted for something in Canada. The town knew them as good citizens and friendly neighbors. Mrs. King's treasonable origin had been forgiven or forgotten.

Already there was being planted in young Billy a certain attitude of mind which he could never quite outgrow. For all his pride in his grandfather and all his love of his parents, he secretly suspected as he grew older that Conservatives, while wrong politically, were socially superior to Liberals. Such were the mores of that time and King was their product. A kind of upside-down snobbishness, a well-hidden but nonetheless powerful inferiority complex, clung to him throughout life.

When the first son was eight years old, the family moved from the modest house of his birth on Benton Street to "Woodside," a ten-room establishment on Spring Street at the outskirts of the town. John King had been getting on. His new home, set among acres of lawn and spinney, was almost a mansion by prevailing standards. Its gables and vine-clustered windows had an old-fashioned English air which exercised an influence upon the son much deeper than a boy could realize.

Young Billy King experienced his first touch of good living early and never lost the taste for it. The future radical was brought up in something like privilege, enjoyed it, and always claimed it as his right, but secretly it pricked his conscience. The contrast between his home with its two maids, gardener, and carriage and the poverty of his schoolfellows might disturb him, would unconsciously fashion his public policies; it never would drive him to surrender a fragment of his own comfort.

At Kingsmere and Laurier House he tried later on to reproduce the atmosphere of "Woodside," which had established his domestic climate. Without his mother, or a successor, the old home could not be revived.

Still, in one side of his nature—the conservative side always at war with his radicalism—King never quite outgrew "Woodside." The rather stuffy decorum acquired in infancy colored his manners and part of his mind until the end. He was born and remained, contrary to all his public policies, a gentleman and an essential Victorian. This fact, one of the most decisive and revealing in his career, was established in those formative years of his boyhood which few men ever outgrow.

In the best traditions of greatness Billy displayed no particular talents at school. The teacher observed a very commonplace boy, squat, plump, moon-faced, gregarious, and mischievous. When reproached for standing too often at the bottom of the class he replied, with a certain naïve sophistry which would serve him well later on, that somebody had to stand there. The teacher could find no answer to that. There was seldom an answer to King from then on.

At the Presbyterian Church he was in the habit of mimicking the preacher for the amusement of his brother and sisters. At Sunday school he once tied the teacher's bustle to her chair and, when she stood up, watched the skirt burst apart to the admiration of the pupils. He played hooky and stole apples. He liked to ramble in the woods, to swim in the brook and ride a pony. He was indifferent to athletics (though he finally made the high-school soccer team and played some cricket). In all, an average boy, distinguished only by an iron constitution, his largest asset for the future. To his family he was known as Willie, to everyone else as Billy.

There was in Billy more than met the eye, even the eyes of his parents. The mother who hoped so much for him must have wondered if the plump boy had the makings of another Rebel. The father, busy with his legal practice, was satisfied if Billy remained healthy and well-behaved. Probably neither parent realized how much Billy absorbed, stowed away, and pondered from the evening talk at the dinner table, from the local politicians who were always dropping in to gossip, and from the incessant arguments of a family which thoroughly understood the simple affairs of the day. Billy was learning, as he always would, by ear, and he forgot nothing.

He learned by the written word also. When other boys were reading *Ivanhoe* and the *Leather-stocking Tales* Billy was beginning to pore over his grandfather's musty papers and such histories of the Rebellion as were then in print. He learned by heart the words of the Royal Proclamation offering a reward of £1000 for the Rebel's capture. (As man and Prime Minister he proudly framed that faded document and hung it in his house where all visitors could see it.) He memorized Mackenzie's speeches and such editorial outbursts as "Not to gain the wealth of the Indies would I now cringe to the funguses I have beheld in this country, more pestilential in the

---

Town of York than the marshes and quagmires with which it is environed!"

This was strong medicine for an imaginative boy. Mackenzie's oratory had an antique savor which the grandson adopted for himself, never quite catching the original fire.

Thus King was becoming vaguely in his own mind a product of history and a future maker of it.

Soon the kids at school started to call him the Rebel. He wore the name with a swagger and tried to live up to it. Already bragging that some day he would be a statesman like his grandfather, he was constantly getting into fist fights with his rivals. It is hard in our time to think of him, the conciliator and compromiser, in any kind of physical combat, but so the youthful record stands. This is another primary fact too often forgotten, especially by his enemies—King was a fighter with a courage as fierce as it was concealed. From the childish fisticuffs of the schoolyard to the contest of wits in the cabinet chamber, his life was destined to be an endless fight. He seldom lost. He never forgave a victor.

Even when Billy reached his teens, the age when distinction should begin to show, he remained unmarked by any apparent talent except a slight gift for argument in the debating club. To his friends he was still only a youth who liked to go camping, to dance with the girls (but never to "go steady" with any of them), and, above all, to read.

The habit of reading, which must be accounted another of the basic facts, grew steadily from the example of his parents. His reading was a strange mixture of the Bible, the romantic poets, and dull history. The Bible he read every day of his life, even in the hardest days of office, memorized much of it, and scribbled endless comments and explanations of God's word on the margins of the book. He read ravenously also of politics. Through the books and the talk of the home he was already in love with politics, the only abiding love he was ever to know. When he said he would be a politician it was more than a boy's boast. He guessed early where his path led.

To understand his later work it is necessary to remember the state of Canadian politics in which he was raised. Confederation was only seven years old at his birth. Macdonald, its chief architect, had foundered on the Pacific scandal the year before. The dour Liberal stonemason, Alexander Mackenzie, was struggling, with a hard, uncompromising stonemason's mind, to retrieve the disaster of Macdonald's railway to the west. The Liberal Party, as King's father must have thought, was at the beginning of a long term of government and reform, based on the lofty principles of Gladstone, the sound economics of Adam Smith, and the glories of laissez faire.

The artless beauty of this automatic system, the divine right of Liberalism and the arrogance of reformers who would make men good in spite of themselves, were instilled early into King, and with them that central belief of nineteenth-century Liberalism, the inevitable progress of mankind.

When King was four years old something went temporarily wrong with the Liberal dream. Macdonald, that incorrigible and indestructible old man with the red nose, tired eyes, and spacious heart, had returned to power. His dream outshone Mackenzie's. It stood above principle, geography, economics, and logic. It encompassed a nation too big and too diverse for any textbook.

In Canada the greatest Canadian of the century began to build Canada with his railway, from coast to coast. If Macdonald had ever heard of the plump boy in Berlin young Billy would have appeared to him as among the least likely of all Canadians to inherit that nation and give it dimensions beyond the original architect's wildest hope.

The orbits of the two major Canadian luminaries, the one rising, the other on the wane, were not to touch in life. Assuredly, they came together after the older star had set. King, the Grit, imitated in all essentials the political methods of Macdonald, the Tory. He followed Macdonald's perpetual search for compromise. Like Macdonald, he knew the paramount importance of timing. Like him also, he could set his principles aside until the time was ripe and meanwhile improvise *ad hoc* remedies without principle and often without consistency. King could not make men love him as Macdonald could but he manipulated them just as well. He accepted Macdonald's dictum that a ruling party must hold Quebec. In short, King knew, like Macdonald, that Canada is a difficult country to govern, can never be governed by logic or any single theory.

Old Tomorrow, neck-deep in the congenial conspiracies and huge constructive labors of Ottawa and often deep in liquor; the commonplace and unknown youth in Berlin; the founder of Canada; the future custodian of his handiwork—there was a chancy combination of circumstance worth pause and pondering. Some commonplace youth in an unknown corner of Canada today, King's heir, would be worth pondering also, if we could identify him. No one identified the boy in Berlin. But to him and his family Macdonald was clearly identified as the most dangerous old rogue in Canada. Time and experience would show King the folly of these boyish prejudices.

He was, like all men, the product of his age. Until he went to college he remained strictly conventional, orthodox, Liberal, and Vic-

c

torian. The issues of those times—the railway, the tariff, the British connection, the autonomy of Canada—were all he could know. The greater issues were still far off. They had appeared on the British horizon, where the Socialist movement loomed as a minute cloud in the blue sky of Capitalism, but they were invisible to Canadians, laboring in their wilderness.

That King was to rise above this environment and perceive earlier than his contemporaries the emergence of a new world was the true measure of his quality. That he remained emotionally a Victorian, that the drowsy airs of Woodside still flavored him, that he was forever a gentleman of the old school and the small town, is not surprising and explains much. That the other side of his nature was secretly aflame with the legend of rebellion few could suspect when he left home.

For in this age of automatic progress and the approaching perfection of mankind, what was left to rebel against? At college King soon found the answers. Mackenzie's work of Canadian Liberalism was far from complete. And, to the sheltered youth's horror, the old enemy, the poverty of his mother's childhood, had reappeared, more virulent and wider spread than ever, to engulf the best of all possible worlds.

3

The Apprentice Rebel

ARRIVED AT THE UNIVERSITY OF TORONTO IN THE AUTUMN OF 1891, the small-town boy confronted the disturbing spectacle of life. It was a good time to begin that study.

Sir John A. had died a few months before. A dull man, Abbott, was in office, first of the four successors who were to perform the long obsequies of the Conservative regime. Its magician had gone, the magic of the National Policy had worn thin. The country was depressed in business and in spirit. A shaky young Confederation was consigned by its self-appointed prophet, Goldwin Smith, to inevitable absorption by the United States. A time of disillusionment, confusion, and despair, when the original energies of the Canadian people seemed palsied and many began to think that Smith might be right.

The new magician had been cheated of an election by sheer accident. To the public eye he was an untried young man—lank, handsome, and melancholy—brooding in the Opposition benches. While the Macdonald epoch, though outwardly secure in the constituencies, was ending in futility and decay, the epoch of Laurier was unconscionably long in getting born.

The university lecture halls and the rooms where King boarded with two other Berlin boys, A. L. Breithaupt and Shannon Bowlby, were comfortably insulated from the passing malaise of Canada, as the life of Toronto usually has been, but King soon broke out of his new environment in a surprising fashion.

We see him now in faded photographs as a seventeen-year-old, with lavish mop of hair parted in the middle, a round, solemn face, a large, homely mouth, a fashionable wing collar and flowing cravat. He is sicklied o'er with a pale cast of thought but has not lost the name of action.

His fellows at university called him Rex. Apparently he was no

19

longer the sort of person to be called by the familiar nickname of
Billy. He took himself and the world with excessive gravity. A boy
who was glad to escape from the athletic field into his books, who
hung his memoranda of the day's work on his bedpost to read as he
undressed and to reread as he dressed in the morning, who recited
his lessons as he walked to class and seldom joined in the week-end
rambles or the students' parties, was likely to succeed in his chosen
profession of the law but not to be a leader among men.

Much more promising students could be observed at Varsity,
among them a gaunt youth, named Arthur Meighen, who crossed
King's path briefly in students' debates and would cross it many
times again in mutual dislike, ripening, on King's part, into the deepest hatred of his life. Between the two, had anyone paused to measure them, there could have been no doubt about the winner in the
lifelong race. Meighen had all the gifts of speed, toughness, ambition,
eloquence, and icy intellect. Yet the race would go to the dull youth
with the memoranda on the bedpost and the schoolbooks under his
arm. The classic contest of the hare and the tortoise was under way,
neither contestant yet aware of the half-century course ahead.

Even in those callow undergraduate days a penetrating spectator
might perhaps have sensed something odd, unorthodox, and a little
droll in the tortoise. He had broken through the University's bars of
convention; he had formed a newsboys' club where he lectured on
Saturday nights; on Sundays he told stories to the patients of the
Sick Children's Hospital, who apparently came to love their curious
visitor. This was out of character for a college boy and somewhat on
the effeminate side, but it had the ring of sincerity in it and a stumbling search after life. While other boys were playing football or
chasing women, King was discovering humanity. The discovery
appalled him.

The world of tattered newsboys, of crippled children and the
Toronto slums was not like the neighborly streets of Berlin, the sweet
security of "Woodside," or the textbooks of classic Liberalism. As in
his grandfather's day the modern York, that "blue-devil haunt," still
contained its Family Compact of wealth and a proletariat more root-
less and miserable than the Patriots of Montgomery's Tavern. There
was room and need here for another Rebel.

How soon King cast himself in the role, as prepared by his mother
from the beginning, we shall never know. It must have possessed him
early, for halfway through college he abandoned the law, was thinking of the academic life, but found himself irresistibly drawn toward
economics, government, and hence, inevitably, politics.

He learned from books, he learned from the politicians who gathered at the home of his father—now living in Toronto as a lecturer at Osgoode Hall—he learned from the next-door neighbor, the oracular Goldwin Smith, now riding the current of his great fallacy. Here one pauses again to observe another chancy conjunction in a career which would present many—the venerable "Sage of the Grange" who prophesied the certain doom of Canadian nationhood, the boy who listened and would soon defy the prophecy. Poor Smith, preaching indulgently over the teacups to the neighbor's youngster, was hatching a heretic.

A mind less self-centered than Smith's might have seen—perhaps King's father and almost certainly his mother already saw—the heresy in birth. A boy who mooned over the poets and worshiped at the feet of Duncan Campbell Scott, who thought the state should subsidize dramatists and song writers, who took a summer job as a newspaper reporter and was horrified by what he saw in the police courts, might be regarded as merely sensitive and naïve, and no doubt would soon settle down to the respectable certainties of the Victorian age. But what was one to say about a boy who, winning a scholarship at Chicago University in 1896, elected to live at the Hull House Social Settlement of Jane Addams, rise at 6 A.M., and travel seven miles by the elevated railroad and on foot to his classes? While the hare was running ahead in the profession of law, the tortoise at last was moving, dogged in look but now filled with an inner fire almost too hot for containment.

In the reek of Chicago's poverty the boy from Berlin saw the real world face to face. If Toronto had appalled him, Chicago drove him to dejection and then to the first agonies of original thought. The imprint of that year in Hull House was forever stamped on him, the most honorable mark of his career and perhaps its truest explanation.

The discovery of laissez faire in action, the Liberal theories of his home and training translated from the pages of Adam Smith into the squalor of tenements, the look of human faces under the wheel of the North American system must have been, for a sensitive youth, quite shattering. For the first time, one supposes, the poverty of his mother's childhood, up to now a mere family tale, began to live in the son. He fancied himself then, and continued to fancy himself even when he was a millionaire, as a man of poverty, dedicated to the poor. Here at last was the mission handed on by his grandfather, a new aristocracy of wealth to be assailed, not with pike and blunderbuss, but with the deadlier weapons of pen, oratory, and politics. Here was the final phase of the Rebellion for him to complete.

That first fire burned deep. By the time he was sixty, rich and powerful, King had almost persuaded himself that, like his mother, he had been reared in privation on alien corn. One recalls the night when some Opposition heckler sneered at his reformer's zeal and the Prime Minister, white with anger, leaped up to shake his soft little fist and shout that he knew poverty at first hand because his mother had often gone to bed hungry in her exile—this a score of years before he was born in comfort.

The poverty which he had never known, except in others, was always the abiding illusion of his life and yet its best inspiration. Still, his separation from the actual experience of humanity, his streak of dilettantism in the ordinary affairs of men was the great lacuna in the masterpiece. In odd moments he knew it.

Wealth, power, and self-doubt were still a long way off when King returned to Toronto in the summer of '97 under a full head of sociological steam. Now to put his new theories of poverty and reform to the test.

Disguised as a reporter for the *Mail and Empire* (the encrusted Tory organ unwittingly nourishing a Liberal viper in its bosom), King studied the poor of Toronto and somehow fell among the sweated laborers of the garment industry. As he had suspected in Chicago, laissez faire and the divine dispensations of the free market reduced his boyhood theories to travesty. The textbook market, which was supposed to enrich employer, worker, and consumer alike, had built the first big fortunes of Toronto and turned women into needle slaves at three and four cents an hour. Free competition had not raised but had debased the workers' standards, as the lower standard was always played off against the higher to the benefit of nobody but the owner. Hence came what King would later pronounce in his own heretical textbook the "Law of Competing Standards."

Not such reasoning, but mere chance, plucked the youth out of the textbooks and the abstract study of poverty, plunged him into practical affairs, and planted his feet firmly in the paths of personal ambition.

In his examination of the textile industry King stumbled upon Government contracts for postmen's uniforms. The contractors, well paid by the state, were brutally sweating their labor. The state, then, the new Liberal state of Laurier, was a partner in the conspiracy of Competing Standards. The postmen's uniforms were a microcosm of the whole deadly business, a denial of all the old theories, a symbol of iniquity at the very hour when Liberalism had just returned to office. On this discovery the boy began his career in politics. No one ever traveled so far in a postman's uniform.

The facts of the Government's contracts were reported to a friend of King's father, William Mulock, Postmaster General in Laurier's new "Cabinet of all the Talents." As the elder King and his nervous son gave Mulock the facts, that ferocious lion paced his cage in anger and cigar smoke, muttering profane threats against the profiteers.

What could be done? Prepared, as he always would be, in advance, King suggested that he make a study of all Government clothing contracts, for the postmen, the Militia, and the North West Mounted Police. Mulock agreed. When the report was filed, the Government, on King's recommendation, inserted in all future contracts a fair-wages clause to protect the worker.

In his Sunday-afternoon meeting with Mulock, King had gone further than he knew. He had caught the eye of the Liberal Government and made a powerful friend who saw in him unsuspected promise. Two years later Mulock needed a lieutenant to start a department of labor and he remembered the bright young man with the postman's uniform. Where was King?

He was in Europe. After a postgraduate course in political economy at Harvard, he had won a traveling fellowship in 1899, had studied the poor of London, met Ramsay MacDonald, that white hope of the Labour Party and its lamented backslider, had imbibed, though skeptically, some Socialism from the ardent spirits of the Fabian Society, had roamed Europe as an admirer of scenery and a student of society, and had showed his mastery of sudden crisis, when the whole staff of a Swiss hotel lined up to receive his tips, by solemnly shaking each outstretched hand. Thus polished by travel, he had arrived in Rome.

There Mulock reached him by cable with the offer of a job as editor of the Labour *Gazette* and actual administrator of the new Department of Labour. Having just received the chance of a teaching post at Harvard, the puzzled traveler stood at the crossroads of life—the rough-and-tumble of government or the shelter of the university? He wandered about the ruins of Rome under an oppressive sense of destiny and finally decided against government. A second cable from Mulock and the advice of a professor friend at Cambridge changed his mind. In September, 1900, the young Utopian was back in Ottawa as Deputy Minister of Labour. At twenty-five he had crossed his Rubicon.

His eight years as a civil servant who soon became a politician on the side were full of accomplishment, at which one might pause now, were it not dwarfed by much larger things later on. Suffice it to say that King and his alter ego, the tragic Henry Albert Harper, with a secretary or two, a burning belief in reform, and a habit of reading poetry together at night, began Canada's first attack on the problem of labor's place in society, which was to become perhaps the paramount social problem of the century.

With almost comical belief in the power of conciliation and the reasonableness of mankind, King wrote the Industrial Disputes Investigation Act. He raced about the country settling strikes, some forty in all. He sat up all night in hotel rooms with owners and labor leaders; argued the theories of Marx with miners on the wooden sidewalks of grimy towns out west; cracked down on employers who had never felt the touch of the state before; compiled endless statistics; delivered endless speeches; once told the wondering Gatineau farm wives that any woman who hung her laundry in the back yard was a better citizen than she who hung it in the front; and framed the central principle on which his whole career as a domestic statesman would be based: "In any civilian community private rights should cease when they become public wrongs. . . . Either the disputants must be prepared to leave the differences which they are unable amicably to settle to the arbitrament of such authority as the state may determine as most expedient, or make way for others who are prepared to do so."

This, in the prevailing climate, was heresy, but the young heretic was so smooth, so genial, so reasonable, and so persuasive that few suspected—perhaps he did not suspect himself—the revolution under way. The work of conciliation was not so spectacular as the pike and blunderbuss of Montgomery's Tavern, but the end was the same—the emancipation of the common man. As the Rebel of the nineteenth century dimly grasped the tyranny of a landed aristocracy, his grandson grasped with a student's colder eye the tyranny of industrial capital in the twentieth.

The importance of these years to King, and to the Canada which he would soon manage, lay in the simple fact that he recognized, earlier and more completely than other statesman, the part which labor must play as an essential estate of the modern realm; recognized also that the Community, the sum of its estates, must be their final master or must be destroyed by their quarrels.

He was still pretty hazy about it. His intuitions, as always, preceded his reasons. He had yet to crystallize his theories into social principles and then, in office, to alter the social principles as the higher principles of politics demanded.

At that age he was a more attractive figure than he seemed later. His habits of industry, sobriety, and worship were exemplary. He worked his little staff hard, scrawling his letters in minute longhand, with insertions, deletions, and marginal scribblings which only that overworked secretary, Francis Giddens, could decipher, but he was a good boss. In his office he was learning the craft of detailed administration by which, in mature life, he could manage effortlessly the whole apparatus of government.

He had become a minor but agreeable fixture in the tedious and well-stratified society of the Capital. He danced, skated, rode horses, and was a deft hand with a cup of tea. Society liked him as a friendly young man with youthful fervors of reform which would pass with age. Harper worshiped him as the prophet of the new world. And the perceptive, humorous eye of Laurier had seen in him material which might be useful.

While still on its fringes and fascinated like a new-hatched moth by its beckoning light, already King must have given his heart to politics. At all events, he had given it to no woman. The only steady affection yet visible—apart from his devotion to his mother and to Harper—lay across the river in the Gatineau country of Kingsmere. There he and his friend used to ride their bicycles and later, when they could afford it, a hired buggy.

By agreeable accident, this enchanted region of lake, hill, and hardwood forest bore his own name. To one whose ego was rapidly expanding, that probably was an attraction, but King loved Kingsmere for itself. His first investment was a decayed farm and typically enough, where another man would have plunged with shovel and pick into the earth, King flung open the doors of his farmhouse to sit alone at a broken table and compose a speech. It was a prophetic gesture. In these environs he would do all the major work of his life and there end it.

For a man in his early thirties he had made a good start. As head of a government department, a modest country squire, a recognized scholar, and a bachelor useful to any hostess, he was on the first rung of the slippery Ottawa ladder and climbing fast. In the tight hierarchy of the Liberal Party he had a small but promising place. His mother, summering with him at the Kingsmere cottage, saw her work unfold according to plan.

Then, without warning, fortune's beamish boy felt the touch of death and never again escaped its presence.

Traveling back to Ottawa from the west, King found himself one morning with only a nickel in his pocket, decided to buy a paper instead of a sandwich, and, even as the train passed Harper's house at Barrie, he read the news of his friend's heroic death. At a skating party the previous night Harper had seen a girl fall through the ice into the Ottawa River. As the bystanders tried to dissuade him from a futile sacrifice, Harper cried, "What else can I do?" and leaped into the current.

"What else can I do?" The words were seared forever on King's spirit. He broke down completely under the most honest emotion of his life. He had lost his best friend, who was never to be replaced.

With a naked outpouring of anguish, such as he would not permit himself again, he paid his tribute to Harper in a tortured little book, *The Secret of Heroism.* Through its turgid and self-conscious style, from which King's oratory never could emerge, one glimpses still the bouncing, successful young man who has just made life's inevitable discovery:

"It is, perhaps, impossible to convey, save to those who have known the experience, any conception of what a constant association of this kind with Nature really means. It proves, to use Harper's own words, 'how beauty, grandeur, sublimity and purity in God's world find a ready response in the human heart unfettered.' Yet it is this perception of God, this communion of soul between the creature and the Creator as He is revealed in Nature, that is the conscious or unconscious secret of all the refreshment and joy which comes from a contact of this kind. Harper's nature was one that could share and did share it to the full."

From now on there was no one, except the aging mother, who could share King to the full. "What else can I do?" With Harper's last words King's capacity of selfless love seemed to die; a part of him drowned in the Ottawa.

In honor of Harper a bronze figure of Galahad was reared on Wellington Street, just outside the walls of Parliament Hill. From the Prime Minister's office King often must have glanced at it and doubtless wondered whether the better man of the old friendship had survived. He must have pictured his own future statue on the Hill, the two friends joined again in public memory. By then King expected a personal encounter with Harper in another world.

A few years ago Grant Dexter and this writer, finding the Prime Minister in a confiding mood, asked him about Harper. His reply was surprising. He mumbled that Harper was a nice young fellow, waved the question aside as unimportant, and went on to talk gaily of other things. Whether he was comforted by the thought of seeing Harper again, whether the old grief had been assuaged by his own success, or whether he still could not bear to discuss it, we were unable to judge. Dexter, at least, who had been deeply touched by the old story, was shocked at this nonchalance.

Within a year or two, King had outwardly recovered from his first serious hurt. There was plenty to keep him busy: the problem of Asiatic immigration into British Columbia; the suppression of the opium traffic; membership in the International Opium Commission; and, to fulfill these new duties, a leisurely tour around the world.

He was now the Government's handy man, to be used wherever a scholar's learning and a rare gift of conciliation were required. It was still only apprenticeship but the master workman was ready to give him larger tasks.

Foreseeing them, King often considered the selection of a partner in life and discussed marriage in an unpleasantly practical fashion with his intimates. To one of them he outlined the specifications of a perfect wife as he might reckon the prospects of an election. She must be a woman of means (since he had none), she must be beautiful and educated, of course, she must understand politics, cherish culture, love the outdoors, but she must not be one of "those doggy women in tweeds and low heels."

There were many flirtations, hand-holdings, and fugitive embraces in the moonlight but at the decisive moment the suitor always retreated, being addicted, as one of his sweethearts says, either to shyness or, in other cases, to excessive flattery.

Toward the end he protested, rather too much, that he had not married for the simple reason that, while supporting his family, he could never afford the luxury of marriage. When he could afford it the habits of bachelorhood were too firmly fixed to be broken.

Had he desired a wife he could have supported her, like many other men much poorer than he. The plain fact was that he did not encounter the ideal partner (who could by such a bloodless calculation?) and, short of that imaginary paragon, he would not damage his prospects by assuming an extra burden and sharing his career with anyone. He was too self-centered for marriage and did not miss its satisfactions.

4

Flood Tide and Ebb

IN THE ELECTION OF 1908, WHEN THE LIBERAL GOVERNMENT WAS over its first twelve years, was already invisibly started downhill. and could think of no better campaign slogan than "Let Laurier finish his work," King was summoned to the Prime Minister's office and invited (that is to say, commanded) to run for Parliament in his home constituency of North Waterloo.

It was a Tory stronghold but it could not resist the magic of Laurier, the power of the Liberal organization, or the hometown boy back from the world which he had made his oyster.

In his first campaign King learned how to manage committees, shake the hands of voters, kiss babies, flatter women, ring doorbells, and visit Sunday schools. He mastered the art of political organization down to the last name on the voters' list and became a greater master than his teachers.

On the platform he was a competent but uninspired performer. In photographs of his first big meeting, he basks, round, grinning, and innocuous, in the glow of Laurier's knightly figure. When called upon to speak, he imitates the tail-coat costume, the sweeping gestures, the antique style of his idol, but cannot, and never will be able to, imitate the elegance of phrase, the timing and nuances of Laurier's oratory.

While any voter could see that the pupil had a long way to go, he was Laurier's choice, he was the hometown boy, and still the wonder grew that one small head could carry all he knew.

He was elected easily and next year, when Laurier took him into the Cabinet as Minister of Labour, was confirmed in the subsequent by-election by acclamation. The career of politics had been launched; nearly two-score unbroken years of it now stretched before him.

The Laurier Government, which unwittingly had acquired in King its residuary legatee and vindicator, seemed now at flood tide. Its leader did not yet suspect, nor could his protégé, that the tide was beginning to turn.

At the edge of the Liberal Party's sprawling and garish encampment could be noted a young camp follower, notebook in hand, the most reliable chronicler of the times. His name was John Wesley Dafoe—a rumpled, reddish giant and one of the greatest of Canadians.

In those days Dafoe was a prejudiced partisan, dazzled by the white light beating upon Laurier's throne, but later, his youthful illusions lost, he could see in retrospect the certain doom of that glittering dynasty, already ordained.

In his definitive work on Laurier, he would write that "A government well entrenched can usually outstay its welcome by one term of office." That final, unwelcome term the Government was now occupying and, said Dafoe, "Its last few years were given up to a struggle against the inevitable fate which was visibly rising."

Visibly in retrospect but invisibly to most of the contemporary spectators. To King the Government looked good for years yet. Laurier was now the institution, outwardly fixed and unshakable, which King would some day become. His was a personal government—serene, confident, inhabiting a lotus land where it was always afternoon.

As Dafoe says, the ego of the Prime Minister and the country had become interblended in his mind: "A Prime Minister under the party system as we have it in Canada is of necessity an egotist and autocrat. If he comes to office without these characteristics his environment equips him with them as surely as a diet of royal jelly transforms a worker into a queen bee."

Into this congenial beehive King, the young worker, who had yet to taste the royal jelly, fitted perfectly. He was the leader's pet, the familiar of the great man and his adoring wife at Laurier House, the guest at week-end parties in the country, the promising boy well liked by the rulers of the tired hierarchy and apparently no threat to them.

Being young and fresh he could do more work than his older colleagues. When a difficult situation must be analyzed, when a laborious report must be written, when some complex problem must be thought out, King was always available and eager. His mind was proving itself as good as any in the Government.

Probably few but Laurier yet guessed its capacity, but Laurier was not ready to pick a successor, though King may have done so. There was plenty of time. Meanwhile, neither Laurier nor King seems to have detected the wide gulf of political philosophy yawning between master and pupil, between the unchallenged Whig, whose days of rebellion were over, and the new Rebel, who had not yet charted his rebellion. Laurier had said that the twentieth century would belong to Canada. He could not have imagined that Canada would belong politically to his youngest colleague. And anyone who had ventured to suggest that the apprentice worker was potentially the bigger bee would have been laughed out of the hive.

No one could suspect that fact in the Ottawa hive which droned comfortably within four years of world war. The busy worker was content with the few drippings of honey that fell from the Queen's table. Still, even then, he must have had his eye on the royal jelly.

In such sunny surroundings the Minister of Labour could not be expected to sense a smell of mortality. As the Government doubtless would win another term of office he set about using the leisurely years to build his labor reforms and the still more congenial structure of his own career.

His apprenticeship in the Laurier Government did not distinguish him greatly, but it taught him more than he realized then.

It taught him, first, the anatomy of party politics, the most useful lesson he ever learned. It taught him, in Dafoe's classic definition, that "parties, in reality, are organized states within the state. They have their own dynasties and hierarchies; and their reason for existence is to clothe themselves with the powers, functions and glory of the state which they control."

In mastering that inner organism, the state-within-the-state, King was learning future mastery of the state itself. This was essential knowledge, for the lack of which both King's major opponents, and many minor aspirants, were to perish. His experience under Laurier might seem, in the barren years of political exile, a waste of time. If they had taught King nothing but the management of a party they would have been among the most valuable of his life. In fact, they taught him much more.

The Laurier Government had attacked many domestic problems and solved some of them. It had begun with a moderate reduction in the tariff and the invention of the British Preference (which would dog King's footsteps to the end). It had opened up the west with the daring immigration policy of Clifford Sifton. It had started to build railways, doomed to early bankruptcy.

Its largest domestic achievement, only possible under Laurier, had been to subdue, for the time being, the lunatic Nationalist fringe of Quebec, to tame the Roman Catholic Church, and, having captured French Canada mainly because the Tories had hanged Louis Riel long before, to give the two Canadian races a deceptive appearance of unity.

Behind that elevated national policy lay partisan calculations of the most realistic sort. The Liberal Party had reached and retained office by French Canadian support. It was determined to hold Quebec at all costs, even though Quebec, voting Liberal for Laurier and Riel, was profoundly conservative by history and education. The central paradox of Canadian politics was by now a working principle of government and was destined to live on through King's times into St. Laurent's.

All these things King learned early as part of his daily work. He was absorbing the anatomy, the possibilities, and the limitations of Canadian politics by living in them.

Equally important, as things would turn out, he was mastering in the same fashion the issue which would first mark him as a historic figure in his own right. That issue was the place of Canada in the family of nations.

Laurier had entered politics as an admitted colonial, hoping that at some distant time Canada might become an independent nation. Quite unprepared, he had quickly been hurled into a new attempt to prevent the overseas colonies from reaching independence. Discovering that the colonies were not "wretched millstones hung about our neck," as Disraeli thought, Britain was desperately trying to recapture them after a period of neglect. To capture them for Joseph Chamberlain's new Imperialism it was first necessary to capture Laurier. The impressive but abortive effort to consolidate the Empire in London, under some vague kind of central legislature and government, was in full cry and hard to resist. In Laurier's words:

"One felt the incessant and unrelenting organization of an Imperialist campaign. We were looked upon, not so much as individual men, but abstractly as colonial statesmen to be impressed and hobbled. . . . It is hard to stand up against the flattery of a gracious duchess. Weak men's heads are turned in an evening and there are few who can resist long."

Even the handsome, cool head of Laurier was briefly turned when, in a regretted moment, he declared that "it would be the proudest moment of my life if I could see a Canadian of French descent affirming the principles of freedom in the Parliament of Great Britain." After a few such lapses Laurier resisted the Imperial pressure affably, patiently, and cold-bloodedly to the end.

King was beside him in those years. He was warned against the duchesses by the older man, who had felt the perfumed and deadly power of the drawing room. When his own test came, King was prepared for the flatterers and for the open Empire consolidators like Churchill. He was ready to carry on Laurier's work. Even King, however, was to have his own lapses at the end before the charming domestic spectacle of a young King and Queen, with two irresistible daughters.

As the Laurier Government's tide ebbed quietly, few spectators could suppose that King's was at the beginning of its flood. To King himself, after three years in office, the Liberal ship must have appeared battered, barnacled, and near the final beach.

In 1911 the sudden chance of rescue appeared. The Reciprocity Agreement with the United States was, in Dafoe's words, "not nearly so much a belated attempt to give effect to a party principle as it was a desperate expedient by an aging administration to stave off dissolution." At first it seemed certain to succeed. Reciprocity with the United States had been the general objective of Canadian policy since the lapse of the first trade agreement in 1866. The end of the Laurier era was still unimaginable. Nevertheless, in Reciprocity the Queen Bee had laid her last egg. It was crushed by a strange conspiracy.

Robert Borden, the slow-starting Conservative leader and, like King, an underestimated man, now saw his chance. His method of grasping it was risky and cynical. But it must be grasped, for it was the only chance available to a leader who seemed doomed to perpetual Opposition. Perhaps Borden did not realize then, as he would later, the unnatural and temporary character of the political marriage he was about to contract. With all party leaders the capture of power justifies almost any expedient. To destroy Laurier a man might swallow anything. So the conspiracy was launched, the marriage consummated.

In English-speaking Canada (with the help of indiscreet speeches by American politicians) the Conservative Party appealed to every Imperialist instinct by damning Reciprocity as the beginning of annexation to the United States, as a wedge to split the Empire. In Quebec the Conservatives allied themselves with Laurier's enemies, the Nationalists, who hated England and the Empire almost more than they loved Canada and who saw in Laurier the French Canadian apostate. Overcome by the duchesses, was Laurier not planning a navy for England and betraying his own people? As against this racial betrayal the Nationalists were ripe for the Conservative marriage of convenience.

The new Conservative combination was unreal to the point of purest fantasy: in the English-speaking provinces the old Imperialist appeal, in Quebec the opposite appeal of Nationalism, both under the same blurred banner. Fantastic but unbeatable. With the flaming Henri Bourassa, Laurier's former friend, uncomfortably in his pocket, Borden was elected and Laurier found himself at the end of the road.

In that debacle no one paused to note the obscure passenger who had been unloaded, after a bitter little campaign, by the electors of North Waterloo. For King the defeat of Reciprocity and his own defeat was a staggering blow, beyond belief. In the committee room of Berlin it appeared as a mere accident, casual and unjust, but after a few days of thought its victim recognized it as an inevitable confluence of Canadian forces, too strong to be dammed. At a later time, when it was urged upon him, he would not risk Reciprocity again.

Meanwhile he seemed to be with Laurier at the end of the road on which he had barely started. Behind him stood two monuments, the Industrial Disputes Investigation Act and the Combines Investigation Act, which he had erected. They were more than most cabinet ministers erect in a whole career but they did not seem to point toward further accomplishment. By all practical reckoning King was through. The second Rebel's exile had begun.

At the last meeting of the Laurier Cabinet its youngest member sat writing steadily while routine business was completed and the good-bys were said. He was writing to his father and mother a letter which they kept to their end and which turned up in King's own files a few weeks before his death. The old man read it then in tears.

In what may be called a final testament to his youth, King wrote that he did not foresee what the future held for him but he felt in every way a better man for having served under Sir Wilfrid and was now equipped for larger service to Canada. He could not resist the feeling that he would be engaged again in similar meetings around the Cabinet table, enriched and strengthened by the lessons learned at the great chief's knee. Mislaid for nearly forty years, that letter contained a sure prophecy. King was leaving but he would return.

He left with $2,000 in the bank, no job, no prospects, and no doubt about his high destiny.

D

5

The Rebel in Exile

BY NOVEMBER 11, 1918, THE GREAT WAR HAD BEEN WON, BUT THE Liberal Party of Canada lay prostrate in defeat. It had been smashed by Laurier, its maker. King appeared the man least likely to put the pieces together again.

For seven years the pupil had watched helplessly the tragedy of the master. In this period of exile King did little but observe, meditate, write, and wait. He could not foresee that the Party's ruin would be the making of him.

After the debacle of 1911 he organized the Liberal Information Office as the future nerve center of the Party, edited the Liberal monthly, and headed the General Reform Association of Ontario. Since an opposition party was too poor to pay him a decent wage, he found himself, for the first time, hard up. When he could least afford it, his father went blind and required his support. Misfortune was only beginning.

Macdougall, the well-beloved brother, now a physician in Ottawa, contracted tuberculosis and he, too, must be helped. With no family of his own, King found two families largely on his hands. By the eve of the war, his life seemed to have reached its nadir. He was rescued by his customary luck. The Rockefeller Foundation, whose sponsors were engaged in a ruinous war with labor out west, had heard of the great conciliator. It offered King the post of Director of Industrial Research. He leaped at the chance of a substantial salary and work which he probably could do better than any man in America.

For a long time it would be said that King fled to the neutral United States while other men of his generation were marching with Canada's army in Europe. That smear hurt him deeply and was clearly false. The plump recluse, now forty years old, would have been useless and absurd in uniform; doubtless would have ended as a political colonel (a proliferating species at that time) in some back

34

office. By agreement with the Rockefellers, he never gave up his flat in Ottawa or his work in the Liberal organization. All but a few months of the war years were spent in Canada.

With his peculiar talents and physical limitations he could have undertaken no job more useful than the settlement of strikes in vital American industries, among them the bitter two-year struggle between the Colorado Fuel and Iron Company and its miners. In Colorado he compelled the aloof John D. Rockefeller, Jr., to descend into the mines and see the abuses of his management for himself, to meet the miners, to dance with their wives. That experience transformed Rockefeller and his industry and gave King a lifelong friend with a lavish and open purse.

Those years were comfortable enough but heartbreaking. The death of King's sister Isabel was followed in 1916 by that of his father. In his Ottawa apartment his mother was nearing her end. His brother was dying in Denver. The decree of lifelong loneliness had been issued.

Meanwhile, as the familiar of Laurier House, he watched helplessly the ruin of his leader and his Party.

The Liberal Party seemed to rebound almost overnight from the defeat of 1911. The marriage of Borden's true-blue Tories with Bourassa's anti-British Nationalists was headed toward inevitable divorce. The new Government, though led by one of the most honest men in Canadian history, quickly found itself floundering in the scandals of wartime administration. The Liberals felt sure of carrying the election due at latest in 1916.

Neither Borden, Laurier, nor King understood the forces now in play.

Not since Durham discovered "two nations warring in the bosom of a single state" had Quebec and English-speaking Canada moved so far apart. To Quebec the war was British, alien, and remote. To all the other provinces it was a crusade which kindled the nation's passions as they have never been kindled before or since. This, with massive hemorrhage of blood and deep purge of the spirit, was Canada's finest hour. Unable to turn back the clock, Quebec shrank into spiritual isolation. It had been long reconciled by a French Canadian leader but now the old conflict of race, religion, and instinct welled up, raw, to the surface. In a clash which he had not expected and could not control, Laurier found all his plans disintegrating.

He had loyally supported the nation's war and expected to complete it in office. Like everyone else, he misjudged its length and cost. When the bloodletting of Europe required conscription to fill up the Canadian army's ranks, Laurier faced overnight the most terrible decision of his life, he must choose between office and his own people.

Borden offered him a place in a coalition, conscriptionist government which, with his talents and prestige, he would certainly have dominated. But to accept office meant to break clean with French Canada. It was solidly against conscription as a symbol of racial inferiority, the final outrage of the conqueror.

Laurier had won back Quebec from the Nationalists. Even Bourassa was giving him grudging support as the protector of the French Canadian race. If he approved conscription he would throw that race back into Bourassa's hands, perhaps fracture the nation beyond repair.

That was the political dilemma of a man who, more than any other of his time, had unified Canada. A still deeper motive was at work in the old leader's mind. He had heard the irresistible call of his blood. If he joined Borden now, he would surrender forever his place as the idol, father, and legendary folk figure of his own people.

He had powerful national reasons for refusing to quarrel with Quebec. He had partisan reasons as well. In the end the reasons of instinct decided him. He would give up the chance of office, hold the country together, if he could, and remain for all time the greatest French Canadian.

That decision involved the destruction of his Party and he knew it. Already the Liberals of Ontario and the West had quarreled with him, some secretly, some openly, on the question of bilingualism in the Ontario schools which he had forced into Parliament, against their advice, to demonstrate his French Canadianism. Now, when Borden formed his Union Government and invited the Liberals to join him in the European crusade, the Liberal Party fell apart.

No one saw the impending catastrophe as clearly as Dafoe. That ubiquitous reporter and wisest counselor pleaded with Laurier, told him bluntly that the war must be placed ahead of any party or personal consideration, and devised a dozen formulas, compromises, and accommodations. All in vain. Laurier had made his choice. With serenity, courtesy, and stubbornness, he refused to abandon the ship on which he was sinking. One by one he saw his lieutenants—the men he had discovered, educated, and made—turn to Borden. Like Harper on the river ice, what else could they do when their sons were dying in Europe?

Sifton, Laurier's ablest lieutenant in the old days, emerged from retirement and, with his editor, Dafoe, functioning as a skilled negotiator, trusted by both sides, was one of the chief architects of the conscriptionist Government, which included such eminent Liberals as N. W. Rowell, Frank Carvell, James Calder, C. C. Ballantyne, and T. A. Crerar. Laurier, with what remained of the Liberal Party, could not hope to beat this widespread coalition.

And so, on December 17, 1917, the deluge. In a House of 235 Laurier had 82 supporters, 62 of them from Quebec, 10 from the Maritimes, and 10 from the Ottawa River to the Pacific Coast. In one day Liberalism had become a Quebec rump. But Laurier had won racial immortality. In this fading sunset he waited patiently for the end.

King had not remained altogether a spectator of these events. He was learning from them and unconsciously preparing himself for their recurrence twenty-seven years later when he would be in Laurier's shoes and would face Laurier's decision. In 1917 he chose to stand by his leader in the most hopeless constituency he could find, North York, the seat of his grandfather. Like Harper, what else could he do? He was Laurier's friend, his spiritual son, and hoped to be his successor.

On election night the successorship did not seem worth much. Next day King returned to Ottawa and on his way received the news of his mother's death. It was the blackest day of his life. At her own request, he had left his mother, ill, to make his gesture in North York, but he could never quite forgive himself his absence at the last hour.

The deepest attachment of his life had been broken. The only woman in it was gone. Laurier would soon be gone, too. King faced a dark and endless gulf of solitude.

A wiser man would have thought his future hopeless. Liberalism could no longer pretend to be a national party. King was numbered among those who had opposed conscription, was suspected of lukewarm enthusiasm for the war, and the few who had not forgotten him altogether remembered him incorrectly as a man who had left his country to take a soft American job. He saw farther than his friends. On the night of the 1917 election, when he beheld Laurier's destruction, King said to his closest confidant: "This will make me Prime Minister."

The aged man who heard that prediction considered it adolescent and absurd. So it seemed then. Laurier would leave to King—if indeed King was his intended heir and even that was doubtful—a bankrupt estate. It included the possibility of the Liberal leadership and not much else. The secret assets, unknown to testator and legatee alike, were far larger than either could calculate.

By hanging Louis Riel, a French Canadian half-breed, the Mac-

donald Government handed Conservative Quebec into the Liberal
Party's custody. By invoking conscription, Borden confirmed the
transfer. From Riel and conscription the Conservative Party has
never recovered to this day, since no party can long govern Canada
without at least substantial support in Quebec—a fact discovered by
Macdonald and bitterly relearned by all his successors.

Laurier thus had planted a time bomb in the enemy's camp. He
had handed to the next Liberal leader the first essential base of
political warfare.

At the moment, if King knew that, he had no hope either of seizing
the base or expanding it. After its nation-wide sweep, the Union
Government looked solid. Borden—his profane mésalliance with the
Nationalists finished—surprised friend and foe with his firm management of the war, with his assertion of Canada's status in the Commonwealth, and, later, with his stout independence at the Versailles
peace conference. He had his heir, too.

Meighen, who had entered Parliament with King in 1908, was now
Minister of the Interior, had piloted the conscription law through
Parliament, and, with Borden determined to retire on the signing
of peace, seemed launched on a long term of power. The hare, running faster than any competitor in his own Party, had left the Liberal
tortoise leagues behind. But the Quebec bomb was ticking quietly a
little way along the track. Out west, still less suspected, a slow
agrarian fuse was burning.

For the moment the tortoise abandoned the race. He denned up in
the Roxborough to collect his ideas and put them into a book. His
amanuensis, critic, and friend was F. A. McGregor, a gentle soul
with a core of steel, who would become one of Canada's pre-eminent
public servants.

How curiously the lives of King and McGregor crossed, separated,
and met again with powerful effects on both! In his youth McGregor
worshiped King and King took cruel advantage of that worship.
Overworked, unconsidered, and harassed as King's secretary, Mc-
Gregor quarreled with him (according to legend, threw an ink bottle
at the Prime Minister in a much envied gesture), and quit. Yet when
he could not do the bidding of a later Government against his conscience, McGregor took his troubles to King and the early friendship
was relighted, warmer than ever. It was to McGregor, his last
familiar, that King left the management of his estate. He left also a
precious memory.

That curious idyll began with King's first venture into serious
authorship. As King dictated and McGregor recorded, the naked
confession entitled *Industry and Humanity* was born with laborious

gestation of twelve months. Every paragraph was typed, edited, pondered, and typed again. Every obscurity of the author's profuse style was clarified by the professor's pen of McGregor, who liked his English plain. Hence a book of crystal clarity in the writing, if not in the content, quite unlike King's speeches.

When *Industry and Humanity* was published in 1918, it made no great stir. The nation's mind was on humanity's more urgent business. Some years must pass, the author must test his written theories in office, before the book could be recognized as the most important ever written by a Canadian statesman, the key to King's career and the explanation of an era.

Were it not for the evil connotations of that title, *Industry and Humanity* might be called King's *Mein Kampf*. While it was in all respects the antipode of Hitler's work, a Christian's challenge to everything Hitler and all other dictators stood for, still, it parallels Hitler's testament in its basic design. It exposes King's final thoughts on politics as he would never expose them again. It accurately forecasts his future. In retrospect it makes cold logic of a career which seemed to be a catalogue of inconsistencies. And, more accurately than any other document, it proclaims the current revolution in Canadian life.

Without a study of King's book it is impossible to understand his work. Had the politicians of Canada read *Industry and Humanity* they would have known what to expect from its writer when he moved from the Roxborough into the East Block. Had the managers of the Liberal Party read it, or believed it, they probably would not have made him their leader. For in almost every respect this book repudiates the historic Liberalism of Canada, denounces the economic system which Liberal politics have nourished, proposes a society of an entirely different sort, edges uncomfortably close to the theories of the Socialist C.C.F., and announces King as a far more formidable Rebel than his grandfather.

It is doubtful that any man who expected to lead the Liberal Party would have written such a book. One can only conclude that King had given up hope of political success, was determined to fly his true colors as a revolutionist, and intended to work for reform outside elected office.

Incredible as it seems now, most of the conservative-minded men who made him their leader and kept him in leadership for twenty-nine years either did not read, or understand, or believe the heresies of King's masterpiece. How to explain, otherwise, the presence in King's Cabinets of men like Fielding, Gouin, Graham, Crerar, Cardin, Ralston, Howe, Ilsley, and many other traditional Liberals who

rejected almost every thesis in *Industry and Humanity*? The explanation, as will be seen later, lay in the infinite patience and flexibility
of the author and in the incredulity of his followers.

No one took the book seriously. Everyone wrote it off as the callow
yearnings of a young man who would learn better in the practical
affairs of life. In one sense the practical politicians were right—King
never tried to implement his theories in their entirety. In a larger
sense the politicians were wrong—King went further with his theories
than any Canadian statesman and, unlike most, he knew at every
step where he was going, even when the step was temporarily back-
ward or sideways.

The colleagues who were baffled by his apparent change from a
traditional Liberal into the designer of a Welfare State simply had
failed to do their homework. If they had read and believed the book
they would have understood King and their own policies. *Industry
and Humanity*, now that we can place it beside the career of its
writer, tells us more about modern Canadian history than any other
document. It is the Rebel's true testament. The seeds planted in it
never ceased to grow. They are growing still.

None of this history could be surmised by the two men toiling
unnoticed in the Roxborough. Being unnoticed, King wrote as a solitary philosopher exactly what he thought, something he could
seldom do as a politician in office. By the current social standards, his
writings on the folklore and the mores of Canada were sheer
iconoclasm, yet, as things turned out, highly practical politics.

His work was that of a political thinker far deeper and wider than
Laurier. Beside it the thinking of Meighen, though equally clear,
was hopelessly out of date, the eleventh-hour conversion of Bennett
to an improvised New Deal was a mere grasping after the straws of
power, and even the actual New Deal of Roosevelt was a blind collision of irreconcilables. Laurier had said that "young King has the
best brains in the country." In his book King confirmed that judgment at the expense of repudiating the brains of his mentor.

What Laurier thought of his pupil's essay the record does not
show. Probably he, like the others, supposed that young King would
settle down when he grew old. That was the cardinal mistake of
King's friends and enemies alike. He refused to settle down, except in
public.

Industry and Humanity begins with an indictment of modern
industrial society possibly more penetrating than the indictment of
Marx, since it is written by a member of the privileged classes with
a surer grasp of economic forces, with a more realistic understanding
of society's slow speed and limitations, with an infinitely better

judgment of human beings, and with a theory of the future conceivably within man's limited reach.

Writing in the presence of the First World War, King announces abruptly that international war is only the symptom of the consuming disease within the bodies of national societies. Civilian war between master and man in industry becomes military war between master states, which try to make one another their slaves. The process, King says—this more than two decades before the atomic bomb and the subsequent bisection of the world—will destroy civilization if it is not arrested.

Moreover, within the process is a vicious circle of destruction. Mankind's unreason produces industrial and then military war. Military war produces a worse state of unreason. In a new preface to his book, not long before his death, King reasserted his earlier thesis: "Men cannot be taught for years to think and act in terms of Force and then be expected, at the moment superior force has won the day, to place their confidence in Reason as a more effective alternative."

Foreseeing as early as in 1918 the broad outlines of man's present plight, King asks where its root cause lies. It lies, he says, in the divorcement of man from the laws of the universe. The universe is harmonious, ordered, legal. Man's society is anarchic, suicidal, and illegal. Between the two forces, Good and Evil, which, by polar attraction, hold humanity in balance, modern man more and more tends toward Evil in his industrial system. The purely materialistic interpretation of life, he declares over and over again, is false, but man, having largely accepted it and rejected the spiritual interpretation, lurches from one evil to another.

These should have been startling words to a society which thought it was already approaching perfection, provided it could repel the challenge of German militarism. The obscure Martin Luther of the Roxborough had hardly begun his arraignment of the industrial papacy.

Evil in society, he goes on, enforces the Law of Competing Standards, which he had first suspected in the Toronto sweatshops. As by Gresham's Law of coinage good money is driven out of circulation by bad, so by the Law of Competing Standards the good employer is driven out of business by the bad. The underpaid workman replaces the well-paid workman. Unrestrained competition debases not only the life of the worker but the wealth of the whole community.

Therein lies the final flaming heresy of the book. It denies at the outset the historic economic base of the Liberal Party in Britain and

Canada. It attacks openly the sacred theory of competition as the
breeder of wealth, the builder of civilization, the salvation of man.
From the Roxborough King assailed the very ark of the Liberal
covenant.

Even a few random quotations will illustrate King's assault on
orthodox Capitalism for which his Party stood. Capitalism "is ready
and willing enough to secure itself in ever-growing aggregations
against the hazards of smaller units. It gives little heed to the individual lives that suffer or are sacrificed by its rapid transitions; it is
slow to concede to Labor, in Labor's struggle against world forces,
facilities of combination like unto its own."

In this system workers "find themselves . . . possessed of little
save their skill and energy—human beings who work with equipment
which belongs to others, in establishments owned by others, upon
materials the property of others and who leave to others the disposition of the wealth they have helped to produce. Working men and
women have come to realize that, in the ever-changing conditions of
Industry, they exist as atoms in a human tide so vast, and subject to
such ceaseless ebb and flow, that the effort to secure collective stability becomes the first requisite of existence itself."

While machines, division of labor, and industrial efficiency increase output, they "ignore personality and are dehumanizing to
the extent to which they make Labor's part in Industry mechanical,
and tend to destroy initiative and resource."

The large-scale organization of Industry has uprooted humanity,
scattered Labor derelict across the world, spawned the modern
city of slums, and "has rendered inevitable the commercial depressions, the financial panics and the violent industrial crises which
have become recurring phenomena of our times."

The worker lives "subject to the play of forces wholly beyond his
control" while wealth, in the form of liquid capital, lives securely.
Such a system was suitable to the age of cottage industry and self-
contained communities but it is no longer tolerable or workable in
a system "which has substituted world for local markets and inter-
dependence for self-sufficiency in Industry and Trade."

The ancient philosophers of laissez faire and even Adam Smith,
spiritual progenitor of Liberalism, cannot escape the volcano welling
up within the staid Roxborough. Political Economy, says King, is
well enough in its field but its field does not begin to cover the complexities of the modern industrial society since it is not concerned
in the least with morals, the real basis of society.

Though the style here grows a little ponderous, despite Mc-
Gregor's editing, the heretical meaning of the next sentence is

beyond doubt: "Being avowedly the science of wealth, Political Economy of itself affords the strongest of reasons for adopting, as respects human well-being, courses of action quite at variance with assumptions and principles which relate primarily to material considerations." King had hurled Adam Smith out the window.

Up to this point, *Industry and Humanity* seems only the echo, in moderate tones, of the older attacks on Capitalism voiced by Marx, by many subsequent prophets, and by the Socialists and Communists of these times. King, however, had isolated the central fact which the mere protestants had overlooked—control of Industry, the title deeds to the productive machine, mean nothing of themselves.

Control under any system, he says, can produce good or evil, depending on the morals of the controllers. There must be control, for good or evil, whether Industry is owned by capitalists or by the State. The capitalist form of Industry must remain even under a state system, for only this form—a huge complex of materials, machines, and men—provides a workable method of producing a maximum supply of goods. The form must remain but the manner of control can change.

The Communist and Socialist would place control under the State, which might be and often has been more evil than the private owner. The Syndicalist would put control into the hands of the workers in every separate industry, vainly hoping that these industries would cease to debase each other merely because different owners operated them. All these easy blueprints King rejects out of hand. A generation ahead of his contemporaries he foresees the failure of all simple solutions which depend entirely on the good will of the State or on the intelligence of the workers. Something much larger is involved— an entirely new conception of Industry.

Up to now, Industry has been regarded by Capitalists as their private possession, by Management as its tool, by Labor as its oppressor. All of them have forgotten the fourth partner, which is the Community. It is the Community, embracing all men, Capitalists, Managers, Labor, and Consumer, which must now assert its rights. But how?

King proceeds to lay down his own blueprint. He would have the Community represented on the directorates of private enterprise. The directorates—though not the management, which must be technical—should include representatives of Capital, Management, Labor, and Community. Thus jointly the four partners should repeal the Law of Competing Standards, should substitute the welfare of the Community, which embraces all, for the debasing process of the unrestricted market, and should go on to establish a National Minimum standard of life for all men; more than that, since nations undermine one another through an international Law of Competing Standards, the new Community societies in the various nations should co-operate in international commerce as the four partners co-operate in domestic commerce.

Here King foresees the obsolescence of national sovereignty in a world knit together by Industry; he advocates an international authority like the League of Nations, which was only a year ahead, but he can hardly imagine himself as one of the founders of the United Nations thirty-seven years hence.

That, in simplest form, is King's concept of the only kind of human society which will work and endure. It is nothing less than revolution—peaceful, based on Reason, moving slowly, gaining here a little, there a little, a process of decades, enforced by Good Will, but revolution nevertheless.

It is tempting to explore the detailed mechanics of King's approach to the problems of Labor as the victim of Capitalism, of the Community as the hope of the new system controlled by four imaginary partners in place of the old Liberal market. The massive content of King's future career leaves space here only to say that he proposes expanding state services to supply the Minimum Standard of life, that he places his faith in investigation of social evils, in mediation, conciliation, arbitration as a last resort, and, above all, in publicity to create an informed public opinion.

This faith in the final judgment of the common man returns King, by a circuitous route, to Liberal principles transcending the mere economics to which Liberalism had grafted itself in the previous century. Faith in man, yes, but not in material man; faith in man only as the child of God: "Material force may conquer material force, but where there is conflict between the material and the spiritual, because God-like in his nature, man will never rest until spirit is supreme. . . . We have based our reasoning on this as a material universe, when, in fact, so far as human personality and its possibilities go, the universe is meaningless apart from the life of the spirit. We have thought of Industry as an institution of purely material significance, of Nationality simply as an abstraction; whereas the unfolding of spiritual capacities which both should further is the only true end of life."

After thus giving his considered verdict on economics, politics, and life, King went off to England with McGregor for a holiday. The war was over. The Union Government, though shaky, had at least two more years of life and might easily win another term. King still saw no immediate political prospects. He had defied the mores of his Party and his nation. He was a self-proclaimed rebel and therefore exiled from politics. That exile seemed likely to continue to the end of his days.

On February 17, 1919, death came to the archbishop of Canadian Liberalism. *"C'est fini,"* murmured Laurier to his wife and, serenely, as he had lived, quitted his life.

For Liberalism this was more than a man's death. It was the death of all hope. The queen bee gone, the workers huddled in despair. Laurier had ruled so long, had so dominated the whole Liberal Party, had so held in his own hands its past, present, and future, had become so like a god that party life without him was unimaginable.

After the first days of shock and numbness the Party prepared to go on alone somehow. A convention already had been called to meet in Ottawa on August 5.

Amid his interminable social studies in London King prepared rather idly to return to Canada. As Laurier's heir-apparent he would automatically enter the convention to seek the Party leadership but the outlook was depressing. He had been long out of the public eye, was almost a forgotten man. Older men, who at least looked bigger, were ravenous for the great chance.

Fortunately nobody seemed to have grasped the meaning of *Industry and Humanity.* Few Liberals realized King's inner thinking. His radicalism was no barrier to preferment. The real barrier was King himself—too young, too inexperienced in office, too remote from the Party machine, too distant from the nation's recent war, and a little too precious. King arranged to cross the ocean not in triumphal return but in obscurity and in forlorn hope.

He almost failed to return in time. A maritime strike had held up his ship. To the worried McGregor, King said there was no need for haste. The strike would be settled, the ship would sail. It did not sail. But King's perpetual luck held. McGregor, that indefatigible man who thought of everything, had secretly booked passage on another ship. In the nick of time King reached Ottawa. The exile was finished.

6

The First Hurdle

THE SWELTERING AND UNCERTAIN DELEGATES WHO MET IN HOWICK Hall, Ottawa, on August 5, 1919, could hardly pretend to represent a national party as judged by the last election returns. Liberalism was hived in Quebec. The conscription wound of 1917 had yet to be healed. Moreover, the country now wore the hectic flush of a brief postwar boom; the boys were coming joyfully home from the war; peace had been won forever and Canada was feeling its oats after four long years of bloodletting—a favorable climate for any government in office.

Still, in the music of peace there were encouraging overtones for an opposition party. Labor trouble had culminated in the great Winnipeg strike, with sympathetic strikes elsewhere. The farmers, west and east, were restive and apparently going into politics on their own. One by one Borden had seen his Liberal ministers leave the Government and he was ready to leave it also. Under these conditions the Liberal Party at least could hope to begin its recovery if it could not strike for office—provided it could find a leader.

There were plenty of aspirants but no man who seemed to possess the adequate stature. After Laurier any successor must appear puny. William Stevens Fielding, the gray, bearded patriarch of Nova Scotia, had all the necessary qualifications of experience as Laurier's chief lieutenant and treasurer, of intellectual power and national prestige. On the record he was the old chief's logical heir and, though King always claimed Laurier's blessing, Fielding's friends insist to this day that he had it. But Fielding was then seventy-one years of age when youth was needed for the long pull ahead. As a supporter of conscription he had earned the enmity of the true-blue Laurier Liberals. Anyway, he did not want the leadership and was persuaded to seek it mainly under the pressure of the eight Liberal premiers of the provinces.

George P. Graham, another veteran of the Laurier Government, was beloved of every Liberal in the country (who could resist this nature's gentleman with his inimitable after-dinner stories?), he was supported by a noisy organization, he came from Ontario where the Party must win or lose, but he looked little like a Prime Minister, and he suffered from the report, which he denied, that he was the nominee of Sir Clifford Sifton, one of the builders of the conscription Government.

William Martin, premier of Saskatchewan, was popular, able, young, and a rising name in politics. He might well carry the convention if he would run.

D. D. McKenzie, of Nova Scotia, had been chosen temporary Liberal House leader and thought his position should be made permanent. If his own suit failed, he might have enough support to decide the alternative.

Sydney Fisher, a devoted Laurier supporter, was vaguely mentioned. Alexander Smith, Laurier's organizer and political handy man, would be given a complimentary nomination.

Finally, there was King—not the dignified old gentleman whom most Canadians remember, but a stout, bouncing figure with boyish, unlined face, a manner almost too jovial in a congress of practical politicians, and a mind almost too well stuffed with technical information and Christian ideals. Besides, he was not quite forty-five yet, relatively inexperienced, callow, and theoretical. Still worse, he had opposed conscription while the great bulk of the Party outside Quebec had supported it. Worst of all, he was suspected, quite unjustly, of slacking in the war when other young men were fighting. Except to himself and a few friends he looked neither like a Prime Minister nor an election winner.

As usual in his early life, before his abilities were known, he succeeded mainly by the weakness of his opponents. The popular Martin refused to run. Graham, it soon became clear, had the convention's affection, but not its votes. The more rabid Laurier Liberals and most of the Quebec delegation would not have Fielding, who had broken with the old chief on conscription. McKenzie obviously lacked stature.

King's assets, however, were by no means all negative. As anti-conscription candidate in 1917 and as Laurier's supposed protégé, he had most of the Quebec vote; and he had unsuspected powers within himself. His speech to the convention was hardly under way when the surprised delegates realized that there was far more to this youngster than they had guessed.

It was a typically long, discursive speech, but well organized, minutely prepared, meticulously memorized, above all, superbly contrived to avoid divisive issues like conscription, to appeal to every sector of the Party, to offend none, and it was delivered with passion in the grand manner.

Some of his economic heresy, but not too much, a few resounding phrases from *Industry and Humanity*, were permitted a discreet appearance. "Human personality is more important than any consideration of property. . . . Human considerations ought to stand above considerations which are purely business or national. . . . Industry exists for the sake of humanity, not humanity for the sake of industry." This would sound well on the political stump in a nation restive under the high cost of living and guaranteed a new life after its victory. If it was not precisely Liberalism as the old-timers understood the word, it probably would do no harm, change nothing, and win votes.

For the old-timers, King presented, with satisfactory ardor, the familiar Liberal doctrine of the low tariff (but not low enough to disturb the Party's Tories and protectionists), economy in government, retrenchment, and reform.

This young man might nourish a social revolution in his bosom, but to implement it by gradual persuasion he must first gain office. Since country and Party were not ready for it, the revolution could be temporarily forgotten and indefinitely postponed. Both personal ambition and practical politics demanded a middle way which diverse men could follow. After the centrifugal pressures of the war and conscription, Canada required more than anything a new cohesion, a centripetal pressure to pull its divided groups together. This, evidently, the young man could supply, and with it a kind of guileless moral fervor, breathing new heat into a Party long cold and moribund.

This was not another Laurier—the contrast between the two was painful. The old magic, the towering natural grandeur, and the seigneurial patina were lacking, but maybe they would grow in time. Meanwhile, when King's long, convoluted paragraphs surged to their climax and he turned, reverently, with a worshiper's humble genuflection to Laurier's portrait on the wall, as a pilgrim bows before a shrine, the convention was half won by a single tour de force. King would seldom equal it again.

On the afternoon of August 7, when the balloting began, King sat impassive in his seat. Though it was youthful and unlined, he already had acquired a poker face which would serve him well. He knew as clearly as anybody that this was the decisive hour of his life. On it hung all his ambitions, his long training, his mother's hopes, his grandfather's vindication, and much more that he alone in the crowded hall could vaguely glimpse—the future of the nation and the great boyhood dream. So he waited, outwardly unmoved, with inward agony, doubtless praying for himself and the nation which, to him, were now almost identical.

Five names had been placed in nomination—King, Fielding, McKenzie, Graham, and Smith. For King the first ballot was encouraging but indecisive, when a majority was required. Of 949 votes, he had 344, Fielding 297, Graham and McKenzie 153 each, with two ballots spoiled. Having received his compliment, Smith dropped out.

The second vote gave King 411, Fielding 344, Graham 124, and McKenzie 60. Apparently the corner had been turned.

Graham retired and his votes could go where they chose. McKenzie retired also but not without dictating the final choice. That hard, blue-nosed Scot could not win with the Maritimes' votes but he could destroy Fielding, his fellow Nova Scotian, whom he detested as the betrayer of Laurier. Not that he loved King more but Fielding less, McKenzie threw the Maritime delegation to the new man. As would happen so often again, King's career turned on the flip of a single human coin.

When the scrutineers completed the last count and passed King of their way to the platform, one of them whispered into his ear: "You're in!" The poker face registered nothing.

It was a close shave, 476 votes for King, 438 for Fielding. The young man who rose to accept the leadership knew that nearly half the Party was against him, doubtless a majority was skeptical of his chances in the country, the great schism had yet to be closed, and the public, reading his name in the newspapers, would hardly recognize it. The boyhood dream had survived its first test but it was still a dream only. All the solid flesh of political victory had yet to be found. The convention beheld an untried leader; a platform so confused between high and low tariffs, between old-fashioned Liberalism and extracts from *Industry and Humanity*, as to have no visible meaning; a nation which had all but exterminated Liberal candidates outside Quebec; unrest in agriculture and labor; and something else dimly visible, the lineaments of a strange new world.

These things the new leader knew better than anyone in the convention hall. He knew that he had yet to master the Party and, a long way beyond that—many years, as it turned out—he had to master the nation. Mastery he would have, but it could wait. To his lips now came only the clumsy mutterings of the dream. And beside him in his first moment of triumph stood the old ghost of the Rebel.

"I can never forget, and I hope you will permit me to mention it

E

on this occasion, that my grandfather . . . and Papineau in Lower Canada were seeking to bring about that change in the relations of the executive to Parliament which would subject the executive to the will of the people as expressed through their representatives. Ladies and gentlemen, I hope that in making mention of these things, which are part of the traditions of our Party, and also a part of the history of this country, I utter words that are prophetic of that greater unity which is to prevail between the sister provinces of Quebec and Ontario—indeed between all the provinces of this Dominion."

Through these uninspired and self-conscious sentences few could discern the secret of the man. No matter if the Rebel was a curious companion to introduce into a country which had just fought a war for the Empire, the practical Liberal politicians saw that infallibly the new chief had hit upon the kind of obscure, nebulous issue which conceivably might win an election in a divided country. National unity after division, healing after a deep psychic wound, a sense of recovery after shock, with no need of consistency or positive policy—these hopes King seemed able to exploit.

No one knew exactly what wares he would offer, King himself did not know, but perhaps he could sell the Liberal Party to Canada again. Therein lay the Party's great gamble. It was no more than that.

Thus as the sovereign healer, the skilled physician, the humble pacificator, the scholar-in-politics, and, in his own words, "the willing servant of all," King was fully launched on the flood tide leading to fortune. Alone now, more alone than the convention could guess, he must sink or swim and the Party with him.

7

The Battle Is Joined

INSTALLED AS THE LIBERAL PARTY'S YOUNGEST LEADER, KING FACED three immediate tasks. He must win his spurs publicly in Parliament and prove himself as a statesman. He must repair the broken Party machine in the constituencies. He must impress his own personality on the Canadian people and begin to build a personal myth.

The first task would be the easiest. In Parliament King felt instinctively at ease. It was his true métier, his natural climate and spiritual home. Since he must use the sounding board of Parliament without delay, he accepted an acclamation in the safe seat of Prince County, Prince Edward Island, with a promise to run at the next general election in his grandfather's doubtful seat of North York.

In Parliament, where Borden's illustrious reign was now closing, King's unsuspected qualities of boldness and dash instantly revealed themselves. He had re-entered the Commons under the shadow of the conscription crisis, against a quiet but general public feeling that somehow he had shirked his duty in the war. That hurt him, how deeply only his intimates knew, and he would never cease to complain of its injustice to the end of his life. Also, it hurt politically. How to lay the persistent ghost?

The chance came in the spring of 1920 and King seized it. Some forgotten little man in Montreal had publicly attacked the new Liberal leader as a "bachelor and capable of bearing arms and only a young man," who had deserted Canada in time of crisis to fatten on the payroll of Standard Oil. King's answer was painful and toilsome, embarrassing in its nakedness, probably disgusting to the blunt and manly Borden, but to any fair-minded Canadian it was conclusive.

He had done during the war, King said, the work he was best

equipped to do, the promotion of labor peace in vital war industries, he had never worked for Standard Oil but for the Rockefeller Foundation as a salaried expert only, he had never closed his home in Ottawa and he had never left the country for more than a few weeks at a time. Then came that kind of huge, unnecessary documentation which he always liked to pile upon the parliamentary record—letters of tribute from industrialists in Canada and the United States, attesting his notable services to the Allies' cause.

Most men, a man like Meighen for instance, would have found such a recital too humiliating to be borne, but King trudged through it to the end. He was using his own method and he knew what he was doing. The record, the full record for easy reference by Party speakers later on, must be set down and the public must understand it well before an election.

Finally, with emotions so full that he did not dare to speak extemporaneously but craved the right to read an account of his most intimate affairs, King answered the charge of cowardice. In detail which the House must have found ghastly, he recounted the story of his life. He was called young, he said, but in fact he was in his forty-sixth year. At the beginning of the war he had already reached forty and had been overwhelmed by family responsibilities. The blindness and poverty of his father, the dependence of his mother and unmarried sister, the illness of his brother (described in minute medical terms), the sister's death, then the father's and finally the mother's—the whole family record of misfortune and the son's long struggle to support it were spread across the pages of Hansard, capped with this final testament, which his hearers would regard as hypocrisy or nobility, according to their taste:

"As I look back upon those years of the war, so full of poignant suffering for the whole of mankind, I cannot but experience a sense of gratitude, that in the world ordeal it was given to me to share, in so intimate a way, the suffering of others, and with it all, so large a measure of opportunity to do my duty, as God gave it to me to see my duty, at that time."

A humiliating performance, truly, but it destroyed the charge of cowardice. This man had done his duty by his country and by his dependents and done it well. It took a peculiarly high form of courage to face the slander and reveal in answer the things which no man, even a politician, should have to reveal. A bigger man with less ambition might have ignored the whisperers and marched on silently to defeat. The politician who was determined to succeed must clear his name before the nation at any cost to his own private feelings and to the usual code of public manners.

THE BATTLE IS JOINED

That done, the secret enemies answered, King was ready to face the outward enemies of Parliament.

The paramount and permanent enemy had now appeared. Meighen succeeded Borden in the summer of 1920 and, at forty-six, the youngest Prime Minister since Confederation, seemed assured of a long term. With King facing him in the Opposition benches, the interrupted race between hare and tortoise was resumed in the full view of Commons and country.

The race still was going, apparently, to the hare. As a politician, Meighen had every essential item of equipment—brains, scholarship, courage, twelve years of administrative experience, an encyclopedic knowledge of government, shining integrity, unequaled oratory, corrosive satire—everything except a gift for politics and an understanding of people. This lack proved fatal.

It was undiscovered then. From the treasury benches, Meighen, the gaunt figure, ascetic face, brooding eye, and incisive tongue, appeared to be, like Gladstone, master of the House and of himself. Understandably there was a tinge of arrogance in him as he glanced across the aisle at the dumpy little man who looked less like a statesman than a Sunday-school teacher or the president of a small-town Rotary Club. The hare, as usual, underestimated the tortoise. That was to be his ruin.

Firmly in office, with a huge majority behind him, Meighen could afford to treat the new Opposition leader with a mixture of chivalry and condescension. He saw no danger from such an enemy. King had no chivalry in him but his parliamentary manners were perfect, with exactly the right combination of moral protest, truculence, and humility. To Meighen, who could hardly hide his distaste, King was always the reincarnation of Uriah Heep, a very humble man with a deadly purpose, relieved now and then with touches of a youthful Pickwick. To King the Prime Minister was at first a dangerous adventurer, later on a conspirator against democracy, and finally a personal devil.

The duel which was to last for a full score of years began quietly enough in the session of 1921. Nothing could have been more disarming, deceptive, and pleasantly hypocritical than King's opening gambit. Turning to Meighen a moon face full of friendliness, he said: "Perhaps the Prime Minister will permit me to say in public what I have already said to him privately, that on personal grounds it was to me a source of both pride and of pleasure to learn that His Excellency had chosen as his first adviser one who in university days was a fellow undergraduate, and whose friendship, through a quarter of a century, had survived the vicissitudes of time, not excepting the

differences of party warfare and acrimonies of political debate. . . .
I can promise him that in seeking to fulfill the demands of public
obligation I shall strive with him to preserve the highest traditions
of our public life, and to be governed in all things by its amenities
and never by its animosities."

Those obese phrases had not been prepared without the burning
of midnight oil. It was the salute before the lunge.

By now King knew that his own Party's policy was too tortuous and
conflicting to be defensible, at least in an election. If, out of the
contradictions of the convention platform, he contrived a clear
policy, he would break the Party's brittle unity at the beginning. If
his tariffs were too low they would defeat him in the protectionist
constituencies of Quebec, if too high they would lose the prairies.
If he moved too far left by dredging up the heresy of his book, he
would antagonize business and the sources of campaign funds; if
too far right, he would affront the labor unions, which were satis-
factorily enraged against the Government. The only defense, therefore, was attack.

The attack was devised with a skill which showed the measure of
King, the strategist. He attacked on a front which would not divide
his own forces or reveal their inward quarrels and in a fashion at
once so audacious and so vague that no government could successfully answer it.

The supreme issue, he said, pulling it suddenly out of his hat, was
the Government's usurpation of power. In his definitive speech of
May 19, 1921, he observed that the Union Government of Borden
had been elected for one purpose and one purpose only, to win the
war. (This statement was buttressed with the usual array of quotations from the enemy.) The war over, the Government had no
mandate to govern in peace. Indeed, the Government itself was not
governing at all, but had become the mere tool of big business.

"The Government is not a free agent in the matter of either intention or action. Its members in truth do not constitute the real government of Canada today. In word and act it is but the visible expression of influences and forces which dictate the policies, aye, and in
large measure are controlling the destinies of Canada today—forces
and influences which constitute the real though invisible government
of the Dominion." This charge was supported with a long and grue-
some list of contracts awarded by the Government to its friends, a
detailed anatomy of interlocking directorates which held the country
in the grip of an octopus, and a grisly picture of power, centralized
by the war, now running wild.

What was the Liberal alternative? It was to return government to

Parliament and people. It was to cut down swollen expenditures, reduce taxes and the cost of living (all admirable generalities with
which no one could quarrel), and to reform the tariff. The tariff, as
it always had been, was a ticklish business, especially for a leader
who needed the protectionist East and the free-trade West, but King
had the advantage of a Government which candidly proclaimed its
protectionism. Meighen proposed to enforce Macdonald's National
Policy, which must greatly damage him in every agricultural constituency; whereas King promised a tariff which would suit farmer
and manufacturer alike.

How this circle could be squared he did not say, since he did not
know. He was careful, however, to explain, and repeated it in every
subsequent speech wherever he went, that the Liberal Party did not
stand for "free" but "freer" trade. Free trade, he said, was a canard
which the desperate Conservatives had tried to hang about the
Liberal Party's neck and frighten legitimate business. No legitimate
business would be harmed by a Liberal tariff but the consumer would
benefit by lower prices on the necessities of life. On the other hand,
the Government and its secret masters wanted "protection for these
favored interests not for the great mass of the people," and wanted
it so badly that the promised tariff revision had been abandoned and
even trade with Britain, to which Conservatism pretended to be devoted, was being strangled.

Having politely retired the convention platform as a mere "chart"
of general directions, King now erected by formal amendment to
the budget resolution the much simpler and less controversial platform on which he proposed to fight the election. It called for the
"encouragement of industries based on the natural resources of the
country," for tariff changes gauged "to reduce the cost of living" and
the price of implements of production, and for a drastic reduction in
public spending.

This, then, was the Government—autocratic, reactionary, the pup-
pet of the trusts, and now masquerading under the new name of the
"Liberal and Conservative party." And this was the true Liberal
Party—dedicated to the supremacy of Parliament, lower prices, a
reformed tariff, economy, and prosperity.

Years later, King told this writer that he had always objected to
detailed platforms "which give the other fellow something to shoot
at." By the summer of 1921 he had reduced his platform to a series
of resounding generalities which the most skillful marksman could
not hope to hit. Meighen, for all his glittering sarcasm and crashing
invective, could never find the mark. Fighting with King was like
fighting with a feather pillow.

Thus, entirely misjudging both King and country, Meighen marched forward under Macdonald's old banner of protection, continued to ignore the tide rising against him and prepared confidently for his re-election. He had underestimated his enemy, and now he underestimated the depression which began, after the postwar boom, in the autumn of 1920. To the Government it was far more dangerous than King. The world-wide economic collapse came just in time to provide the climate on which all opposition parties thrive. King hastened to make the most of it, blaming its effects on the Government (a cry which, nine years later, would defeat him in turn). His progress so far had not been spectacular, had kindled no flame, but, on the whole, it was satisfactory to his Party.

8

The Prairie Fire

AFTER HIS APPRENTICESHIP UNDER LAURIER IT WAS NOT DIFFICULT for King to rebuild the local machines. That was a mechanic's job. His real stature as a leader was tested when he faced the problem of the conscriptionist Liberals who had deserted Laurier. By meeting that test he showed himself an abler man than most of his friends suspected.

Some of the old chief's closest colleagues would never forgive the deserters of 1917. They must be punished and banished from King's counsels. Only the loyal followers who had stuck with Laurier in wartime defeat must have any power in the reorganized Party.

Such advice King had flatly rejected from the convention platform and afterward regarded that decision as the most important of his life. Had he acted otherwise, his own career and the Party's future, he believed, would have been doomed from the beginning.

His task was to resurrect a Party now in an advanced state of decay. Anyone who could help him was welcome, and no questions asked. Publicly he made it clear that he held nothing against the conscriptionists. They had done their duty as they had seen it. Their patriotism could not be doubted:

"The Liberals who stood with Sir Wilfrid in 1917, if they are to be true to the first principles of Liberalism, must be as ready to accord sincerity of purpose to those who differ from them as they are to demand like attitude in themselves."

He buried the old quarrel at the price of antagonizing some. Laurier Liberals forever. That price he considered cheap if the Party could be revived. Its revival must be his supreme work since all other works depended on it.

Most of the conscriptionists returned to the Party's ample bosom. What of the conscriptionist voters? Would they, the great majority of the nation, forgive an anticonscriptionist?

57

In parts of Ontario and throughout the prairies a more alarming question had arisen. The farmers, as King had feared, were up to their ears in politics of their own making. Vainly he tried to dissuade them. He approached farm leaders as Liberals who were getting out of line and argued that they could not hope to achieve half as much if they nominated separate candidates as if they remained in the Liberal Party and leavened it with their truly Liberal ideas. He hurried through the prairies, carrying his argument beyond the leaders to the farmers. It was no use. His appeal to the West proved an obvious failure. The prairie fire, known as the Progressive Party, was alight.

Its origins went deep and, in the historic sense of the word, were Liberal.

From the beginning of North American history the core of politics had usually been the contest of the man on the land against the man in the city, beginning in Jefferson's struggle with Hamilton, recurring in the Jacksonian revolt, and repeated by Bryanism.

In Canada, Laurier had felt the same immemorial pressure from the land and had tried to satisfy it with Reciprocity in 1911. That failing, a farmers' revolt could be foreseen. Though it was postponed by the war of 1914, which produced a farm boom, it was bound to appear as soon as grain prices fell in the first days of peace when the farmer, after incurring heavy debts in his acquisition of more land, found himself once more in the grip of the eastern financiers, ill paid for his labor and mercilessly milked by the tariff and high freight rates.

The perpetual struggle between city and country was well under way in Canada when the war ended. It now emerged in a new world climate which would change its course in an unforeseen fashion. Perhaps King foresaw it—the new climate was implicit in his book— but it was no time to quarrel with the West, to offer *Industry and Humanity* in the place of lower tariffs, interest, and freight rates. He could only watch the fire and try to keep ahead of it.

The first tremors of the revolt could be noted in the last days of the war. The farmers were promised by the Union Government that if they voted for conscription their sons would not be taken from the farms, where they were needed to produce food. The promise was soon repudiated and the boys drafted into the army.

The farmers besieged Ottawa and were coldly rebuffed. When Harry Gadsby, a press-gallery humorist who looked with urban condescension on the vulgar workers of the soil, wrote of their ill-fitting clothes, their boorish manner, and the straw protruding from their ears, the farmers went home in fury. They had been betrayed, as they thought, by the Government, and held up to contempt by the city press. Since they could expect no help from the existing parties, they must form a party of their own.

Once the war was over and times growing hard on the farm, the rise of the National Progressive Party was a process of spontaneous combustion, from rural Ontario to the Rockies, with a few spot fires as far east as New Brunswick. All the diverse farm organizations which so far (like the labor unions) had avoided politics fused overnight in a conflagration which their leaders had not planned and could not direct. The prairie fire was out of control.

From it sprang some unlikely figures who, briefly ignited, would soon fade out or carry their diverse torches into new movements and, a little later, divide the West and destroy the general revolt. For the moment the movement centered around Thomas Alexander Crerar, a Liberal, a businessman, a thinker, and, above all, a farmer, with the prairie sun luminous on his face, the labor of the plow visible in his tall, lean figure, the original doctrines of Liberalism unshakable in his mind, a delicate honor legible in every public and private act.

Crerar, the farm boy who had somehow acquired an education, an abiding love of the classics, and an unshakable belief in Liberal economics, became the manager of a grain firm, joined the Union Government in 1917 to represent the prairies in the conscription issue, and, at the war's end, quietly resigned because he would not accept Borden's tariffs. The parting of these two men—Sir Robert, the scholarly statesman whose world was passing, and Crerar, the classical Liberal whose world seemed to be returning but in fact was passing also—is one of the heartening memories of our politics. Such men obeyed a code now unhappily old-fashioned.

Crerar and a few friends who thought with him did not rejoin the Liberal Party but sat on the cross-benches of the Commons where that untamable individualist from Red Deer, Dr. "Red Michael" Clark, and a few others christened themselves the Progressives. Without their bidding the prairie fire leaped up around them.

From then on, until his last days, King was never free of Crerar. Repeatedly, and at last in the largest crisis of his life, King found Crerar's classic Liberalism quarreling with the new doctrine, dividing the Government, and standing like a rebuke from the past. Though they quarreled, though they disliked each other, fate held them in uneasy partnership to the end, not by mere accident of politics as it seemed, but because each represented a separate force in Canadian life which King was perpetually trying to coalesce in the new Liberalism.

Just after the first war, when a farmers' government already had
been elected in Ontario and the national revolt was fully under way,
Crerar attended a local farmers' meeting in a Calgary beer hall.
There he encountered Henry Wise Wood, a bright-burning, erratic,
and short-lived meteor who had flashed into the Canadian sky from
Missouri. He brought with him to Alberta the doctrines of Populism
and had lately combined them with an evangelical religion and some
notions extracted at long distance from the recent Russian revolution,
to produce his own private theory of a corporate state, in which the
curse of party politics could be replaced by a true people's government.

While the farmer delegates at the Calgary convention discussed
the evils of the time, between frequent draughts of beer, Crerar and
Wood fell into talk. Each saw in the other an original, perhaps a
complementary, human force. Each would soon be disillusioned.
The water of Crerar's Liberalism could not mix with the oil of
Wood's imaginary Utopia. For the present, two such natural leaders
out of the prairie soil were thrown together, willy-nilly, and borne
along by a current the end of which neither could imagine.

Thus to his amazement Crerar found himself at the head of a new
political party, chaotic and unorganized, but united in its antagonism
to the financial power of central Canada, in its demand for low
tariffs, reduced freight rates, justice to agriculture. It was, to all
appearances, a resurgence of classic Liberalism. The Progressives, or
at least Crerar and his friends, were going to rescue Liberalism from
the Liberals who had betrayed it.

So the movement was regarded by Dafoe, the ablest political
thinker in the Liberal Party. On the Progressive Party, said Dafoe,
he could hang his hat for the time being. The movement might not
last but maybe it could drive the Liberal Party back to its original
base.

Through his intimate friendship with Crerar, Dafoe became the
philosopher of the revolt and the Winnipeg *Free Press* its forum.
Backed by Dafoe's famous "Sanhedrin"—such formidable figures as
A. B. Hudson, a scholar of politics, Frank Fowler, that wisest of
counselors, who could reduce any political riddle to a barnyard
phrase, and H. J. Symington, the brilliant man of law—the Progressive Party was now equipped not only with rural anger, but with
some of the best brains in the country.

It also had in Norman (now Senator) Lambert, that unusual combination, a skillful organizer, a trained journalist, and a student
steeped in the history of politics.

All these men were Liberals, in rebellion against their Party, but

only to save it from itself. Whether that meant saving it from King
or whether he would join in the rescue remained to be seen. Meanwhile no one saw that within the new granary of pure Liberalism
some curious seed was sprouting. It would grow into such shapes as
Socialism and Social Credit and finally would be absorbed in something else which may be called Gardinerism, to splinter the West
and repeal its power.

By the summer of 1921, King was watching the conflagration,
powerless to extinguish or even to divert it. He had failed to lure the
West back into the Liberal Party by all his gestures toward a lower
tariff. Perhaps the elected farmer candidates could be persuaded
into his Government after the election. That chance he was already
considering, and so were Crerar, Dafoe, and the Sandhedrin—provided King would begin his return to Liberalism as the West knew
it. For the present the fire must run its course.

9

The New Team

I N THE SUMMER OF 1921, MEIGHEN WENT TO THE EMPIRE CONFER-
ence in London, planted there a bomb which would burst in
King's face a year later, and, on returning to Canada, called the
election for December 6.

His prospects were hopeless—Quebec solidly against him as the
surviving author of conscription, the Maritimes impoverished, the
West and rural Ontario in flames, the whole country shaken by what
seemed in those days to be a great depression. Only urban Ontario
offered fighting ground for Conservative candidates.

Meighen, always aware of every fact except the facts of politics,
does not seem to have grasped the approaching shape of disaster,
from which he could never recover. He plunged into the campaign
with vigor and outward confidence, sincerely regarding himself and
his revival of the National Policy as the country's only chance of
salvation.

His Party's blundering propaganda department tried to present
him as the one essential man and thus made him the issue, precisely
as King desired. Able as he was, Meighen could never be built into
a popular figure. He was always to have the people's respect, never
their affection or a majority of their votes. He dominated every
meeting, gave Canada the best oratory it had heard since Laurier,
overshadowed King on the platform, and carried his honor high,
but his Government was dead with the world which had borne it.

King's prospects appeared better but not nearly good enough.
Knowing that it could not popularize him, his Party wisely concentrated on issues, on the depression, and on Meighen's unpopularity.
King's assets included a solid Quebec, which the Conservatives had
lacked since the hanging of Riel and finally outraged by conscription; substantial support in the Maritimes; perhaps a few seats out
West; and, with the conscription issue out of the way, the prospect
of recapturing some traditional Liberal seats in Ontario.

The destruction of the Meighen Government, the plight of the new Liberal leader, were of small moment in history. What appalled every man who understood and loved the nation was the evident dis-integration of its politics. Canada, as diagnosed by the state of its political organs, was sick as it had not been in modern times. The quarrels of politicians, not serious in themselves, seemed to repre-sent—in the contest between town and country, in the antagonism of East and West, in an isolated and smoldering Quebec—a Confedera-tion but half a century old and already falling apart. The symptoms of that malaise were superficial. They could grow more alarming still ten years hence without destroying the nation's basic health. At the moment, however, they daunted the young Liberal physician.

As he started his breakneck campaign tour in September, his blurred and noncommittal speeches, his attempt to be all things to all men, his amorphous policies, all could be defended in retro-spect as the desperate labors of a statesman who must reunite the nation at any temporary cost to his principles. This man knew, like the elder Pitt and like Meighen, that the nation must be saved and only he could save it.

If *Industry and Humanity* was forgotten, if King appeared a safe man to eastern business, a low-tariff Liberal out West, and every-where the champion of Parliament, democracy, and the people's rights, and if he nowhere said precisely what he intended to do in office—if, in short, King was making friends of everybody while Meighen was making enemies, his conduct could be excused, by his friends, on the high ground of national necessity. His critics will always say that he was merely winning an election and building his own career out of mud.

At any rate he was fighting with two and three speeches a day. To the nation one campaign was an incident. To King it was victory or the end of all his hopes. The Party which had reluctantly put itself in his hands would certainly choose a successor if he failed in his first attempt.

By now he had found his political alter ego. Beside him on the platform stood an unknown giant, Ernest Lapointe. He was gigantic of figure, with a shock of black curls, a walrus moustache, and a humorous eye. His mind matched his body in magnitude. He had come to Parliament early in the century without a word of English, had painfully taught it to himself, and now, with a fascinating inflec-tion and a quaint misuse of words, was almost as good an orator in English as Meighen, almost Laurier's equal in French. As a human being he was several sizes larger than King.

Rather like a vaudeville team these two moved about the country

—the huge, swarthy French peasant with his superb accent and sharp phrases, the tiny figure of the future Prime Minister with his interminable, spongy speeches and sprawling perorations. Together, representing the two great races of Canada, they held the future in their hands and would hold it for a generation. The team of King and Lapointe was the successor of Baldwin and Lafontaine, of Macdonald and Cartier, of Laurier and Fielding.

Few realized that in 1921. King was not widely known outside the East, Lapointe nowhere outside Quebec. The policies they presented were not electrifying, even when the deep reverberations of Lapointe's matchless voice invoked the Liberal spirits of the past and the name of Laurier. King was playing safe. The Conservatives could not budge him an inch from the vague line he had laid down at the start.

The sovereign issue, he kept repeating as the campaign closed, was the restoration of Parliament. This was traditional Liberalism to rally the Party's original strength. For the man on the land he increasingly attacked the protective tariff. For manufacturing Ontario and Quebec he rejected free trade just as vigorously. Business had nothing to fear from him. On the other hand, some discreet extracts from his book appealed to labor. Reform of the Senate, which he mentioned now and then as an added tidbit, appealed to everyody except the Senators. All taxpayers, even Senators, could understand the promise of economy and lower taxes.

Thus at Brantford, November 24: "The real issue is not protection or free trade. It is whether for the next five years we shall have a Liberal policy of government of the people, by the people, and for the people or its alternative of continued autocracy, or government for and by a class."

The Liberal Party, in a word, offered the only people's government. The Conservatives offered the dictatorship of money, the Progressives government by a single class.

So rolled the campaign—turbid, contradictory, without visible meaning or direction. The country watched it in bewilderment. But one thing was clear—the only leader who had a chance of power was King. He had almost mastered his Party already. He had begun, only begun, to master the nation.

On the night of December 6, King heard the election results in Ottawa. They told him that his Party had elected 117 members, the Conservative Party 50, and the Progressives 65, with three independents. King was one vote short of controlling Parliament but he had accomplished a prodigy, unexampled and almost unbelievable. He had held all Quebec's 65 seats, had taken 21 in Ontario, 25 in the

Maritimes, 3 on the prairies and 3 in British Columbia. The Quebec rump left by Laurier's disaster four years before had expanded once more into a national party, still too strongly based in French Canada, almost powerless in the West, but the only truly national party left.

At Laurier's death, Dafoe had written, the age of the great parties had closed. For once the oracle was wrong. On the shaky foundation laid in 1921 King would finally erect the largest and most successful party Canada has ever seen and shatter every other party in the process. On election night, all that was far ahead but, for the first time, the tortoise had passed the hare.

F

10

The Royal Jelly

TO SURVIVE WITHOUT A PARLIAMENTARY MAJORITY, A TEST WHICH no Canadian Prime Minister had faced before, King must have the support of the Progressives. Better still, have them within the Government. The election vote had hardly been counted before Andrew Haydon, the Liberal organizer, turned up, incognito, at a Winnipeg hotel to begin negotiations with Crerar.

Like King's the position of Crerar and his advisers in the Sanhedrin was delicate. The farmers would suspect as outright betrayal any move to dilute their new-found and heady power by merging it with the Liberal Party, from which they had just escaped. Crerar had no mandate, no established organization to provide it, no chart for the future, no particular confidence in King or in the long-term future of a purely sectional movement such as he now headed. Amazed at the Progressive sweep, he could not see where it led or where he should attempt to lead it. King, on the other hand, was ready to take the farmers into the Government if they came as reconverted Liberals but not—so he said later—to form a coalition of two parties.

On this uncertain basis the Winnipeg negotiations began in utmost secrecy, the sagacious Hudson keeping a faithful record of every conversation, the massive form of Dafoe sprawled like a tired lion in the background, the Sanhedrin in perpetual conference. Sheer chance soon snatched these events from the hands of the negotiators.

A Dr. Rambeau, Winnipeg veterinarian, Laurier Liberal, and hater of the Progressives, learned through a leak in the local telegraph office that a steady stream of telegrams was going to Ottawa, signed only by the initials "A.H." To a seasoned politician they stood for only one name. By searching the hotels Dr. Rambeau discovered Haydon and confronted him with the charge that King was selling out Liberalism to the farmers. When the story reached the newspapers, the negotiations blew up. At this stage Crerar could not be sure of his followers' support for union with King and King could not afford to antagonize his eastern Liberals by appearing to flirt with western radicalism.

A second attempt was made in Ottawa but again the secret leaked out, apparently through an eavesdropper in a Chateau Laurier bedroom. Probably the kind of union that King wanted was impossible at the moment anyway. The immediate objective of Crerar and the Sanhedrin was to wring from King concessions to the West. For them, if they were large enough, the Progressive leaders were ready to pay the price of keeping King in office for the time being.

The arrangements finally reached to this end were meticulously noted in Hudson's papers but have never been published. Their result was clear enough—for the next four years the Progressives, without love of King but with horror of Meighen, saved the Government whenever it was in danger.

This suited King well. So long as the farmers voted right in the Commons, he could afford to have them in technical opposition and await the slow dissolution of their Party. This probably was assured when the Progressives refused the right of official Opposition and left it to Meighen with his handful of fifty followers. From then on, the Progressive Party could be regarded as a sectional protest only and a temporary phenomenon. It could be nothing else unless it was prepared to become a national party and thus surrendered its agricultural ideology.

The Cabinet which King presented to the Governor-General on December 29, 1921, was a strangely mixed bag and a rather sad falling off from Laurier's "Cabinet of all the talents." Still, it contained the relics of the great age, the venerable figure of Fielding in Finance, Graham in Defense, Charles Murphy (whose subsequent hatred of King is an interesting psychological study) in the Post Office, and the grand seigneur, Raoul Dandurand (a counterpart in look and temperament of Frontenac) without portfolio.

These were the last of the old crop, inherited from Laurier. King's new crop did not look promising and most of it did not last long.

On the far right stood Sir Lomer Gouin, a former Quebec Premier, and a strong man soon to be proved a total failure in federal politics. How any government containing this encrusted Tory and high protectionist could be called Liberal by any known definition King did not try to explain. He needed Quebec and Gouin seemed to control it.

The low-tariff Liberalism of the West was represented by W. R. Motherwell in Agriculture, one of the three elected prairie Liberals—

dear old Daddy Motherwell with his white goatee, kindly spirit, and love of rough-and-tumble fighting.

In between these extremes the Cabinet generally was competent but mediocre, except for James A. Robb, in Trade and Commerce, and, of course, the indispensable Lapointe, who, for the moment, was stowed away in Fisheries, awaiting his promotion. With this motley assortment King was far from satisfied and intended to dispense with the weaker sisters when he could. Meanwhile, his official family provided the compromise between opposites which the state of the Party and of the nation demanded. The Party was passing from one era into another. The nation was divided, confused, and angry. Of which the Cabinet was a pretty accurate mirror.

Parliament watched its new master skeptically and wondered how long he would last. A young man who bobbed into the House of Commons with deferential look and hesitant gait, who seemed to shrink behind his desk, his fingers playing nervously with the stub of a pencil, who had a habit of hitching his shoulders spasmodically when he stood up to speak, and then spoke in a mild, professor's voice with a dullness obviously studied and deliberate—could such a man hope to succeed the patrician figure of Laurier? Could he even control his own restive Party? And could such a soluble substance endure the cold blast of Meighen across the aisle? The times certainly were out of joint. King hardly looked the man to set them right.

The Hamlet of that drama, as it turned out, was not King but Meighen. While the Conservative leader spent the next four years in introspection, inquisition, and destruction, King from the beginning adopted the role of a friendly and judicial Polonius. Meighen's approach was acid, corrosive, and elegant—the withering interjection, the ironic aside, the upright figure of ice. King was all sweet reasonableness and round, cherubic good will. Thus, as politics became largely a personal trial of strength between two men, the race of tortoise and hare entered what was to be its decisive lap.

Meighen's first gambit was to test the strength of the evident agreement between King and the Progressives. He got a quick answer—the farmers supported the Government on the first confidence motion.

The details of Meighen's maneuvers to drive a wedge between the Progressives and the Liberals, his attack on the Government for failing to reduce tariffs as it had promised and then for damaging industry by reducing them too far, the many nonconfidence votes, amendments, and subamendments, and the usual thrusts of an Opposition feeling out a Government's strength are too lengthy to be told here.

Through them, however, the mature figure of King, the Prime Minister, can be seen emerging slowly, deliberately, and irresistibly.

On the surface he might appear to be an awkward acrobat on a tightrope, his balancing pole moving to right or left as his changing equilibrium required, without regard to principle, consistency, or political morals. In part that analogy is sound but there was a plan behind it; not a clear plan, to be sure, for King was groping in unmapped territory, darker and more mysterious than his Cabinet or Party suspected, an untraveled world in Canada and everywhere else, but a plan nevertheless.

His plan, like most acts of statesmanship in great affairs, could not afford the luxury of principles or consistency, and not even too strict a code of political morals. It was, in brief, to find, after the dislocations of the war, a common denominator in Canadian life, to unite a splintered people, to chart a middle course which certainly could satisfy no one, but would be accepted, grudgingly perhaps, by all as the best available alternative, to give the country a breathing space and convalescence.

This was bound to be unspectacular and generally unpopular. To win long-run gains King must take short-run losses. He could not hope to grow suddenly into personal power and had seen too many men like Meighen collapse after a swift start. How much of his pedestrianism came out of his own nature, how much out of his cold appreciation of the weather in which he lived cannot be assessed. At any rate the long-run gains far outweighed the short-run losses, for King and Canada.

While his general objective—a nation united on any compromise so long as it was united—remained clear in his mind, he had to follow many detours. More than detours, he had to pursue deliberate distractions and dissimulations. His entire strategy of the early years, seen in retrospect, was to divert the public mind from issues which could not be settled then one way or the other and which, if pressed, would split the nation anew.

Canadian society, inseparable from the changing society of the world, was feeling the first quiver of the world-wide revolution. It could never be the same again. King knew that, it was written in his book and seldom absent from his mind, but this was not the time to reveal what he knew. Lest change come too soon and too fast for a strained nation to absorb it, he had to act like a man who was returning Canada to what President Harding even then was calling "normalcy."

King, like Harding, repeatedly mouthed such slogans. Unlike Harding, he did not believe them. He could not, being educated. It was enough for him, at that point, to see the country growing in physical and spiritual strength, no matter how it grew, in preparation for the deeper changes and larger trials already under way.

It would be absurd to say that King understood what was happening to the world. No man understood it then, now, or any time. He did understand that a universal process of change was in flow, that Canada could not escape it and must accommodate itself to the deep tide. His business was to accommodate himself to the superficial tide of practical politics, even when it flowed in an opposite direction.

Hence, in his first Ministry, the concentration on simple issues and traditional Liberal Party policies, which would cause the least disturbance, would seem to promise the revival of the cosy prewar world and, of course, would hold the Party together and him in office.

Those policies were mainly economy in government, immigration, the construction of railway branch lines, and, above all, the reduction of the tariff. Those who are interested can reread the budgets of Fielding and his able successor, Robb, who managed to cut expenditure, to give Canada in 1924 its first revenue surplus since 1913, and even to reduce the national debt.

They may also read with a certain nostalgia for simpler times the prolonged debates on the cost of a wharf or an icebreaker, which our modern Parliament would dismiss without a word, and the angry exchanges between King and Meighen over a few wasted dollars.

Suffice it to say here that the King Government economized successfully after the deficit budgets of the war and immediate postwar years. It restored a flow of immigration. It built railways. It provided uninspiring, businesslike administration in place of inevitable wartime extravagance.

The tariff still seemed to be the central issue of politics as it had been more or less from the beginning of the nation. Though King must have known that other larger issues were beginning to outweigh the tariff, it was essential, in diverting politics temporarily from wrenching decisions, to concentrate the public mind on the old familiar ground. The tariff had been forced to the front by the Progressives and it was a serviceable lightning rod.

King used it with skill. The tariff was reduced enough to keep the Progressives in line without disturbing the manufacturers too much. Even that took courage since in a world of hog-wild autarchy Canada was the only nation to decrease import duties since the war. The British Preference was extended. The Government made a broad offer of Reciprocity to the United States. This offer may have been sincere, though subsequent events make that doubtful, but at least it was safe, since the United States already had erected the topless towers of Messrs. Fordney and McCumber and was moving on to the higher lunacy of Messrs. Smoot and Hawley.

To many observers, especially historians, this long battle over the tariff appears to have been a sham battle. True, the customs duties moved up and down little in percentage points but there was no sham in the political pressures which even this movement produced. A minute tariff change, insignificant on paper, may have profound effects on the direction and volume of trade and on the lives of countless people. Trade in that autarchial world was restrained by formidable dams. Even an inch shaved off their top released a sudden torrent of goods.

Measured by the course of international commerce, by the political pressures within the nation, and certainly by the records of other governments, the first King Government—whether it was dominated by its principles or by the threat of Progressive revolt—achieved slow but solid progress in tariff reform. This was only the beginning of a process which has made Canada the third trader of the modern world.

The moderate adjustments of the tariff, the return to the Reciprocity policy of 1911, in gesture anyway, were accompanied by a rousing invocation of Liberal traditions, with all the old battle flags unfurled.

In the Liberal Party's devotion to low tariffs and the world market there had always been a certain repulsive piety, and King laid it on with a trowel. The Party's assumption of God-given authority in economic affairs (which are only one minor aspect of Liberalism), its sublime patience with those who cannot see the light, its assertion against all recorded history that free trade is the norm of human behavior and all behavior to the contrary a temporary aberration, its worship of tariff principles too sacred to be sullied by implementation—this holier-than-thou attitude, by which the Government now seemed to replace the divine right of kings with the divine rightness of King, was as hard for the thoughtful Canadian to take as the Tory's instinctive assumption of his natural claim to power.

In King's mouth the promulgation of the Liberal economic myth was particularly glutinous and Pecksniffian. Never had Parliament seen a Prime Minister so pious, so certain of rectitude, so charitable, and so eager to convert the lost high-tariff sinner even while the Government itself remained almost as protectionist as its predecessors.

Again and again King would distract the Commons from some specific tariff item by a schoolmaster's lecture on the theories of

Adam Smith, by a parade of the golden names like Peel, Bright, and Gladstone, by the assurance that, in principle, the Government favored universal free trade, the natural state of the world, but could not throw the Canadian market open while all other nations were closing their own.

Nothing in this period is more revealing than King's laborious speech of May 23, 1923. It is filled with documentation to prove that he had made good his election promise to reduce the tariff without damaging anybody, to disprove the charge that the Government was protectionist and the contrary charge that it was exposing industry to dangerous foreign competition. The speech is heavy with figures, tariff schedules, cotton cloth, flannel underwear, sugar, and drain pipes, but all this strange assortment of goods in the shop window cannot quite hide the man behind it.

That man already was feeling the loneliness of his perch on the tightrope. He compared his isolation to that of Pitt, Peel, and Gladstone in "their days of darkness, disappointment and of difficulty." Could the House not realize that these statesmen "knew what it was to feel solitary and alone in their inability to realize within a limited period of time the ideal which was so strong in their own minds?" He pleaded for patience while he struggled toward the far-off horizon.

Meanwhile he urged "reasonable stability" not merely in the tariff but in the whole nation, since, after the "titanic convulsion" of the war, in this "trembling world" the highest duty of statesmanship was "to seek, so far as it lies within the power of every nation, to restore in the minds of all classes of the community, a feeling of certainty, a feeling of confidence, a feeling for that which, for lack of a better word, we describe as stability." He wanted a "nation of united optimists." There in a nutshell was the task he had set himself. Until stability had been re-established and united optimism had dawned, other tasks could wait.

That same speech wrung from King an admission of his secret struggle, which was little noted but is the key to his whole career. A statesman, he said, must operate in the "real" and not the "imaginary" world. He was operating politically in the real world, wherein the ideals of his Liberalism must be postponed and the heresies of his book must be forgotten. King the private person must not interfere with the work of King the public servant. It was in this real world that he was to win his fame. For him the imaginary world contained a deeper reality. The real and the imaginary—King moved day by day and hour by hour from one to the other.

In the real world King's methods by now were well known to

Parliament and public—the gentle and cumbersome reply, the long and heavy-laden speech, the rambling sentence, the politeness to his enemies. Parliament and public also had found, to their surprise, that the man of peace could fight.

Year in and year out he maintained his running fued with Meighen across the floor of the House. The Opposition leader, hardly hiding his contempt under the amenities of debate, continually flung questions at the Prime Minister, interrupted his speeches, leaped up to argue every detail. Usually King, well briefed by his secretaries, had a reply to the most obscure question, a statistic or quotation to match Meighen's. When Meighen caught him out in some factual error, his method was to assert blandly that "the facts are as I have stated them," or "I hold, Mr. Speaker, to my statement," or "the record will bear me out," and then to hurry on to something else.

The lawyer's needling questions from Meighen, King's sweeping assertions, usually with a side kick at the Conservative Party's record, fill the pages of Hansard and bring again to life that forgotten day with all its irrelevancies, inconsequential arguments, vain hopes, and unfounded fears. Throughout the record can be seen no indication that the Canadian Parliament or public had begun to glimpse the larger events now marching. Hitler's beer-hall putsch had foreshadowed the Nazi war. Communism had firmly seized on Russia. America was reeling drunkenly toward the great depression. And in Parliament Meighen and King quarreled over wharves and icebreakers, drain pipes and commas.

King was winning the quarrel but that was not yet clear. He suffered under Meighen's pinpricks as he never suffered from any other opponent. As soon as Meighen stood up to speak, one could note from the gallery the Prime Minister's sudden congelation. His pencil stub began to tap on the desk. A line of scarlet rose slowly up the back of his neck until it had flooded his bald scalp. As Meighen, erect, gestureless, and glacial, poured on his vituperation, King oozed pure hatred. The friends of student days had learned to loathe one another.

The public impression thus created by King was not too favorable, but it produced a minimum of animosity. While Meighen aroused his Party to belligerence he seemed bent on destruction when the people wanted constructive policies, wanted mostly to be left alone in peace.

In any case, Meighen's ground of attack had been crumbling under him. The country which he had pitied in its Liberal ruin was soon prospering again after the 1920 slump, trade had reached new heights, taxes had been reduced, unemployment had diminished, and the biggest boom in history was beginning to roll. Those "whispers of death" which a Montreal newspaper had made the watchword of the Conservative Party hardly penetrated the ear of a vigorous young country now well recovered from the war. By his air of sackcloth and ashes Meighen was made to appear a superfluous undertaker while the corpse seemed to be in excellent health.

King was profiting by good times. If his policies had not entirely created them, they had certainly helped. Considering that he lacked a majority, he was giving the country remarkably sound day-to-day government. More important, he was gradually succeeding in his larger objective—stability, unification, convalescence, a new equilibrium.

Through all this labor of detail—despite the handicaps of physique, a bumbling style of speech, and his technique of deliberate blur—King had proved himself an unequaled manager of Parliament. He lacked Meighen's chiseled phrase, Borden's rugged look of integrity, Laurier's charm, and Macdonald's humor, but he perfected a unique method of his own, compounded of patience, conciliation, stubbornness, and mastery of fact.

The management of Parliament, however, occupied less than half his thoughts. Above all he had to manage the Party. It was mainly through the instrument of party that King did his work for Canada. It was as a party leader that he became supreme.

Better than any contemporary he understood the Party as a living organism, something larger than a machine to win elections, distribute spoils, and punish enemies. To him national parties formed an essential engine of the state. They were the great invention of the British parliamentary system. Without them the system could not function.

Of the Canadian party system, Viscount Bryce once said: "Party [in Canada] seems to exist for its own sake. In Canada ideas are not needed to make parties, for these can live by heredity and, like the Guelfs and Ghibellines of mediaeval Italy, by memory of past combats."

King would have denied that definition. For the moment it was true that the Liberal Party had no fixed set of principles, or at least no fixed policy; it had to live, in its shattered condition, on the memory of past combats and in preparation for new ones, but under King's management it had gradually acquired a corpus of doctrine, a direction, a record of achievement, and more potential success than was good for it or the state. Perhaps unconsciously, King was founding a Party so broad and powerful that it would soon occupy the entire center of the road, moving right and left from day to day sufficiently to thrust aside all competitors on either side. It was becoming, in fact, something more than a party—a vast and expanding coalition of almost sovereign powers which only a leader of unquestioned authority could hope to control.

King was not that kind of leader yet, and he knew it. He must build his authority slowly, with infinite patience and attention to political minutiae. The business of government might be left to his Ministers. No business of the Party, however small, was allowed to slip out of his hands. He personally made every appointment of Senators, judges, deputy ministers, and even lower officials. He was in constant touch, by an unending stream of personal letters, with local Party organizations and, beyond them, with local leaders outside the Party. Much of his unquestioned political intuition was a mechanical process of good staff work, the making of useful friends, the conciliation of rebels. Like a cobweb his power grew outward in a ramifying and generally invisible net. Many flies were caught in it.

There is no mystery about his management of the Party in English-speaking Canada, which he understood. His management in Quebec was still simpler. King never understood the French Canadian mind. He had a Protestant's deep distrust of the Catholic Church and of clericalism in politics. Never able to learn Quebec or even its language, he left it to Lapointe as a kind of local governor, almost autonomous in his powers.

Lapointe could have anything he wanted in Quebec, both in patronage and policy, provided it did not infringe too much on patronage and policy elsewhere. Within the limits set by King's national policy, within the great compromise which he was trying to establish, Lapointe was independent and sovereign. This division of power probably is essential in a nation of two races. With King it worked smoothly until the moment when Quebec's demands collided with those of English-speaking Canada and threatened to destroy the compromise and the unity of the nation altogether. That was still far ahead.

King's highest achievement at this stage was his gradual domination of the Party while appearing always to be its servant. He was tasting the royal jelly. He would finally become the queen. For the first five years at least he remained a worker, laying up a store of honey for the future.

Managing with one hand the far-flung organization of the Party, with the other King contrived his own method of managing the Cabinet at the center. That method was not heroic, was often disagreeable and always deadly, but it worked.

Every Minister was left alone in the management of his own

department. King seldom asked or wanted to know the details of administration except as they affected the politics of the Party or touched some essential feature of policy. So long as a Minister did not embarrass the Government he could do pretty much as he pleased.

Nevertheless, in essentials King showed from the start that he was boss. In council he listened to all sides of an argument, invited opinions, was diffident in expressing his own until, at the end of interminable discussion, he summed up the "sense" of the meeting, and his summation, though it might not represent exactly his own view, was then unquestionably the policy of the Government.

With him the Cabinet solidarity thus achieved was even more fictitious than in most governments. His Ministers were constantly quarreling among themselves and he tacitly encouraged their quarrels. Divided, they could not unite against him. Angry at one another, both sides had to come to him in the end for support. His method was domination by division which he turned into a public look of unity. Many of his Ministers he actively disliked. Some he loathed and made no secret of his loathing. They loathed him in return, with equal candor, but, as professionals, they could keep their business and their feelings in separate compartments. Only once would the continuing rifts come into the open.

The Liberal Party was now healed of the conscription schism. The farmers' revolt had opened a new gulf which might prove almost as serious. It must be closed before King could begin to consider himself master as Laurier had been.

Having failed to seduce the Progressive Party, King proceeded to destroy it. Since it could not be destroyed from the outside, he bored from within.

Publicly, he continued to plead with the farmers to abandon their hopeless class movement and work from within the Liberal Party, their true home. Piece by piece he paid in tariff and freight-rate policy the minimum price of Progressive support in the Commons, going as far as he could without disrupting his own Party in the central manufacturing areas. Privately, he wooed the Progressive leaders with a subtlety of approach and an evident sincerity of purpose which few men could resist.

This campaign was facilitated by his usual luck. Crerar, poor after his years of public service and overwhelmed by a cruel family bereavement, retired from the Progressive Party leadership and went back to his grain business. His successor, Robert Forke, a simple and admirable old gentleman from Pipestone, obviously would be easier to convince.

At first, Forke resisted King's blandishments and the offer of a cabinet portfolio, and one day, as he told this writer at the time, rebuked the Prime Minister with insulting Western language. King took this abuse in silence and stood looking out the window while the familiar flush crept up his neck.

However, as King suspected, Forke could be had on honorable terms later on. Within three years of the 1921 election the Progressive Party was crumbling, its members were creeping back into the Liberal fold, the movement had accomplished at least part of its objective and King could foresee the end of the revolt. Another revolt already was brewing and would last longer.

In King's first Parliament there appeared, almost unnoticed, a new political force which perhaps he alone could reckon. Its spokesman was J. S. Woodsworth, à former Methodist minister, an ex-longshoreman, a scholar, a saint-in-politics, the conscience of the Commons, and the portent of a new age in Canada.

Woodsworth had been precipitated into politics by that unsuspected catalyst, the Winnipeg strike of 1919. Prosecuted for reading some verses from Isaiah to the striking workmen, thrown briefly into jail, this gentle soul emerged a blazing prophet of social justice.

He looked the part. The beautifully chiseled face, the pointed, graying beard, the luminous eye, the delicate hands, and the organ voice instantly made him a force in the House, though he was backed by only three other independents.

What he portended could not be gauged by numbers. Without yet knowing it, he spoke for the largest force of the contemporary world. He was the voice of the new Canadian proletariat coming by accident from the agricultural West. He was the first formidable leader of the Left in Canada. And, always in opposition, he was closer to King in his social theories than any member of the Cabinet.

By now the peaceful revolution which King had predicted in his book and then conveniently forgotten while seeking election was moving everywhere. It moved more slowly in Canada than in most countries, but it moved. The Winnipeg strike, apparently a local dispute, had meant to those who could see beyond next week end the emerging power of organized labor. Defeated locally, it was beginning a steady advance. To those who, like King, could see still farther ahead it symbolized that world-wide movement away from individualism to collectivism which would alter the whole complexion of American civilization in the next twenty years and which only awaited some economic disaster to launch it.

That disaster was not far off. Meanwhile the society of Canada was changing drastically, to most eyes, imperceptibly. A rural,

frontier country was becoming urban and, in a few places, metropolitan. The center of political gravity was shifting from the country
to the town, from agriculture to industry, from the farmer to the
wage earner. Crerar and the Progressive movement expressed the
last dying convulsion of the old age. Woodsworth, none too clear in
his thinking and often wrong in detail, proclaimed the birth of the
new.

Ironically enough, the man who had predicted and advocated the
revolution on paper sat in the treasury benches opposed by the man
who proposed to do something about it in fact. Woodsworth, an
independent with no party behind him, could afford to speak his
mind. King, with a Government, a Party, and a nation on his shoulders, could foresee events but could not hasten them without endan-
gering all three, and himself also. Nevertheless, step by step, King
and Woodsworth came together by natural chemistry, since their
minds were composed of complementary elements. Both were seeking the same end in a good society, freed at last from the old Liberal
market and the Law of Competing Standards.

In the end the general theories of Socialism which Woodsworth
was trying to articulate and put into a Canadian setting had more
influence on King than the orthodox dogma of Liberalism as that
word was used in Canada. This was not surprising, since King had
actually rejected Liberalism of that sort long ago. The political organ
soon to be founded by Woodsworth and his friends ostensibly failed,
as it was bound to fail in the contemporary climate of Canada. It
affected Canadian society, the policy of the Liberal Government, and
the daily course of King more profoundly than the official Opposition
and the Progressive movement combined. In short, temporarily unable himself to carry the torch which he had lighted in his book,
King was glad to find it in Woodsworth's hands.

In King's first Parliament the Welfare State was only a random
arrow from Woodsworth's quiver. Industry and Humanity were still
abstractions in King's mind, safely postponed. The great depression
which would catalyze these things was still well hidden within the
skyscrapers of Wall Street. The new society could wait.

11

Calm before Storm

NOW THAT HE WAS PRIME MINISTER BY CONSENT OF THE PROGRES-
sives and Liberal leader by consent of his Party, the personality of King seemed to change. Actually, the real King was
just appearing.

Where he had been gregarious and sociable he became solitary
and difficult to see. His celebrated remark that he could deal with
men best when he saw the least of them, his studied attempt to save
himself from the spoils seekers and hangers-on, were merely part of
his job. He needed time to think. The deepening solitude on which
he now entered came from other causes within him.

For all his traveling, handshaking, and tea drinking, he had always
been alone, as his nature had ordained; alone with his ambitions, his
God, and his dream which, in his mind, were all part of the same
thing, his mission. Public appearance and the dust of the arena
having served their purpose and put him where he intended, he
could afford to be himself.

The product of "Woodside," the old-fashioned, rather Tory gentleman who lived inside the radical found a natural refuge in Kingsmere. The original bush farm had been expanded by the continual
acquisition of neighboring farms into a broad estate, with seven
houses in all. The two largest were rebuilt, the owner drifting between them as the humor seized him, one for creature comfort, the
other for the noble view of the Ottawa Valley. Each was heaped up
with antique furniture, pictures of indifferent taste, and bric-a-brac
to suit an old maid's fancy. King loved every bit of it, fussed over the
installation of a new bathroom, relished his evening fire of good
Quebec maple, wore tweed caps, jackets, and knee breeches, carried
a stout cane, and hovered over the hired men.

He liked to think of himself as a simple countryman. In middle life
he did some physical work about the property and later on he would

sometimes hold a young tree as the gardener shoveled in the earth. He walked constantly about the Gatineau meadows to nourish his soul on this soft, comfortable scenery and to arrest the obesity which was beginning to worry him. The farmer's physical love of the earth he never felt. Kingsmere was not a piece of land but a monument, and as a monument he upbuilt it.

Since wooden houses and even living trees would not last long, later on he began those incredible stone ruins which perhaps tell more of the man than any official act. He gathered stones from demolished buildings in Ottawa, a hotel window arch, the wooden sash still clinging to it, the front entrance of a bank, some chunks from the burned Parliament Buildings, a carved stone hand—any lump of masonry which caught his eye. On the shoulder of a hill above his lake he watched the masons as they reared his queer masterpiece, in form rather like the remains of Melrose Abbey, directing every stone to its place, even playing with trowel and mortar now and then.

The result meant nothing to the masons—a series of ragged arches arranged in a square upon the turf, some fragments of walls as he had seen them in Britain—but it meant much to King and still more to those who wish to understand him. Clearly he knew now that he belonged to the ages and must leave his mark, vivid to all future Canadians. By a typical paradox, his mark, a poor imitation of foreign ruins, was written in an alien language.

In this heart of Canada, in Champlain's valley, nothing could have been less Canadian and more like King than this contrived antiquity. The man who was mediocre in everything but politics was trying to be an artist. As was inevitable in his nature, he failed. But he had his monument and, always obsessed with eternity and his brief span upon the earth, he seemed to find comfort in it.

Though made in foreign design, this enterprise contained a certain inverted Canadianism. By its very incongruity it reflected the inner conflict of Canadian life. The Canadian (as that penetrating prophet, Mr. Arthur Irwin, has said) is half a geography man, clinging to his own land, and half a history man, perpetually looking back with secret nostalgia to his origins in Europe. Such a divided creature was King. The earth and the politics of Canada pulled him on one side and, on the other, he felt always the heavy heritage of his ancestors in the old world. Hence unconsciously his Scottish monument beside the Ottawa expressed, among other things, the ambivalence of the Canadian mind.

When Lady Laurier died in 1921 and left her home to King—not to the Liberal Party, but to King personally—his domestic equipment was complete and the heirship legitimized. The ugly but commodious old pile on Sandy Hill was run down, all its furniture had been given to other heirs, and it lacked modern conveniences. King had no money to refurbish it. Happily, his admirers were only too proud to pay the bill.

There was no secret about these gifts. To any visitor King would explain that when he had envied a neighboring farm at Kingsmere his good friend Peter Larkin had delivered him the title to it a few days later and then, with other rich men who loved Liberalism more than money, had rebuilt Laurier House, installed the elevator, constructed a strong room where secret papers could be locked up, and turned the attic into that cluttered eyrie where the Government of Canada was henceforth centered.

By the time King had restored his mansion with this friendly assistance, it was, to most men's taste, a horror, a Bleak House straight out of Dickens.

The drawing room was crammed with gilt and crimson plush, with gigantic vases and glass-covered tables to hold worthless ornaments, in all an assemblage of expensive junk sufficient to stock a high-class secondhand store. No piece was ever moved an inch. Everything, threadbare and with upholstery protruding, remained unchanged to King's last hour.

A reception room on the other side of the massive hall contained items of sculpture, bas-relief, and painting which King had collected in Europe, most of it hideous.

The dining room, darkly paneled, with dim oil portraits of Laurier, Gladstone, the Rebel, and King's other predecessors staring down from the walls, was a candlelit cavern where a guest was likely to feel spirits at his elbow.

A chamber of contemplation was provided on the second floor, also packed with collected knickknacks, through which a visitor threaded his way with care.

In his bedroom King slept in Laurier's antiquated brass bed. Beside it on the floor, a warm basket housed the beloved Irish terrier, Pat, and his successors. On the mountainous bureau lay a brush, a comb, a bottle of eau de cologne, and a marshaled row of pencil stubs which King always liked to fondle nervously in his fingers. The bureau drawers were heaped to the top with shirts, socks, underwear, and the familiar high stiff collars, each item in its proper compartment. In the clothes closet suit on suit, from Windsor uniform to country tweeds, hung perfectly pressed and hardly worn. Twenty pairs of shoes, from dancing pumps to brogues, were arrayed in meticulous rows on their stand.

G

In the upper hallway, where no one could overlook them, hung a flattering oil portrait of King in the gown and hood of a university graduate and beside it, the most precious relic, a framed proclamation of the Queen's governor, offering a reward of £1,000 for the capture of the Rebel.

On the third floor, its door cunningly concealed in the oak panels, was the "dark room." Here King was amassing the leaves of his daily diary and scrapbooks a yard square of newspaper clippings, invitation cards, Christmas cards, dance programs, and every sort of empty souvenir which anyone else would burn. Nothing was forgotten, nothing lost. When King died he left several large packing cases full of Christmas cards in the basement where his secretaries had persuaded him to move them, to make more space in the "dark room."

Finally, on the third floor, reached by the new elevator, King had made his study the perfect image of himself. It was lined on all sides with books, many of them in leather-bound sets—good, heavy books and classics all, none of the detective stories on which the great are said to relax. Most of this library had been read and reread. It contained on the margin of every second page a fine, illegible scribble in King's handwriting. Even the Bible, in fourteen stout volumes, was penciled with his comments to remind himself and others after him what the Word meant.

Though spacious, the study was almost completely filled with tables, desks, chairs, a gigantic leather chesterfield, and various oddments like a cougar skin with a stuffed and snarling head to trip the unwary feet.

Every table top carried a cargo of silver-framed and autographed photographs of famous personages and other trophies of the chase. As King did not smoke, a box of pipes surprised the visitor. They were his father's. Nearby stood the piano which his mother had bought from her earnings as a music teacher. Her portrait in oils rested on a special stand to the right of the fireplace. It showed an aged woman of rare beauty who gazed wistfully into her own fire at Woodside. A shaded light, never turned out, gave this picture the look of a shrine. King could worship it at ease from the chesterfield, in which the great decisions of the nation's life were often made.

Here as nowhere else was he at peace. Everything had been done to make that peace perfect. The secretaries, stowed away in the barren rooms to the rear, could be summoned at any moment to take dictation. The housekeeper would bring in tea on a silver tray and set the crumpets by the fire. Nothing to assure the master's comfort was neglected.

About all these little attentions he showed a woman's proprietorship. As if it were his own invention he would point proudly to the special table which had belonged to Matthew Arnold and now stood beside his desk, free of papers, so that it could carry a biscuit and a glass of milk when he desired them.

All his personal wants were supervised by that jewel of a messenger, valet, and factotum, John Nicol, who devoted the last thirty years of his life exclusively to King's service. If there were trousers to press, and they were never worn without pressing, Nicol pressed them. If King wanted a book from the parliamentary library, Nicol would get it. If, while traveling, King took a taxi it was usually charged to Nicol's account, paid by the Government, to keep the Prime Minister's expenses low on the public record. King could get along without any of his colleagues. He could hardly have survived without the ubiquitous and silent Nicol beside him, night and day.

Thus he settled into a bliss of domesticity, lacking nothing but a wife and intimate friends. These he did not miss. What he had undertaken to do he must do alone. More and more he thought alone, worked alone, and lived alone until, at the end, he was almost a hermit.

At first his isolation was fairly well disguised. He could not yet afford, either in his Party or in the country, to be as remote as he desired. While he refused to lunch with his colleagues at the Rideau Club, the gossip center of the capital, or in the parliamentary restaurant, where political enemies fraternize, he was punctilious in attendance at banquets and receptions, he sometimes entertained select guests in Laurier House, and frequently dined out.

He never failed to write a note in his own hand to any associate who suffered bereavement. He sent flowers to any acquaintance who fell ill. He distributed Christmas cards by the hundred. A substantial part of his time was spent on an endless and ramifying personal correspondence with obscure people all over the country who could help the Party and tell him candidly what was happening at the grass roots.

Men of importance to him he invited for the week end at Kingsmere, where they could talk without interruption or publicity. Now and then, fancying company, he would invite lighter folk and could be observed with a good-looking matron on the arm of his chair, but always in the presence of others.

In public a model of discretion and understatement, in private King became increasingly imprudent. If he trusted a political intimate or even a newspaper interviewer he would damn his Ministers, chortle over their troubles, and, with a Puckish talent, would mock anyone from the Prime Minister of Britain down to his youngest colleague.

As the new Government gradually shook down into working order he could afford to relax a little for the first time in his life and satisfy an occasional whim. Walking home from his office one summer evening, he was encountered by a nervous but determined youth, named Carl Goldenberg, who had come to Ottawa from college to study government at first hand. Goldenberg brashly introduced himself to the Prime Minister, and King, indulging a sudden whim, invited him to walk down Rideau Street. While the excited Goldenberg explained his theories of politics and King listened, this strange pair arrived at the doors of Laurier House. King asked the boy to dinner, remarking that he had just received a shipment of lobsters from New Brunswick.

With a gaucherie that makes him blush even today, Goldenberg retorted that he did not like lobsters. King said he thought something else could be provided. They dined alone and King, setting aside his usual work, listened to his new friend until midnight.

That chance friendship grew into intimacy and lasted until King's death. It was typical of him that he gave freely to Goldenberg, as to others outside his official family, confidences such as he seldom trusted to his Cabinets. In these extramural relationships King sometimes showed a playfulness which he never permitted himself in office hours. When Goldenberg, now an eminent lawyer, in middle age, married a beautiful young wife, he received from the Prime Minister a note congratulating him on his "successful feat of cradle snatching."

As such incidents showed, King had begun to regard himself as something more than the head of government. It would be years before he could attain a higher and intangible position as leader of a people, above politics and party, but he was working slowly toward it. Thus he once ventured outside his usual narrow orbit and lectured his fellow townsmen of Kitchener on the evils of what had become known as flaming youth: "It is not the girls who drink cocktails and smoke cigarettes and spend their evenings between the movies and the dance halls, any more than it is the women who spend their afternoons at bridge who make the mothers of men who rise up and call them blessed."

This fatherly admonition apparently was out of character, it touched a side of life unknown to King, but undoubtedly was part of this bachelor's sense of national fatherhood. In these respects he lived up to his own rules of conduct. He never smoked and when he took whisky, wine, and cocktails on occasion, he was never drunk. Food he loved and ate voraciously.

Most of the time he was working. He is reputed to have worked harder than anyone in Ottawa. In fact, he never strained himself. He had learned to work with the least possible strain by regular habits, a long night's sleep, a nap during the day (he could stretch out anywhere and be instantly asleep), and by sweating his assistants.

His hours of work were no longer than those of his colleagues but they were unorthodox and peculiarly hard on his secretaries. Rising late, reading his Bible, spending an hour on his diary or dallying over a book, he hardly got well under way before noon and was seldom in high gear until evening. As he rarely left his office until seven o'clock, his staff was always late for dinner and the elevator man in the East Block must remain on duty to carry him down one story.

After dinner the real work of the day began. Almost every evening secretaries and stenographers were summoned to Laurier House and infrequently left before midnight. Being a bachelor, King had no notion of other men's domestic arrangements, cared nothing for their inconvenience, worked them unconscionably, and was amazed when a daring secretary asked a night off to see a hockey game. There was no rest even on Saturday afternoons when all government offices were closed. If the Prime Minister dined out he might summon an assistant from his bed in the middle of the night.

One secretary who waited on duty at Laurier House for King's return after a banquet foolishly sent a girl stenographer home. King was furious at this presumption. As a penalty he kept the unfortunate man working until three in the morning.

Another time King tried to find a letter for himself in the filing room and, baffled by the files, strewed them about the floor. Such fits of temper were unusual with him. While he constantly felt aggrieved by the failures of his assistants, he usually punished them without words by a manner of patient rebuke, a sort of silent treatment impossible for most men to bear.

No wonder his secretaries seldom lasted long. One new secretary after another was hired, broken by the strain, and released. Most of them left with resentment against King the man, and admiration for King the statesman. Some, like McGregor, were quietly promoted into bigger jobs.

King was capable at once of sudden kindness and unbelievable meanness.

A chauffeur who awaited him in his outer office one evening was instantly dismissed because he smoked a cigarette. After curtly ordering the man out of the East Block, King sent a secretary to rehire him.

Another chauffeur who had just returned from town to Kingsmere with a guest showed by his manner that he was suffering from some secret anxiety, observing which, King asked him what was wrong. On learning that the man's little boy had suffered a terrible injury in an accident, King sent the father to him, paid all the hospital expenses out of his own pocket, and went without a car for the week end.

On the death of two unknown children in a tenement fire he walked in the funeral procession, hardly noticed by the crowd.

When his brother Macdougall died in Denver, King hurried there in his private car, reciting "In Memoriam" and talking of death to an embarrassed young secretary, brought the body home, buried it in Toronto under a headstone shaped like that of Louis Pasteur, one of his heroes, and supported the widow and her children.

His generosity, his stinginess, his hardness, and his sudden fits of sentiment all were unpredictable, and all were related to a fact much deeper than those around him had yet begun to detect. That fact was King's direct communion with the dead.

In this period he began to apply, almost by accident, his method of political action to the larger concerns of his personal life. As in politics he first reached his big decisions by intuition and then sought visible reasons to support them, so he had made up his mind on the position of man in the universe and was always seeking proof of his conclusions.

For him the universe was God's creation, organized by invariable laws and governed by pervading divine intelligence; man was God's creature, placed in that creation for special purposes and gifted with an immortal soul. The life of politics seldom offers any striking evidence to that end and often pretty bitter evidence to the contrary. In the life of his own mind and in its outward expression, the Christian religion, King found invisible confirmation of a philosophy much older than Christianity, he was devout in his worship at the Presbyterian Church, he continued to read his Bible daily and to make his prayers, but he was eager for any outward assurance in the world of visible facts.

Corroboration, and perhaps the most important event of his life, occurred in a curious fashion. The widow of a Canadian Senator and a friend of King's was looking for her dead husband's lost will. Mrs. Etta Wriedt, a celebrated spiritualistic medium, was consulted. She conferred with her supernatural authorities and announced that the missing document would be found in a house in France. There it was found.

This greatly impressed King, who had always been fascinated by the occult and eager to believe that some human beings could span the gulf between the two worlds. He began to dabble in spiritualism with various mediums. A little later on, he pursued his studies more extensively whenever he visited Britain, where they could proceed without danger of detection.

Secrecy was essential and it was safely guarded. There were constant rumors in Ottawa of the Prime Minister's reliance on fortune-tellers but few of his closest confidants suspected that he was a practicing spiritualist. One or two secretaries necessarily knew the secret since they arranged appointments with the English mediums, but others, who were not supposed to know, wisely said nothing, being moved to admiration or mirth, according to their natures.

If the public learned that the chief of state was conferring with advisers in the other world and supposed that he was basing government policy on this advice, it is easy to imagine what an Opposition would do with that piece of news. Among the thoughtful, King would have seemed an unreliable sort of leader in the practical affairs of life; among the profane, he would have become a laughing-stock.

The mediums who were questioned by Mr. Blair Fraser, the able and ubiquitous reporter of *MacLean's Magazine,* three years after King's death, all agreed that he had never consulted the spirits of the departed on the business of state but solely on personal affairs. Helen Hughes, of London, who frequently acted as King's intermediary, says she had no idea who he was when she first met him and did not realize for some time that he was a famous statesman. Geraldine Cummins, another medium, thought he was a New York clergyman. These and others testify that King sought to communicate with his mother, his brother, and his youthful friends on matters so intimate and often so trivial that they have no place in public print and should not be subjected to further inquiry. A statesman, even a dead statesman, has some rights of privacy.

It was typical of King that he kept the spirit world in one compartment of his mind, the physical world of government in another. When he had told Parliament of the real and imaginary worlds his definition thus went much further than any of his listeners supposed. With him the imaginary world became increasingly the only world of actuality and real importance, as his later adventures in spiritualism were to show.

While it is evident that King made his politics on the mundane plane and cannot be charged with governing Canada through spiritualistic seances, it is nevertheless true that his approach to every problem, personal and political, was conditioned by his belief in immortality as first revealed by religion and now confirmed by medium-ship. Nothing about him, either as a public or private person, can be fully understood until that broader frame of reference is taken into account.

Whatever he did—and he did many things hardly calculated to improve his position in the other world—was done as part of his preparation for the ultimate adventure. Even the disagreeable things could be explained away to others and to himself as the operations of an inscrutable Providence, with him as its agent. Death and the life beyond it were the governing factors in his approach to every problem. They were not abstractions to be remembered on Sundays but facts as practical and imminent as the affairs of daily life here and now.

King once said to Helen Hughes, the English medium, as reported by Mr. Fraser, that "people who don't believe in survival haven't yet begun to live." For his part he felt himself living in end-less time, of which his years upon the earth were a small part and his years of politics a tiny fragment. Yet with the other half of his mind and with his corporeal body he valued this life and its rewards of power so highly that he was unwilling to abandon either. Like Thoreau, he proposed to face one world at a time, but he never doubted, as he grew older and more experienced in the spirit world, that it was waiting for him and would judge him.

The public in those early days of his first Government had no notion of his real thoughts. The man who was chiefly concerned with the affairs of that other world and preparing himself for it appeared as a highly practical politician only, even his political talents as yet unmeasured, as a religious man in outer forms, but, like most politicians, as a worldling who enjoyed the world which he was now making his oyster. Except by a few mediums, the final explanation of his life was never guessed until he was dead.

With this philosophy to sustain him, with his comfortable habits of work and his careful habits of health, King wore out other men but saved himself for his own high purposes as directed, he did not doubt, by God. Thus progressing outwardly and inwardly, he began to feel a new sense of security in politics and life. By the middle 'twenties the country was prospering again. The Party was quiet. The Cabinet was as harmonious as cabinets are ever likely to be. King was enjoying at last the prerogative of the royal jelly. Even he was deceived by its flavor.

12

The Fatal Blunder

AT MIDNIGHT OF FRIDAY, SEPTEMBER 15, 1922, A CODED TELEGRAM
reached Ottawa from London. In its result it was one of the
most important messages ever sent across the Atlantic to
Canada. It would alter the whole course of Empire, establish Canada's new position in the world, reveal the true stature of King, and,
for all his apparent triumph, launch him into the worst mistake of
his life. This telegram, so heavily freighted with human events, lay
unread for twelve hours.

King was in North York attending a political picnic. Before the
telegram reached him he read the news in the Toronto newspapers,
cabled from London—Britain was seeking Canada's aid in a new war.

He was irritated by the British Government's lapse in manners, its
announcement of a policy involving Canada before he had been told
anything. That, however, was a small matter. King knew that in the
British policy he now confronted, like all his predecessors, the
sovereign test which no Canadian Prime Minister could escape. As
always in moments of crisis, the nation and its leader were torn
between the compulsions of American geography and British history. King and Canada had reached a fork in the road. There could
be no turning back.

In those bleak autumn days Kemal's Turks were driving the Greeks
out of Asia Minor. Britain stood alone at Chanak in defense of the
Straits. It was confronted here, quite unaware, by those new forces
of nationalism which, in stronger hands, would soon produce universal anarchy. Also, it was now encountering the old force of North
American isolation which made the anarchy inevitable. And at
Chanak Britain was to discover, through the agency of King, that
the kind of Empire which it had long taken for granted already was
dead.

With all his subtlety, Lloyd George, the architect of victory and of
peace, could not gauge the momentum or direction of the forces

now in motion. Certainly he quite misjudged Canada and its new leader when he sent his secret telegram to Ottawa, asking for Canadian troops in the expected war with Turkey. It is not surprising that he could not grasp Canada's new position in the Empire and the world. The Canadian people had not grasped it. Nor had King. The change had been too sudden and too quiet.

Only eight years before, when Canada entered the war of 1914, it had no foreign policy, no diplomatic relations with other states, no power to make treaties, no national status, and only three officials in its Department of External Affairs. It enjoyed an actual autonomy in its internal business but it dealt with the world through London and was content to be left alone.

The war changed all that forever. Canadians now realized for the first time that, through a British Foreign Office over which they had no control, they could be sucked into battle anywhere in the world. The First World War they accepted as theirs, by sentiment and by vital interest, and all their resources were thrown into it. What of the peace to follow? What of other wars later on?

The inward doubts, the new awareness, and the growing nationalism of Canada were clearly spoken by Borden when he complained to Britain that his people, despite their contribution of blood and treasure, were treated in London as "toy automata." If Britain so regarded Canada, said Borden, it was harboring a "dangerous delusion."

That delusion Borden destroyed at the Paris peace conference in the great work of his life. By insisting that Canadian representatives be included in the British delegation, as a rough compromise between complete sovereignty and mere colonialism, by signing the peace treaty and making Canada a full-fledged member of the League of Nations, Borden evidently had erected a new Canadian status. But precisely what status? If Canada could no longer accept automatically the foreign policy laid down in Downing Street, how was a common Empire policy to be devised, by what form of consultation, with what advance commitments, under what central executive to enforce them?

The Imperial War Cabinet, including representatives of the Dominions, had worked reasonably well, it seemed to offer a model for the future but, though the wartime Empire conferences agreed to consider a new Empire constitution of some sort after victory, the problem was evaded as insoluble in logic and law. Actually, while the statesmen debated the letter of the law, a new constitution was evolving illogically by a higher logic.

If the Dominions were to be sovereign in their own affairs and yet enforce with Britain a common foreign policy, logic demanded the creation of an Empire parliament and executive. Even Laurier, in an unguarded moment, had toyed with this notion. The Round Table school in England had devised an Empire federalism on paper, but it was never practical politics in Canada. What, then, was the alternative?

The Canadian people had no answer to the question and little apparent interest in it. For all their obsession with national autonomy, they were sick of war, eager to escape the world and return to what the genial ostrich of the White House was still calling "normalcy." When Borden brought the peace treaty to Parliament and with it an obscure new Canadian status, Parliament approved the document without bothering to understand its implications for Canada. The nation demanded status in the Empire. It was not ready for responsibility in the world, which that status must compel it to accept.

Parliament and people would waste no time on constitutional abstractions, but some men were thinking on these things. Already a deep division had opened between them. King would have to stand on one side or the other. His stand as the leader of the most powerful Dominion must prove decisive in the Empire's future.

On the one side, Borden, the nationalist who had made Canada something more than an automaton, still believed in a common, single Empire foreign policy. Before going to the Washington disarmament conference as the delegate of Meighen, his successor, Borden had argued that "the voice of the British Commonwealth in foreign affairs must not be the voice of the United Kingdom alone but the voice of all the British self-governing nations." Alas, "the precise method by which it shall be worked out in actual practice has not yet been fully determined and is surrounded by difficulties of undoubted gravity, but not incapable of solution." There Borden was wrong. The problem, in those terms, was insoluble.

This King already knew but Meighen did not. As Borden's successor Meighen attended the Imperial Conference of 1921 and there persuaded Britain to end the old alliance with Japan solely because the American Government regarded it as an alliance against the United States.

Meighen acted in this issue as a North American, ably fulfilling the historic Canadian role as a mediator between America and the old world. Nevertheless, Meighen stood with Borden for a common Empire policy and a "single voice." The secret proceedings of the 1921 conference have never been published. King interpreted them as a considered attempt to consolidate the Empire in foreign affairs, almost as a conspiracy between the Lloyd Georges, Balfours, and Churchills of Britain and the Tories of Canada to turn back the clock of Canadian independence.

The telegram of September 15, 1922, instantly confirmed that suspicion. Meighen, in King's view, had tried to commit Canada to the "single voice" and now, in Chanak, the new plan of consolidation was being given its first trial. Lloyd George quickly received a surprising answer from King—the Canadian Government could not think of sending troops to Chanak without consulting Parliament, and it was not even sure that the situation justified the summoning of Parliament.

This was a polite but firm way of saying that King regarded a war in Turkey as sheer madness, that the automatic commitment to fight at Britain's side anywhere, any time, was now finished for good. King had reversed the direction set by Borden and followed by Meighen. It was the largest decision he had made so far. From it flowed consequences, good and bad, far beyond his sight.

Meighen took his stand also. Loyal to his convictions and to whatever tacit undertaking he had given in London the year before, he acted with his usual courage. He knew what King's answer meant and he demanded the opposite answer. Canada, he said, should tell Britain: "Ready, aye, ready; we stand by you." It was his most memorable phrase and it misconstrued the whole course of Canadian history. Canada was not ready.

King's convictions were as strong as Meighen's, he was prepared to fight for them, and he had the Canadian people behind him. Lloyd George in England and Meighen in Canada both had been left behind by the unnoted march of Canadian nationalism. King now led that march and thought he knew where he was going. Actually, just when the future seemed to open clearly before him, he was as lost as Lloyd George and Meighen, on another blind road.

Britain settled its trouble with Turkey at the Lausanne conference, from which Canada and the theory of the single Empire voice were ostentatiously absent. The Chanak incident, however, did not end the latest attempt to reconsolidate the Empire.

When King reached London for the Imperial Conference of 1923, he found, to his consternation, that the old drive, attempted in countless versions and colorations for half a century, was under way again. Apparently nothing could discourage the centralizers of London.

Now at last the Empire would take the measure of an untried Canadian, a Prime Minister without a majority, a lucky youngster who had stumbled into office, a social theorist, and a fledgling in world affairs. A telegraphic invitation from London proposing an adventure which the Canadian people had no intention of accepting could be rejected with little political risk. How would the fledgling stand up to the grandeur of London, which had almost overwhelmed Laurier; to the "flattery of a gracious duchess" which, as Laurier confessed, turned men's heads in an evening; to the wining and dining "by royalty and aristocracy and plutocracy and always the talk of Empire, Empire, Empire"; to the "incessant and unrelenting organisation of an imperialist campaign," in which Canadians were "looked upon, not so much as individual men but abstractly as colonial statesmen, to be impressed and hobbled"?

The techniques might be different, the purpose better masked, the duchesses more discreet, but in London the young King felt the same pressures which had almost turned the head of the young Laurier. They did not move the young King. In his old age they were to make him almost an avuncular appendage to the Royal Family.

The Governments of Britain and the other Dominions naturally underestimated the Prime Minister of Canada, with his deceptively mild look. The Canadian people so far had made the same mistake. Still, King already had revealed, in the Chanak affair, some of the iron behind the flabby exterior and he had followed up his success there by asserting for the first time Canada's right to contract foreign treaties on its own account.

When Lapointe went to Washington in 1923 and signed the halibut treaty, concerning Canada and the United States solely, a momentous precedent had been set, the changed status of Canada was now written down in binding language, and evolving sovereignty, though blurred, was evidently moving in a new direction, away from the single voice. Despite this obvious intransigence, King appeared to the British as a man who could be changed, mollified, and swerved from a course fatal to the Empire.

The old dream of Joe Chamberlain, as King soon found in London, was still alive, in its final phase. Churchill (who was temporarily out of office and had yet to discover that the Empire could not be held together by "bits of string") was calling the meeting of the Empire governments an "Imperial Cabinet." This, in King's eyes, it certainly was not and could never be. The *Times*, which had yet to understand either Canada or King, hailed the "executive authority" of the conference throughout the Empire. The conference had no authority, executive or otherwise, so far as King was concerned. It could discuss. It could not act for Canada.

The official records of the conference tell nothing of the real story or King's decisive part in it. Fortunately, King took with him a meticulous reporter who noted every play in the large game, and, moreover, understood it better than King. Every evening King returned from the conference to tell Dafoe of the day's developments, which will be revealed sometime in Dafoe's published papers. It is a story of persistent, relentless, and almost irresistible pressure by the Governments of Britain and the other Dominions to persuade King to accept some form of Empire consolidation, some method of common foreign policy as conceived at the former conference two years previously.

The old objective was presented in many new forms and disguises. King saw through them all. He was friendly, accommodating, cooperative, and obdurate. His answer to every proposal which seemed even indirectly to whittle down Canada's independence of action was a polite and invariable "no."

The British Government had never encountered this kind of quiet, reasonable, and unyielding opposition before. Finally, in desperation, it appealed to Smuts of South Africa. He was an autonomist like King, the representative of a conquered people with no reason to love England, but he was a man of cosmic views, an Empire hero, and seemed altogether a more potent man than King. Smuts undertook to reason with the rebel. It was no use. After a long evening of fruitless persuasion, Smuts rose wearily from his chair, remarked, "Mr. King, you are a very stubborn man," and left, baffled and defeated.

When Dafoe saw King a few minutes later he knew that the struggle had been won. Also, he perceived in King a more substantial figure than he had formerly supposed. And yet, unknown to either of them, the paths of King and Dafoe were now dividing, for the issue of London in 1923 was infinitely larger and more complex than either then understood. At the moment they rejoiced together.

The official record shows only agreement in London. All the struggle of those critical days is hidden by a solemn declaration of principles, unanimously accepted. Even that document could not hide a drastic change in the constitution of the Empire, or the Commonwealth, as it was now being called. Confirming the precedent of the halibut treaty, every Dominion now assumed the right to make its own treaties as it saw fit. What was left of the single voice, the common foreign policy?

Very little, in pure logic, nothing that could be written on paper. Words on paper, however, have seldom explained the nature of the English-speaking family.

King had been concerned for the moment only to repel a counter movement back toward a centralized Empire. He did not know the nature of the alternative and was ready to let it appear somehow in its own time.

Dafoe had thought his way through this constitutional jungle already. As early as 1920 he had written to his friend Borden that "the only possible status for Canada, in my judgment, is that of complete nationhood on the basis of equality with Great Britain. Our relation to the King then would be identical with the relation of Great Britain to the King; our relations to one another would be identical. The executive government in Canada would be vested in the King advised by his Canadian Ministers."

There, unheeded at the time, was the germ of a new Commonwealth, the draft of a constitution as workable as it was illogical, the fantastic invention of a monarch divided into half ·a dozen or more separate official persons.

After 1923, the seed planted by Dafoe was certain to grow. No alternative to a Commonwealth of equal states, which might or might not achieve a common foreign policy from time to time, was now available. King had made sure of that in London. He had thereby established himself overnight as a durable figure in British and Canadian history. "More than any other statesman," says Professor A. R. M. Lower, our greatest Canadian historian, and no special admirer of King, he had become "the architect of Canada's present position of national independence."

It is typical of Canada that it little noted nor long remembered and so far has not fully understood the proceedings of London in 1923. King understood their meaning well enough but, on his return to Canada, made no attempt to share his knowledge with Parliament or · people. He knew that events would declare themselves in due season. Meanwhile, the people were satisfied that their status had been protected. There was no need for King to quarrel with the imperialist minority who wanted Canada to retreat into its mother's womb.

Here, with a new national status and the rout of the centralizers, King paused—paused disastrously, as things turned out. For what Dafoe saw, what King failed to see until too late, was that the new Commonwealth, however free its members, was of itself unworkable, indefensible, and nonviable. Without a much wider setting it was doomed.

The necessary setting already had been provided by the League of Nations, but King saw that much less clearly than Borden. Of all Canadians only Dafoe had fully grasped the meaning of the League to the Empire and to Canada. "In a Leagueless world," Dafoe wrote, "the British Commonwealth would be subject to strains of unpredictable violence . . . the conception of a British peace maintained by

the pooled power of the British nations, would not be realized. . . .
Difficulties practically irreconcilable about Empire relations would
emerge." The interests of the Commonwealth nations, now sovereign,
were so conflicting that they could be resolved only in a world
authority strong enough to prevent war. King's error from 1923
onward, the cardinal error of his life, was his refusal to admit the
possibility of war.

At London, Dafoe had seen King as a Canadian autonomist. He
had yet to see that King, in his autonomy, was moving toward isolationism. Now began the most dismal chapters of King's life. The
beginning was invisible. For the moment his course seemed clear
and triumphant.

The new autonomy of the overseas British nations, won by Borden
and defended by King against the single-voicers, was proclaimed in
the Balfour Declaration of 1926, and codified by the Statute of
Westminster in 1931. The larger dream of a world ruled by law
and protected by a system of collective security already was fading
and would soon perish. It was there that King failed utterly.

Still, the failure was common to nearly all Canadian statesmen.
Even at the Paris peace conference, Borden had attacked the essential Article 10 of the League Covenant, which would guarantee collective action against an aggressor. Repeatedly, at League meetings
in Geneva, the Canadian delegation tried to water down that article
by various ingenious interpretations, the most obscure and subtle of
which King wrote in his own cumbersome style.

This movement to extract the League's teeth almost succeeded on
paper as it soon succeeded in fact. Canada was not the only League
member which was appalled at the commitments it had accepted in
the Covenant.

In Canada two motives were at work, one sound, one impossible.
Canada wanted to rebuild the League in a shape innocuous enough
to attract the United States, which had rejected its own child; it
was trying to operate in Geneva, as in London, as the link between
the old world and the new. That motive was sound. The larger
motive was sheer escapism and isolation, the doctrine of Dandurand
at Geneva, that Canada lived in a "fireproof house" and needed no
League to protect it.

Hence Canada's rejection of every attempt to strengthen the
League, including the Draft Treaty of Mutual Assistance and the
Protocol for the Pacific Settlement of International Disputes. Hence
also its refusal to participate in or give an opinion on the Locarno
treaties of 1925, under which Britain guaranteed France and Germany against each other.

In this increasing isolationism King had most of the nation behind him. After Meighen's "Ready, aye, ready" speech nobody seriously questioned the Government's course. Canada was withdrawing into the fireproof house built of straw.

The lacuna in King's thinking was noted by few Canadians except Dafoe and by few others even when, in the Locarno treaties, Britain bound itself to maintain the boundaries of Europe, if necessary by a war which inevitably would involve Canada. Assuredly, under these treaties made by Britain alone, the single voice had disappeared, but Canada, without consultation or agreement, was definitely committed to the ultimate results of war or peace.

In this sense, as Professor G. P. de T. Glazebrook argues in his classic work on Canadian foreign policy, "Canada had willingly dropped back into the position under which high policy was made in London." Only for the moment, however, and only because King, the isolationist, did not realize that a policy, in fact, was being made and involved Canada.

He continued to deny to the people and himself the possibility of war. He felt safe in his straw house. He construed the League of Nations as a debating society, an organ of conciliation, and regarded with horror any attempt to make it into a law-enforcement agency. After rejecting a single Commonwealth foreign policy and having none of his own, he sought refuge in the utterly meaningless doctrine of no-commitments. "Parliament," he said over and over again, "will decide."

Sheer escapism, since the Government must advise Parliament and take responsibility for a definite policy in any crisis. The solemn nonsense of no-commitments could serve for the moment, when the world seemed at peace. It must be destroyed by the first outbreak of trouble. King failed to see—a failure common to the statesmen of most democratic countries—that only collective security, only a strong League, could prevent trouble or repel it if it came. His mistake was to weaken the League, so far as it lay in his power to do so. His final blunder was to betray the League altogether. But he always had the people behind him. At times, indeed, only Dafoe appeared to be against him.

That slippery road to ruin still stretched dimly ahead as King reached the end of his first parliamentary term. Abroad, affairs apparently were settled. At home, the Government seemed proof against fire, either foreign or domestic. Contrary to appearances on both sides, it was in a highly combustible state. Despite his success at London and his reasonably good record at home, King was lurching toward the supreme crisis of his life.

H

13

Low Tide

B Y THE SUMMER OF 1925, KING FELT PRETTY SECURE IN PARLIA-
ment and country. In less than four years of government he
had reorganized his Party, healed the conscription wound,
almost completed his leisurely digestion of the Progressives, and
lived safely through the postwar depression.

If nothing spectacular had been achieved, Canada was reasonably
satisfied, the sectional feuds of 1921 were quiet, the Government had
learned how to operate a vast system of bankrupt railways free of
politics, Parliament was so dull that the Government's trumpery
plan to subsidize shipping on the Atlantic and break a freight-rate
combine had been the only serious issue of the 1925 session. Even
in this absurd affair King's luck held—the owner of the subsidized
shipping line obligingly dropped dead in Ottawa and extricated the
Government from an impossible bargain.

With a solid Quebec, with no conscription issue to sour English-
speaking Canada, and with the Progressive Party apparently a spent
force, the Government was ready to risk its first public trial of
strength. King called the election for October 29 and awaited the
result with confidence. For once he had underestimated Meighen.
Also, he had overestimated his hold on his own Party.

The election campaign of 1925 was as dull and apparently as insignificant as any in the nation's history. A delayed explosion was
buried within it.

King could not provide, nor did he desire, a clear issue. He stood
on the record of his Government, a fair record of expanding trade,
taxes reduced 25 per cent, the country prospering in a world at
peace. "Unity, moderation and progress," for lack of a policy more
exciting and dangerous, were his watchwords, along with such harmless platitudes as "The moderate course, or the middle of the road,
so that the greatest good may reach the greatest number," and no

"extreme measures of almost any description," which might "shatter" Confederation. These were platitudes but, like all platitudes, were true, and accurately described the slow, steady course King had set himself.

The main practical questions before the people, he said, were taxation, transportation, immigration, and the tariff. He proposed to reduce taxes further; to give the Canadian National Railways a fair trial under government ownership, without political interference, and to resist their amalgamation with the C.P.R.; to encourage immigration; to maintain a tariff which rejected the "chimera" of free trade, which provided revenue "with no harm to essential industry" but with maximum relief to the consumer.

At the last minute he resurrected the good old reliable bromide of Senate reform, which he had used with some effect in 1921 and then forgotten. He did not say how the Senate would be reformed, since he did not know, but he assured the country that he was appointing, as rapidly as the long-lived Tories died off, new Senators who favored reform of some sort. When he thus had built a Liberal majority in the upper House, "we could count upon our suggestions for reform going through."

(If the Senate was not reformed, King transformed it by his appointments until the Liberal Party had left the Opposition with about a dozen Senatorships. These, death might soon hand on to good Liberals, all in favor of the reform which King never attempted.)

King asked, in short, another mandate to carry on his existing policies.

Meighen fought on the clear-cut, historic issue of tariff protection. Without middle course, moderation, or fear of extreme measures, he demanded a revival of Sir John's National Policy. He declared that King's low tariffs were ruining business, throwing workers out of employment, driving the young people of Canada into the United States, and threatening national "disaster." He would end the "vacillating and compromising" courses of the Government and revise the tariff "upon a definitely and consistently protective basis" to safeguard the home market for Canadians and retaliate against the Republican tariffs of the United States, "brick by brick." If any Canadian manufacturer took advantage of protection to raise prices —which, curiously enough, Meighen did not expect—the tariff would be reduced, or the product would be penalized by special excise taxes. In other words, a return to well-tried Conservative principles and no nonsense, disguise, or compromise about it.

Meighen also condemned the wild extravagance of the Government, especially on the railways. He promised drastic economy, railway subsidies to aid the Maritimes-and the prairies, a vigorous immigration policy. But the tariff, the home market, the discouragement of competitive foreign imports were for Meighen the essential issue of the election, and without a "strong, stable government" to enforce protectionism "we may perish and mayhap—though God forbid—endanger our nationality."

The familiar pattern of Canadian elections when there is no vital issue now reappeared like a faded picture in a family album. The Government represented the country as recovering from the Conservative Party's mistakes, only needing another term of Liberalism to complete the cure. The Opposition conjured up a national crisis in which Canada "instead of going forward has gone behind" and now rested in "the still, back waters." Said Meighen in a phrase which contained his future destruction: "To devise ways and means to provide bread and butter and comfort for the people is, to my mind, more important than frothing about constitutional rights."

There was no crisis, the country was going ahead steadily, but the people were confused, found no magic in the pedestrian figure of King, and felt no particular confidence in Meighen. Altogether the election was worse than average in unreality.

The deep, significant, and enduring movements of the day—the emergence of labor as a major force in society, the increasing power of the state, the gradual substitution of the community for the sovereign individual, the first small shudders of the great change only four years off—perhaps were unknown to Meighen. If King suspected them he ignored them on the platform. He left *Industry and Humanity* at home.

The big decision he had made and enforced at London he was happy to forget at the moment lest it irritate imperialist voters, just as Meighen was still happier to forget "Ready, aye, ready," which irritated every Canadian nationalist.

There was nothing, save Meighen's high tariffs, for the voter to get hold of. Nothing, that is to say, in the way of policy or issue. The personal contest between the two leaders, however, was as vivid as ever, a kind of national sporting event.

Though King had not yet reached the peak of his style as a campaigner and needed time, the lines of age, and the patina of office to counterbalance his portly, prosaic look on the platform, he could fight, he seemed to have an unsuspected vitality, he was no longer a temporary accident but had become one of the hard facts of Canadian life. Meighen was already at the height of his powers, near the climax and anticlimax of his career—gaunt, saturnine, eloquent, and alarming. For the most part the people did not vote on issues. They voted on these two opposite personalities, with little enthusiasm for either.

Out of these doldrums came a shattering storm. It was not visible on election night.

No party had a majority, but the Government had been morally defeated and Meighen had won his only moral victory. The Liberal group of 117 in the last Parliament had been cut down to 101. The Conservatives had risen from 50 to 116. The broken Progressive Party elected only 25 members. Considering that he could not break into Quebec, Meighen had performed a miracle as remarkable as King's in 1921. He had swept English-speaking Canada. Thus vindicated, he saw a long era of office opening before him. The triumphant hare again underestimated the defeated tortoise.

The election had produced a temporary stalemate, an atmosphere in which Meighen, with his rigidity, rectitude, and arrogance, was at his worst, and King, the conciliator, at his best. In the subtle and prolonged chess game now opening, Meighen made every mistake, King none. Thus, while King seemed to be at the end of his career, which actually was just beginning, Meighen, by his own blunders (or by his honesty, as his friends believe), already was doomed.

The election result was staggering to King. He had expected a Government victory. He seemed to have lost his Liberal-Progressive majority and had been defeated by his own electors in North York. He had prided himself on being the best judge of public opinion. He had quite misjudged the humor of the people. He had begun to feel his mastery of the nation and the nation had rejected him.

Better than anyone else he knew that the damage to him personally was much more serious than a passing defeat could be to the Party. The Party would go on, in government or opposition. He had been leader up to now on sufferance, had yet to master the Party, and in his first electoral test he had failed. By all the calculations of politics there would be a new leader and, for King, no second chance. Happily, his luck was incalculable, but he did not know it then.

What had gone wrong? If King didn't know, some of the best brains in the Party thought they did and were not surprised. To them the experiment of the 1919 convention had not paid off. King had been tried and proved a failure. Even before the election, a small group of men who dominated the Party in the West had quietly prepared for King's defeat and departure. They were ready with a substitute in Charles Dunning, Premier of Saskatchewan, the immigrant boy from England, the dirt farmer, whose real instincts would lead him surely into the city and the board rooms of high finance.

King knew and liked Dunning. During a western tour he had found the handsome young boss of Saskatchewan beside him on a public platform and, on a sudden impulse, told the audience that he wanted Dunning in his Cabinet. That, as he tells the story, was the first Dunning heard from King, the embarrassing invitation to a national career.

Whether Dunning knew it or not—and such a penetrating politician could hardly fail to know it—the plan to make him King's successor was well under way at the 1925 election. It was sponsored by Liberals of probity and power who had nothing to gain for themselves, who were thinking only of the Party, and who did not yet know Dunning for the honest and genial conservative he was at heart. The documents proving how well this movement was organized and how powerfully supported are safely locked away and may yet be published. The names attached to them will surprise most Canadians, just as Dunning's ultimate progress surprised his friends.

Ignorant of this threat, knowing only that Dunning had been elected in Regina while he had been defeated in York, and that he now led the second group in Parliament, King was crushed and thought of resigning forthwith. The story of his life seemed at an end in its fifty-second year. After a day or two, however, the old bounce returned. King resolved to play out the game to the end. While his position appeared hopeless, both in Parliament and Party, there was the chance of another act of Conservative suicide. On the past record that was always a good chance.

King's first step was to consult with the Governor-General, Baron Byng, then his close friend, soon to be his bitter enemy.

Exactly what passed between Governor and Prime Minister may never be known. King always said that he had asked only for the chance to meet Parliament, prove that he could govern with the support of the remaining Progressives, and, failing that, to resign in favor of Meighen. Byng, a soldier and a man of honor, accustomed to gentlemen's agreements, and wholly ignorant of government and of Canada, took out of the conversation far more than King intended, or afterward said he intended. The ensuing dispute, which rocked Canadian politics and dogged King to his grave, centered around the meaning of King's word.

To King it meant that if he could get a majority in Parliament he was entitled to seek dissolution and another election when he pleased. If he could not govern, and only if he could not govern, he was obligated to make way for Meighen.

To Byng the famous conversation meant that the Prime Minister had given a binding contract by which he must make way for Meighen at any time, without dissolution or election, if King once lost the confidence of Parliament.

In the quarrel between the statesman and the soldier everything turned, so far as personal honor was concerned, on the time limit of King's promise. How many votes of confidence must he secure before he had demonstrated his right to office and, if necessary, to dissolution? To King there were definite limits in the bargain, to Byng none. And Byng, the blunt soldier, died with the conviction that King, the tricky politician, had betrayed him and was no gentleman.

For the moment, neither man foresaw the quarrel as King, with the Governor's consent, prepared to meet a doubtful Parliament, to maintain a minority Government, and to find a seat for himself.

The seat was finally found in Prince Albert. From Ontario to Prince Edward Island and out to Saskatchewan, King had journeyed far and the journey was not yet ended.

The Cabinet, with some of its familiar faces missing, was reorganized and strengthened by the arrival of the able and ambitious Dunning, now close to the throne which his friends expected him soon to occupy.

In the same weeks of shock and recovery, two other events were changing King's position for better and for worse.

On one side of King's ledger Meighen inserted a large asset with the celebrated Hamilton speech. The wartime conscriptionist, desperate to break into Quebec, was ready at last to compromise with French Canadian isolationism and, at this critical juncture, win a by-election in Bagot, which King could not afford to lose.

With characteristic ineptitude, Meighen chose Tory Hamilton, on November 16, 1925, to deliver the most foolish utterance of his career. In the event of war, he said, "it would be best not only that Parliament should be called but that the decision of the government which, of course, would have to be given promptly, should be submitted to the judgment of the people at a general election before troops should leave our shores. This would contribute to the unity of our country in the months to come and would enable us best to do our duty."

At one stroke this made nonsense of the single-voice theory. What hope for a concerted Commonwealth foreign policy if it were to be at the mercy of election politics? And what was left of Parliament if it could not decide on the issue of war or peace? Meighen, in fact, had reversed the historic policy of his Party, his own policy in London four years earlier, the policy of his British friends; he had calmly repealed the "Ready, aye, ready" theory of Chanak; he had proposed to override the constitutional power of Parliament.

Was it only to win a by-election? Meighen's motives doubtless were mixed. He thirsted for the cup of power now at his lips, he was outraged at King's blind clutch for office, but there was more to it than that. As he once explained to this writer, Meighen had concluded, after his unhappy experience with Quebec, that Canada could never enter a foreign war united without a national verdict in advance. As a politician he yearned for power and offered a sop to Quebec. As a statesman he yielded to the nation's isolationism, hoping, by a new and heretical constitutional theory, to cure it. In this clumsy straddle he lost his by-election, made no impact on Quebec, and delivered himself into King's hands.

King was too busy with another and more dangerous matter to exploit Meighen's sudden apostasy. That could wait and be utilized in good time. The other matter, too long delayed, might prove fatal.

For more than a year King had known that there was something very wrong with his Customs Department under the genial, sick Jacques Bureau. He had started to investigate through private detectives and was considering a royal commission. He did not yet realize that he faced the worst scandal in the Party's history. He did not know either that Meighen was already in possession of the facts, had handed them over to H. H. Stevens, M.P., of Vancouver, and that Stevens, the ablest private detective in politics, was preparing to dump the whole fetid mess on the floor of Parliament.

Thus, reeling from the election result, without a seat in the House, threatened by the formidable rivalry of Dunning, sitting on the volcano of the Customs scandal, misconstruing the mind of the Governor-General, but heartened a little by Meighen's incredible performance at Hamilton, King hastily prepared for the parliamentary session and ordeal by fire.

Few of his friends, observing him *in extremis* and foreseeing greater shocks ahead, could picture his survival. Without his ingenuity, courage, and sheer luck, without another and larger error by Meighen, survival was out of the question.

Fortunately, King had greater resources of character than his friends yet realized, and the lonely, acid mind of Meighen contained the final, necessary blunder. As at every point in the long race, the hare would never fail the tortoise and the tortoise would never fail himself.

14

The Great Assize

WHEN PARLIAMENT MET ON JANUARY 7, 1926, KING WATCHED IT from the gallery. On trial for his political life before a national assize, he sat, as it were, in the prisoner's box.

Below him lolled the dark bulk of Lapointe, chief counsel for the defense and temporary leader of the House—lolled with deceptive calm, his body sick, eye tired, but mind on hair trigger, ready for the attack which must come soon. Across from him the ramrod figure of Meighen, the prosecutor, seething with impatience for the kill, but outwardly as casual and Arctic as ever. And beside him Harry Stevens, the graduate grocer of Vancouver, a square, compact little man, who held behind his hard, beach-pebble eyes the secret evidence to convict the Government.

Neither accused nor accuser, though both guessed already the evidence of that trial, could imagine the final verdict.

For the prisoner in the gallery, who had survived many black nights, this must have seemed life's darkest hour. The darkness would deepen before the dawn.

His fortunes for the moment depended upon a handful of Progressives, on Woodsworth and the uncertain band of four independents. King had been their friend, or at least their sympathizer. Would they stand by him now? Every vote counted. No member could leave the House for fear of a sudden division. The whips were refusing to grant pairs. Quarter would not be asked or granted on either side.

Until he could re-enter Parliament, King's strategy was delay, which Lapointe ably executed. Delay suited the Opposition. It needed a little time to prepare a new indictment as yet unsuspected by the public, assemble evidence, and collect exhibits. By March, King was back in his customary chair as member for Prince Albert, ready to prove that, with a minority of followers, he could govern. Out of the prisoner's box, he was still on trial. Would the House vote

confidence in him by the formal adoption of the Speech from the
Throne? That seemed to be the final test. Actually it was a mere distraction from the trial now opening. The real contents of the session
lay hidden in Harry Stevens' brief case and, without the Governor-
General's knowledge, in Rideau Hall.

For the Government the debate on the throne speech was a measurement of its strength among the farmers and labor members. For
the Opposition it was only a feint. On both sides it was conducted
stubbornly and with skill but words counted little. How would the
votes fall? Two months must pass in this shadow boxing before a
vote could be reached, before any of the country's business could
move.

Meanwhile, on February 2, Stevens had opened Pandora's box.

By this time King had learned in general what that box contained.
Stevens obviously knew something about the Customs Department.
There had been leaks from the Government's own investigators. How
much did Stevens know?

When the graduate grocer rose in his place, it was clear at once
that he knew too much. To a stunned House and squirming Ministry
he delivered an indictment of corruption the like of which had not
been heard since the Pacific Scandal. This was no general charge. It
related the laches of the Customs Department in complete, sordid,
and reeking detail. It gave names, dates, and facts. It accused
Bureau, the Customs Minister, of gross dereliction, the Government
of connivance with criminals, the Liberal Party of debauchery.

The Treasury benches listened in pallid silence to the grating
voice of Stevens. Meighen sat with blank, imperial look, awaiting his
chance, which would never come. The Progressives, as King anxiously watched them in the southeast corner, the innocent farmers
who had yet to see the dank underside of politics, were restless,
shocked, and incredulous. Woodsworth, the saint who had fallen
among politicians, stared at the square form of Stevens with undis-
guised horror, feeling, as he said, that he had been plunged into a
mud bath. Agnes MacPhail, the only woman in the House, began at
that hour to lose her faith in human nature.

As presiding judge, Mr. Speaker Lemieux, impassive, white, and
majestic in three-cornered hat, black robes, silk knee breeches, and
silver shoe-buckles, shrewdly observed the faces of the jury. He was
a Liberal politician, he had been King's boss and friend in Laurier's
Labour Department, but he would do his duty without fear or favor.

The charge had been read and must be answered. The Government immediately moved for a select committee to study Stevens'
evidence. For nearly five months that committee—four Liberals, four

Conservatives, and a supposedly neutral Progressive—labored day after day, reading documents, questioning witnesses, sifting truth and falsehood, exploring the dark nooks and crannies of Bureau's broken department.

The corruption of the Customs service was soon established. The Liberals on the inquiring committee made no attempt to hide it, nor King to deny it. Officials were guilty of condoning and assisting a ring of smugglers from coast to coast. The Government, on Bureau's advice, had modified or quashed the sentence of criminals convicted in the courts. Liberal hangers-on, the scum which every party collects in office, were fattening on contraband, mostly liquor, which flowed in swelling cataract north and south across the American border. King had known that the Customs Department was weak, inefficient, and friendly to the underworld. He now saw that it was rotten.

To cleanse it, his first act, taken the previous September, had been characteristic, courageous, and indefensible. He dismissed Bureau for his failure and elevated him to the Senate for his long service to Liberalism. Here, in the scoffing of parliamentary lobby and street corners, was the promised reform of the Senate. It was to be re-formed, then, by the presence of a politician who had disgraced the Commons and betrayed the Government. A reckless act for a Prime Minister on the verge of ruin, an affront to Parliament and nation, but loyalty to a friend.

Bureau had let King, the Government, and the Party down. Yet he was forgiven. For once, King had put human charity above politics and his own safety—indefensible, outrageous, and still, in a tortured fashion, generous, almost noble. Not too noble, though. Bureau was still popular in Quebec.

The Opposition could exploit King's insult to public morality but was rather glad to have Bureau safely out of the way. He was an engaging, jolly, and weak man, the victim of his own friends, perhaps more sinned against than sinning, whom everybody secretly liked. The freemasonry of politics had no wish to dredge up his private peccadilloes.

In Bureau's place young George Boivin had been given the Customs Department. It was a high honor and a sentence of death. To repair the wreck left by Bureau, Boivin literally killed himself with work before the end of the summer.

Parliament droned on with its legislative chores. Its real business, and the future of politics, were concentrated in the Customs Committee, whose findings might well save or smash the Government. Meighen had no doubts on that score and in the meantime regarded any act of the Government as fictitious, farcical, and subject to his repeal. King was looking beyond the committee for a loophole through which he might escape into that larger court of public opinion where new issues might be raised, the present indictment forgotten.

At last, on March 3, the first hurdle was safely passed—the House divided on the Speech from the Throne and the Government was given a vote of confidence, 111 to 102, the Progressives and labor men hardly loving King more but Meighen less.

It was a narrow vote, but it would do. If it showed no great confidence in the Government, it showed less in the Conservative Party.

When Robb's sunshine budget of drastic tax and tariff reductions was approved by a majority of thirteen in Parliament and by most of the nation, when King could claim Parliament's support in sixteen separate divisions, he felt that his understanding with Byng had been fully redeemed. The Government had demonstrated its ability to govern.

Meighen doubtless expected nothing else for the present, having no friends in the cross-benches. These votes were still preliminary skirmishes. The crucial struggle awaited the report of the weary Customs committee.

While the committee slogged through a quagmire apparently without end or bottom, the House managed to make some progress with the country's business. In that agenda was an item of lasting importance to Canadians. King introduced the first old-age pension system, which added to his growing structure of social reform, insinuated *Industry and Humanity* further into the society of Canada, and, more important at the moment, assured Woodsworth's essential support in the vote now approaching. The Conservatives of the Senate made that certain by vetoing the pension bill. It was thus postponed for one year only.

Though the fact was obscured by the shadow of the Customs scandal, that session of 1926 also approved King's work at the Imperial Conference of 1923, formally asserted Canada's right to sign its own foreign treaties, and, perhaps without realizing it, repudiated the single Empire voice. In normal times this would have been a triumph for the Prime Minister. Now it was hardly observed by the public and less understood. Before the end of the year, King's policy would be confirmed by the assembled Commonwealth in Balfour's declaration, asserting the equality of all the partner nations, and, five years later, in the Statute of Westminster.

King used this introduction of foreign policy skillfully as a brief but effective diversion from his domestic troubles. The moment had arrived to turn the Hamilton Speech against its author. King became, for an agreeable half hour, the prosecutor, Meighen the defendant, in an issue infinitely more vital to the nation than any temporary corruption of a government department.

During the election campaign of 1925, Meighen had dismissed King's interest in constitutional issues as mere "frothing." In constitutional froth Meighen was now sinking, and would soon drown, when he seemed to be climbing safely to power. If he could only have realized it, the attack on the Hamilton Speech was the first stroke of a strategy which would ruin him and defeat his Party.

At London two years before, King had stilled the single voice and finally established Canadian autonomy. Meighen, having lost Quebec in the general election of 1925 as a suspected imperialist, had countered at Hamilton, in the subsequent Quebec by-election of Bagot, with the strange new doctrine that Canada must never fight abroad again without a vote of the people. To recapture French Canada he had tried to outdo King's nationalism. Now King showed the nation where the Meighen doctrine would lead and Meighen had no answer.

The Hamilton Speech, said King, meant that, in the event of war, the existing government would decide for or against intervention and submit its policy directly to the people in a kind of plebiscite. Parliament would be by-passed, ignored, and stultified in the paramount decision of national life.

Nothing of the sort, Meighen retorted, but for the first time that session he was in confusion. He had never contemplated, he said, "that the government would make the decision [on war] irrespective of Parliament." Under King's relentless cross-examination, he contradicted himself with the statement that "if the people have to be appealed to it is perfectly worthless to appeal to Parliament first. The people will decide and Parliament, when elected, will approve."

King pounced on that contradiction. Meighen, he said, would not seek Parliament's approval but would "precipitate a khaki election after the government had reached its decision and allow a condition of affairs to arise at a time of war abroad which might be equivalent to civil war itself in parts of the Dominion at a moment when the nation should be united."

For King there could be only the ancient constitutional practice of leaving the decision of war or peace to Parliament. To the doctrine of Hamilton he opposed Parliament supremacy.

Hoist on his own petard, and having antagonized many imperialists without winning Bagot or any strength in French Canada, Meighen now tried to brush his blunder aside, asserted lamely that King was misrepresenting him, and never answered the basic question. What answer could there be to the constitutional absurdity of Hamilton, to the theory that the nation must argue for two months on the hustings while the enemy advanced at leisure?

All constitutional froth, and Meighen had no time for it. He was awaiting the verdict on the Customs scandal. That would place him in office and then he would know how to manage the nation's foreign policy, Hamilton happily forgotten.

Constitutional froth, but the stuff out of which King would yet contrive Meighen's end and his own power for nearly two more decades. Constitutional froth, but touching the deepest emotions of a people whom Meighen could never understand. Constitutional froth, used now to make nonsense of the Hamilton Speech, to be used within the week to rescue the Liberal Party from imminent disaster, rebuke the Crown in Canada, and establish an unshakable precedent for the whole Commonwealth.

Not froth in fact, but the very substance of Canada. Dazzled by the prospects of the Customs inquiry, Meighen could not perceive the larger issue. And so, borne along momentarily by the side-eddy of scandal, he was sinking in the central tide of Canadian life, the tide which King always grasped and rode to fortune.

It needed a perceptive eye, much sharper than Meighen's, to see that tide as the sub-jury of the Customs committee drafted its verdict for the full jury of Parliament. King knew the verdict in advance, everybody knew it, but when the committee finally reported on June 18, the public saw for the first time that the Government was guilty, pretty much as charged. The verdict was unanimous. No other was possible on the evidence.

The Customs Department was convicted of "slowly degenerating," Bureau of failure to discharge his responsibilities, many officials of incompetence or worse, many companies and individuals of wholesale smuggling.

Was the Government as a whole guilty? The committee did not attempt to say. The Conservative members had fought for such a total verdict, and failed against the Liberals and the neutral, D. M. Kennedy, Progressive, of Peace River. The Opposition must now persuade the House to expand the verdict and unseat the Government entire.

All other business forgotten, Parliament had become indeed a court to convict or acquit but by no means an impartial court. Its verdict would be decided by politics, not justice. Both major parties would vote for their own interests, which both regarded as the interests of the state, without a break in party line. What of the Progressives and the labor men, now become suddenly the fulcrum of the future? Their votes would be decisive and, unfortunately for the Government, they might vote on the evidence.

There lay King's danger, Meighen's hope. King had been courting the Progressives and labor men with increasing ardor. Every possible pressure, promise, and persuasion had been applied to them these many months. Some were wavering. Few, if any, wanted Meighen in office. Others showed an alarming disposition to put the facts and their own integrity above the Government's convenience.

Prosecution and defense, in final appeal to the jury, prepared to capture the half-dozen waverers who could decide everything. Both sides were also addressing the appeal court of the electorate, to which the case must soon be carried. King, the layman, despite his present humiliating posture, knew that court better than Meighen, the lawyer.

For the moment the report of the investigating committee was damning enough. The Liberals had signed it and King had accepted it, since he had no option. With a little charity it could be called a vote of censure on Bureau only, not on the Ministry.

When Stevens rose on June 22 to sum up the case, it was clear that Conservative charity did not extend that far. True, Stevens spoke "with all the sympathy that one human heart can have for another" but he quickly dispatched Bureau, went on to demolish Boivin, the new Customs Minister, and condemned the whole Government for interfering with the course of justice to protect its friends, the smugglers. It was an able and crushing speech.

The boundless sympathy in Stevens' heart was not allowed to interfere with his final duty—he moved to expand the committee's report into an outright vote of censure on the Government which had yielded to "improper pressure from the underworld."

The Stevens amendment, as King knew, must be defeated at all costs. Were it passed, the Government, condemned by Parliament and with the albatross of the Customs scandal around its neck, faced extinction at the polls, presuming that it could even reach them intact. For two days King and Meighen watched in silence while the junior counsel wrangled.

Young Boivin's own defense was quiet, honest, and impressive—he had inherited corruption and was laboring to exterminate it; laboring, as it soon appeared, to the point of suicide.

Dugald Donaghy, Stevens' fellow townsman and personal enemy from Vancouver, a bristling little terrier in debate, followed with five hours of argument, sheaves of documents, and endless official correspondence to defend the Government or, that failing, to impugn the good faith of its accusers. This marathon of invective and sheer political pleading ended tearfully with a Biblical quotation—who dared to throw the first stone?

All the facts of accusation and defense were now known, could only be repeated, chewed over, and regurgitated. The liquor-laden barge "Tremblay"; the schooner "Ellice B."; the motor boats "Cozy" and "Jeanne d'Arc"; the bootleg ships that sailed legally from Halifax for Peru and returned miraculously from their voyage next morning; Daivey Waisberg and Moses Assiz, energetic enterprisers in the liquor business; J. E. A. Bisaillon, a Customs official who had made himself a small-time Bigot, a spider fattening at the center of the Customs web—these names and many others became overnight the headlines of the press and the household words of the nation.

In Parliament, sitting through the night and into the dawn, this was no longer a debate. It was an endurance contest and a brawl.

On the Conservative side, moral indignation, hints of deeper crime yet to be revealed, rumors of nine filing cabinets secretly abducted by guilty Ministers, suggestions of personal misconduct which no gentleman would mention.

On the Liberal side, points of order, argued by the hour until no one could remember their origin; questions of privilege spread over ten pages of the record while the Customs Department was forgotten; appeals to natural justice, to Burke, to the constitution, to the Bible, to cricket, to Lycurgus, and to God.

From the cross-benches of the Progressive Party old Bob Forke rising in sudden fury to denounce John Stevenson, correspondent of the London *Times*, for threatening him if he failed to vote against the Government, and invoking, as from one Scotsman to another, the glorious names of Scottish history; righteous displeasure, rather overdone, from the Prime Minister, with threat to discipline Stevenson; icy rejoinder by Meighen, Stevenson's friend, who asked King what he proposed to do about it and got no answer; timely insults from Daddy Motherwell; glum sarcasms from A. W. Neill, of Comox-Alberni, master of the deadpan; legalities from the massive C. H. Cahan (known to the Press Gallery as Dinosaurus); interruptions, heckling, cries for order; wrangling in the lobbies until Mr. Speaker could not hear the wrangle inside.

A House unwashed, unshaven, red-eyed from loss of sleep, a Government reeling toward the abyss, a nation deafened by too much sound.

In all this clamor it might be forgotten, but the Stevens amendment still hung like an axe over the Government's neck. Clearly the Government lacked votes enough to remove it. At this moment of crisis it found in Woodsworth a friendly neutral who might dull the blade.

The saint-in-politics had been sickened by the spectacle of the organized Pots calling the organized Kettles black, his stomach was turned by the smell of evil, his soul revolted, as he protested, by a society which put a man in jail for stealing a loaf of bread and promoted a Minister to the Senate for debauching a department of state. Though revolted, Woodsworth kept his head. He did not propose to leap from King's pot into Meighen's kettle. The Government should be rebuked but, having offered old-age pensions, with the promise of more reform to come, it should not be thrown out. The tortured reformer therefore proposed an amendment to the Stevens amendment by which a royal commission would continue the Customs inquiry.

King doubtless knew beforehand of this diversionary movement and accepted it as a small interim dividend on *Industry and Humanity*. The Conservatives also saw Woodsworth's intent—if his motion passed, the Stevens' motion of censure would be smothered. Assured of labor support in the House and Woodsworth's moral influence in the country, the Government might yet escape. The Liberals breathed easier. Meighen, watching the axe tremble, grasped it more firmly in his hand, and denounced Woodsworth as out of order.

The main issue was forgotten again as Lapointe, Cahan, and the other lawyers argued in parliamentary death grip the legitimacy of the Woodsworth motion. Mr. Speaker listened, but after nine hours in his chair was almost past hearing. He pleaded for mercy, postponed his decision on the point of order, and tottered to rest at 1:14 A.M. of Thursday, June 24.

Now the immediate fate of the Government dangled uncertainly between the Stevens and Woodsworth motions. Much more hung there than the House yet realized. This fitful fever would pass but Woodsworth's action had aligned the Left in Canada with the Liberal Party as a lesser evil than the Conservative. King's early radicalism, generally forgotten, had built a tacit alliance which might save him now, would certainly profit his Party in due season. He had won support where his enemies could not hope to find it. And because it had to in a tight spot, the Liberal Party was moving leftward. It would move much farther than Woodsworth dared to hope.

All these larger forces in Canadian society were overlooked as the House waited for Mr. Speaker's decision. He gave it the next day— the Woodsworth motion was in order.

Here was King's chance and he seized it with one of the ablest speeches of his life. He had long played Pecksniff. For the last two

I

days he had played Uriah Heep. Now he played Galahad and before he finished was thundering in the accents of Jove.

It was useless to deny the corruption of the Customs Department. He had already admitted it. He argued, however, with infinite quotation from the record, that he had known of the corruption and had begun to cure it months before Stevens had heard a whisper of scandal.

Briefly switching to the role of Sherlock Holmes, King recounted a tale of detection more improbable than any thriller, yet true—the net thrown around Bisaillon, the secret Cabinet meeting on a Saturday afternoon, dispatch of detectives to Montreal, closing of the net, seizure of damning documents, arrest of smugglers.

While the Government, said King, has thus saved the country by its own ruthless investigations, Stevens had merely received an unpardonable leak from a Government investigator, had rushed out into the streets to raise a cheap, political sensation, to butcher the Ministry and make a Roman holiday. How could the Government be guilty when it alone, without the help of Stevens or anyone else, had fearlessly unearthed the guilt of its own department, reckless of consequence to itself; had, as it were, performed an amputation on its own limb to preserve the body politic? The guilty party was not the Government, which pursued the corruptionists, but the Opposition, which sought to profit by the misfortunes of the country.

True, Bureau had been lax, but King defended him—a sick man, wearied by good works, well deserving the haven of the Senate. In the role of Galahad, King pleaded for chivalry toward the fallen and when Sir Henry Drayton nodded his head approvingly, King clutched at this straw and praised the belted knight of Opposition for his knightliness—a worthless straw. Neither the chivalrous Drayton, nor Stevens with all the sympathy that one human heart could feel for another, nor any other Conservative could find a spark of mercy for Bureau.

If there was to be no mercy then, said King, let there be at least justice. A royal commission would be appointed to continue the Customs inquiry (and, King intimated, might well find some dank spots in the record of previous Conservative Governments). Before this commission Bureau would appear, prove his innocence or resign from the Senate. No man would be destroyed without trial. Let the House beware of "slaughtering" innocent public servants, ruining homes, and bringing shame upon defenseless wives and children.

White with passion, fists clenched, hair damp and disheveled, King played Galahad, suddenly finding the strength of ten because his heart was pure, whatever the state of his Ministry. Like all successful prime ministers, he could also play Machiavelli, and in that role he executed his final stroke of confusion.

He had come into court as defendant. He now presented himself as the prosecutor of those who played politics with the nation's honor, whose purpose was to prevent an honest Government from completing the Customs inquiry, who sought to grasp power solely that they might fasten high tariffs upon the Canadian people.

At this wild irrelevancy of the tariff issue in the middle of the Customs scandal, the Opposition laughed. It laughed too soon. For among the Progressives there was magic in the tariff, relevant or not. It might fail now. It could be exploited with sure effect later on.

The Opposition laughed still louder when accused of greed for office. Again it laughed too soon. That greed would soon be its undoing.

The Opposition laughed and shouted "Shame!" but its laughter and shouts could not hide its nervousness. The disheveled little man with clenched fists was doing well, too well, considering the case he had to argue. Without evidence he was constructing a counter-indictment perhaps sufficient to rally the Progressives. Without straw for his bricks he was building a house which, frail and temporary as it appeared, might shelter him through this storm, until he could build better.

The Opposition jeered but could not still the final appeal of that impassioned voice. The country, King shouted above the hubbub, was not interested in the Conservatives' tawdry cabal, only in the reforms which the Government, alone and fearless, would yet wring from the entrenched enemies of progress.

Thus, as always in critical moments, the return to *Industry and Humanity*. Thus Galahad pursuing a Grail (unfortunately dripping with contraband liquor). Thus also the subtleties of Machiavelli in the pinch. And lastly, the sanctimonious quotation from Holy Writ: "For with what judgment ye judge, ye shall be judged; and with what measure ye mete, it shall be measured to you again!" When the Tory benches roared with new merriment, the diminutive prophet flashed back his final prophecy: "They laugh at Scripture! They laugh at anything and everything but they will find the truth of the words I have just used because those words have stood through many centuries and will stand for many centuries to come."

To this outburst of fire Meighen replied with the drip of an icicle. His speech proceeded systematically to stand the Prime Minister on his head. This was not difficult when Bureau had left him with no feet to stand on.

Where King had staggered blindly in all directions, Meighen's argument was built on lines of classic architecture, stone on stone, without ornament or digression, a lean tower and unassailable. Where Stevens and the others had lost themselves in documents and digressions, Meighen took the corruption of the Customs Department, the failure of Bureau, the whole sorry spectacle of the Government, and ushered them in faultless procession before the jury. Gestureless, his voice quiet, his face serene, he moved pitilessly from one perfect extemporaneous paragraph to another which still stand in the record like considered prose.

The jury retired at 12:50 on the morning of Friday, June 25; no one could foresee its verdict. When it returned on Friday afternoon King's whips could tell him only that it would be a close thing.

The Progressives, it was soon evident, were not as solid as King had expected. The debate of that fateful Friday had hardly begun before he saw his agrarian alliance falling to pieces under Meighen's blows. Kennedy, who had sat on the investigating committee, already was counted with the Opposition. Now M. N. Campbell, of Mackenzie, was on his feet to denounce Woodsworth for appeasement, apostasy, and something like sheer cynicism. Where the Conservatives had accused the Government only of a general corruption, the fiery Campbell was soon talking of the "real criminals higher up" and, through the shrieks of protest from the Liberal benches, refused to withdraw a word.

A close thing, too close. As King watched, he was meditating already a dash for freedom if Woodsworth's whitewash motion failed. Meanwhile, to contain the Progressive desertions, he ordered a concluding rear-guard action. It was led by Dunning.

That redoubtable young dirt farmer, with bushy black mustache, chiseled features, dark suit, and gray spats, looked exactly like an old-fashioned advertisement for gents' superior clothing. Behind this urban disguise was the ablest rough-and-tumble fighter of his time, and he thirsted for revenge on Meighen. On entering Parliament he had flung a flip remark at the Opposition and received from Meighen a memorable spanking which still rankled. This was his first chance to retaliate.

For Dunning there could never be defense, only attack. Before he had been speaking five minutes he had dragged up the Conservative graft of the Great War; wrung from Campbell an apology for the mention of "criminals"; arraigned Meighen for trying to raise the tariff and encourage the very smuggling business which he condemned; turned the House into screaming turmoil; produced the planned chaos through which the Government might somehow escape; and compelled the exhausted Speaker to plead again and again for order. There was no order and there would be none that day.

As Kennedy joined Campbell against the Woodsworth motion and in favor of Stevens, King could see the end. The division bell rang just before midnight. When the "yeas" stood up for the Woodsworth motion, the clerk counted only 115 of them and a moment later 117 voted "nay."

Technically the Government had not been defeated. Practically it was finished.

Meighen had reached an understanding with some Progressives who would support him in office simply to rescue Parliament from paralysis and complete the sessional business. Though King always denied this later on, there was now no hope of voting down the Stevens motion. The dike had been breached by the destruction of the Woodsworth amendment and the flood must pour in.

It soon appeared that the Government had lost all control of the House. Two Progressives, Fansher, of Last Mountain, and Coote, of Macleod, moved to expand the Stevens motion by deploring the practice of politicians in recommending mercy for criminals. The Liberals, judging that the Fansher-Coote motion was aimed at them, called it out of order. So it was, said the Speaker, but on division he was overruled by 118 votes to 116, even Woodsworth opposing the Government—a second defeat within ten minutes. The Government could not survive another.

King's personal fortunes had reached rock bottom. His power in his own Party was evaporating by the hour. In the corridors and in the upstairs rooms where Liberal members, their wives and hangers-on ate, drank, and argued to while away the dreadful night, everyone talked of his leader's ruin, some with regret, some with delight.

The Dunning movement was now in the open. Its sponsors planned a Dunning-Lapointe Ministry, modeled on the lines of Macdonald's union with Cartier, and Baldwin's with Lafontaine (forgetting Lapointe's fierce loyalty to King). Dunning seemed willing to do a disagreeable duty, if necessary. He, too, was loyal to King and took no step to unseat him, though that would not be too difficult. Still, he must have felt the sudden surge of destiny, perhaps the throb of an honorable ambition. It was a heady moment for the immigrant boy. He kept his head and in answer to all inquiries remained, as his friends recall, "in the hands of the boys."

The boys had not reckoned with the elastic and the steel in King, nor with his guardian angel. From rock bottom his fortunes were about to reach their zenith within four days. Who could believe that? Not even King.

As the dreadful night wore on, as debate guttered in the House and the members drank upstairs, as the first light glinted on the Ottawa, King knew that he must break out of Parliament, where the Progressive switch had made his position untenable. He was beginning to meditate, as yet vaguely, another plan. With luck and a merciful Conservative error, it might succeed. While he planned, the House droned on with the Fansher amendment.

It was daylight of Saturday morning when King decided to end this farce with a motion to adjourn. Meighen would not be cheated of the kill. With the dissident Progressives the Opposition voted the adjournment motion down, 115 to 114. A Government which could not even adjourn the House was dead. And still the axe of Stevens hung over its head.

At 5 A.M. King undertook his last maneuver as leader of the Government, accepted the Fansher amendment and interpreted it as an insignificant addition to that of Woodsworth. Through C. G. Power, a young man who could get things done, he again called for the adjournment of the House. Again Meighen objected, but the House, prostrate with fatigue, carried the adjournment motion by one vote— 115 to 114. King went home at 5:17, to all appearances a broken man. In Laurier's bed that morning he decided on his dash for freedom.

15

The Brief Candle

WHEN THE HOUSE MET ON MONDAY AFTERNOON NO ONE COULD read on King's haggard face the hectic events of the week end. Even the back benches could see that something big had occurred. Tears welled up in King's eyes as he rose to speak, tears of mortification and defeat.

All his old plans had gone wrong and, so far, he had no new ones. He could not guess that, in falling from office, he had escaped certain annihilation. How could he guess it? How could he suspect that Meighen was about to annihilate himself?

Afterward, King could claim to have foreseen everything, to have planned Meighen's downfall and his own elevation. His face that day contradicted such foresight. It was the face of a lost man. He had not discovered a way out of the prison. Just when he did discover it, whether Lapointe discovered it for him, as many suppose, or whether he blundered upon it blindly when Meighen offered him the chance, we may never know. King's own diaries doubtless will show him omniscient then as always. His colleagues knew on that decisive Monday that he was at the end of his tether.

His first words to the House, as the moisture of despair oozed from his eyes, were low-pitched, disarming, and brief, but they altered in a single paragraph the political history of the nation.

"Mr. Speaker," he said in the humble voice of Heep, "I have a very important announcement which I wish to make to the House before proceeding any further. The public interest demands a dissolution of the House of Commons. As Prime Minister I so advised His Excellency the Governor General shortly after noon today. His Excellency having declined to accept my advice to grant a dissolution, to which I believe under the British practice I was entitled, I immediately tendered my resignation, which His Excellency has been graciously pleased to accept. In the circumstances, as one of the

members of the House of Commons, I would move that the House
do now adjourn."

So this was the end. The Liberal regime had died not with an
explosion but with a whimper. So thought Meighen, his ice melting in
a dizzy moment of sunshine. No, not the end, but the beginning—
the beginning of King's final mastery of Canada.

That impossibility Meighen could not conceive in the intoxication
of his Pyrrhic victory. Even this frigid man found himself stumbling
and grasping clumsily for words: "Mr. Speaker, if I caught the Prime
Minister's words aright, they were that the House adjourn; that the
Government has resigned. I wish to add only that I am . . ."

King cut him short: "I might say that this motion is not debatable."

Meighen, now Prime Minister in everything but name, could only
retort that there should be a conference between him and King to
arrange the conclusion of the sessional business. A reasonable request, surely. Even this slight courtesy King did not propose to
grant. He could not tell how this battle would go but he was giving
no inch of ground to his enemy. Probably without realizing it clearly
himself yet, he was laying a fatal trap which neither Meighen nor
anyone else had the wit to see.

In the same toneless and Heep-like voice, King remarked that "at
the present time there is no government. I am not Prime Minister; I
cannot speak as Prime Minister. I can speak as only one member of
this House and it is as a humble member of this House that I submit
that inasmuch as His Excellency is without an adviser, I do not think
it would be proper for the House to proceed to discuss anything. If
the House is to continue its proceedings, someone must assume, as
His Excellency's adviser, the responsibility for His Excellency's refusal to grant a dissolution in the existing circumstances; and until
His Excellency has an adviser who will assume this responsibility
I submit that the House should not proceed to discuss any matters
whatever."

Thus appeared the glimmering of a strategy which might work if
Meighen failed to grasp it in time. It was a wild chance, but King
had no other. "Responsibility for His Excellency's refusal to grant a
dissolution"—those were chilling words in any but a deaf ear. King
could not look far ahead but he had made his first move and
Meighen, always deaf to his opponent, ignored it. There his tragedy
began.

"Responsibility for His Excellency's refusal." Would Meighen
accept it? Would Parliament support him in accepting it? If not, did
he sense what it would involve? Did King sense it yet?

That, too, we may never know. Events were now moving solely within the minds of two men, without public record, probably without full recollection in either, certainly without knowledge of Parliament's mind, which was not made up. But consciously or unconsciously, King had now baited the trap and Meighen still ignored it.

Again he suggested that he confer with King. Again King retorted, with irritating correctness, that "There is no Prime Minister. . . . When there is a Prime Minister he may come to this House and announce his wishes."

And then while Meighen rose, regnant, on the wings of a long-sought triumph, while King played Heep but already was preparing to play Hampden if he got the chance, the dazed House adjourned.

Now everything depended on Meighen, and King knew it. What would Meighen do? King was confident that he would make the mistake of accepting office and "responsibility for His Excellency's refusal." So far, so good. But if Parliament supported Meighen, he would still be safe. The trap would not close.

Meighen had disappeared and was busy with larger affairs and darker doubts than even King imagined.

Among the Liberal members that day a Canadian legend took root and has flourished ever afterward. King, it was said in the smoking rooms, had subtly courted Byng's refusal of a dissolution. A legend only. On the contrary, King had sought a dissolution at three separate interviews with the Governor-General, beginning on the Saturday and continuing until noon Monday. He wanted to go to the country as leader of the Government, not as discredited leader of the Opposition. He strove until the last moment, against Byng's soldierly, stubborn, and mistaken refusal, to dissolve the House and escape the censure of the Stevens motion.

True, he would go with that motion avoided but hanging over his head. He would lead a Government already found guilty, in part, by its own confession before the parliamentary jury. At least he would go as the head of the Government and could argue that it had never been fully censured or found completely guilty.

He must have known, for everybody knew, that the Government could not be re-elected. Honorable defeat at the polls was better than destruction in Parliament, which would lead to a Liberal rout. King, with Dunning ready to succeed him, was playing for his own political life. The chances, bleak in any case, were better as Prime Minister leading a forlorn hope than as Opposition leader expelled by Parliament.

To read the record otherwise is to assume that King was insincere in seeking a dissolution and wanted Byng to refuse it. Such an assumption would spring instantly to the minds of King's enemies. It is denied by the facts. For had King desired the Governor-General's refusal, he would have recommended dissolution only once. He would not have taken the chance of asking it the second and third times, lest Byng change his mind.

Certainly he would not have urged Byng to seek instructions from London, since this course, though quite proper, must make King appear to be recognizing Britain's authority in Canada, contrary to his whole record and to the whole constitutional argument which he now proposed to raise.

No, King had wanted dissolution desperately. If he had received it he would have been defeated in the election and replaced by Dunning. That was the closest shave in all the incredible accidents of his life.

What happened on that black week end has been told by Byng to his friends.

When King asked dissolution, Byng was shocked and incredulous. He reminded King of their gentleman's agreement. King had promised, said Byng, that if he could not govern he would make way for Meighen. Now King proposed to repudiate the agreement. As a gentleman Byng could not credit such a breach of honor.

King replied that the agreement had been fulfilled and terminated. He had proved that he could govern for the last five months. Having proved it, he was entitled to dissolution. And so the wrangle of King and Byng—both mistaken, as it proved, Byng in constitution and King in strategy—stretched through Saturday, Sunday, and half of Monday.

In the end, enforcing the gentleman's agreement as he understood it, and violating the constitution as King understood it, Byng accepted the Prime Minister's resignation and called on Meighen. For Byng and Meighen that call assured disaster.

Meighen, however, was not the mere bungler of the Liberal myth. Within an hour of King's statement to the House, Meighen perceived his own danger. Arrogance and patriotism combined in the man of ice to underestimate that danger. The underestimate was to prove mortal.

Most of the Conservative Party, jaws slathering for office after the hungry years in the wilderness, saw only the great chance—an easy election, a long term of power. A few men knew better. One of them was R. B. Bennett, who had gone reluctantly to Calgary to fulfill a personal promise, who always said afterward that if he had been in Ottawa that Monday, Meighen would have refused to form a government. There were others who warned Meighen against King's trap. All such warnings were rejected.

Meighen believed, in the first place, and still believes that his constitutional position in taking office was sound. He could not agree that it was wrong in principle, much less that the Canadian people would think it wrong or take any serious interest in it. The public, he thought, would vote against a Party which had corrupted the Customs Department. That would be the sole issue and the result could not be doubted. Constitutional froth would make no votes. As always, Meighen knew all the facts except the only fact of importance to a politician, the public mind.

There were far graver considerations which Meighen, to his honor, has never yet revealed. Byng had dismissed King. If Meighen refused to take King's place, the Governor-General, the Crown, the principle of monarchy would fall between two stools and be discredited. To expose Byng to this humiliation and force him to call King back to office, to make a laughingstock of the Throne, was unthinkable to Meighen, the patriot, or to Borden, the elder statesman, who had been called in for advice. It was just as unthinkable as defeat in an election on some issue of constitutional froth.

As a politician, Meighen was too impatient to postpone his golden chance. As a patriot, he could not refuse to rescue the Governor-General. Thus lacking a seat for himself—since he must resign from Parliament on taking cabinet office with a salary and then seek re-election—lacking a majority but never doubting either his rectitude or his success, Meighen answered Byng's call.

On Monday night he was sworn in as Prime Minister. He had accepted the responsibility of Byng's decision in calling him. Unwittingly he had accepted with it the disruption of a great career.

It was yet too early for King to count on that. Though Meighen would find it almost impossible to form a viable ministry, he might survive a few days in Parliament, call a quick election, and still escape the trap. At least Byng and Meighen together had made the first necessary blunder. King's spirits rose.

When Parliament met on Tuesday afternoon, the new Meighen Government seemed to have a good chance of survival. It required all King's genius and a last unbelievable stroke of mere chance to engineer the essential defeat without which King's career, not Meighen's, must end.

His seat in the House vacant, because he had accepted a salary from the Crown, Meighen watched with confidence the performance of his deputy, Sir Henry Drayton, and four deluded colleagues who thought they formed a Government but would soon be sadder and wiser men.

King watched also, but the moment had not come to strike. Before striking he launched his last attempt to expurgate the Customs affair and thus remove if he could the heavy load of scandal before he faced the election, now evidently ahead.

In Meighen's absence the Conservative vote had been reduced by one. Some Progressives, already wobbling, and appalled at the prospect of a Conservative Government, might switch to the Liberal side if they were given a respectable opportunity. King gave it to them in a motion moved without warning by the brilliant Fernand Rinfret.

Rinfret proposed that all the censure of the Stevens motion be stricken out, that a royal commission pursue the incomplete Customs inquiry to the end, examining not merely the work of Bureau but that of his Conservative predecessors.

Here was a gambit dangerous to both sides. The Conservatives knew it and sought refuge in the rules of order. That was Drayton's first mistake. When the Speaker ruled the Rinfret motion in order, the new Government's first division was called and it was defeated 115 to 114.

By upholding the Speaker, King had demonstrated within an hour of its appearance that the Meighen Government did not control Parliament. Equally important, King had seized the initiative at one stroke, was now demanding a Customs inquiry wider than the Government could accept, had leaped from the prisoner's box, and was acting the prosecutor.

By the middle of Tuesday afternoon the whole course of events as planned by Meighen had been turned upside down.

It was only a beginning. King's larger strategy lay ahead. In it he would play Hampden. For the present he donned again the armor of Galahad with another superb speech demanding that every dark corner of the Customs Department be exposed, that all the laches of his own Government and its predecessors be ruthlessly tracked down. He threw in just sufficient hints of Conservative corruption to alarm the Government, sufficient condemnation of high Conservative tariffs to scare the Progressives, and sufficient hints of his larger strategy to alert any Cabinet Minister who was not living in blind euphoria. Alas for Drayton and his five colleagues, they were too euphoric to heed the warning.

They seemed to have good reason for their assurance. King's first gambit failed miserably. Enough Progressives and even Miss Mac-Phail, her woman's faith in all political parties now shattered, voted with the Government to defeat the Rinfret amendment 119 to 107. The axe of the Stevens motion, long fended off, edged uncomfortably nearer to the Liberal Party's neck.

Five minutes later it fell. Now that their old friend and ally, the Liberal Government, was dead, the Progressives had no practical

reason for defending it posthumously, and again enough of them—
members like Garland, Campbell, Coote, Kennedy, and even the
heartbroken Miss MacPhail—voted with the Conservatives to pass
the Stevens amendment 119 to 109. To King this was outright
betrayal by the farmers whom he had served so well. He must now
face the electors bearing a post-mortem verdict of guilty. However,
he still had Woodsworth and the little labor group with him, and
that alliance, strong under fire, cast a long shadow ahead.

Next day, King tried his second gambit. Without warning he
moved a want-of-confidence motion declaring that the high-tariff
policies of the Government would "prove detrimental to the country's continued prosperity and prejudicial to national unity." This
was an obvious snare to catch the low-tariff Progressives—too obvious. After hours of wrangling which fought the election issue of
tariffs all over again, the Progressive group, having voted condemnation of the King Government, refused to reverse itself. These tortured
men hated the Conservative high-tariff policy, they wanted a tariff
lower than King's, but they voted with the Conservatives because,
they said, they wanted clean government above everything else,
they wanted to get on with business and go home. Anything, even
Meighen, was better than the present chaos. King's motion failed by
101 votes to 108.

This second betrayal was a bitter blow and King showed it on his
face. Too discreet to quarrel openly with the dissident Progressives
—for he had an election to win on the prairies—he allowed his lieutenants to express his feelings. The mighty soul of Lapointe burst in
anger against the traitors, Motherwell flung his best insults across the
floor, and Dunning demanded flatly, amid a tumult of shouting, what
bargain the Tories had made with the Western apostates.

King let this wrangle go on until late in the evening of Wednesday,
June 30. Everything up to now had been mere skirmishing, to test
out Meighen's strength. Now he was ready to launch the main
attack.

As he stood up with blank face to ask a simple question, few
suspected—least of all Drayton and his colleagues, now corpulent
with success—that he was about to deliver a lethal blow. He only
wished to ask, he said in a rather tired voice, whether the gentlemen
in the Treasury benches had "complied with constitutional practice
in the matter of assuming office." Had Drayton, for example, taken
any oath of office?

Now the trap was closing. Poor Drayton fell into it head over
heels. Had Meighen been in the House that night instead of governing from behind a curtain, he would have seen at once where King's

questions were leading, he would have demanded with crushing invective by what right a dismissed and discredited Ministry questioned the bona fides of an honest successor. He would have rammed the Customs scandal down the Liberal Party's throat. Meighen had been too busy to foresee King's strategy, to warn Drayton, or even to build a legal government. In those few seconds between King's question and Drayton's answer the whole future of Meighen was decided. King guessed it as soon as Drayton opened his mouth.

No, said Drayton, he had not taken a new oath of office. He had long been a Privy Councillor and that, he thought, was enough to entitle him to sit as an acting Minister, in receipt of no salary, in Meighen's Cabinet.

Without a word of comment or change of face, King closed the trap on Drayton with a click so silent that neither the quarry, Parliament, nor country heard it. Drayton, satisfied with his candid explanation, looked on composedly as King trapped the rest of the Government.

One by one he asked the other Ministers whether they had taken an oath of cabinet office. Like marionettes on a string, each of them jumped up to make the same reply—all were Privy Councillors, none had taken a cabinet oath. Perley, Manion, Stevens, Guthrie, all found themselves dangling on the fine, invisible cord with which King would hang them. For the moment they felt no pain. The House, suddenly alert, the members pouring in from the smoke rooms, beheld but could not yet comprehend the first withering blast of the constitutional issue.

The Meighen Government safely hooked, King played it at leisure. With the confession of the Ministers in his hand, he proceeded to indict them for kidnapping the Government of Canada. They had taken no oath of office, they could not without resigning their seats in Parliament as Meighen had done, and thus destroying the Government's majority. Either they had no right to govern their departments or they had no right to sit in the House. As mere Privy Councillors, without power, they had walked into the Cabinet chamber, sat around the table, and passed out portfolios to one another. Meighen, therefore, did not head an acting Ministry. He headed an illegal Ministry which was no Ministry at all. It was a shadow, a phantom, an usurpation, defying the constitution, making nonsense of a thousand years of British history.

If this counterfeit Government of shadows could vote itself money through a supine Parliament, what was left of the constitution and the parliamentary system, "what guarantee have we of future liberty and freedom in this country?"

This seemed grotesquely overdrawn. The House had not yet seen how deep King's issue went. The country (safe abed that night) would need time to awaken. Perhaps only King foresaw the anger of its awakening. Already the shadows on the Treasury benches, dimly aware that something had gone wrong, squirmed painfully. They had felt only one half of the double trap. The other half was being set for the Governor-General.

The flustered Drayton protested that everything so far as he knew was in order. Perley argued feebly that there had been acting Ministers in King's Governments. Cahan, a tough legal mind which soon perceived where this was leading, rushed in to the Cabinet's defense with a ferocious attack on King, who, with no sense of honor, had refused to confer with Meighen and facilitate the erection of a Government in the usual way.

The Liberal benches laughed with a quick inward relief. They saw now, for the first time, why King had resigned without a word to Meighen, leaving him to sink in constitutional froth. The mordant Motherwell gave it as his solemn medical opinion that the umbilical cord of the Government had been cut too short at birth, dooming it to premature death. "Keep cool, boys," Lapointe chortled. "It's only the beginning."

Yes, only the beginning. The little man standing stolid above the storm was physically exhausted. For more than a week King had worked day and night, quarreled with the Governor-General, watched his Government dismissed, his Party thrown into opposition, his own career perhaps wrecked, and all that time, except for Lapointe and a few others, he endured his agony alone. This, he knew, was the watershed of his life. The present hour would make or break him. All that had gone before was preface only. By tomorrow's dawn he must win or lose everything.

The combined fear, courage, despair, and glory of that hour sustained his tired body. Pecksniff, Galahad, and Heep he had played with ease. Now he was swept along at the side of Hampden, with all the Roundhead armies at his heels. As the savior of Canadian liberty, he was once again, as in his boyhood, the reincarnation of his grandfather. Parliament listened to the Rebel that night.

King's speech was perhaps the greatest of his life. Certainly it was his bravest show. It grew in stature with every attempt of the Conservatives to suppress it. Each question, each jeer, and the continual gales of laughter which hid the Conservatives' uneasiness only served to open up new avenues for King's argument, to supply him with more devastating retorts until the whole effect was overpowering, like the denouement of a stage play.

Manion spluttered and scoffed. Drayton could think of nothing but a few gauche sarcasms. The back benches flung pitiful taunts. Only Cahan had the sense to see that the issue raised by King was fundamental, striking to the roots of the nation's life. In vain Cahan tried to argue it. King overbore him. The little prosecutor had started quietly with a punctilious legal manner. Now he was ablaze as the House had never seen him before.

Step by step he went over the events of the last five days. He had found it impossible to govern, but since no one else could govern, since a majority of the electors had pronounced against Meighen's tariff policy, since Meighen obviously could not survive in this Parliament, the only proper course was dissolution and a new election. Had there been any chance for Meighen, King would have been the first to recommend him to Byng, but Meighen had no such chance and the present spectacle proved it, just as King had foreseen.

"What spectacle?" cried the Conservatives, and King flung back: "A country being governed by a Cabinet in which there is not a single Minister of the Crown in Parliament and in which there is no Prime Minister with a seat in the House. . . ." The jeers drowned out his voice. Only for the moment. The enemy could not shout him down.

The nation, abed at this midnight, would not hear the news until the morning. Meighen, tongue-tied behind the curtain, still believed that King's new issue was bogus, irrelevant, and politically ineffective. There were some men in that House who understood and it was to them that King was appealing now as he would appeal to the nation tomorrow.

The dissident Progressives who had broken with him on the Customs scandal were restless in their seats. They at least knew that King had pushed politics far beyond the scandal. It was already a faint spot of dirt on the road and receding every moment.

King did not spare the traitors. Sure that most of the Progressives were still with him and that on his new issue he could win an election without them, he damned the little group which had voted against him on the Stevens motion, abandoned the appeal to their old friendship, and drove them to his support by constitutional logic which these men, by their proved honesty, could not reject. If they could be switched, King would bring down the Meighen Government.

Such was his immediate objective on the midnight of this last day in June. It seemed too ambitious. That within three hours he could elude the Customs scandal, turn Parliament and country inside out, and destroy a Government scarce one day old was unimaginable. King gambled everything on that chance.

He gambled on the one thing he knew better than any statesman of his time—the deep, inarticulate, and unshakable instinct of the Canadian people whom Meighen never understood, the instinct of a people who had struggled for more than a hundred years to establish responsible government and would never give it up, would punish without mercy any government which infringed it. And at this midnight the bewildered Conservatives rushed in to complete King's case, to place him in the center stream of the nation's history, and to paint his issue in the garish, human colors that the public could not fail to understand.

For now there came from the Government benches the very cry that King needed to consolidate and dramatize his case, to lift it out of the constitutional froth and lay it complete and unanswerable on the breakfast table of Canada tomorrow.

"You are thinking of '37!" shouted some frenzied Conservative, his name lost in the hubbub.

"Yes!" cried King, as the history of his grandfather, his mother, and his own youth surged up in him. "Yes, I am thinking of '37 and I tell my honorable friend that I was never prouder in my life than to have the privilege of standing in this Parliament tonight on behalf of British parliamentary institutions denouncing the irresponsible government of his Party. Do the honorable gentlemen opposite advocate that we go back to a condition of affairs in Canada worse than anything that existed in 1837?"

There it was—the whole past of his family, the grandfather's exile, the mother's alien corn, everything he had labored for, the secret dream conjured up in blinding vision.

All the days of his life seemed to have been lived solely for this hour. The schoolboy of Berlin, the pallid university student, the amateur of social reform, the dilettante of Ottawa drawing rooms, the apprentice politician had merged into the Rebel's grandson aflame with the Rebel's cause. The Tories, like the Tories of '37, might jeer, but King held them in his hand because he believed in that vision as he had never believed in anything, and he knew that the Canadian people would believe in it also.

The glory of that moment was almost too much to be borne. Groping for words, he could only shout again: "1837 was bad enough but it was not a circumstance on the present condition of affairs. If, at the instance of one individual, a Prime Minister can be put into office and with a Ministry which is not yet formed be permitted to vote all the supplies necessary to carry on the Government of

K

Canada for a year, we have reached a condition in this country that threatens the constitutional liberty, freedom and right in all parts of the world!"

It was a turgid sentence, a feeble attempt to distill the real essence of this crisis and it drew the issue in lines of gross hyperbole, but wanton, clumsy, and pompous as they were, his words would arouse the ghosts of '37, they would awake the racial memory and unfailingly penetrate the Canadian mind.

Yet for King there was peril in them. In that heady flow he had let fall a dangerous phrase—"one individual" at whose instance an illegal Government had come into office. The panting Conservatives seized on it. Who, demanded Leon Ladner, was that "one individual"? It could be only Byng, King faltered in the midst of a general outcry, realizing that he had dragged the Crown into debate, an unpardonable offense by the rules not merely of Parliament but of the British constitutional system.

Hastily, as the shouting died down, he explained that "the individual to whom I refer has, I believe, acted according to his conscience, honestly, sincerely, truly, I have nothing disrespectful to say of him in any particular. I have the greatest admiration for him . . . a gentleman for whom I have the greatest affection possible. . . ."

This was dangerous ground. It could not be avoided, for King was ready to close the other half of his trap and Byng perforce was inside it. The illegality of the Government was one charge, already proved to King's satisfaction. The other was still graver, involving the whole function, power, and limitation of the Crown in Canada. Graver and, politically, much more devastating. The public might forgive Meighen for knocking together a temporary and questionable Government in a single afternoon, because he had no alternative. It would never forgive the Crown for invading the rights of Parliament or its adviser for recommending this invasion.

King had Meighen fatally impaled. It was much more tricky work to thrust home the blade while sparing the Governor-General. As King now risked everything on that thrust it was soon clear that Byng could not escape. Laboriously, over and over again, King repeated his respect and affection for Byng (who by now had no respect or affection for King), he blamed Byng's actions on Meighen, who must take sole responsibility for them, but clearly the attack, however it might be disguised, was on Byng himself.

King said he had tendered sound advice when he proposed dissolution to Byng. The advice had been refused not by Meighen, but by Byng. Undoubtedly Byng had acted in the honest belief that Meighen could govern and for that belief Meighen perhaps was actually, as he was constitutionally, responsible. But who had made the original mistake? Only Byng. King might blame Meighen as Byng's adviser. He knew that the country would blame Byng and, unable to punish him, would punish Meighen.

King had come thus far without a slip. Then, though no one observed his accident, he fell at least halfway through the thin ice.

His midnight fall, unnoted by Parliament and forgotten by the public in the succeeding spectacle, was recorded by the unerring stenographers of Hansard. Within a week the Liberal Party, King at its head, would launch its crusade for responsible government on the charge that the Crown had refused the advice of its Prime Minister and thus placed itself above Parliament and people. That was the sole issue which struck at the foundations of democracy.

Hansard reveals no such charge. On that frantic midnight King raised no such issue. Fumbling his way through a constitutional forest without path or precedent, depleted by days of unbroken crisis and hours of ceaseless speech, shouting to make himself heard above the tumult of the House, either he did not yet perceive the final sharp point of his weapon or did not dare to use it in Parliament as he later used it in the country.

The record shows how far the whole constitutional issue, clear in Parliament, was distorted on the hustings. Under the cross-examination of the Government benches King said specifically that he did not question the Governor-General's right to refuse his advice. On the contrary—in denial of the Liberal campaign in the following weeks—King agreed that the Governor-General had the right to refuse that advice, provided he could find a new Prime Minister able to govern. If Meighen could not govern, he must return to Byng and resign, admitting his mistake in taking office. Until Parliament determined whether Meighen could govern, King would "wait and see what His Excellency does before I judge of the motive which governed with respect to the non-acceptance of the advice which I tendered and which motive up to this moment I have never questioned."

Again: "I have no objection that the right honorable gentleman who is today Prime Minister of Canada should be given his chance, if you wish to call it such, to carry on the business of the country at present."

Byng's actions up to that moment had not been questioned. There was the core of the issue which the election would garble. It remains unalterable on the record—King had not disputed the right of the Crown to refuse a Prime Minister's request for dissolution if an alternative government could be found.

The Conservatives now had the chance to pull the sting out of

King's election issue. They failed either from stupidity or because they thought the issue not worth their trouble. As a result, the Liberals could fight the election on the proposition that the Crown could never refuse its Prime Minister's advice without imperiling the constitutional system, even though King had admitted the contrary.

In the clamor of midnight, as it passed into the first hours of Dominion Day, all these fine points were blunted. Even now they still lie buried under the rubble. That King himself saw them clearly at first is doubtful from the confusion of his speech. Certainly Parliament did not, and the nation was asleep. For the present confusion, contrived or accidental, suited King well. It gave him the chance to prepare his last decisive blow and, exhausted as he was by argument, passion, and hunger, he delivered it with an impact certain to reach the Canadian mind from coast to coast on the nation's birthday.

Who, asked King, was defending the Crown? Who was dragging it into the mire of party politics? He paused a moment for an answer and received only a few nervous guffaws from the Government benches. Then he answered his own question—he was defending the Crown, he was rescuing the constitution from peril, while Meighen, by bad advice to Byng, by pretending that he could govern when clearly he could not, had dishonored the Crown and installed an illegal Government.

And now the ultimate crusher: In Britain for a hundred years no King had ever refused the advice of a Prime Minister. If the King's representative in Canada could refuse such advice then such a theory of government "reduces this Dominion of Canada from the status of a self-governing Dominion to the status of a Crown Colony."

Those words contradicted the earlier statement that Byng had done no wrong. They opened up an entirely new issue. No matter that the House failed to see the deft shift of ground. They were words to touch the deepest Canadian instinct. They raised the old emblem of national independence which the dullest Canadian could understand. They asked Canadians whether they were citizens of a free country or the colonists of England. If that question was valid, there could be only one answer from Parliament and people.

Left thus, the question was full of danger, too. If it conjured up the ghosts of Canadian nationalism it also raised the ancient love of England. It thrust Canada headlong between the two contrary poles of its being—the pole of geography and the pole of history. The geography men of nationalism would rally to the call of Canada. The history men would hear the call of their origins in England. The nationalists would vote for King because he was one of them. The imperialists might vote for Meighen because King, despite all his protests, might seem to be attacking the British connection.

This danger King had foreseen before he uttered a word and he was ready to forestall it. And so the final stroke: Who, he asked, was defending the British Empire, who dividing it? Again the same answer. King alone was the Empire's defender. "The issue that we are face to face with at the present time is one which affects all parts of the British Empire and it is, amongst other reasons, because of my belief in and my love for the British Empire, that I take the stand that I do in this matter. It is only by a recognition of the fact that the British Empire rests upon the corner stone of responsible self-government in each of the Dominions and the Mother Country that this great Empire can endure."

Meighen, by usurpation, by infringing responsible government, by dragging the Crown into politics, by placing Byng in a position of "great suspense which he must be in at the present time with respect to whether or not his act has been constitutional or justified"— Meighen was the underminer of the Empire, King its savior. Meighen was also the true enemy of Byng. King was his friend.

Here, in a few awkward sentences, was the crowning masterpiece of King's strategy. He had made himself at once the Rebel of Canadian nationalism and yet, by miraculous combination, the Empire's champion in Canada. He had outflanked Meighen from both sides. At that instant he had chemically combined, as it were, the opposite instincts of the Canadian people into a single force that must prove irresistible. Everything in King's life up to midnight of June 30 had been weary plodding. This was political genius in a sudden flash. It made King. It ruined Meighen.

When King slumped at last into his chair, he was sure he had turned politics upside down, with himself on top.

The Conservatives, thoroughly alarmed by now, finding themselves no longer on the attack but huddled in defense, vainly tried to answer King. Stevens undertook solid argument on grounds of reason and common sense—arguable grounds, no doubt, but who could hold them against the emotions unloosed by King? Cahan, that magnificent dinosaur of the law, followed with legal analyses. It was no use. None of the Conservatives was prepared for this crisis, none was properly briefed, and Meighen, who might have improvised a holding action, was somewhere behind the curtain, listening, but speechless.

At ten minutes past one on Dominion Day Drayton moved an adjournment. King went home almost sick with success. The Conservatives repaired to the library to search the history books and find before dawn some answer to his attack.

By Thursday afternoon, July 1, it was clear to Parliament and country that the whole situation of the preceding months had been reversed and was now strained to the bursting point. The smear of the Customs scandal was all but obliterated. The Governor-General had been catapulted into politics for the first time since Elgin. The legality of existing government had been indicted, the endurance of responsible government itself questioned. The independence of Canada within the Commonwealth had shouldered aside all other public business.

The people, stupefied by these events, were not ready yet to judge them. King had no doubt of their judgment when they got their mind around the facts. Yet much depended not on these larger issues but on the immediate practical politics of Parliament. King had executed his attack. Its impact might be lost if Meighen could postpone the election. In practical politics it was essential for King to strike now while the iron was hot.

There was more to it than the immediate calculations of parliamentary votes. If Meighen proved that he could govern, the whole constitutional issue would evaporate. King was the prisoner of his admission that the Governor-General had done no wrong, that Meighen had given good advice, provided Meighen could command a majority of Parliament. Hence, all last night's triumph and all the future turned on King's ability to unseat the Government, get an election before the iron cooled, and prove beyond doubt that Meighen's advice had been bad, Byng's decision wrong, and the constitution imperiled.

This July 1, Canada's anniversary, was to be the day. Both King and Meighen knew it. The Government would stand or fall before another dawn.

They both knew also that it would be a very close thing. The whips of both sides had been busy. They reported that the dissident Progressives again were in doubt. Some of them already had been converted by King, had forgotten the Customs scandal, and would vote on the constitutional issue. By noon, the best count indicated that the Government's fate probably hung on the doubtful vote of George Coote, the U.F.A. member for Macleod.

That gentleman was deeply troubled. Like many others who saw little choice between Meighen and King, he felt that the country must soon crack under an intolerable strain which only an election could relieve. An election there must be, and a fresh start, under one government or another.

If Meighen were defeated in the House, would he call an election? That was all Mr. Coote wanted to know. At lunch he asked the question of the two ablest newspapermen in the capital, Grant Dexter, of the Winnipeg *Free Press*, and Grattan O'Leary, of the Ottawa *Journal*. They could not answer but agreed to find out.

O'Leary, a close friend of Meighen, sent a note to the Prime Minister asking bluntly if defeat would be followed by an election. Meighen scribbled a reply. Certainly, he said, there would be an election. Mr. Coote had his answer. When Dexter and O'Leary showed him Meighen's note the fate of the Government was settled.

No one knew that then. The Conservative whips still believed, and rightly, that even with Coote against them they might achieve a tie vote. An Opposition motion of censure would then fail. They had not counted on King's unfailing luck. It was wild and impossible beyond counting.

As soon as the House opened at two o'clock King sought a showdown. The first maneuver was executed by Lapointe, who, on a question of privilege, argued that the Government had been illegally established, all its acts were invalid, and all votes cast by its members in the House must be expunged.

Until six o'clock and well into the evening the argument on Lapointe's question of privilege threshed over again all King's original accusations and ramified far beyond the legal position of the Ministry into the whole constitutional system.

The Conservatives, after a night of study, had come prepared this time with piles of evidence, legal precedents, textbooks, and the entire history of the British Crown to prove that the Governor-General had done no wrong in refusing King's advice. Guthrie argued the law. The irrepressible Manion quoted ancient authorities. Drayton protested the innocence of the Government and appealed to common decency. Cahan stated the obvious fact that King had resigned to escape a vote of censure. This King flatly denied. He said that no such vote would have passed had he remained in office, that it had passed afterward only through an intrigue of Tories and farmers, all eager to escape an election.

Between them the politicians, turned into constitutional authorities overnight, covered most of the history of Britain, the Empire, and Canada. Pitt's quarrels with a recalcitrant Parliament, the Governments of George III and Queen Victoria, the Pacific Scandal, Macdonald's Double Shuffle, Asquith's statement that the King could refuse dissolution to any Prime Minister, the behavior of forgotten governors in remote British colonies—all this and much more was crammed into the debate to shift the doubtful fulcrum of the Progressives to one side or the other.

Already with Garland's superb speech denouncing the illegal Government, it was pretty evident which way the shift was going. Only a little shove was needed to tilt this precarious balance against Meighen.

After listening for three hours in silence, King undertook this shove.

His final speech clarified in a few minutes the issues which he had taken most of the previous night to expound. He said that he had known from the beginning what would happen, though of course he could not know. He had warned Byng that Meighen could not govern. He had foreseen the wretched subterfuge of the Shadow Government. He had anticipated that Meighen, ravenous for power, would attempt just this outrage on the constitution. Now that the Government obviously could not govern, all his warnings had been confirmed and Meighen's advice to Byng discredited. Byng should have granted a dissolution to King. No British monarch in more than three hundred years had ever refused such advice from a prime minister.

This was a sticky line of argument, since King already had said that Byng could not be criticized if Meighen could prove his ability to govern. In the fury of the moment no one saw that contradiction. Anyway, Meighen's advice had been proved wrong because he had lost control of the House. His plain duty, said King, was to tell Byng so and it was Byng's duty to call King to office again; for assuredly the Governor-General could not refuse a dissolution to King and, in the same week, grant it to Meighen, who was responsible for the original blunder.

That logic was devastating and, better, it was safe. Meighen would never advise King's recall and Byng would not humiliate himself by accepting such advice if offered. King was in no danger of heading another Government which would enter the election on the defensive, with all its old sins revived. He could urge his own recall, he could remind the Governor-General of his duty in a blunt fashion which Parliament had never heard before, he could attack Meighen for dragging the Crown into politics and tying its representative to one political party, but King's real chance was to face the electors in opposition, to appear as the champion of the constitution, the one man who could rescue the country from an erring English Governor and his power-hungry Minister. In such a crisis who would care about a minor Customs scandal? In the presence of the new Hampden, who would remember Moses Asiz and the Barge Tremblay?

Even the House had forgotten them by eleven o'clock on the night of July 1, and it was now time for King to test his constitutional theories by an actual vote. If he could outvote the Government, his original charge would be vindicated, Meighen's advice to Byng would be proved wrong, the Meighen Government would be illegal by the declared verdict of Parliament. There must be such a verdict or the great indictment would fall in Parliament and would be blurred if not lost in the country. King had taken a long chance on the wavering Progressives. The moment had come to count the chips.

Robb, because he had the friendship of everybody, was chosen to call the Government's bluff, or, as it might be, King's. So Robb moved the vital motion declaring that the Shadow Cabinet, if legal, had no right to sit in the House, if illegal, had no right to transact business. There, after two days and nights of wrangling, was the question which Parliament must decide, and Parliament, weary unto death, was relieved at the prospect of an end.

Two more hours passed in the last fevered efforts of both sides to convince the Progressives. Behind the scenes the whips aroused the sleeping members, registered their solemn pairs and wrestled with the recalcitrants. In the lobbies the din of private argument rose so high that the Speaker, still the superb neutral, protested that he could not hear the proceedings of the House. And once again when the hour of decision approached the nation was asleep.

At 2 A.M. of July 2 the vote was called on Robb's motion. The division bells clanged in the empty corridors. The members prepared to be counted and no one knew how the count would turn out. One by one the clerk noted the Liberal yeas. They totaled 96. The Treasury benches stirred anxiously. They had foreseen 95 Opposition votes. The Conservative nays stood up and mustered only 95.

The Meighen Government had been defeated as no Canadian Government had been defeated in Parliament before. But how? Where had that fatal extra vote come from? Red-faced and ashamed at a breach of parliamentary honor, T. W. Bird, Progressive of Nelson, rose to confess "with extreme regret that I was paired with the honourable member for Peace River [Kennedy] who had retired from the House on account of indisposition and I cast my vote inadvertently."

The sacred parliamentary pair had been broken, an offense unpardonable, but Bird's vote stood on the record. Without that vote the Government would have survived on a tie. The vote could never be deleted. Meighen's evil star had betrayed him again. King's infallible good luck had rescued him in the great gamble of his life—rescued him for two more decades of power.

In the face of overwhelming and unnecessary disaster, Drayton proceeded imperturbably to perform the obsequies of the shadows.

"In the first place," said he, "let me congratulate my honourable friends upon the partial success they have achieved."

"Partial!" screamed the derisive Liberals, who knew the success to be utter and complete.

"Yes," said Drayton with unchanging countenance, "upon the partial success they have achieved which was made possible by the accident which has occurred. . . ."

Amid the hoots of the Opposition he managed to get in a lame rebuke: "There were two ways of fighting; one we believe in and one we do not believe in. . . ." Then he moved an adjournment so that the beaten Government could consider its position.

King was instantly on his feet, the triumph of the moment well hidden under the face of a poker player who had already seized the entire pot. "I shall assume," he remarked coldly, "that the Prime Minister will immediately advise His Excellency that this House has declared that his Government has no right to be in existence and that he has found it impossible to carry on."

"I assume," Drayton retorted in a last hopeless fling, "that the Prime Minister will have to tell His Excellency that in this House his Administration stands at least nine votes better than my honourable friend's Party."

It was a despairing gibe and meaningless. Meighen, watching from behind the curtain, knew that the game was finished. A new game must be started with an election.

That prospect did not daunt him. He had nothing to fear from this constitutional froth. So Meighen slept well, and, on rising, advised Byng to dissolve Parliament. Byng, consenting, granted to the defeated Meighen the dissolution which he had refused to King, though King had never been formally defeated in Parliament.

For King—thanks to an unfortunate Governor, an erring adviser, and a broken parliamentary pair—the issue was now perfectly shaped, the election as good as won. The double trap had closed, containing within it Byng and his ill-starred Minister. But, like Waterloo, it had been a damned close thing.

16

On the Watershed

ON JULY 23, IN OTTAWA, KING ENTERED THE ELECTION CAMPAIGN as the leader of a minority party in opposition, as the former head of a discredited Government found guilty by Parliament, as a failure in the eyes of many Liberals after five years of trial, as nothing more than a political manager in the eyes of the people. By a single speech he began to make himself one of the major figures in Canadian history. Within a month that project would be complete and unassailable. And he was to construct it single-handed.

The practical politicians of the Liberal Party were doubtful from the start of their leader's strategy. It might serve in Parliament, it might be valid in law, but these finespun arguments would make few votes in the back concessions. King, they thought, was trying to lift the campaign into the ether, far above the head of the common man.

What a party needed for victory was not an abstract issue which few could understand, in which fewer still would be interested, but something simple, familiar, and earthy like the tariff, taxes, prosperity, or, best of all, a scandal to be turned against the enemy. King, it appeared, was obsessed with his tangled abstractions, he was leaving the safe old pastures where the Party had long grazed and fattened, he was following a new, unmarked trail, and, worse, it was now the enemy who had the scandal on his side, the most deadly scandal of modern times.

Already Meighen had seemed to confirm these doubts by his first devastating speech. In his usual erosive style he swept aside the constitutional issue as mere quibbling. He called it a disreputable quarrel between an ambitious politician, hungry for office, and a wise Governor determined to preserve the parliamentary system. He said that King had tried to filch a dissolution only to avoid the final vote of censure, a telling and probably an accurate charge. There was only one issue worth considering: Should the nation be governed by a Liberal Party defeated in the last election and condemned in Parliament or by a Conservative Party untouched by suspicion and able to govern?

Meighen's speech looked good to his own Party and to the Liberal managers. His speeches always looked good—for about twenty-four hours. In a Liberal Party which smarted from its lacerations and felt the ache of defeat already in its bones, King alone saw Meighen's campaign as a flaring rocket soon to descend into the dark. King refused to hear the Liberal doubters, he locked himself up to write his own speech and prepared to light a bonfire which would burn long after the rocket was forgotten.

As King started to speak in the crowded Ottawa auditorium, his audience was disappointed, the Liberal managers depressed. For this was not a campaign speech at all. It was a lawyer's brief. So it was intended to be. The oratory and oversimplification of the stump could come later. First King must establish as a kind of manual and chart for his candidates throughout the country, and as a record for future history, the legal foundation of his own case. That case, however it wearied the first-night audience, must be complete, documented, and watertight. It must omit no favorable point, however dull, no Conservative blunder, however small. Alone it would make few votes, as King well knew, but it would kindle, he hoped, a flame which, growing by the hour, would consume Meighen and Byng together.

Knowing Meighen's first point to be perilous, King denied outright that he had sought dissolution to avoid a vote of censure. Unblushingly he asserted that if he had not resigned, no vote of censure would have been passed. The Stevens amendment, as he had "the best of reasons" to know, would have been rejected because the wavering Progressives would have voted against it. King had not resigned to escape censure, which he had no reason to fear, but solely because Parliament was in chaos and the people must be given the chance at another election to establish a workable government.

This was stretching the facts pretty far. King proceeded to stretch them farther. He said his Government had never been censured at all, either in office or after its resignation. The Stevens amendment, he explained, without blinking an eye, was not a vote of censure since the word "censure" did not appear in it. The motion only used the words "wholly indefensible" and "utterly unjustifiable" against the

Liberal Government. Therefore, Meighen misrepresented the record when he said the Government had been censured.

This quibble, stretching the facts out of joint, was King the sea lawyer at his worst, for if the Stevens motion did not mean censure it meant nothing. And if it did not mean censure, why had King struggled so frantically to vote it down? While he must have known that his quibble would not wash with the public, it was essential to the defense brief and, once recorded, could be forgotten in the prosecutor's case which he was now ready to launch.

The sudden reversal from defense to prosecution was the sole purpose of the Ottawa speech. For sheer recklessness and skill it must be counted a maneuver unequaled in the record of our politics.

Even in the Customs scandal King managed to appear as the real inquisitor, who only sought by judicial inquiry to find the whole truth and let the chips fall where they might. Such matters, and even the tax reductions of the Robb budget, old-age pensions, and the other reforms of the Liberal Government were incidental now. The single, sovereign issue, as King came to it at last, was the preservation of Canada's liberty.

Meighen was busily coining his phrases and electrifying his audience elsewhere that night. He did not hear and would not have listened to the simple proposition by which King proposed to smash his career: "Mr. Meighen says there is no constitutional issue. Let me tell the present Prime Minister that he will find before the present campaign is over that there is a constitutional issue greater than any that has been raised in Canada since the founding of this Dominion."

That was the political proposition which King proceeded to prove, step by step, like a theorem in Euclid.

His first premise was undeniable and lethal: Byng had accepted from Meighen the very advice which he had refused from King two days before. King, though undefeated in Parliament, had asked for a dissolution in vain. Meighen, defeated in Parliament, had been granted it.

The Ottawa audience and the back concessions understood that inconsistency at once. It was the most telling cry in the Liberal campaign. When King turned from the groundlings to the intellectuals and entered the deeper constitutional argument, he was confined, by the admissions of his parliamentary speeches, to a narrow and twisted channel in which he squirmed painfully. Fortunately, few observed his discomfort.

He contended that the core of the election issue was Meighen's attempt to form an illegal government. This proved a much less effective argument than the simpler thesis that an English Governor and a Tory Minister were trying to reduce Canada to a colony. King saw that the second arrow in his quiver was by far the more penetrating. He concentrated on its use.

His reasoning went in this fashion: A prime minister like Meighen, rejected by Parliament, should instantly resign and make way for a successor. He was not entitled to advise dissolution and remain in office until an election had been concluded. This confirmed King's previous admission in Parliament that if Meighen could have secured a parliamentary majority he was entitled to govern and Byng was entitled to let him form a government. It contradicted, of course—though hardly anyone noticed it at the time—the next argument which was to become the decisive factor in the election— namely, that the Governor-General, like the King, must always take the advice of his prime minister under all conditions.

Ignoring his own inconsistency, King went on, with elaborate documentation, to prove that no sovereign of Britain had ever refused a dissolution to a prime minister since the time of Pitt, who had been granted it even though defeated sixteen times in Parliament.

A narrow passage, but King made it, thanks to his opponents' stupidity and the short memory of the public. He knew precisely what he was doing every inch of the way. He could not go back on his earlier admission, he could not vary his original hypothesis, but, having restated it for the record, he concentrated the public mind entirely on the much clearer and safer principle that the Prime Minister of Canada must be supreme, that if the Governor refused the Prime Minister's advice then the Crown was seeking to dominate Parliament and nation and, in fact, had entered party politics on the side of the opposition. That was easy to understand and had the added advantage of being true.

From the Ottawa speech onward, the Liberal Party and King himself forgot all their contradictions and focused the campaign on the single fact that a Governor from England had tried to govern the affairs of Canada.

It was essential for King, however, to deny that he had quarreled with his dear friend Byng, the beloved commander of Canada's army in France and "a gentleman for whom I had the greatest affection possible." The public, or enough of it, saw, as King intended it to see, only the spectacle of an English Governor treating Canada as a colony. "That," as Dafoe wrote, "was the argument that did the business." Behind the figure of King with his legal brief case stood the old shadow of English domination. Meighen, who unwittingly had provoked it, could not survive the shadow.

It was dangerous to King also. He could not afford to attack either Byng, the man, or the Crown which he represented. Accordingly, in a superb stroke of agility and footwork, King proclaimed himself the defender of the Crown against Meighen, who had dragged it into politics. To be ousted from office by the Governor, to arraign the Crown for this crime against the Constitution, and then, in the next breath, to appear as the Crown's champion—that was a feat of daring to make Meighen writhe and to convulse the gods. But it did the business.

Similarly, King could not appear to quarrel with the British connection. He argued, therefore, that he was the defender of the British parliamentary system "inherited from the Mother of Parliaments" and now "treated as a scrap of paper, to be torn to shreds by a self-appointed dictator."

The transposition and new synthesis were complete. King was, or claimed to be, the champion of Canadian independence, and yet, by that very fact, the true anchor of the Crown and the Empire holding Canada close to "those little islands of the North Sea," while Meighen, the usurper, threatened not only that independence but the Crown and Empire as well.

In a last sprawling but deadly paragraph King declared that Canada was the custodian of the Crown's honor in every part of the Empire, for "free representative institutions cannot be threatened in Canada without their being everywhere threatened." If Meighen's act went unchallenged "we may question on behalf of all self-governing British communities whether the British Constitution may not become a phantom to delude to destruction instead of being, as we believe it is, the day star of our dearest liberties."

King had pre-empted the best of both possible worlds. With his left hand he conjured up the spirit of Canadian nationalism, a half of the Canadian nature. With his right he invoked that other half, the nation's racial memory, its attachment to its past in Britain. If he could ride both those streams at once, what was left to Meighen? Nothing but the side eddies of scandal 'and denigration, which Meighen took for the main current.

Canadian independence, the honor of the Crown, the unity of the Empire, the survival of the Constitution, the protection of human liberties—of all them King was the true defender and Meighen their enemy. That proposition, if accepted, must guarantee King's future career and end Meighen's. So the business was done.

There had never been a more audacious maneuver in Canadian

politics and none so ably executed by a single man. Before its outcome is examined, King's unfairness to Meighen should be noted.

King's case was that Meighen had formed a Government knowing that it could not survive in Parliament. His offense against the Crown was the willfully bad advice which he had foisted on Byng. In truth, Meighen had thought he could survive in Parliament. He had every reason to think so and would have survived but for a broken pair in a close vote. The charge that he proposed to govern while knowing he could not was false. There were plenty of sound arguments to be turned against him without this spurious after-thought.

Again, King belabored his charge that Meighen had caused Byng to dissolve Parliament without the formalities of prorogation, a gross breach of manners and an insufferabe affront to Parliament; yet, within fourteen years, King would do precisely the same thing.

(It should be noted also that many eminent authorities maintain to this day that the whole constitutional issue of 1926 was spurious and nothing more than a smooth piece of political deception. No opinion is offered on that question here.)

Filing his lawyer's brief with its endless bill of particulars, King left the courtroom and mounted the stump. For fifty consecutive days and nights he scurried about the country, addressed mass meetings where he could, talked to half a dozen railway workers from the rear platform of his car, shook hands with the knot of people at country stations, and enjoyed every minute of it.

In his two earlier compaigns he had appeared of necessity as a pallid compromiser with a vague doctrine and a dim policy of con-ciliation. Now at last he had a cause which the ordinary voter could get his teeth into. In 1921 he had been compelled to defend the Liberal Party's wartime record on conscription. In 1925 he had de-fended his precarious minority Government after four dull years of office. Now he was on the attack. For the first time the nation saw a new and unbelievable side of him. This benign little creature, it appeared, was a fighting man. The figure of dough had turned into granite. The mouse had grown into a lion.

On every platform he reduced the complexities of the constitu-tional issue to a straight fight between independence and colonial-ism. The unsuspected flame in him grew brighter and fiercer with every appearance. Canada had witnessed no such campaign as this in modern times.

King, the sedentary student, tired out all the ex-farmers and athletes in his entourage. His colleagues were soon exhausted. His secretaries wilted. But he, snatching a few minutes' sleep wherever he chanced to lie, was unworried, tireless, and completely confident, for he had found what was almost too much to ask from Providence, the perfect political circumstance, a situation exactly shaped to his temperament. Best of all, he had a cause in which he believed utterly. Released from the clutch of compromise, he soared.

As he began his tour he had placed all his documents in a big, black wooden box. His secretary forgot to load it on the train. King had foreseen this accident and now triumphantly produced a duplicate box from under his bed. He really needed no documents. His memory contained every fact of record. The whole story of the constitutional crisis was burned into his mind and he could present it every day in a new and sharper light.

At first unaware of his dilemma and never admitting any offense whatever, Meighen regarded victory as already won. It was inconceivable to him that the Liberal Party, disgraced and rejected, could recover in the space of a month. He continued to brush aside the constitutional issue as a political trick, invalid, insignificant, and shabby. He relied on the Customs scandal, on his policy of protection, on the dire economic plight of a country (which, in fact, was surging into its largest boom), and on his own fatal gift of eloquence.

His phrases were never better or more ineffective. King had "constitutional fleabitis" and had tried to cling to office·"like a lobster with lockjaw."

It was no good. The campaign went against Meighen not by accident but by the sure logic of history. He had lost Quebec by his conscriptionist record to begin with. Now, in the rest of the country, he was caught between the deep cross-currents of Canadian life, between those who suspected him of surrendering Canada to an English Governor and those who feared that his actions struck at the British constitution and damaged the British connection.

Toward the end, Meighen realized what was happening to him. Desperately he tried to turn the tide. It could not be turned, because it welled out of Canada's whole past. Wearily he dragged himself through Ontario, with three or four speeches a day, until his voice grew hoarse, his face grew haggard, and his wit failed. Even he, a poor judge of voters, saw the tide rising.

The campaign had become the contest of two men, the hare and the tortoise on the home stretch, with the tortoise a long way in the lead, the hare's days of politics already numbered.

King was happy and untired because he knew he was winning, because he believed he deserved to win, but, most of all, because he

L

was now able for the first and last time in his life to feel in himself the reincarnation of the Rebel, fighting the same cause and finally vindicating his grandfather.

Meighen was cast down not by approaching defeat but by its injustice. He had slain the King Government in honest combat. He had saved the Crown from humiliation. He had been rejected in Parliament by the accident of a broken pair. Now he beheld his enemy recovering on what he believed to be a counterfeit issue, a brazen distortion of all the facts. It was almost more than flesh could bear. Meighen bore it without a whimper.

His Greek tragedy closed and King's triumphal progress opened on the night of September 14. The verdict of the polls was more decisive than it looked on the face of the figures. The Liberals had won 116 seats, the Conservatives 91. King could count, however, on the general support of 11 farmer candidates from Alberta, the 13 surviving Progressives, and 9 Liberal Progressives. He had 60 of Quebec's 65 seats; was a little stronger in the Maritimes with 9; had raised his Ontario support from 12 to 33 (the real turning point of the election); had held 23 in the prairies against the Conservatives' single Alberta victory; but had been almost driven out of British Columbia, where the Conservatives had taken all but one seat.

While the Liberal vote was not overwhelming, it was widely distributed, whereas the Conservatives were hived in the Maritimes, Ontario, and British Columbia and the Progressive Party was no longer a national power. For the first time since 1911, the Liberal Party, its sins forgiven, could claim to dominate Canada and after this recovery could hold office, with one fortunate interruption, to this day. The next election would disguise the fact but the long decline of Conservatism had begun. Meighen's career was broken, as a final attempt to repair it later on would show.

The Liberal Party's escape from the jaws of the Customs scandal was unbelievable enough. King's own escape was still more improbable. The Party, failing then, could have come back later. For King, the election had been not only a constitutional issue but a personal issue of political life or death. Since he, singlehanded, had engineered the escape, showing himself abler than all the managers and practical politicians combined, he was now the Party's master as no one but Laurier had ever been. No one could challenge his regnancy or suggest a substitute. The Dunning movement was dead. From then on King could remain as long as he pleased, resting on the single miracle of 1926 and surrounded by his own aura of infallibility.

What, in actual fact, had he accomplished in those seven years since the Liberal convention of 1919?

He had transformed Liberalism from a rump to a political dynasty dominant throughout the nation.

He had extinguished the Progressives' revolt within the Party, unhorsed Meighen, and left the Conservatives so shattered that they could win only one election in the next quarter of a century.

He had begun rather gingerly but surely to apply the theories of *Industry and Humanity* by a corpus of social reforms which was still growing.

He had lowered the tariff, balanced the budget, reduced the debt, and nurtured, if he did not create, the nation's returning prosperity and rapid growth after the war.

He had stilled the single voice in London, established Canada's autonomy in the Commonwealth, and settled for good the position of the Crown in Canadian affairs.

Sweeter than all his works, his victories, and his permanent place in history was his personal vindication. He had justified the Rebel and himself. He had paid his debt to his mother. There would be no more alien corn.

After such a watershed surely he would find nothing but level ground ahead. King's penetrating eye failed to see a dark gulf not far off, and behind it new heights to be scaled.

17

A Spell of Blindness

BYNG WENT HOME TO ENGLAND, BELIEVING HIMSELF BETRAYED. No public word of this ever crossed his lips but he told his friends that King had succeeded solely by sharp practice against the Crown.

One of King's former Ministers, Charles Murphy, who had made a life work of hating his leader, undertook to compile and circulate privately a substantial literature, all designed to document the great betrayal.

Among other exhibits in this record of diligent venom is the choice tidbit of Byng's later return to Ottawa as a private citizen, a meeting with his old enemy, King's servile confession of guilt, his plea for mercy, and finally his breakdown in tears of remorse at Rideau Hall. The truth of this and other gossip probably will never be known. In those heady days of 1926, King could afford to ignore Byng and Byng's friends. With the ex-Governor in England, Meighen in defeat, and the Liberal Party safely in his own hands, King was monarch of all he surveyed.

A political leader who had plucked victory out of the jaws of defeat was unassailable in his Party and in Parliament. The great corner of King's career had been turned, his personal crisis solved by the solution of the constitutional crisis. There could be trouble ahead but never again any serious challenge to his leadership. The successor must come from another generation (and the actual successor was then quietly practicing law in Quebec, with no interest in politics).

King was thus more than Prime Minister; he was almost the whole nation's accepted leader, above party politics, and needed only a few more years to achieve that mastery which only Macdonald and Laurier had ever possessed before him. Now Dafoe's royal jelly took its final effect, turning the ordinary bee into the reigning

148

queen. By Dafoe's definition the democrat now became the autocrat. The *primus inter pares* was actually the boss, and for the first
time.

Nothing could threaten him except a national disaster. Who could
imagine a disaster in the late twenties? The nation prospered. Its
industries were expanding, its product rising, its cities swelling
after a decade of war and depression. The era of the Bull Market,
the ticker tape, the silk shirt, and the higher lunacy had begun. In
the White House sat a small-minded and taciturn man from New
England, now the established saint of the American Way of Life,
who, uttering the final wisdom of the world's most enlightened Government, pronounced the permanent conquest of poverty.

King maintained his former policies and floated with the golden
tide. He was deceived by the general deception. It is perhaps the
most incredible fact of his life that he accepted the mythology of
the great boom. The student of history and economics, the rebel
against capitalism, the Liberal heretic who had long foreseen
where his Law of Competing Standards would lead, went temporarily blind. The Conservative prediction of disaster had proved
so absurd, the "whispers of death" had been so drowned in the
rattle of the tickers that, for the moment, King seemed to imagine
that the good society of his dream already was coming to life—this
only three years before October, 1929.

The Cabinet solidified by the victory of 1926 was rather abler
than its predecessor.

The great Lapointe remained as King's first and essential lieutenant.

Dunning, no longer a threat, provided at once high administrative
capacity, a rare skill in politics, and a sound conservative look,
warming to the heart of business, especially when he succeeded to
the Treasury on Robb's death in 1929.

Ralston accepted the Defence Department soon after the 1926
election and gave the Government not only competence but a kind
of transparent intellectual honesty rare in public life and, behind
that, a core of iron. No one could guess then that this man, so self-
effacing, so loyal and charitable—the perfect specimen of the
Christian gentleman—would deliver the largest defeat in King's
experience.

The presence of Forke in the Government (the grand old man
of the soil having swallowed his former pride) proclaimed the end
of the Progressive movement, the merging of the Liberal Party's
eastern and western wings. When Crerar finally took over the Railways Department the West was represented by its most typical son.

Younger men were coming along, too. P. J. A. Cardin, in Fisheries, was an orator almost Lapointe's equal, a more attentive machine politician, and he aspired to succeed Lapointe as leader of the French Canadian race. On the outskirts of the Cabinet were youngsters of ability eager to get in, among them C. G. Power, one of the wisest politicians and finest characters of his generation; James G. Gardiner, now outswelling the premier's seat in Saskatchewan; James L. Ilsley, the Nova Scotia granite in him just beginning to harden.

The still younger crop, the Pearsons, Abbotts, Claxtons, and Martins of our time, had not yet pushed through the ground. Meanwhile King was attracting to him little affection but ample talent. He encouraged it so long as it never threatened his supremacy. The queen required workers but tolerated no rivals.

A few weeks after his return to power, King went to another Imperial Conference in London, secure in his new stature. The conference heard him as the first overseas statesman of the Commonwealth who had taught the Crown a lesson, destroyed the last vestigial remnants of the royal prerogative in the issue of parliamentary dissolution, and established the equality of the Dominions and their British mother beyond question.

With all this history behind it, the Conference of 1926 completed the logic of 1923 by formally proclaiming in the Balfour Declaration that the British nations were "equal in status, in no way subordinate to one another." This theory would be crystallized into law by the Statute of Westminster five years later.

King's work as a Canadian autonomist was done. He could turn to the easier business of domestic politics, the quiet life of Laurier House and Kingsmere.

His country estate (he hated that word, preferring to call his property a modest retreat) was growing like the nation, of which it had become almost the summer seat of government. He considered his land a sound investment, as it was, and all his savings went into it, unlike those of his friends who plunged into the stock market. Acre by acre, he picked up the patches around him at bargain prices, traded a band of unprofitable sheep for a brook and waterfall, continually added to his houses, talked to neighboring farmers about crops and weather, raised pigeons and bees, shooed bears away from his hives, planted trees, installed two street lamps which had once stood outside his birthplace in Kitchener, hung up a ship's bell from a Nova Scotia schooner, erected an English sundial, and enlivened his lawn with a life-sized china donkey from Spain and a china rooster three times life size.

At Kingsmere he could relax in rough tweeds, stick in hand, as the country gentleman. He loved that pose—a replica of Gladstone at Hawarden, but he never wielded Gladstone's axe. When a reporter wrote a sketch about him and submitted it to King for approval, the squire of Kingsmere added a revealing phrase about himself: "The day's work done, he roams the hills." As a hill roamer, as a simple countryman he wished to be known to the public and had almost come to believe the legend himself.

In part it was true. King roamed the hills in odd moments. Most of his time was spent in the labyrinth of politics and in the meticulous care of his Party. He watched over it like an anxious father, listened to its faintest mutter, applied soothing syrup or parental discipline as required. The Party was less his child than his instrument, his craftsman's tool, and most of his life. He might quarrel with the tool but there was no other. It had many handles and assorted blades with two edges. King had learned to use them all, ambidextrously.

Other statesmen might hesitate to call themselves professional party politicians. King gloried in his profession, fitted into it as into a pair of worn slippers, and enjoyed, like any other craftsman, every detail of his craft.

How jealously he guarded the prerogatives of the Party leader, the appointment of Senators, deputy ministers, and judges, the promotions within the secret hierarchy, the demotions and punishments, the correspondence with remote Party managers, the organization of constituencies, the arrangement of by-elections, and all the laborious minutiae which might disgust him as a statesman but delighted him as a born politician!

Working in the labyrinth he managed, even in his own disillusioned mind, to glorify the Party, to make it appear better, purer, and larger than it could ever be. He knew its sordid side and before long would involve himself in its most sordid act, but for him these were necessary evils, human nature being what it was. Above the Party and nourished by its dark soil stood the noble growth of Liberalism. The amateur farmer knew that the fairest flowers grew sometimes out of the dung heap. The city politician, though he prayed night and morning for guidance, knew that elections were not won by prayers.

It was an easy time, the last easy time that King or the world would know until the present day, a time when the master of all he surveyed could find leisure to organize his private thoughts and clarify the Liberalism which had grown rather puzzling and confused of late.

To give it an up-to-date habitation and a name, he appeared
before a Liberal women's convention in Ottawa. Among such innocents he could afford to think aloud. His soaring thoughts might
make the practical politicians of Liberalism smirk, but they were
sincere. That was the point which his friends and enemies never
understood—King was always sincere, even in his most misleading
moments, for, whenever the occasion required it, he could mislead
himself and believe almost anything.

The gossamer of his speech on true Liberalism to the Liberal
women is worth noting, to show not only his infinite variety but
something more important. Here he was trying not only to lift
Liberalism out of party politics, to rescue the soul, as it were, from
the vile body, but to reinterpret it in the light of modern society. Yet
within two years he would find that he, the 'supposed radical, was
years, perhaps a whole generation, behind the times. This speech is
a forgotten landmark in his mental evolution.

Liberalism, he said, was the Future struggling against the Past.
The Past, of course, was Conservatism. The Liberal Party was the
champion of the Future, and he as its prophet already had changed
Canada forever by his social legislation. He was thus a long way
ahead of original Liberal laissez faire, in accomplishment as well
as thought. And if he was a long way behind *Industry and Humanity*,
so far at least he had not forgotten it.

The actual fact, however, so clear in this long, abstract, and high-
sounding speech, was that in the comfort of office he was losing
touch for the moment with the stream of history which he had always
understood so well up to now. The ideals of *Industry and Humanity*
had become for him partly a mere exercise in nostalgia and partly,
as he thought, an accomplished fact in society through his reforms.

Hence he saw a "vast gulf" between his Liberal doctrine of the
Future and the Conservative doctrine of the Past. What he did not
see, what nobody saw so far, was the gulf between King and the
Present.

The Present, so rich, gaudy, and comfortable, even then was beginning to slide into the deepest depression of all time. In that
April of 1928 a few rocks only had been dislodged, unheeded by
King's Government or any other. While America was still climbing
to new heights, the avalanche was moving imperceptibly. King
should have suspected that movement. The sensitive seismograph
within his skull should have recorded some faint shocks. He cannot
be blamed, however, for failing to discern his two improbable
passengers on that landslide, the one from Calgary, the other from
up-state New York, both destined to change the course of his life.

Perhaps if he had not felt so solid on his own mountaintop he might have perceived that his Government, while preaching the Future, already belonged in its thinking to the Past. That discovery was just two years off.

In the spring of 1928 he looked forward to Liberalism's most glorious summer. By the calendar of history it was already late autumn. The glow which he took for dawn was sunset.

Those innocents of the Federation of Liberal Women saw an infallible prophet who announced that "Our God must be a God of the living not of the dead. A God of love, not of hate. A God who holds the future in His hand." All this King certainly believed. In these timeless beliefs he never wavered. In his timing of politics, the application of his religious principles in practical affairs, he had begun to falter badly.

Another side of him—indeed several—was revealed in this period of ease, to the general surprise. His speeches on the Diamond Jubilee of Confederation and at the dedication of the new carillon in the Victory Tower showed him at once as a scholar of Canadian history, a proud burgher of Ottawa, and a suppressed poet.

His account of the fire which destroyed the Centre Block in 1916 is first-rate picturemaking. He told of the clock sounding the hour as the fire billowed through the original tower and "still the old sentinel stood on guard. At midnight the crash came. In an endeavor to strike the final hour it fell, its belfry demolished, its voice silenced. . . . In a few minutes it will be our privilege to bear witness to the immortality of that spirit. When the clock which is now installed begins to sound forth the hours of this day it will take the flaming torch, thrown to it over a space of years by the old sentinel at midnight and, holding it aloft, will strike at high noon the hour of twelve in commemoration alike of birth and resurrection."

Party managers might well wish that he could daub an occasional gout of color like that upon his platform speeches. A vain wish.

Or again, this phrase as he recounts the history of Canada and pauses at his grandfather's rebellion: "It failed on the field of battle but won on the field of principle."

Still another side of him, an important side which later would be dominant at a critical moment in Canadian history, was visible to the discerning eye in that carefree summer.

Welcoming Edward, Prince of Wales, who was to unveil Laurier's monument on the Hill, King for once abandoned his bulbous sentences and delivered a tribute to his old chief as chaste, classic, and moving as the bronze statue before him. In a few of its sentences that oration approached poetry. He pictured old folks and children playing at the base of the monument in the quiet of the evening, perhaps looking up now and then at "the old man, with his bare head and his white hair, standing alone, fighting for the right as God gave him to see the right."

That style of speech was surprising in him but the more surprising thing went generally unnoted until long afterward. The Prince of Wales, then so youthful, so charming and unspoiled, had touched the history man in King, called up that racial feeling for the Old Land which is dormant in all Canadians, and lighted a tiny flame of royalty in the Rebel's grandson. King began during Edward's visit to see himself as the Canadian watchdog of the Royal Family. It was a congenial role. He thenceforth cultivated it with remarkable results.

The speeches of this period show King's method of speaking finally set. Many attempts to alter it were made by his assistants. All failed. King guarded his method as jealously as he guarded his private life. He hired a succession of writers and in the end wrote all his own speeches. If the original draft prepared by other hands showed the slightest variation in his fixed style, if it contained a single phrase or word which seemed out of tone, he altered it.

Later on, when he employed the ablest Canadian speaker of his time, Leonard Brockington, of the golden voice and the purple passage, the experiment was a fiasco. Brockington's repeated efforts to insert even a faint wash of color were expunged. The brilliant hues of that superb orator were systematically dulled into a steady gray. King refused to be a purple passenger on another's wings. He walked on the ground. Because he knew it would sound false in his mouth, he rejected the great phrase, the epigram, and any metaphor but the familiar and trite. He did not usually wish any single statement to be remembered. He wished the public to remember only the general effect. By converting the strong meat of his assistants into a bland gruel and transforming the thunder of Brockington into a faint rumble, far away, he achieved exactly to the effect he desired.

The object was to state all the facts accurately while avoiding commitments and later embarrassments. Wherever possible, his declarations of policy were put into such an open-ended form that they could be reinterpreted to mean something else at another time. When he was sure of his position he could be as clear as daylight. When no policy was involved he sometimes could be as light as air.

On rare occasions he could rise to jest, satire, and whimsy. For the most part he kept his speeches muddy until his writers asked one another who would have thought the old man had so much mud in him. Muddy or clear, no man could read his speeches or hear his sibilant voice on the radio and doubt that this was King.

It did not surprise Ottawa, therefore, when Brockington quit in despair. Long before that, King had found the ideal speech writer in John Pickersgill, who will soon appear in this record as one of the decisive influences on King's life. Mr. Pickersgill has explained in *Queen's Quarterly* his chief's technique of construction and the intention behind it.

The technique was slow, toilsome, and agonizing for King's assistants. Four or five original drafts were subject to endless hours of revision, to quibble over a sentence, a word, or a comma, until Mr. Pickersgill often grew faint with hunger while King forgot both time and diet. Against every attempt to change it, he maintained his own antique style of classic rotundity, convoluted sentences, occasional florid passages, grand and wooden gestures, the starched-cuff manner which he took from Laurier, his mentor, losing Laurier's magic in the imitation.

The verbal anachronism was an essential part of his legend. In public diction, as in many of his instincts, he remained a late Victorian. The style of his speeches was out of date but King clung to it because he knew his work to be dateless. He was addressing the ages. His words, like his ruins at Kingsmere, were to be monuments of stone. They must be carved to fit and to endure.

"Mr. King," says Mr. Pickersgill, "believed firmly that what really mattered in a speech was the meaning rather than the sound. . . . Yet he scarcely ever read a written speech in public without previously reading it aloud to see whether the sound conveyed to him the meaning intended." He refused to use the familiar tricks, hesitations, and asides of the orator to give a prepared speech a look of spontaneity.

Mr. Pickersgill denies, however, that King ever used his cumbersome sentences to convey a deceptive impression. He had a passion for accuracy. Often he would spend hours searching for the phrase or word of precisely the desired shade of meaning. As Mr. Pickersgill often told King, these minutely accurate subordinate clauses and elaborate reservations frequently did convey to the public an impression much less accurate than it would have taken from an oversimplified version.

Mr. Pickersgill "tried to persuade him that it would be much better to be approximately right and understood than completely right and ignored." Mr. Pickersgill failed. It is true, he adds, that King, while accurate, was not always candid. He knew that some things could not be discussed and must be blurred. Mr. Pickersgill never knew him to put into his speeches anything which he thought false or even misleading. He would not use lies. He reveled in evasions.

Anyone who heard them often will agree with Mr. Pickersgill that King's extemporaneous speeches were by far his best. A few were masterpieces. Why, then, did he insist on preparing in advance his massive testaments which, in their preparation, seemed to stretch in an endless coil of paper from one end of his house to the other and to contain, as has often been said, everything but the kitchen stove, which also appeared now and then?

Mr. Pickersgill answers, surprisingly enough, that King lacked confidence, was always nervous before he spoke, and needed a text as an insurance policy. Few listeners could suspect that. King never looked so comfortable as when he stood on the platform, using speech not to create a passing atmosphere but to build his aura of quiet authority, the true source of his power.

While King basked in the sunset which looked so like the dawn, the wounded Conservative Party was beginning to heal. Or so it seemed then before the depth of its wounds was suspected. At the convention of 1927, Meighen retired forever, as he thought, from politics. Nothing so became his public life as his taking leave of it, with a speech which could have won him another term of leadership if he would have accepted it. The lonely eagle soared into the silences, bruised but unbroken.

His return was not foreseen at this moment of reborn hope when the convention installed in his place another bird, equally rare, but very different. Richard Bedford Bennett had been a conscriptionist in 1917 but a minor figure who escaped the anger directed on Meighen by French Canada. He had escaped also those dreadful hours of the Shadow Government, being fortunately in Calgary. While he always said that if he had been in Ottawa he could have saved Meighen it was now apparent that he probably would have destroyed his own chances of succession. These might-have-beens were forgotten in the flamboyant arrival of the new leader. To King, the old eagle's perch seemed occupied by a peacock. Those gaudy feathers were deceptive. The Conservative Party at last had found a winner.

At the age of fifty-seven, Bennett, like King, was a bachelor, but an admirer of women. Like King, he was deeply religious with an assertive Methodist piety combining a sincere love of God and an appetite for money. Unlike King, he was rich and could personally finance an election campaign.

The differences between the two men went much deeper than that.

King was the Rebel's grandson and never forgot it. Bennett came out of United Empire Loyalist stock in New Brunswick and while he lived in the western cowboy town of Calgary his spiritual home was in England, to which he was inevitably drawn to die, an English lord. King was a scholar and a mystic. Bennett had spent his life in business as a corporation lawyer, understood finance (but, unhappily, not economics), and imagined that the Businessman, in partnership with God, could build the new Jerusalem. If King's timing for the present was inaccurate, he understood history. Bennett never sensed his place or the place of Canada in historic time, he failed, like most businessmen, to see where the hands of the clock then stood, and believed, with a pathetic faith, that he could turn them back.

Both men were profound egotists. Whereas King hid his egotism not only from the public but from himself, Bennett's was paraded nakedly. King relied on thought, to which public speech was only a prop. Bennett, with his pipe-organ voice and rolling cadences, seemed to think that he could solve any problem by a piercing utterance. King made speeches. Bennett pronounced judgments from a court of final jurisdiction. King was a politician, Bennett an oracle. King appealed to Providence. Bennett seemed almost to command it.

In appearance as in character the new Conservative leader was as much a contrast to King as Meighen had been. His face, round and smooth, with the glint of porcelain, his eyes gleaming through pince-nez of antiquated design, had a look of obvious power, courage, and honesty, qualities that no one could deny him. His figure was tall, rotund, and elegantly tailored in old-fashioned tail coats of varying hue, often changed several times a day. He took no exercise. He took no liquor or tobacco either, his sole vice being rich chocolates, which he consumed by the pound. With the aid of a daily massage he avoided all exercise and enjoyed robust health. Beside this handsome and glistening extrovert King appeared small and fragile.

King gradually realized that Meighen was the greater man but that Bennett might be harder to beat. Meighen's faults of judgment were obvious. His record, though honorable, had proved fatal in Quebec. He looked what he was, an unrepentant Tory. While Bennett was a Tory, too, in his policy and in his soul, he carried no conscriptionist smear and he had a knack, almost as able as King's, of fogging issues and dissolving contradictions in a gust of platitudes.

Also, he could give platitudes an air of life, as King could not. Meighen's oratory had cut like a clean knife. Bennett soon showed that he could overwhelm King with a kind of vague and fuliginous vapor, impossible to grasp or answer. In the end, this kind of oratory must consume the orator. King awaited that outcome.

Nevertheless, Bennett was a considerable figure in our history and a man of parts—wildly generous to some, small and mean to others, honest to all, and filled not only with his own sense of rectitude as an instrument of destiny but with the will to enforce it. He had a vast store of knowledge, most of it thin and amorphous. In his ceaseless monologues—for he never ceased to talk in public and private—he surged from the immediate business of Parliament to the pottery of the Ming Dynasty, the history of Rome, or the career of Disraeli. Despite his talents, and he had many solid ones, he suffered from an incurable weakness—he wanted to do everything himself. Therein lay his tragedy.

Bennett, King realized, might be harder to beat than Meighen, but was not King himself unbeatable?

Bennett was equally confident. He began at once a crusade to liberate Canada. From what was not clear, since the nation had never appeared in better health. Alone Bennett could not hope to liberate it. Unknown to him an ally was approaching, far stronger than King or any government in the world.

As Bennett busied himself with the work of liberation in the summer of 1928, King made his first serious venture into world affairs, outside the Commonwealth. It was hopeful, naïve, and, in retrospect, a little fatuous.

At Geneva he attended the League of Nations Assembly and at Paris signed on behalf of Canada that gesture against war, the Briand-Kellogg Pact. He was completely deceived by Europe's outer look of peace and the nations' vow to reject war as an instrument of policy.

In the autumn he returned to tell a meeting of the League of Nations Society in Ottawa that there were now "no wars to be averted, or rumors of war to be quieted." He expressed an almost childish delight in the ceremonies of the Paris treaty signing, described them to his audience in minute detail, and showed that in a garish international charade he was flattered to be a minor actor.

The world was striking an attitude about a year before it collapsed. King struck the same attitude in Canada. "How mighty," he cried, "has become the power which now holds the peace of the world as the most sacred of all moral and national obligations!" And "what the world chiefly needs today, in my judgment, is to cast aside suspicion and distrust as between nation and nation and not merely to feel greater confidence in each other but to display it."

To those who knew that the world was not like that, to anyone who could discern Hitler already scheming in his basement or the Japanese plotting the rape of China, King's pose as a dove of peace perhaps seemed natural enough at this time of general posturing. Actually, the pose was more significant and cast longer shadows ahead than King, his friends, or his critics could yet suspect.

Even Dafoe, watching him through his telescope from Winnipeg, did not then perceive that King's public posture was his private posture also, that he might glory in the outer panoply of the League and mouth the slogans of peace but was quite unprepared to support collective security in the pinch. In the pinch he would desert the League.

That was some years ahead. The posture would serve in those last golden hours before the dark.

Like most statesmen, King continued at this point to misconstrue the economic as well as the political climate of the world. As late as April 9, 1929, he gave Parliament one of his dreary and documented speeches proving by statistics that Canada was prosperous as never before. There was no cloud in the sky, nor any sound in this serenity but the merry upward click of the tickers in Wall Street.

True, he said, the genius of the Canadian people had made this prosperity but it was possible only under a wise Government (a dangerous boast, since in reverse he must accept the responsibility for any depression). He could see no chance of failure and so felt safe in claiming full credit for the success.

He had indeed a good report for the board of directors. The Government's revenues were in surplus, taxes had been slashed, the broken private railways had been amalgamated in the Canadian National system, branch lines had been built, the tariff had been cut, people's wages and the profits of business were at record levels, industrial peace reigned, and the future was secure. No wonder, he said, that the people felt complete confidence in the Government after it had managed such a miracle.

One looks back on King's figures of that day with a certain nostalgia. Government was costing only $385,000,000. In the age of innocence even the national income was unknown. There were no central planners, cyclical budgets, and hardly an economist in sight. The Canadian economy was primitive but it was rich by all previous standards. Considering its condition when King took office, considering the fact that his Government was spending, apart from the remaining costs of the war, less than the Conservatives had spent in 1914, considering also that under his predecessors the nation had been sinking dangerously into debt and had not paid even its non-war costs out of revenue, King's record was solid and impressive. Against it "the whispers of death" appeared only ludicrous.

"We have prosperity at which we have aimed," said King, "and we intend to maintain it, and, if possible, to increase it."

Bennett, listening in Opposition, could not meet that boast, could not successfully advocate protectionism when the nation obviously needed no protection, could not hope for office unless the climate changed. Still, rather hopelessly, Bennett did urge, even then, a rise in the tariff to match the rise on which a Republican Congress was now bent, in the last ecstasies of Smoot and Hawley.

Even with prosperity at home, the American tariff was putting King in an awkward corner. He could not long resist higher Canadian tariffs if American statesmanship continued its march into economic lunacy. As long as possible he fended off a decision, lest Canada provoke the Americans into a lunacy still more extreme. To Bennett's demand for a "red-blooded attitude" of reprisal against the United States King replied that the Conservatives were jingoes advocating a tariff war. What was needed, he said, was not a red-blooded but a cool-headed attitude.

Nevertheless, though he saw no danger of depression or anything like it, he did foresee political danger. The Conservatives, he knew, had allies in the American protectionists, who could force Canada into retaliation. Bennett had struck a profitable vein in the Canadian character by denouncing "domination by Washington."

There was the germ of Bennett's next election campaign. By his labored attempt to answer, it is evident that King was trying to crush this high-tariff movement before it could sprout. He was careful, however, to leave the Government plenty of elbow room, with hints of possible action if the Americans went too far.

King was speaking more to Congress than to Parliament, he was warning the United States against the economic suicide which Congress seemed determined to commit. King at least would not provoke that act. And as always in this basic issue of Canadian politics, King appeared not as a high-tariff or low-tariff man, but as a pragmatist, ready to do anything necessary when the occasion arose.

So Parliament adjourned in the summer of 1929 in the glow of the big boom, in the false dawn of the Briand-Kellogg Pact, and in the first inconclusive encounter between King and Bennett.

On October 29 came the earthquake. The brokers who leaped from their skyscrapers into Wall Street that day were accompanied by an invisible companion. King, like them, had been caught short. Still he did not begin to glimpse the dimensions of the general debacle and his own.

Perhaps the most puzzling single fact of his public life is his failure to understand the meaning of the stock-market crash, to realize that it was a mere symptom of a much larger process. Why did he continue for six months longer to regard the deepening depression as a passing readjustment, a stern but necessary purge of an inflated world economy? Why did the author of *Industry and Humanity* fail to recognize, not a familiar shake-out of private enterprise, but the culmination of those very forces which he had long ago predicted would end in catastrophe? Why could he not see that an era had ended in October, 1929, that society in America would never be the same again?

Those questions may never be answered. A student of his life is inclined to conclude that the explanation was really quite simple— King's timing, for once, was wrong.

He had understood as well as any man in his time that the capitalist system, like all others, contained the seeds of its own destruction. He had seen where the purely economic philosophy of traditional Liberalism would lead. He had realized from youth that a society, if motivated solely by profit and governed solely by the market, could not long endure. The profit motive and the market were essential elements. They were not all the essential elements. There must be something much stronger animating the society and reconciling the conflicts of profit and market.

Rather too simply he had foreseen in his book the new synthesis of an economy governed not alone by capital, not even by capital and labor, but by these two with the public somehow represented. He was not preaching either Guild Socialism or the State Capitalism into which Socialism usually drifted. He really foresaw, without knowing that he foresaw, something like the North American society which is now emerging out of the depression and the succeeding war. But his timing was wrong.

The crisis of capitalism had come long before he expected and long before the alternative system was ready to reform capitalism. Beguiled by the apparent success of the existing system, beguiled also by the assumption that the system had plenty of time to reform itself gradually into the better society of his dream, he did not realize yet that no such time would be granted. It was far later than he thought. Society, for all its outward flush, was sicker than he could imagine.

Hence, the very man best equipped by his previous thinking to deal with the crisis failed to meet it because he could not quite believe in it.

One of the first effects of the depression was to make Canadians,

M

like Americans, examine their existing system for the first time. What had happened? What had gone wrong with a machine which had worked so smoothly that nearly everyone took its continuing success and harmony for granted? Where government had been for North Americans a distant force, almost an irrelevancy and generally an unavoidable nuisance, the people now looked to government to rescue them from the pit where they had been plunged by a system they had never understood.

King understood that system, none better, and government also. He was among the last to see, or at least to admit, that the system had been injured almost mortally, that government could wait no longer for the slow emergence of his ideal society and must step in now to effect immediate repairs before the system broke down altogether. The old-time Liberal in him, with the nineteenth century's faith in inevitable progress, could not surrender the dream of a new society evolving quietly, without breakdown. That a quiet evolution was no longer possible if revolution was to be avoided he could not bring himself to admit.

Refusing to surrender the dream, he persisted in believing that this accident would pass and the old evolution would be resumed. He was not trying to turn back the clock. He was simply not ready to see where the hands already pointed. It was now the eleventh hour when he thought it was still midafternoon.

Moreover, his error in political thinking was exaggerated by his personal thinking. That he had come all this way and surmounted all these obstacles, only to find the nation in danger of immediate collapse—this thought was more than his vanity could bear. He had become, in Stalin's phrase, dizzy with his own personal success. He was a little drunk on royal jelly.

For the rest of the parliamentary term he refused to take any fundamental measures against the depression. He would vote a little money, grudgingly, to relieve the unemployed, while insisting on the narrow legal point that the provinces were solely responsible for relief. His old-time Liberalism was still strong enough to make him believe that the federal budget must be kept in balance and that, with sound money, the nation could ride out the storm. In the last gasp of the pre-Keynesian era, the notion that the state should deliberately spend more than it collected to create purchasing power for idle goods was wildest heresy. That the state should underwrite the private economy was unthinkable. So the Government floundered through 1930 and the nation sickened by the hour.

Even weaker was the thinking of Bennett. That unfortunate man now seemed to be the darling of fortune. He had found his essential ally in the depression and used it with energy and skill. The short-run gains would soon be canceled by the long-run losses. Bennett understood less than King what had happened. King had foreseen a changing society. Bennett could suggest no remedy except a return to society's worst errors. If those errors had reduced it to prostration, he would apply more of the same.

He made a garish show of them as he surged through the country prescribing as cures the most violent poisons that society could drink. For him there was no historic process at work, no fundamental disease, nothing which could not be healed by the good old-fashioned spring tonic of high tariffs. If capitalism was temporarily sick, it would recover by a return to its worst vices. If the world economy was suffering from the pernicious anemia of a slump in international trade, he would nourish it back to health by bottling up trade still more. If Canadians could not sell their products, he would see that no foreign products competed with them.

Under the impression that he uttered some great new truth, Bennett careened from coast to coast uttering the oldest Tory doctrine of protectionism, self-containment, and international economic war. Imagining that he wrote a charter of new birth, he wrote his own obituary by announcing that he would "blast" Canada's way into world markets and, by this new magic, as old as history, would "cure unemployment or perish in the attempt." In Bennett's crusade of 1930 there was at least one element of indisputable truth—he would perish.

King watched the performance with revulsion. He knew that Bennett's nostrums were worthless. Caught short in his own thinking, he could offer no alternative.

By the spring of that year the depression, now growing worse, was not nearly as grave yet as Bennett alleged. The year of 1930, indeed, was not a very bad one for Canada. There had been many worse years before. Still, the public instinct was sound in its belief that this was only the beginning. In the nation's present humor, Bennett could exaggerate the emergency far beyond the facts and convince most of the people that they were already close to destitution. Their real misery had yet to come.

Preparing for an election, King followed Bennett on a nation-wide tour. He was ready to admit now that Canada must retaliate against almost impenetrable American tariffs. It must extend the British Preference, trade with nations willing to trade, and withdraw its business as much as possible from countries which penalized Canadian goods. The accent was still on foreign trade. By Dunning's 1930 budget the Preference was extended on the proposition, as Dunning said, that "we do not intend to meet other countries of the British Commonwealth of Nations in a spirit of petty bargaining, but rather in the broad spirit of willingness to become in ever-increasing measure good customers to those who treat us in like manner."

Bennett favored Commonwealth trade also but on a very different basis. He would reduce no tariff and make no concession, even to the Commonwealth, which "will destroy any industry indigenous to Canada." He was horrified by modest butter imports from New Zealand and made them appear to the Canadian dairy farmer almost as the sole cause of his poverty. All goods coming from any outside source were damnable. Bennett damned them from every platform in the country. The export of Canadian raw materials for manufacture elsewhere simply meant that "they've got the jobs and we've got the soup kitchens."

So ignorant was the great corporation lawyer of elementary economics, so numb was the country from the hurt of unemployment, that this palpable nonsense was widely accepted. An age-old fallacy was regarded as a blazing new truth. Bennett, a sincere man intoxicated by his own honor, undoubtedly believed his own errors and his own cures.

In the 1930 session of Parliament Bennett found firmer ground. He demanded that the Federal Government assist the provinces and municipalities to finance adequate relief for the unemployed.

King—such was the measure of his miscalculation—argued, with pitiful splitting of legal hairs, that the federal treasury had no such responsibility under the constitution. Incredible as it seems in retrospect, he denied that there was a national unemployment problem or any emergency.

Then, goaded by the Opposition, tired, cranky, and overwhelmed by a crisis which he had not grasped and could not control, King proceeded in one paragraph to deliver the next election to the enemy. Probably it had been delivered anyway by the depression, but King made that certain by crying out in his anguish: "So far as giving money from this federal treasury to the provincial governments is concerned, in relation to this question of unemployment as it exists today, I might be prepared to go to a certain length, possibly, in meeting one or two of the western provinces that have Progressive premiers at the head of their governments . . . but I would not give a single cent to any Tory government."

As the gleeful opposition screamed "Shame!" and thanked God for a one-cent piece beyond price, King, now beside himself, shouted back: "May I repeat what I have said? With regard to giving moneys

out of the federal treasury to any Tory government in this country
for these alleged unemployment purposes, while these governments
situated as they are today with policies diametrically opposed to
those of this Government I would not give them a five-cent piece!"

That was the first serious verbal slip of his career, and the last.
The man who had steadfastly refused to make phrases had made a
phrase to hang the Government. Not a five-cent piece for unemployment relief! No co-operation with a provincial government which
happened to be Conservative! The victims of the depression to be
relieved only if they voted Liberal! This was not what King meant
or what he actually was doing but the country would not forgive
him.

By the end of that dismal session, it is said that King knew the
jig was up, that he called the election without hope or even wish
of winning it, that he panted secretly for escape to Opposition and
was glad to dump his troubles into the willing lap of Bennett. The
truth is that King expected and wanted to win the election. Only
when he had lost it did he soothe himself and expand his reputation
for omniscience by encouraging the legend that he had planned his
own defeat.

The nation's desperation had assured Bennett's victory. He made
doubly sure by repeating the successful Conservative strategy of
1911, which had defeated Laurier. The old alliance between the
true-blue Tories of English-speaking Canada and the anti-British
nationalists of Quebec was resurrected with new personalities and
the same results. Through the back door the Conservative Party
was re-entering French Canada. It would not remain there long.

King had lately made just about every imaginable mistake in
thought and speech. At the last minute his Party contrived one
more. To finance the campaign the empty Liberal treasury was repaired by funds from private power interests which had received
valuable hydro rights on the St. Lawrence. While King denied any
knowledge of the mephitic Beauharnois deal, nothing in his life
was to cause him so much humiliation.

On the night of July 28, Bennett found himself with a majority of
137 members against 88 Liberals and 20 assorted farmers and independents. King had lost 28 seats, surprisingly few in such a climate.
It was the only election he ever lost and one of the luckiest. For with
his majority Bennett also had inherited the depression. Now he
could blast and perish. This he proceeded to do with a sincere and
suicidal energy.

18

The Valley of Humiliation

OPPOSITION WAS CERTAINLY THE MOST COMFORTABLE RESIDENCE for any statesman during the black 'thirties. After the first bitter and unexpected sting of defeat, King settled down philosophically at his country place and remarked to an early visitor that, all things considered, the election had been a blessing in disguise.

It meant more to him than he yet knew. Opposition was to prove in many ways the most important period of his life. By changing his whole course in politics it changed the Liberal Party and perhaps saved it from extinction. The society of Canada would have been changed in any case by the impact of the depression. Its change was conditioned, if not dominated, by the change in King; or, more accurately, by his return to his old faith.

Free of responsibility, he now had the chance to think things out. What had happened to his Government, to the nation, to humanity? As he diverted himself by building up the synthetic ruins of Kingsmere, fussing with trowel and mortar among his hired stonemasons, designing his square of broken walls, inserting in them stones and carvings from the old Parliament Buildings, gazing at them rapturously in the moonlight or reading in their noonday shade, he grappled with the fundamentals which he had neglected in office. More than fake ruins was being built at Kingsmere. There, so far as King could control it, the future of Canada was under secret construction.

Those close to King soon perceived the change in him. The confidence, grown almost into complacency through the fat years, was gone. In its place appeared a sudden humility, a new kindliness to his colleagues and assistants, an air of apology and an appetite for advice.

He knew now that he had grossly underestimated the depression, that it did not fit into the old philosophy of Liberalism as a mere period of readjustment nor even into the theories of *Industry and Humanity*. In that early thesis he had foreseen a crack-up of some sort. This was worse by far than anything he had expected. It was almost beyond belief. The remedies, therefore, must be more drastic and much quicker than any he had prescribed. Long ago he had dismissed original Liberalism as antiquated. His own advanced version obviously would not serve either. To build a new structure of policy for the future while he built stone monuments out of the past he sought help wherever he could find it, and in some queer places.

Bennett, on the other hand, needed no help or advice from anyone. Now Prime Minister, Minister of Finance, and the autocrat of a Cabinet which contained only assistants and no real colleagues, Bennett knew a sure and painless cure for the depression.

At the Parliamentary session of autumn, 1930, he raised all tariffs beyond any known level to prevent the importation of goods that Canada could produce itself, regardless of cost. Having thus struck a swingeing blow at British goods, among others, he went to an Imperial Conference in London and proposed an Empire *zollverein* in which the British nations would trade together with a maximum exclusion of foreigners. Since he proposed to surround this trading preserve by still higher tariffs against the foreigners, not by reducing tariffs within the Empire, the Labour Government of Britain, still almost a free-trade country, refused to enter an empty cage. It saw in tariff-bounded Canada and in the other Dominions no market to compensate it for the losses which it must suffer by breaking off its business with the world and confining its trade to Bennett's Empire club of genteel poverty.

In a calculated and famous indiscretion, J. H. Thomas, the Colonial Secretary, called Bennett's plan "humbug." The London conference was a failure. Bennett was stung to the quick by Thomas' phrase and left for home with the blunt warning that if Britain wished to do business with Canada it must change its policy. Fortunately for him, Britain soon changed its government. Installed as mayor of Ramsay MacDonald's palace, Stanley Baldwin might be willing to do business on Bennett's terms.

After leaving Bennett alone for nine months, King opened his first guarded attack on June 16, 1931. His speech in Parliament showed that at last he understood the dimensions of the depression, though he was still far from seeing its cure. Now the man who refused a five-cent piece to a Tory government denounced Bennett for failing to relieve the unemployed. King was on slippery ground here. When he reached the old tariff issue he was treading a terrain familiar from his youth.

Bennett, he said, had contracted a psychopathic horror of all foreign trade, he was strangling the Canadian economy by his restrictions on imports, was worsening the depression which he had guaranteed to end. Moreover, in the theory that prosperity at the top would trickle down to the mass of the people, Bennett's budget had reduced the taxes of the rich and increased those of the poor. Bennett, in short, was ruining Canada.

This might sound like political claptrap then. King was in no hurry. In time the nation would accept his warning.

King could offer no advice more practical than a return to the Liberal remedies that had cured the depression of the early 'twenties—obviously a frail straw to grasp in this storm—but already a first basic shift can be noted in his policy. While few listened to him then, the old-time Liberals of his Party were disturbed by his admission that the capitalistic system was "under fire, it is on trial, it is being investigated and I hope, indeed, I believe, it is being modified."

Was this also claptrap or was King edging away from the system largely built by Liberalism in the last century? Yes, there was a shift in King's policy. There was, as yet, none in his thinking. He was only coming back in public to the original heresies of *Industry and Humanity*, so long neglected. Hence in this speech the extracts taken straight out of that book: Labor was as much entitled to reward as capital, industry must be a "social service," not a mere earner of profits, and its third partner must be the community.

King was ready to revive his heresy in vague terms. He still was not ready to accept the much larger heresy which John Maynard Keynes was launching into the world with strange results. The notion that the state could cure depression by spending money to create public purchasing power appeared so absurd to King that he condemned Bennett's wild extravagance, demanded a balanced budget, and advocated the gold standard. And in the Governor's mansion at Albany a young man who would conduct Keynes' revolution in America was still thinking, like King, in terms of orthodox finance.

The American and the Canadian, soon to be thrown together in even larger adventures, did not know it then, but they would reverse their ideas of money. For the moment, King could only deplore Bennett's spendthrift policies with one cutting phrase: "The government's promises of yesterday are the taxes of today." Bennett, said King, in an unusually vivid piece of imagery, was like a child in a powerhouse grasping one lever and then another to see how it

would work; like a boy at a pipe organ, pulling out stops at random
and hoping for harmony.

There was a good deal of truth in these similes. Harry Stevens,
King's old enemy of the Customs scandal, and now Minister of
Trade, could think of nothing better than exhortation and was
circulating a "creed" to be hung in every business office, pledging
the owner to buy Canadian goods. Why not hang the creed, said
King, in the churches and Sunday schools? This sort of thing was
merely industrial feudalism, even down to Stevens' oath of fealty
to be sworn by the vassals.

King's spirits were recovering. The spirits of the nation sank
steadily lower. Every month the depression deepened, more industries closed, more workers were unemployed, and the relief rolls,
thermometer of the national fever, continued to rise every month.

Bennett remained undaunted. He was ready to apply his final
remedy and cure unemployment whenever the British Government
would co-operate, and on that score he had good hopes. Meanwhile,
in an outward fashion, he dominated Ottawa as King had never
tried to do. He was not the Prime Minister. As no one before him,
he was the state. He managed every phase of the Government's
business, he treated his Ministers as clerks, he lectured the House
of Commons as a master to a class of schoolboys, and every morning,
after his massage, as he walked from his huge suite in the Chateau
Laurier to the East Block—walked in his exquisite clothes past the
panhandlers and deadbeats of the pavements—he meditated some
staggering new pronouncement to a punch-drunk nation.

His work through the day and most of the night, his ceaseless
flow of eloquence in the House, his kindliness and sudden rages,
his desperate clutch on a disaster which he totally misunderstood,
were one of the highest feats of physical endurance, personal courage, unblemished honor, and inevitable failure ever seen in Canada.
Ottawa had watched great men before. It had never watched the
Great Man myth so nakedly paraded as a theory of politics and a
system of government.

King, a greater man, was alternately disgusted, angered, and
amused by the spectacle, but he knew that the myth could not last
among Canadians. Therefore, he worked contentedly on his ruins
to leave his personal monument of stone, to create a gray myth of
his own image for all future time.

Without warning his new peace of mind was rudely broken. He
was plunged headlong into what he called "the valley of humiliation."

On July 21 a Parliamentary committee considering the affairs of the Beauharnois Power Company turned up a fascinating exhibit. It was a voucher for a hotel bill in Bermuda, paid in the spring of 1930 by Senator Wilfred Laurier McDougald on behalf of himself and King. The voucher was modest for a Caribbean holiday, a mere $283.53, but large enough, it seemed then, to wreck King's career. For McDougald was the front man of the Beauharnois Company and it was accused of bribing the Liberal Party to give it valuable power concessions on the St. Lawrence. If the company had paid the hotel bills of a Liberal Prime Minister, then the scandal, already burning underground in a Parliamentary investigation, had touched King's honor, never questioned before.

He instantly denied any knowledge of the affair. True, he had gone to the hotel cashier to ask for his bill and found it paid for the most part by his old friend, but, on picking up today's newspaper, he had been "horrified" to learn that McDougald had asked the Beauharnois Company to reimburse him for his Bermuda expenditure.

Hurrying to the East Block, King told the facts to Bennett and, in the afternoon, to Parliament. He said he had never discussed the Beauharnois affair with McDougald and "had no connection with Beauharnois in any way." As McDougald's evidence showed, the hotel bill had been sent to Beauharnois by a secretary's mistake, without McDougald's knowledge.

That was only the first tremor of the appalling scandal. The Parliamentary committee was now digging up still more fascinating exhibits. On July 28 it tabled its report, signed by the Liberal and Conservative members unanimously after some frantic and unpleasant interparty bargaining behind the scenes.

In brief, the report found that the Beauharnois Company had long sought the approval of King's Government for necessary navigation rights. It had spent lavishly on its Ottawa lobby to secure "political influence." Altogether, $864,000 was paid to political campaign funds, of which "somewhere around $600,000 to $700,000" went to the Liberal funds, according to R. O. Sweezey, the principal promoter. This money had been handed to Senators Haydon and Raymond, the former being the national collector of the Party and the latter the manager in Quebec. The Conservative Party got about $30,000 and it was indicated that Bennett himself had intervened to prevent the acceptance of more.

In a classic dictum on the law of the jungle, Sweezey said that "gratefulness was always regarded as an important factor in dealing with democratic governments." Campaign-fund contributions, however, had been "very distasteful" to him and he preferred "not to know or remember much about it."

To King, at this point, they were much more distasteful. They might well be ruinous. To the Parliamentary committee they "were shamelessly, wastefully and needlessly made for the express purpose of obtaining favorable consideration of the Company's proposals to the Government."

Haydon's acceptance of a legal retainer and campaign funds from the Company was "strongly condemned."

A stronger verdict was delivered on McDougald. How one holding his office and expressing his "high regard for his public duties should allow his private interest to so interfere with his public duty that he found it necessary, speaking from his place in the Senate, to be 'ambiguous' and incorrect, it is difficult for your committee to understand. Senator McDougald's actions in respect to the Beauharnois project cannot be too strongly condemned." After this, McDougald's resignation from the Senate followed automatically.

The committee did not say so, but the implication, in Parliament and country, was that King's Government had handed over the river rights to Beauharnois in return for some $700,000 in campaign funds to finance the election of 1930. Since the charge had reached him directly through the Bermuda incident, this was much more serious for King personally than the Customs scandal, which had not touched his own integrity. An answer must be made and King, his misery legible on his face, attempted it in the most painful, labored, and ingenious speech of his life.

For months, he said, the Government had considered the Beauharnois project, having no interest but the welfare of the nation in the St. Lawrence waterway. He knew nothing of the identity of the men behind the scheme. To prove that the Government had not been influenced in the least by payments for "gratefulness" he emphasized that the approval of the Beauharnois plans had been given months before the Liberal Party received its campaign funds.

He had made it a strict rule never to discuss with anyone outside, even his most intimate friends like Haydon' and McDougald, any business before the Cabinet and never to know anything about the source of campaign funds. He had not even known of McDougald's connection with Beauharnois. Actually, he added, he had "believed that in dealing with this matter the Government was dealing with a Conservative corporation." The Conservative benches could not quite accept this innocence and laughed outright. It was hard going for King that day.

Nevertheless, he boldly undertook to turn the scandal against the enemy. If it was true that Bennett had refused Beauharnois money, then Bennett, unlike King, must have known who was putting up his Party's funds, perhaps knew of the funds provided by great

corporations already benefiting from Bennett's high tariffs—an in-
nuendo which Bennett instantly denounced as outrageous.

King said he had "implicit faith" in Bennett's integrity and "I
honor him as a man." He did not withdraw the insinuation. Instead,
he pictured the huge expenditures of the Conservative Party—ten
times those of the Liberals. These were open to "misunderstanding"
when the Government was granting favors every day to large business interests.

With rather overdrawn pathos King painted the picture of his
Party's poverty, the impossibility of getting money even to issue a
pamphlet and inform the public of its policies. In these straits it
was understandable that Party organizers, during the heat of a campaign, might do things they would not do if they had time to consider the consequences.

When he asked the glowering Bennett point-blank if a party leader
could be expected to keep track of campaign-fund contributions,
Bennett grunted this crushing reply: "I have always held that the
receiver of stolen goods was a criminal."

The going was getting heavier. King admitted that he was "surprised and pained" to find his friends taking Beauharnois money,
but was every man responsible for every act of his friends? In any
case the committee had found no proof whatever that the Government had been influenced by its friends' extramural activities, though
he agreed that what they had done was "wholly unjustifiable and
cannot be defended at any cost."

To show who was the real offender, King proposed a royal commission to investigate the expenditure of funds in the last three elections and to study methods of reducing campaign costs. He included
also the radical suggestion of compulsory voting by all Canadians.
This, like Senate reform (now caricatured by the activities of
Haydon and McDougald), was never heard of again.

Considering that the Liberal Party had been caught red-handed
in the sale of "gratefulness," King had made the best of a bad case.
His arguments, however, were too long, lasting until nearly midnight, and too complicated for the public to grasp. The public
grasped only his closing confession:

"The Liberal Party has not been disgraced but it is in the valley
of humiliation. I tell the people of this country today that as its
leader I feel humiliated and I know my following is humiliated. I
have told them so in caucus, that we are in the valley of humiliation. But we are going to come out of that valley . . . to higher and
stronger and better ground."

Brave words. Unfortunately, the public did not remember the

higher and stronger and better ground. It saw only the Valley of Humiliation and within it the sorry figure of King and his wretched hotel bill. Few Canadians could imagine then that he would ever climb out. Bennett could imagine that ascent less than anybody. When he replied to King next day in a speech dripping with righteousness, laced with sarcasm and altogether ravaging, Bennett stood on the final eminence of his life. He own quick descent was unimaginable.

He showed in this speech his almost superhuman grasp of business detail, a memory for facts which even King could not approach, the high but narrow talent of the Man of Business ill equipped for the business of a nation.

After outlining the case in business and legal terms, he swept aside all these minutiae. The simple fact was, he said, that Haydon had been told by King to get money. Did King think Haydon could manufacture it or "pull it down from the stars or find it in the earth?" No, Haydon as a practical man had gone where the money was. Beauharnois had provided it and got what it required from the Government.

As for himself, Bennett knew no more of party funds than King. If King would make charges, a royal commission would investigate them. There would be no general fishing expedition. Meanwhile, the Government would take over the Beauharnois canal on the St. Lawrence, protect the investors, and reorganize the company.

So ended the scandal in Parliament with a postscript from Miss MacPhail. She was revolted by the Liberals and suffocated by the self-righteousness of Bennett, who, "when he brings down legislation, he is never wrong, when he withdraws it he is never wrong, no, never wrong."

Unlike Miss MacPhail, the country still saw only the Valley and its prisoner. In the end, however, it showed over and over again that it had not been shaken in its belief that King himself was scrupulously honest. Without that belief among a great majority of Canadians his subsequent career would have been impossible.

In any case, the fetid smell of Beauharnois did not last long. It was overcome by the more powerful odor of poverty and hunger. All Bennett's business talents, his personal honor, his policies, and his appeals to God could not repel the rising whiff of national catastrophe. By the next year King was emerging from the Valley into which Bennett already was descending, now that his old ally, the depression, had turned against him. But on King's soul the word "Beauharnois" was burned deep and he was haunted by the hotel bill, the only piece of sheer mischance in his life.

19

Out of the Depths

A s THE DEPRESSION WORSENED, KING FELT ABLE TO INCREASE HIS attack on the baffled Government. In his pitiless speech of March 31, 1932, he recited with relish all Bennett's election promises, repeated the guarantees to cure unemployment, and then placed against them the chilling current figures to show that unemployment, totaling 150,000 under a Liberal Government, had now reached half a million under a Conservative.

This was monstrously unfair. King had felt only the first breath of the depression when he left office and Bennett was caught in a world panic which no government, least of all the government of a small nation, could hope to arrest. Unfairer still his attack on Bennett for spending twenty millions for unemployment relief in one year, whereas the Liberal Government had spent less than two millions in ten years—as if there were any comparison between the depressions of the 'twenties and the 'thirties. In a climax of injustice, King ignored his own five-cent speech to accuse Bennett of partisanship in relief administration.

King could offer only the same remedies which he had proposed a year ago. He would reduce tariffs, taxes, and expenditures. He dismissed as nonsense the notion of governmental spending to create prosperity. He rejected paper money detached from gold. His finance was more orthodox at this point than Bennett's, but would soon change.

Of this period an eminent Canadian scholar, Wilfrid Eggleston, has said that Bennett was providing circuses without bread whereas King promised bread without circuses. The thing went deeper than that. Bennett at least was trying to feed the unemployed while he blindly widened their unemployment by his economic circus. King provided no circus but had yet to offer the public an escape from Bennett's.

The Conservatives listened with outward calm to King's telling indictment. It was evident, however, that he was striking home when they could think of nothing better than to shout "Beauharnois!" and "Five-cent piece!" across the House. Bennett was not disturbed. He had yet to play his ace.

He played it at the Imperial Conference in Ottawa during the summer. This was to be his triumph and vindication.

The whole Empire family was there in the newly elected Conservative top hats of Britain and the silks of Asia like vivid flowers against the dark oak of the Commons chamber.

Towering over all as host, architect, and prophet was the handsome person of the Canadian Prime Minister with gray tail coat and face of white porcelain, the famous jowls overspreading the famous wing collar; beside him the John Bull figure of Stanley Baldwin with his homely pipe, an indispensable stage property, and the hawklike visage of Neville Chamberlain, the gates of Munich six years distant; and in the gallery, fresh from Kingsmere, in a summer suit of light flannel, a tiny individual who watched the proceedings with expressionless look and prepared to expunge them at leisure.

The story of the Ottawa conference belongs to Bennett's biography. To King it was only his enemy's latest feat of madness. He knew from hour to hour of all the tough bargaining between the Empire partners behind the outward show of Empire fellowship, for nothing in Ottawa could ever be hidden from him.

He knew that the British balked at Bennett's plan, which called upon them and the other Commonwealth countries to raise their tariffs against the world, to tax their people through prices in order to make the Commonwealth a watertight trading compartment.

He saw at once that this was the reverse and caricature of Laurier's Preferential System, which raised no tariffs while reducing those on British goods.

He realized how little Bennett was offering Britain in return for the guarantee to buy Canadian raw materials to the exclusion of cheaper imports from the world market, and he remembered that Bennett started from the premise—fatal to the whole concept of expanded trade even inside the Commonwealth—that nothing should be imported if it could be made in Canada.

Thus King was not surprised when Britain at first refused the bargain, threatened to break up the conference, and then yielded, against its better judgment, to Bennett's alternate persuasion and threat. As the conference signed the treaties contrived to shoulder foreign goods out of the Commonwealth and strike yet another blow at a supine world, King believed that the whole thing was still what Thomas had called it in the beginning—sheer humbug.

Bennett, the victor over the British Government, the U. E. Loyalist from New Brunswick who at last had succeeded, where Joe Chamberlain had failed, in building a new Empire economy, looked on his work and pronounced it good. To him his victory was the biggest thing since the repeal of the Corn Laws, a piece of folly which he had now repealed. Bennett's was to be a brief triumph. Not long afterward, the depression worse than ever, he was trying to extricate himself from the strangling clutch of his Ottawa Treaties.

The year 1933 dawned on a world distracted, hungry, and sick. Looking about him now, King was forced to admit that the thing was bigger than Bennett, bigger than tariffs, and bigger than any remedy that he or anyone else had yet proposed. The whole problem, and all his thinking on it, must be reassessed.

The reassessment had begun already within the Liberal Party.

A new brain trust, headed by an enlightened man of wealth, Vincent Massey, was bombarding King with memoranda, circulating plan and counterplan among the Party leaders, and painfully hammering out a design for a new Liberalism.

At "summer schools" and country week ends the younger and brighter minds (some of whom would soon move into a more radical party) re-educated the old-time Liberals in modern economics and proposed revolutionary solutions which were rejected, revised, and compromised.

Norman Lambert, the master of political organization who had managed the Progressive Party and observed its collapse, was imported as Liberal organizer and began to reduce to some semblance of order the blizzard of paper policies now descending on Kingsmere and its puzzled resident. All of which Dunning, the major conservative in the Liberal Party, watched with interest from his temporary roost in the manager's office of the Seigniory Club on his way to the higher towers of finance.

And out west, unknown at that time, one of the ablest minds of Liberalism, John Pickersgill, was writing his own solitary testament. Printed two years later, it announced that "it is not remotely likely that the decay of orthodox Liberalism in Canada can be arrested for very long." A young man to watch. King had not yet discovered him but presently would be leaning on Pickersgill as he seldom leaned on any cabinet colleague.

The words written by the young professor of history in solitude represented more clearly than King yet cared to say the revolution in his own thinking, now well under way.

Liberal doctrines, Pickersgill wrote, were "potent to destroy po-

litical, social or economic privilege but, having little positive content, they have become politically obsolete as their destructive work
has been completed." The effects of unrestrained self-interest, the
basis of Liberal economics, "far from being universally beneficent,
were often evil and, in some cases, intolerable. . . . It is small
wonder that economic Liberalism is discredited. . . . Classical
Liberalism is dead; as a practical political creed it is bankrupt. . . .
Its apparent survival on this continent is almost completely explained
when it is remembered that it is the only type of conservatism to
which North Americans can turn."

Bankruptcy—that, as King believed, was the state of Canadian
Liberalism now to be faced. The measure of the man in these most
decisive years of his life is that he faced it. Not openly, of course.
Pickersgill, a philosopher, and the other unattached philosophers,
could speak their minds openly. King, the statesman, with a Party to
hold together, a nation to persuade, a new policy to frame, must
work quietly, must appear, while jettisoning his past, to be following
his lifelong principles.

In the art of invisible reversal and elegant somersault he was the
unequaled master, and the Party's radicals knew it. Their only
chance to reform the Party and restore its solvency was to reform
King. So with the reformers clamoring, King listening, and Lambert
organizing, the great change went steadily forward in secret and
King, altering the Party's historic direction, prepared to prove that
he was still marching in the same changeless path.

The Liberal bankruptcy was little noted in the bankruptcy of
nation and world. Nearly a million Canadians were on relief just
sufficient to keep together a hungry body and a despairing soul.
Thousands of men were living in government camps with wages of
twenty cents a day. The railway cars moving through the Canadian
winter bore on their roofs a pitiable freight of homeless and ragged
boys who would wear uniforms of khaki to save this country within
half a dozen years. The Mounted Police, once Canada's pride, were
engaged in the alien work of ejecting from the trains, freight yards,
and hobo jungles their fellow citizens, who had committed the crime
of poverty. Section 98 of the Criminal Code, that dead-sea fruit of
the Winnipeg strike, was working overtime against suspected Communists and other subversive elements, most of whom only wished
to eat. The unemployed waited in dismal queues, too beaten even
to protest, at every relief office in the country, or conducted their
poor processions of protest, becoming day by day a kind of separate
nation within the nation while the employed and prosperous lived in
a mixture of complacency, pity, and fear.

As if the world economic scourge were not enough, nature re-

N

enforced it with a withering drought. It left much of the Canadian prairies covered with thistles and shifting dust for nearly a decade. The farmer now joined the city worker on relief. Almost it seemed that God had turned against His servant in Ottawa. The Great Man image now broken beyond mending, Bennett staggered toward his appointed goal, bearing on immense shoulders the too vast orb of his fate, overloaded with the extra burden of his election promises. He might have lost any semblance of policy. He never lost his courage.

A sick nation in a sick world, whereof the fevers and spasms took many curious forms.

In Washington, Roosevelt, elected on a program of economy and budget balancing, was ushering in his New Deal of gigantic deficit spending, was reopening the closed banks and pronouncing in a voice which had become overnight the most familiar and heartening of recent times that the nation had nothing to fear but fear itself.

Lately he had received Keynes, who tried to educate him in the new economics "with a rigamarole of figures," but Keynes remarked acidulously to Frances Perkins afterward that he had "supposed the President was more literate, economically speaking." Illiterate as he was, Roosevelt prepared to launch Keynes' revolution without understanding it, together with the N.R.A. (though it happened to deny all his principles); to plow in crops while people hungered; to dump little pigs into the Mississippi because the hungry could not buy them; to tamper with the price of gold as he ate his breakfast in bed every morning; and yet, from all this inchoate mass of contradictions and utter whimsy, to shape a new society from which there could be no retreat.

In London the nations met to rebuild the world's trade after the strangulation of Republican and Conservative tariffs, only to find all their plans torpedoed by the free trader of the White House, who had changed without notice into a protectionist.

In Berlin a lunatic with hypnotic eye and comedian's mustache was climbing to power over the corpse of the Weimar Republic and arranging to rescue the world from depression by the simple act of world war.

In Tokyo a military government, having entered Manchuria and mortally wounded the League of Nations two years before, was planning the conquest of China and then of civilization.

In Africa the tribesmen of Ethiopia tilled their land while yet another lunatic was fixing to bomb and gas them in the restoration of the Roman Empire.

A mad world, ridden by lunatics who spoke in the statesmanlike accents of a higher lunacy, a world of Great Men, of Leadership, of Fascism, Communism, Socialism, and Capitalism soon to meet in death grip and produce the next chapter of lunacy in which we now live.

Canada could not immunize itself from the world fever.

In Ottawa some Conservatives meditated their own heresies, for announcement two years hence. The dazed Banking Committee of Parliament, attempting to cram a university course into a few days of public hearings, suddenly stumbled upon the entrancing subject of money and listened, popeyed, to such apocalyptical evangelists as Gerry McGeer, of Vancouver, who, after reading a book or two, could miraculously fix everything by manipulating the medium of exchange and introducing, without knowing it, the system then being perfected by Dr. Hjalmar Schacht.

In Alberta, always the volcano of extraordinary remedy, an eruption of soft money, old as the struggle between frontier and city —old as Intendant de Meulles, who had used playing cards for money in the New France of 1685—was presented as a virgin discovery called Social Credit by Mr. William Aberhart, a pale and mountainous oracle, who mixed modern economics with old-time religion and proceeded thence into office, innocent to the last of any knowledge of his own theories.

Under almost unbearable strains Canadian society held together. Not without deep cracks, which the existing remedies could never heal.

20

Lunge to the Left

PROTEST, DISILLUSIONMENT, AND THE WILL FOR SOMETHING BETTER must find their organ in politics if the political system was to endure. Assuredly the organ would be found, but where? By supplying it, King saved his Party from the collapse of its parent, the Liberal Party of Britain. He also saved himself. In some measure anyway, he saved the nation.

For a brief period it appeared that he was rounding the corner too late. Another leader was ahead of him and, if he succeeded, could permanently pre-empt Liberalism's historic position on the Left, as men like Pickersgill feared.

That leader, inevitably, was Woodsworth. As he had become the conscience of Parliament he was emerging now as the hope of the underdog throughout the nation, especially in the West, where he was known.

The apostate Methodist minister had left the church because, as he once said, he could no longer bury dead babies and pronounce their death the decision of God when he knew that they had died from bad milk. Now he saw a whole nation sick from the poison of the profit motive, the core of Liberal economics.

This frail man had labored as a longshoreman in Vancouver, lifting bales of freight heavier than his own 130 pounds, and he knew, by his own experience, the life and misery of the workingman. To the workingman he had dedicated his life in the search for some amelioration of conditions here rather than in a distant heaven.

His economics were as vague as his ideals were clear. That mattered little to the workers who followed him. Enough that the greatness of the man and the sufferings of his own life were written for all to read upon his face.

Though Woodsworth was doomed to fail by the test of elections, he was to become, next to King, perhaps the most influential figure of his time in Canada, and no man influenced King so much. For it was the pressure of Woodsworth and what he represented that encouraged and then drove King leftward. In a man who had never hesitated, compromised, or feared, King saw the idealism of his own youth and tried to recover it.

Woodsworth was the companion of half King's nature, a rebuke to the other half. As much as King, he was the architect of the New Liberalism.

In history Woodsworth needs no defense. His sainthood stands out like a beacon in the darkness of the depression, undimmed by his lack of a plan to end it. King's defense, if he requires it, is that he could not go in idealism as far as Woodsworth even if he wished to (which is doubtful) without smashing his Party, probably the nation, and certainly his career. Woodsworth, in short, was a prophet and a saint. King was a statesman.

At Calgary, in 1932, Woodsworth ceased to be a lone voice and became the leader of a political party. A gathering of disillusioned Progressives, desperate farmers, labor leaders, and Fabian socialists from England formed what they called the Co-operative Commonwealth Federation and a year later, at Regina, they issued their Manifesto.

It called for the extermination of capitalism but it did not propose an outright socialist state (though that must be the outcome of it). Like most reformers, the founders of the C.C.F. could not anticipate the end of their reform, could not agree on details, and appealed to all discontented Canadians of contradictory feeling. That is to say, they sought to form a national party.

If they succeeded they must destroy, in time, one or the other of the old parties. Since they were on the Left, Liberalism must be the victim unless it, in turn, moved to the Right and destroyed Conservatism. King saw as quickly as anyone that the C.C.F., for all its confusion, might manage to ride the tide of the future. But he knew better than the C.C.F. where the central current of that tide flowed and he sought it instinctively, while the C.C.F., moving too far leftward, would be swept upon the rocks.

Still, the fact that the C.C.F. had arisen at all, and was making evident progress among the discontented and dispossessed, was warning enough of the Liberal Party's threatened bankruptcy. To restore its solvency in the coin of practical politics, Liberalism must move somewhat leftward, must seize some of the votes which the C.C.F. would gain otherwise. How far left? That was the problem which obsessed King throughout the years of Opposition and was never quite settled in his mind.

He was not, of course, a free agent. No party leader ever is. Given sufficient support, King might move almost as far leftward as the C.C.F., or at least as far as M. J. Coldwell ever moved in his own thinking. To move at all, King, while pushed from behind by the radicals of his Party, must manage to hold its conservatives. To combine the older Dunnings and the younger Pickersgills was a delicate feat of balance. Only an equilibrist of King's capacity, a very Blondin of politics, could have done it. And he stumbled, squirmed, and often almost fell off the tightrope.

In his thinking there were two factors of confusion.

First, society had not evolved, as he hoped, by an orderly progress into the ideal state, managed jointly by capital, labor, and the community. Instead, it had broken down. In some countries it had sought refuge in dictatorship. In others like the United States it seemed to be spinning into what, at this stage, King considered mad experiments.

Secondly, though he realized that collectivism in some form was in process of diluting the individualism of the Liberal dream, he could not tell—who could?—how far this dilution would go or how far, in practical politics, he could accept it and still hold his Party and the nation together.

He may also have seen, though there is no public record of it, that the C.C.F. represented another aspect of fundamental change. The Progressive Party, a rural revolt, had failed. Canada was becoming an urban nation. The center of power had shifted from country to city; and while the C.C.F., by the accidents of personality and by the impact of the prairies drought, had arisen in the West, it must be based, if it were to last, on urban votes. There was its opportunity and its danger. If it shifted to the city and became only a labor-union movement, then, at this stage in the nation's life, it could not become a truly national party. Its ground would be too narrow.

Contending with the same forces, King must manage to capture the vote of protest while still occupying ground broad enough to include both city and country, rich and poor, employer and worker. The trick, in short, was to make a transition but to make it quietly, without dislocation, to change enough to satisfy the haves and not enough to alarm the have-nots.

To this, as to all his larger decisions, King applied his invariable method of cart-before-horse. By intuition and mere hunch he reached a conclusion. After that, all his study and then his argument and documentation were used to support the conclusion already reached and to make it appear to be a deductive reasoning from facts, when actually it was the reverse. In this case he had decided on a left

turn. Now he had to contrive public reasons for his intention, to
refine an obscure feeling into an understandable policy. And without
further delay, lest someone get ahead of him.

On February 27, 1933, he crossed his Rubicon. His speech of that
day was the first public proclamation that something decisive had
occurred in him and his Party. It was, in fact, the outline of a new
Liberal policy.

Before his own leap leftward, King felt it necessary to demolish
the C.C.F., his competitor for the leadership in reform.

Woodsworth's little following in Parliament had introduced a
resolution calling for the creation of the Co-operative Commonwealth. Few politicians understood what this meant. Certainly
Bennett did not. King, a scholar who had studied every variety of
political philosophy, understood fully. Among Canadian statesmen
of that period he was the only one adequately equipped to discuss
the Co-operative Commonwealth in practical terms, where most of
its enemies could find no reply better than abuse and sneer.

King began by appealing to the C.C.F. to work within the Liberal
Party instead of forming a futile splinter. It was too late for that
now. Woodsworth and his friends might think King not beyond conversion but they would not trust a Party which contained the Dunnings of the eastern cities and the Crerars of the western plains.

Doubtless aware in advance that his appeal for unity would fail,
King proceeded to analyze the C.C.F. program in a fashion which
would be commonplace today but at that time showed not only deep
knowledge of the past but a rare foresight into the future.

Whether it knew where it was going or not, said King, the C.C.F.
stood for Socialism and Socialism must finally mean the end of
private ownership in all productive enterprise. Did the C.C.F.
imagine that a mere change of title deeds would accomplish anything? It would change owners. It would not change industry. (This,
in 1933, long before the first bloom had been rubbed off Socialism
by the experience of Britain, Australia, New Zealand, and other
countries, was a searching glance into the present world.)

Then followed a penetrating analysis of Socialism as a theory leading in practice leftward into the very kind of bureaucratic, centralized, and unworkable state which Bennett even then was erecting on
the right. Socialism and Toryism thus were sisters under the skin,
both moving toward the same dead end.

Bennett, said King, was haunted by Communism, was trying to
fight with the dirty and useless weapon of Section 98, and seemed
to imagine that the C.C.F. was Communistic. Of course it was nothing of the sort. It was rather a well-intentioned confusion. It did not

preach a violent revolution. It proposed to erect peacefully a system which could not work in any free society.

King was careful to emphasize that the Liberal Party was not opposed to government ownership of industry, where that device would work better than private ownership as in the case of natural monopolies. That, however, was not Socialism, since publicly-owned industries lived within a free-enterprise economy.

After an impressive attack on Socialism, what did King offer in its place? Only the existing system? Not by any means.

The Liberal Party, he said, stood for a fairer distribution of wealth, holding "personality more sacred than property." It regarded Capitalism as an unequaled producer of wealth for the general good but Capitalism was being destroyed by its owners. The depression had been caused by the greed of men, of classes, and of nations. Capitalism was digging its own grave by its lust for excessive profits. The "few men" responsible for this disaster were "criminals" and should be in jail.

This, from a former Prime Minister of a pretty conservative government, was iconoclasm and was intended to be. King was beginning, and only beginning, to carry his appeal to the have-nots.

As the "criminals" destroyed their own system within nations, he went on, so nations destroyed one another by the kind of stifling tariffs imposed under Bennett. Nevertheless, confronted by these enemies in business and in government, the nation would be mad to destroy its well-tried constitution by attack from right or left.

Would a man who is sick from too much drink or food condemn the human constitution which he had abused? Why blame Capitalism, which could flourish if it were properly treated merely because, for the moment, it was crapulous with vice?

If Capitalism continued in its vices, however, if it moved further into monopoly and giantism, it could not survive. As Capitalism, Socialism, Communism, or any other system ended in monopoly, all were "alike doomed," and "in that sense I do believe the capitalistic system is doomed." Monopoly Capitalism, that was to say, was doomed. The monopoly of Socialism or Communism would be even worse because it would be more powerful.

The Liberal Party therefore stood for Capitalism, so-called, but a capitalism drastically reformed. The reforms which he now proposed, in rather haphazard order and in blurred form, showed that he and the brain trust were thinking their way through the depression. They had a long way to go yet.

There must be, said King, an expansion of social legislation to care for the unfortunate. Who could provide it better than the

Liberal Party, author of old-age pensions, combines legislation, industrial conciliation, and many other measures?

The Liberal Party would administer unemployment relief through a nonpartisan national commission during the present emergency and establish unemployment insurance as a permanent protection for the worker.

It would reduce tariffs, revive trade, attack all combines, prevent the issue of fraudulent securities.

King had thus gone far in attacking Capitalism, the handmaiden of Liberalism. He had gone some distance in proposing actual reforms. But the real nubbin of that speech was his proposal to establish a central bank, under public control, to "determine the supply of currency in terms of public need." There, though few realized it then, was the engine of revolution. The revolution could be peaceful. Thus powered, it could not be halted.

Apparently King himself did not realize that yet. Less than a year previously, he had advocated the gold standard, a direct denial of the new theory, and did not publicly abandon it now. In this latest speech he was still talking of reduced public expenditures and balanced budgets. Deficit spending to create purchasing power and prime the pump was still anathema.

He had yet to see that once a central bank was controlling the money system, "in terms of public need," the whole Keynesian revolution would follow. By seizing the central lever of the economic system, the state from then on must control its direction and momentum, for better or worse. The revolution was young then, hardly more than a gleam in Keynes' eye and an answering gleam in Roosevelt's. King did not know what he had got hold of. It would take him and Canada some seventeen years to find out.

The rest of that speech—so little noted or remembered by Parliament and public—was straight out of *Industry and Humanity*, a plea for a society managed jointly by the three partners, the establishment in economics of the same parliamentary mechanism which had solved the nation's political problems.

The more perceptive eyes saw a change in King. A change in his recent tactics there was, but no real change in his philosophy. He was being sucked back into his original philosophy after the years of abandonment. The depression was the catalyst now suddenly clarifying a mind long blurred by mere political success.

No one could foresee then, not even its owner, that Bennett's mind was subject to the same catalysis. A slow process, and nebulous in both men. Yet among all King's gropings for a society not then available or yet achieved anywhere, there remained one hard core. With the acceptance of a state control of money, to be used for "public need," a great divide had been passed. That step taken, society would never be the same again. Classic Liberalism, said the Pickersgills, was already dead. Now King had buried it.

He was on more familiar ground in demanding lower tariffs, an end to government by order-in-council, a return of power to Parliament, repeal of Section 98, the suspension of Bennett's arbitrary deportations, the restoration of liberty of speech and association, and, finally, support for the League of Nations (less than three years before he would betray it).

As usual, he ended by appealing to a higher authority and filed as his ultimate exhibit the Sermon on the Mount. There was no use, he said, in talking about changed techniques in the economic system. Nothing would change it really except a change in the minds of the men who controlled it. Still, "Parliament can do much to help to make it difficult if not impossible for the avaricious man to profit by his greed and the mean man to profit from his meanness."

With the voice of Roosevelt proclaiming the future from his fireside, the voice of Hitler proclaiming the past from the jungle, and the voice of King lost in the northern silence of Canada's misery, the world descended into the abyss of 1933, still finding no bottom to its descent.

Even after he had lost three by-elections in the autumn—sure whispers of death for his Government—Bennett opened Parliament in 1934 with the assurance that the worst had passed, that "permanent prosperity" at last was returning. At which King jeered, asserting that unemployment was wider than ever and trade sunk to a new low under the burden of the Ottawa Treaties.

King was not ready to go beyond his proposals of the previous year. He was waiting to unveil his election platform until he was sure that Bennett would call an election, and this Bennett feared to do. In the meantime King proposed a trade treaty with the United States, now possible because a Liberal presided in Washington (unfortunately not the sort of Liberal he imagined). He did not know then that Bennett, disillusioned with his own Ottawa handiwork, was secretly moving to alter it by a new Canadian-American tariff deal.

King looked to the Liberal in Washington for help but attacked Roosevelt's New Deal theories because Bennett already was copying them in some respects. Among other things he condemned Bennett's attempt to limit Canadian wheat production, and thus to help the farmer by reducing his source of wealth while raising his costs through the tariff. Here King ventured on one of his few essays into heavy-handed satire.

In the days when the Blue Eagle was parading through the American streets, when General Johnson was curing the depression with slogans, dead cats, and wisecracks, when America had become a kind of grim circus with eminent clowns wearing a grin of grease paint, Stevens, in Canada, was still circulating his economic Creed among the bemused businessmen. Let the Creed be revised, said King, to conform to the Government's actual policy, and he read a new Creed solemnly into Hansard:

"O, most merciful Father, Who of Thy gracious goodness has heard the devout prayers of Thy Government and turned our cheapness and plenty into dearth and scarcity; we give Thee humble thanks for this Thy special Affliction; beseeching Thee to continue Thy loving scarcity unto us, that our land may yield us ever less of her fruits of increase, to Thy glory and discomfort."

At this jest, so out of King's character, Bennett was appalled and cried across the floor of Parliament: "That is as near blasphemy as this House has ever heard!"

"I wish," King retorted, "the Prime Minister would try to be a little more composed—there, that is nicer!"

The general tragedy had produced a moment of comedy between the two men of God. Nothing appeared funny to a sick nation any more.

After King's elephantine joke and Bennett's moral indignation, the 1934 session produced one vital change in the Canadian system, or the beginning of it. Bennett created a central bank.

King crowed that the Government had been compelled to adopt a Liberal policy and, as usual, had distorted it. Bennett's bank was privately owned. It did not give the people the control of money. Bennett was trying to restore the gold standard (which King had advocated two years before), whereas Liberalism proposed to manage money "in terms of public need" and "from a social point of view."

Keynes now had one foot invisibly inside the Liberal Party's door. Nothing could stop his complete entry.

King's further confusion was indicated by his praise of Roosevelt's N.R.A. and the codification of wages. He thought he saw there an attack on his old enemy, the Law of Competing Standards. He did not see yet, but soon would, that the N.R.A. was a frontal attack on Liberalism, was tinged with Fascism, and in any case was unconstitutional.

King proposed to introduce something like this experiment in Canada by shortening the hours of work, distributing employment more widely, and raising wages by law.

With an unerring genius for self-destruction Bennett had lately chosen to proclaim the doctrine of Privilege in the winter of discontent by re-establishing titles of nobility, contrary to the will of Parliament as declared by resolution in 1919. He had created noblemen in Canada almost as if he wished to tell the country that he and his belted knights knew what was best for it. His Loyalist instincts had outrun his instinct of survival.

A small thing, perhaps, and irrelevant, but King made the most of it. Here, he said, was a nation ground down by poverty, a million Canadians on the dole, and yet the Prime Minister, defying Parliament, caricatured the depression with his titles of tinsel, his noblemen decked out in ermine, while better men went hungry.

King spoke for four hours and thirty-two minutes, afternoon and evening. He broke no new ground because he was waiting for an election. Bennett refused to give it to him that year.

21

The Man of Business

OUTSIDE PARLIAMENT SOMETHING HAD OCCURRED TO ALTER drastically the political atmosphere in which King must soon operate and to assure Bennett's downfall.

Harry Stevens, with his clear head but weakness for the theatrical, had gone to Toronto and made a speech denouncing the habits of Canadian industry. The creed writer of private enterprise had become disillusioned much sooner than the Man of Business, his leader. If the Government would not correct the abuses of the business system, Stevens evidently intended to force its pace.

The spectacular Toronto speech compelled the Government to establish a parliamentary committee of investigation under Stevens. Before this committee, later translated into a royal commission, the secrets of business—such as wages of $1.50 for seventy-five hours of work, the huge price spreads between producer and consumer, the watered stock and gamblers' profits—crawled like obscene bugs out of the corporate ledgers.

Even when they were presented later in the privacy of the royal commission, these facts somehow reached the press. Every morning the secret documents of the inquiry turned up in an old overcoat hanging beside the desk of Bob Lipsett in the Ottawa press gallery and every night were spread in the Toronto *Star*. Bennett, as usual, found himself betrayed, "betrayal" being his favorite word, and God knew that he had suffered from it more than any man deserved.

The efforts of Bennett to corral all the documents, the suspicion that Lester B. Pearson, secretary of the inquiry and then an unknown civil servant, had handed out the secrets, the sudden call for all papers to be collected in the safety of the Prime Minister's office, the complete vindication of Pearson—all this added an amusing touch to a series of grisly revelations that embittered the entire nation and

189

must play straight into the hands of the young C.C.F. unless King could exploit them.

Here was a situation made to his order. His Law of Competing Standards had been conveniently confirmed by Stevens' inquiry. With such evidence King could do much. He waited to see how far Stevens would go. While King did not know it then, Stevens had got hold of a much larger affair than his Customs scandal and was prepared to go to the point of destroying the Government and himself.

In the summer, Stevens delivered a private speech to a group of Conservative members of Parliament, outlining in naked detail what his inquiry committee had found in its study of business methods. His attack on starvation wages, sweatshops, exploitation of farmers, high prices, and watered stock was calculated to detonate a national explosion of anger if it reached the public.

The speech was reported, edited by Stevens, and widely circulated in a secret pamphlet. As anyone could have foreseen, it soon found its way into the newspapers. Bennett was enraged. He was still the champion of business and here was his Minister of Trade denouncing the sacred cause and, as Bennett suspected, bringing outside pressure on the Government.

It was not until the end of October, however, that Bennett undertook to discipline Stevens. In a letter delivered by special messenger to Stevens' house, Bennett declared that the now celebrated pamphlet was a slander on reputable business firms and its circulation "contrary to every principle of British Justice." Stevens was offered the chance to withdraw his charges and apologize. Instead, he sent back a letter of resignation, accused Bennett of untruth, intimated that the Government was shielding the enemies of society, and proceeded to found the Reconstruction Party of economic reform.

Stevens was a political comet of brilliance but secondary magnitude. There could be only one comet in Bennett's firmament. The collision shattered both and assured three results: Stevens, by breaking with his Party, had lost his almost certain successorship to Bennett and wrecked his promising career; the Conservative Party, already in decline, was now split between its two most powerful figures and could not hope to recover before the next election; King had not only a first-rate political sensation to blot out the sins of his Party but the perfect setting for a program of reform, slowly maturing these last four years.

No government or social system could stand these strains. The break came from the most improbable direction. It came from Bennett himself.

He had been thinking, too, and deeply. In his Chateau suite he had read the works of the seventh Earl of Shaftesbury and, after a lifetime of education in business and of social illiteracy, had suddenly perceived the gap in his political philosophy. What he did not perceive was forced upon him by his own inner brain trust, Roderick Finlayson, long his political factotum, and his brilliant, mercurial brother-in-law, William Herridge, who, as Minister to Washington, had soaked up the confused theories of the New Deal and was haunted by the fear of revolution.

For months these two and no doubt others had been trying to persuade a stubborn Prime Minister that he must reverse overnight the whole course of his life. Bennett, the Conservative, must become the reformer. The Man of Business must be the Roosevelt and New Dealer of Canada. The Match King of the Eddy corporation and the recent architect of Nobility must be the savior of the Common Man. As Brockington chortled out in Bennett's home town of Calgary, the tide of fortune must now be taken at the Eddy. A neat trick which would require some doing.

Bennett resisted a role which his life and record denied. He was still saying publicly that he stood on his promise to cure unemployment, by existing methods, even if no one believed that any more. In the end, he surrendered and suddenly marched out of the Chateau as the champion of reform to out-King King. That was all King needed.

In the first days of 1935, the Canadian people could not believe their radios. From the winter silence boomed the familiar voice of the Prime Minister announcing that society must be overhauled from top to bottom and that he would overhaul it. There would be a New Deal for everybody. In six successive broadcasts Bennett elaborated his reversal as if it had been his original objective, to which all these years in an opposite direction had been only the logical preparation.

This promise of reform was what the people wanted to hear, but would they believe it from Bennett? Would they take the somersault seriously? Such was the only question in practical politics. King had no doubt of the answer. He knew, as well, that while the mass of poor Canadians would not let Bennett conduct the New Deal, it would terrify the Conservative Party's rich friends in business. So it turned out.

Still, Bennett's performance, as a performance, was magnificent. His voice was confident, his courage undoubted, and his honesty, if confused, was transparent. After four and a half years of physical and spiritual punishment such as no Canadian statesman had ever endured, he had achieved something of a miracle. He had survived. He was still alive and dauntless. The wonder, as Dr. Johnson said of women preachers and of dogs walking on their hind legs, was not that Bennett walked clumsily but that, in this unnatural posture of reform, he walked at all.

When he introduced the New Deal into Parliament, King regarded it as superficial, unconstitutional, and phony. In retrospect it appears rather harmless and anemic. There was legislation to limit working hours and enforce minimum wages in all industries; to establish unemployment insurance; to give the Federal Government wider control over the marketing and price of basic materials; to provide relief for farm debtors by a scaling down of mortgages; to police the issuance of securities; to jail swindlers and exterminate unfair practices in business.

At first sight most of the program was *ultra vires* of the federal authority, falling within the provincial sphere of property and civil rights. Here Bennett, the lawyer, showed a rare ingenuity. Since Canada had signed foreign treaties as a gesture toward reform, he proposed to implement them in actual law and he held that the treaty-making power superseded the sovereignty of the provinces.

King at once questioned the validity of this loophole. He called the new legislation an attack on the perimeter of the social problem but he was careful not to damn it, except by faint praise. This was no time, with an election ahead, to question anything which seemed to offer any small relief from the evils of the day. Even though he cautiously questioned the wisdom and legality of the New Deal, and even though much of it was subsequently thrown out by the courts, King actually adopted most of it later on. Today the ghost of Bennett may well be laughing to find a Liberal Government solemnly enforcing many of his policies as its own inventions.

The New Deal, as King saw, was not big intrinsically. It did not seek to treat the inner disease of society, only to soothe some of its outer sores. It was, in fact, a Conservative measure because it sought to conserve the existing system, precisely as Roosevelt, the great conservative, was trying to conserve it against suicide in the United States.

It might be weak in economics, doubtful in legality, and phony in motive, but the New Deal was big in politics, as King knew—big as a symbol of the change ahead. Canada, said Bennett, had reached the end of one era and the beginning of another. In truth it had. The New Deal, coming from a Conservative, stood like a tombstone to mark the dead past. In King's view it was no reliable guidepost to the future. King's problem now was to prove that he and he alone

JAMES RALSTON

LOUIS ST. LAURENT

knew the path. This he undertook to do on January 21, 1935, in perhaps the most important speech of his career so far.

The time had come to reveal the conclusions of the long turmoil in the Liberal Party, to announce the platform which had been chopped and chewed interminably, handed from one draftsman to another, repeatedly caucused, and finally handed to King still in pretty amorphous state, for final treatment.

There was nothing important to add to the actual contents of King's speech in 1933, a tentative outline, which was largely forgotten. Inspired by Woodrow Wilson, another Liberal, King now took the same material and stretched it into a thin manifesto of fourteen points. This was an arbitrary grouping. Extracted from the sprawling letter of his argument, the substance of his policy can be summarized in more convenient sequence as follows:

Unemployment insurance for the long run and a national commission to administer relief in the current emergency.

A reduction in governmental spending and national debt with at least a balanced budget.

Expansion of trade with all nations willing to trade on a reciprocal basis; the elimination of unfair trade methods, price fixing, and the juggling of tariff interpretations; the end of tariff-making by executive action; an extension of the British Preference; the development thereby of basic industries with "state assistance in marketing natural products."

The maintenance of the "integrity" of the Canadian National Railways as a publicly owned and operated system.

A larger share for workers and consumers, "as opportunity offers," in the government of industry.

The repeal of "autocratic powers" assumed by the Government in usurpation of Parliament's rights under such devices as blank-check appropriations and the misuse of the "peace, order and good government" clauses of the constitution.

The restoration of individual rights, violated by the Government, the repeal of Section 98, and the end of arbitrary deportations.

Electoral laws "which will insure a true Parliamentary representation of the Canadian people and such legislation as may help to reduce the cost of election campaigns."

A pledge that the Liberal Party, regarding "personality as more sacred than property," would "devote itself to finding ways and means of effecting a fair and just distribution of wealth, with increasing regard to human need, to the furtherance of social justice and to the promotion of the common good."

A central bank, state-owned, to control the money system "in

o

terms of public need" and not for the profit of financiers—this point, dropped without emphasis among the others, being the unsuspected embryo of a new, or at least an entirely altered, economic system; for the banking policy meant, whatever King's intention might then be, that the state. with this central economic lever in its hand, must guarantee national prosperity at all times.

Apart from the bank, much of this famous platform was vague and dilute to the point of meaning everything or nothing.

None of it was new except the proposal—not considered worthy of inclusion in the fourteen points—that Canada take power to amend its own constitution, and nothing came of that until King had left politics.

Some of the program, like unemployment insurance and control over securities, already was in Bennett's New Deal. That did not disturb King. Where his platform duplicated Bennett's he accused the Government of stealing his policy and could ask who was better able to effect it, the true author or the plagiarist? Moreover, he had contrived his program in his invariably open-ended fashion so that he could interpret it as he saw fit or, in his own ineffable phrase, "as opportunity offers."

To the public, King's New Deal might appear less daring than Bennett's, but Bennett's had the fatal disadvantage of coming from a confirmed Old Dealer, whereas King had behind him a solid record of social legislation and was known as a reformer, if a slow one. Again, Bennett's was a deathbed repentance from a Government obviously in the final stages of decay, whereas King's Party was on the make after winning five successive by-elections (four seats being still empty because Bennett did not dare to fill them).

King made the most of these advantages. His own policy laid down, the time had come for the final attack on the dying ministry. King launched it without mercy.

In a sleazy sort of sympathy he even praised his old enemy, Stevens, for attempting reform, however wrongheaded—this praise being designed solely to emphasize the Conservative Party's split.

There were empty words of sympathy also for Bennett, whose health was breaking under his impossible burdens, but even this human accident King turned to advantage. For, he said, Bennett had never consulted his Party on the New Deal, which was entirely his own idea, and in the event of his retirement no one could be sure that his successors would carry the policy through. Bennett was a dictator who proclaimed that the old order had gone. Yes, said King, the old order of parliamentary supremacy had gone but the Liberals would restore it. The constitution had been "dismantled" but the Liberals would revive it. And as for Bennett's New Order, it was "a pretty cheap order," ornamented by titles of nobility when the people hungered.

The New Order of deathbed repentance, these Johnny-come-lately improvisations of the radio, hardly touched the edge of the problem. It must be solved by the familiar philosophy of King's book (now reappearing as often as King Charles' head in Mr. Dick's memorial). Perhaps, asked King, Bennett at last had read *Industry and Humanity*? Bennett denied the imputation indignantly. That, said King, only showed how little the Prime Minister knew about fundamentals.

Bennett, he went on, proposed state intervention in the economy when his only intervention to date, the tariff, had been disastrous. As for Liberalism, it would use intervention or laissez faire as each was needed. Assuredly it would apply laissez faire to international trade. Bennett had accepted the Liberal theory of a central bank but it was a private bank, still under the control of capitalists, and hence Bennett's talk of an economy planned by the state was non-sense.

Bennett had made the unnecessary blunder of saying that King had never done anything for the poor and in Montreal had used the cheap phrase, "If you don't want minimum wages and maximum hours of work, vote for King." This gave King the chance to parade his record of reform, every item since his first days of public service. Bennett and the Conservatives, of course, had nothing to match it.

Anyway, said King, what was the use of Bennett's talking about the redistribution of wealth when, through his strangulation of trade, there was no wealth left to distribute? What use to talk of shorter working hours to a million Canadians unemployed and on the dole? And who could believe in a New Deal largely stolen from Liberal policy?

One by one he cited the stolen items—unemployment insurance, the last-minute attempt to revise the Ottawa Treaties in favor of increased trade, the pledge to attack the business combines that the Conservatives had always befriended, the control of security issues, support of the League of Nations.

Bennett's proposal to spend more money in pursuit of prosperity assuredly was not stolen from the Liberals. At this late date, while proposing a central bank which was sure to have no other result, King was against spending as a solution. "Prosperity is not brought about by the expenditure of millions of dollars . . . not real prosperity, for once these expenditures cease the last stage may be worse than the first." King was ready, however, to build some "useful public works" to replace Bennett's hated camps for unemployed.

Bennett and King remained in confusion about money in different ways. Neither realized yet where central banking must lead or how the guarantee of full employment, once made, would render most previous policy obsolete. King was able to offer no quick cure for the depression, only the method of expanded trade.

Through the confusion King's purpose was clear. He had wanted all his life to move to the Left. Now he had the chance among a people groaning for reform. More than the chance. A leftward movement was compulsory in politics. With the C.C.F. breathing down his neck and the lunatic fringe of soft money in full cry, King must assert his leadership of reform or lose it. But he must not move too fast or too far. He could not know yet how far he would finally move, or where.

His present hazy policy was designed to move just enough to satisfy the hungry without alarming the rich, both being necessary to his strategy of the middle road. And as the election would show, he was now in process of building something more than a party. He was building a coalition of parties so broad that there would not be, until the present day, room on either side of the road for Conservatives or Socialists. So ingenious was his carpentry, so subtle his shift of ground, that few Canadians knew then what he was about, and the enemies within his Party, the conservative Liberals, found out too late to stop him.

This was mostly practical politics, but not all. Behind it was the considered philosophy which Bennett lacked. The politics were subject to change without notice. The philosophy, often disguised or even flouted, had been long growing and would endure.

In a word, it can be said that King, after nourishing the idea all his life, now felt able to introduce into practical politics the central thesis that the profit motive for the most part was sound and essential but that it was not enough to hold a disintegrating society together. There must be a stronger cement. Society must be held together by a new sense of public service on the part of capital, full participation on the part of the public, and any intervention by the state as might be required. That conclusion would often be dimmed by good fortune in the days ahead. It was never forgotten. Its results were to be larger than King yet dreamed.

22

The Pugilist and the Physician

HIS NEW DEAL WRITTEN INTO LEGISLATION, MUCH OF IT UNCON-
stitutional, Bennett closed Parliament and prepared for the
election. He was worn out, he had been frequently absent
from the House, his heart was strained, but his spirit was unbroken.
Wearily he plodded from one end of the nation to the other. On
every platform his body came suddenly to life again, the face, lined
and chalk-white, took on its old look of authority and the voice
boomed out as deep and confident as before. When Communist
hecklers tried to drown his speeches in Vancouver and Victoria, he
shouted them down, commanded silence by the spectacle of his
courage, and sent his audiences away in admiration, still determined
to vote against the dying gladiator.

The New Deal clearly had not stuck. The public might agree with
it but distrusted its origin. Bennett's personal honesty was everywhere admitted but could such a man, on his record, be expected to
reform the system which had produced him? Could the Man of
Business change his spots? The public doubted it.

Bennett might argue, on the existing figures, that the depression
had lifted a little. It was not enough to make any difference to his
prospects. A bloody clash between the Mounted Police and a band
of unemployed in Regina, midway in their "march on Ottawa,"
seemed almost a rebuke from Providence, since it was at Regina that
Bennett had made his most celebrated jibe at King in the 1930 election: "Nine years of wasted effort before the great betrayal—it didn't
take Judas that long." After the Regina riot, who was the betrayer
now? The whole past was rising up in vengeance against the Man of
Business. Yet Bennett still boasted of his business capacities when
Stevens had made business, no doubt unjustly, the best-hated institution in the land. A Man of Business was the last man that people
would trust.

All Bennett's arguments in this, his last campaign, were perfectly contrived to lose votes. He still defended his high tariffs, still asserted that Liberal tariffs would result in "wreckage of industry, vastly increased unemployment," and this the public had the sense to regard as ridiculous, especially when the other old protectionist, Stevens, was now urging lower tariffs. Bennett's worst mistake was to present himself as the one essential man who "would be more than content if I could believe that my successor might do better for you than I." The nation was tired of the Great Man image, of big promises, excursions, alarms, and one-man government.

When King appeared before it after an absence of five years, the nation beheld a changed man. He was now in his sixty-first year. By careful diet he had slimmed down his figure. The putty look of youth had gone out of a face which had wrinkled and hardened. His eyes sparkled and his smile was friendly. After watching the gallant exhaustion of Bennett, his audiences found King more vigorous and surer of himself than ever. For the first time, a people who had never regarded him as anything but a smart politician began to detect a statesman.

This was neither pretense nor accident. King looked larger because, for the first time, he was advocating a constructive policy and believed in it completely. In 1921 and 1925 he had led a Party quite unprepared to accept his radicalism and, perforce, he had muted and blurred it. In 1926 he had believed in his constitutional issue but he had only used an opponent's blunder to rescue himself from a scandal, and in any case his quarrel with Byng had not touched his dream of a new society. Now he could appear in the role, chosen from the beginning, of a reformer and a rebel. A sober reformer and a safe rebel. The nation being sick of sound and fury, King pitched his campaign in a quiet key of sweet reason.

If he had needed any weapon besides the depression, Bennett had supplied it with the claim of indispensability. To the Great Man image and the one-man government, King counterposed government by an organized party and the joint wisdom of a cabinet. He presented himself not as a master but as a servant and finally he hit upon the most effective and self-revealing phrase of his career: "What this country needs is not the fist of the pugilist but the hand of the physician." A sick nation could understand that.

The Party managers had thought up a slogan more sleazy and effective. They shouted from every billboard in the country that it was now "King or Chaos." Sleazy, but true. With the Conservatives split, Stevens leading his fly-by-night Reconstruction Party, the C.C.F. too young to count, and Social Credit in control of Alberta, it was mathematical that only King could hope to form a government.

The campaign was easy for him but he took no chances. As he had never believed in chivalry on the platform he delighted in the recital of Bennett's pitiful, broken promises. The attack on the Man of Business would not be worth recalling if it had not led King into a memorable, almost classic comparison between business and government, which were confounded in the mind of Bennett as they are in the minds of many current statesmen.

"Business," said King, "is concerned with money. Government is concerned with men. Business is an occupation which has for its objective the success of the individual. Government is an art. It is the art of effecting a maximum of co-operative effort in all that pertains to the state. Business is concerned primarily with present material gain. Government is concerned not less with the future than with the present and with human and spiritual values much more than with material values. It cares nothing for the gain of special privileges and everything for the common good.

"Many so-called business successes have been due to a ruthless disregard of humanitarian considerations. . . . Until industry is regarded in the nature of a social service and sees the necessity of dealing with its problems from the point of view of the sacredness of human life and personality rather than for the accumulation of wealth and material reward there will be and there should be social and industrial unrest."

That, as closely as he dared come to it, was the philosophy King had distilled out of his previous life and these last five years. He had seen, in short, that the profit motive, though essential in business, was not big enough for all the needs of society.

The campaign also forced King to explain the meaning of his state-wide central bank, a new gimmick not understood by one Canadian in ten. He attacked Bennett's privately-owned bank as being of the "Fascist type," an instrument of greedy "plutocracy." After further denouncing Bennett's whole New Deal as "a make-believe affair," he laid down this doctrine which, if enforced, must suck him into a New Deal much larger and more incalculable: "Once a nation parts with the control of its currency and credit, it matters not who makes the nation's laws. Usury, once in control, will wreck any nation. Until the control of the issue of currency and credit is restored to government and recognized as its most conspicuous and sacred responsibility, all talk of the sovereignty of Parliament and of democracy is idle and futile."

No one seems to have realized that this was outright repudiation of the whole economic past of Liberalism. In office King had never found the sovereignty of Parliament destroyed by the absence of a central bank, and he had not thought of creating it. Democracy had not seemed idle and futile under the private management of money according to Liberal theory.

When he said that money was the sacred responsibility of government he could not visualize the day, only sixteen years off, and after his retirement, when government would have robbed money of half its value by the age-old method of inflation, conducted through the new and elegant technique of central banking. And still he could not see that if the state were to manage money "in terms of social need," then, at a time of depression, it must issue and spend more money than it collected in taxes, whereas King was now demanding economy and balanced budgets. Roosevelt had been elected on the same paradox and had rounded the corner afterward with a push from Keynes. King could do the same.

Meanwhile, if his words were turgid, his purpose obscure, the public knew who was the more likely to change society, the physician or the pugilist. At all events, King was the nation's only hope.

By the election eve, when King had used the radio for the first time and thrown in his final warning against the "possibility of war at our very doors," when events infinitely more terrifying than the depression were in full flow in the jungles of Africa, and when Bennett was *in extremis* politically and physically, the people's general verdict at the polls could not be doubted by Government or Opposition. The detailed outcome on October 14 surprised both.

King won 171 seats out of 245; Bennett a corporal's guard of 39; Social Credit, the soft-money doctrine of Alberta, 17; a disappointed C.C.F., 7; the Reconstruction Party, only Stevens' own seat. The remaining ten seats were divided among assorted types of Liberals, Independents, and Labor.

After that King was safe for life. His opponent, Chaos, had been driven out of politics.

On election night King let himself go. A statement prepared confidently in advance called the election a "victory for democracy" over "one-man government, mistaken policies and autocratic leadership . . . it proclaims the end of the superman idea." It also had repudiated the Ottawa Treaties, now to be revised. It had given a mandate for trade and lower tariffs and for a publicly-owned bank. The electorate had declared "that a responsible ministry, not organized finance and international money power, is to control in all matters of state," and that the "collective wisdom of many minds" must replace government "by a single individual." In industry the nation had given a mandate for "democratization" and against dictatorship; in finance a mandate for debt reduction and a balanced budget (another unnoted denial of money issued in terms of public need); in society a mandate for a more equitable distribution of wealth.

King might discern such a many-sided mandate. A puzzled nation had simply voted against Bennett and Bennett's traveling companion, the depression. It had not much faith in King's policies. It knew that the alternative indeed was Chaos. Like all democratic elections, it had been a choice of the lesser evil. With so huge a majority King could interpret his mandate as widely or narrowly as he chose. He had more elbow room than ever. There was plenty of time to devise policies within the foggy outlines of his platform and he assured the nation that its trust "will not be betrayed."

Canada, he said in that moment of dizzy triumph, must have "an end of hysteria and a speedy return to sanity." Yet there was something a little hysterical about his concluding hymn to the sunrise: "A new era dawns today. . . . Poverty and adversity, want and misery are the enemies which Liberalism will seek to banish from our land. . . . We take up at once our supreme task to endeavor to end poverty in the midst of plenty."

No wonder there was joy and a touch of euphoria in Laurier House that night. King had saved his Party by changing its direction so smoothly that the passengers hardly suspected the change. He had avoided political bankruptcy, had established a new and durable solvency, and though all this was in part the outcome of sheer luck and Bennett's misfortunes, King had known how to use his opportunity.

However it had come about in an age now spawning its supermen in the United States, Germany, Russia, Italy, and elsewhere, Canada had dismissed its own superman and pugilist, had recalled the drab little family physician to prescribe his soothing remedies.

His first prescription was a poison, slow but almost fatal in the end.

23

Midsummer Madness

WITH HIS RE-ELECTION, KING HAD SAID, A NEW ERA WAS DAWNING. A new era, to be sure, but not the era he expected. While physician and pugilist contended in Canada and the nation's mind was focused on its own sores, an era of anarchy and bloodshed, the era in which we still live, was dawning all over the world. King's failure to see it, or to prepare the nation for it, is the supreme failure of his career. He plunged headlong into this failure abroad at the very moment of his success at home.

In the Chanak incident he had finally established Canada's status as an independent state, able to enter or renounce Britain's wars. He had not admitted to the people or to himself that new status involved new responsibility. His foreign policy of no-commitments, if it could be called a policy, lacked half its essential content. It declared what Canada would not do. It never intimated for a moment what Canada would do in case of general war. In the autumn of 1935 the vacuum on which the policy was built suddenly revealed itself. The apparent triumph of Chanak caught up with its architect and turned into humiliating defeat.

On October 2, when King was busily extinguishing Bennett's era and re-establishing his own, the Government of Italy ordered its troops across the border of Ethiopia. Mussolini also was establishing an era, in the image of the Roman emperors.

Here, then, was the ultimate test of the League of Nations. It had been terribly weakened, all but discredited, by its refusal to halt the Japanese aggressors in Japan four years earlier. If it could suppress Mussolini's latest crime it might still survive and go on to deal with Hitler, a much more dangerous potential aggressor. At first, the League showed every outward sign of its will to live and enforce peace. It pronounced a verdict of guilt on the criminal and prepared to apply economic sanctions against Italian imports and exports.

The Bennett Government was scattered all over Canada in the last throes of the election campaign. Bennett himself was barnstorming from city to city. King was thinking only of votes. The Ethiopian crisis could not have touched Canada at a worse moment.

Despite these distractions, Howard Ferguson, high commissioner to London and Canadian delegate at Geneva, urged the League to go ahead with its sanctions and "show the world" that it was "no longer to be scoffed or laughed at but that it meant business." Again, on the very day when the Canadian voters were rejecting Bennett's Government, Ferguson called on the League for vigorous action against the aggressor, now enjoying the easy murder of the Ethiopians.

Next day Bennett cabled his delegation at Geneva to suspend further action until it heard from the new Government. Ferguson, as Bennett's representative, retired as soon as he read the election results. Canada was now represented at Geneva, in one of the most crucial moments of history, by Walter A. Riddell, a modest but courageous civil servant. The tragedy of errors which instantly engulfed him is not the tragedy of a man but of a civilization.

King took office on October 23. Four days previously, the League's co-ordinating committee had voted for limited sanctions against Italy and awaited the approval of the member governments, which would have to enforce them individually. Three times Riddell cabled Ottawa for instructions. He got no reply. King was fully occupied in the construction of the new-era Cabinet.

Meanwhile the Italian armies advanced into Ethiopia with airplanes and poison gas to remind the bombed and choking African tribesmen of the white man's superiority. The League had reached its trial of life or death. Among its most interested spectators was the German Fuehrer. He was ready, if the League failed, to launch his armies into the Rhineland and thence across 'Europe at leisure.

"This," in Riddell's opinion, "was the last and best chance that the member states would have of preventing a European collapse and another world war."

From Ottawa he could get nothing but silence on Canada's willingness to take this last best chance.

The silence was broken on October 29 when King announced that Canada had imposed the limited sanctions approved at Geneva, having found "no room for doubt" about Italy's aggression.

By now it was known at Geneva that these sanctions were quite inadequate to halt Mussolini. If sanctions were to succeed, they must include the vital materials of oil, coal, iron, and steel, on which the Italian armies marched. The French delegation was preparing written proposals to enforce such essential sanctions. It was soon evident to Riddell that the Laval Government, already suspected of conniving with Mussolini by long-distance telephone, would not move.

Riddell talked to other delegations, including the British, and found them favorable to enlarged sanctions but hesitant to take the lead. As the issue was to be settled on November 2, he resolved to take the lead himself. It was a bold move and, for him, disastrous.

At this turning point in the human story, hours counted, even minutes. Riddell sent two cables to Ottawa, the first uncoded to announce the arrival of the second, in code, which outlined his plan and asked for instant instructions. He expected the League committee to be occupied until late afternoon on routine business. To his horror he was notified that he would speak before noon.

In an agony of indecision he awaited news from Ottawa. When none arrived he looked again over King's statement four days earlier. To him, as to anyone with a knowledge of English, that message could mean only one thing—the Canadian Government was prepared to apply any nonmilitary sanctions accepted by the other League members.

Thinking he understood the Government's mind and knowing that the future of peace hung in the balance, Riddell rose in the committee to propose that petroleum, coal, iron, and steel be added to the list of goods which the League members would not sell to Italy. After little discussion the proposal was approved unanimously and referred to the various governments for consideration.

If that decision could be enforced, the League would recover its lost power and the world its hope of preventing aggression. Mussolini would have to abandon his Ethiopian campaign or face certain ruin. "If," he said afterward, "the League of Nations had extended the economic sanctions to oil I would have had to withdraw from Abyssinia within a week."

No one could be sure of that in the first days of November. Mussolini maintained an impressive bluff. While Italian women were giving their gold wedding rings to their hero and even the King contributed some of his private hoard, the Government raised a fund of a million pounds to fight sanctions by the piecemeal seduction of the League governments.

Tired by the election campaign, King had set off for Georgia to renew his strength in the southern sun for the rigors of the new era. He had taken with him virtually the entire External Affairs Department in the person of its under-secretary, Dr. O. D. Skelton. Lapointe was left in charge of Cabinet and foreign policy.

The election, the disappearance of one Government, the emergence of another, and King's absence all had conspired to complete the tragedy of errors.

When the Italian Consul-General protested to the Canadian Government against the new sanctions policy, Lapointe at first stood firm. In a reply to Italy on November 27, he said Canada "had no alternative, when confronted with the evidence, which was not in dispute, but to assent to this finding [of Italy's aggression] and accept its implications." Canada refused to retreat from the League's verdict and sanctions. Riddell apparently was confirmed in his action.

The firm posture at Ottawa lasted only three days. By December 1, Lapointe had heard from a Cabinet which could not face serious trouble after its election on the physician's program of national healing. Lapointe had heard also from his own race. The French Canadians, traditionally sympathetic to the Italian people and now horrified at Mussolini's threat of reprisals, felt that Riddell and his sanctions might well produce a second world war, for which Canada would be held responsible.

Lapointe was a politician. He knew the Cabinet, he knew Quebec, and he feared a rupture in the Liberal Party before the new era had even begun. The Cabinet agreed with him. But in a matter so grave, nothing could have moved this man but his own judgment on the wise course for Canada. The wise, the only possible course, as he saw it, was retreat. Doubtless he consulted King by telephone and King agreed, taking full responsibility for his deputy's action.

On December 1, Lapointe repudiated Riddell. A statement to the press said that Canada's position on sanctions had not been modified in any way but had been misunderstood. Canada had not taken the initiative in proposing the extension of the former sanctions. "The opinion which was expressed by the Canadian member of the Committee and which had led to the reference to the proposal as a Canadian proposal, represented only his own personal opinion and his view as a member of the Committee, and not the views of the Government of Canada."

To blame an official who had sought to carry out the Government's declared policy—and this though the policy had been reaffirmed after the official had spoken in Geneva—appears at first sight the single act of moral cowardice in Lapointe's career. It was so regarded in many parts of English-speaking Canada and by the internationalist sectors of the Liberal Party, especially by Dafoe. A second look reveals much else, now generally forgotten.

When he had made his motion at Geneva, Riddell had written to the committee chairman formally advising him that he acted "entirely on my own authority and not on instructions from my Government."

He was naïve, however, to imagine that any proposal from him would be construed as anything but the act of Canada.

It was so construed throughout the world. The "oil sanctions" became, in world opinion, a gallant Canadian policy, for which the Government at first seemed glad to accept credit, until it realized what it had undertaken. Apart from the act of a brave official who obviously had gone too far without authority, apart from local Quebec politics, much larger forces were in motion.

Italy, of course, crowed over Canada's capitulation as a first public break in the solid front of collective security. Actually, there was no real front to break.

In advance of Riddell's act at Geneva, the Laval Government of France was preparing to sabotage the League while ostensibly supporting it, encouraging Riddell, and voting for the oil sanctions. Laval, who was Mussolini's secret weapon in the democracies, soon found allies in London.

On December 6 the British Foreign Secretary, Sir Samuel Hoare, opened secret negotiations with Laval in Paris. He agreed with Laval on a settlement of the African war by the complete dismemberment of Ethiopia.

On December 9 the Hoare-Laval deal burst upon an incredulous world and outraged a British public which had voted almost unanimously in a recent poll for a strong League. Hoare was driven from office. He and Laval were discredited. Their deal, opposed by both Italy and Ethiopia, was dropped. And the League itself was wrecked.

Since none of the great powers was ready to enforce real sanctions, and since the two greatest seemed to be condoning it, Mussolini's crime was quickly completed. The Ethiopian capital fell on May 7, 1936, and was incorporated into the empire of the jackal who, in the Churchillian phrase, would soon yelp and frisk behind the German tiger.

Months before that, Riddell knew, as he writes in his book, *World Security by Conference,* that "the last chance of averting World War II had gone forever." As a first step in that war Hitler already had occupied the Rhineland on March 7. In Winnipeg Dafoe saw the "League destroyed by the Baldwin Government at the instance of a caste," the "hyperbolic war" inevitable, and civilization "ready to crumble" in an era of "international anarchy."

What of the prophet of that other era which had been born on election night and stifled almost within the ballot boxes? What forces operated in King's mind when he confronted for the first time in his life a real international crisis and felt the hot breath of war? Was he merely playing politics to protect the skin of the Liberal Party and his own?

He was doing that, of course, as he always did, but he was trying to do much more. He was trying to postpone war if he could and to deny to the people, and above all to himself, that war could come. The secret of his whole behavior in international affairs from the autumn of 1935 on to 1939 is to be found in the simple human fact that he feared war and could not face it until he had no alternative. The intuitive reason, as always, was the real reason. The public and semipublic reasons were only props of argument for a decision made by instinct, in this case the instinctive horror of bloodshed.

This writer talked to King about the Geneva fiasco a few days after the Hoare-Laval deal was announced. That deal, of course, was an easy out for him. It showed that if he had not been ready to take the initiative in real sanctions, the British and French Governments had been ready even to approve Mussolini's dismemberment of Ethiopia. Morally, King's position was better than that of Baldwin or Laval.

On this occasion King spoke of the British-French plan of appeasement with clenched fists, flushed face, and angry voice. He called it betrayal. He said he could hardly believe his ears when he had heard of it. As he was denouncing it, the dark figure of Lapointe entered the room and listened glumly to the Prime Minister's tale of outrage. I do not recall exactly what Lapointe said, but it was to the effect that his policy had been justified by the treachery of the British Government, for which he could hardly find words of sufficient condemnation.

It was easy to blame the Baldwin Government and the other gravediggers of Europe, now enthusiastically engaged in their work of excavation. King's motives were better revealed by his final remark in that interview. Throwing up his hands in a gesture of incredulity, he asked what the United States would have thought of the Canadian Government if, by pressing oil sanctions, it had precipitated the world into general war? It had been of the United States, he said, that he had been thinking all through the crisis.

He had been thinking, in fact, of his inevitable position as a North American statesman enmeshed in the affairs of Europe and bound at all times to prevent his policies clashing with that of his American neighbor. He had encountered the ancient dilemma of the Canadian, the tug between geography and history, and geography, for the moment, had won. At Geneva he had acted as an American. As such he had acted also as a Canadian and in accordance with the actions of his predecessors, who had tried from the beginning to pull the

teeth and the commitments out of the League Covenant. And he had
acted, quite sincerely, as the appeaser he always was.

Moreover, he was mistaken in his timing of foreign affairs, as he
had been mistaken in his judgment of the domestic depression at its
beginning. Just as he had believed the economic system to be more
advanced and enlightened than it was, so he overestimated the virtue
of western civilization as a whole. He had not realized how thin a
crust covered the brutality of mankind.

It was a mistake common to most Liberals. Their assumptions of
man's natural goodness, the nineteenth-century expectation of perpetual progress, had been shattered once in the First World War. To
a Liberal like King a second collapse of this sort was inconceivable
or, if conceivable, was too hideous to be admitted and therefore must
be denied on principle.

Two main charges are leveled against King in the Ethiopian affair.
Both are false.

It is said that, by refusing to repudiate Riddell, he alone could
have rallied the League and saved the peace. Considering the character and policies of the French and British Governments, this is
palpably absurd. They were not ready for anything of the sort. They
were committed to Laval's plans of peace by surrender, which would
lead eventually to Vichy and national suicide; to Chamberlain's appeasement policy, which would lead successively to Munich, Dunkirk, and Britain's finest hour.

King could not have saved the League or the peace. That was far
beyond the capacity of any Canadian Government, as Dafoe well
knew when he condemned King for cowardice. The true indictment of King on this count was that he could have saved his own
integrity and the reputation of Canada by refusing to scuttle and
run.

It must never be forgotten in appraising these events that King
unquestionably acted as the Canadian people wanted him to act.
They were in no mood to save Ethiopia or the League. They were
opposed by overwhelming majority to any risk of war. They were,
for the time being, as deep in their isolationism, with rare exceptions,
as King himself, probably deeper. If King's trumpet gave out an
uncertain sound it certainly was the sound of Canada in 1935.

The second accusation against King is that he acted dishonestly.
If by dishonesty it is meant that he acted against his conscience and
convictions, nothing could be more untrue. Never in his whole public
life did he act more completely by conscience and conviction. By
conscience, he loathed and feared war. By conviction, at that date,
he was certain that the League's policy of opposing Mussolini could

GENERAL McNAUGHTON

JAMES ILSLEY

not save Ethiopia and might doom the world to war; that, in any case, the League could not keep the peace without the presence of the United States in it.

As Mussolini's later admission shows, King was wrong in his military calculation. So were all the leading statesmen of the day, including Roosevelt, then an isolationist by force of politics. King's courage failed him in the pinch. He could not face the facts of a world now sliding over the edge of the abyss. But he was not dishonest.

His complete private thoughts on Ethiopia were never revealed to the public. In Parliament, on February 11, 1936, he tried to argue that he had not repudiated Riddell, had decided against immediate repudiation ". . . only because we were most anxious not to take any step which might possibly embarrass the situation in Europe or which might appear even remotely to indicate an exception on the part of Canada to what was being done by other parts of the British Empire." This was splitting hairs very fine, even for King.

His real excuse was offered in these words: "I am not at all sure that when the whole story comes to be told it may not be discovered that but for the action of the Government of Canada in this particular matter, at that particular time, the whole of Europe might be aflame today."

He may not have believed that when he spoke but he must have known soon afterward that it was untrue. In the first place, even if Canada had pressed its oil sanctions, the great powers would not have enforced them at the risk of war. Secondly, as events would show within three years, Europe could not be saved from flames by surrender; it could only be made more inflammable when the conflagration broke out.

Parliament apparently was satisfied with this weak explanation. The nation had no stomach for any war but the war on depression. Only a few voices like Dafoe's were raised in protest. They could do little political damage to King when he had an isolationist country with him.

Privately, he treated Riddell with kindness at their meeting shortly afterward in Ottawa and made no attempt to blame him. Riddell says in his book, however, that Lapointe was "cold, critical and overbearing" and did not seem to understand exactly what had happened at Geneva. Lapointe, according to Riddell, expected to succeed King as Minister of External Affairs and his failure in the Ethiopian affair had thwarted his ambition. Therefore, he condemned Riddell more for private than public reasons. That is Riddell's version. Lapointe's friends deny it.

The vindication of Riddell's opinions and the rejection of La-

P

pointe's were not long delayed. When the hour of reckoning arrived, Lapointe atoned for his error. That hour was to be his finest.

The Riddell incident was soon left far behind as events slid downhill with increasing momentum. On June 10 Chamberlain uttered his famous "calculated indiscretion," calling the League's present and worthless sanctions "midsummer madness." The quiet accents of the higher lunacy rebuking madness now announced the settled policies of the great states. Obviously, all sanctions would soon be withdrawn.

Eight days later, King followed Chamberlain by advising Parliament that Canada favored this withdrawal. After his terrible pounding from Dafoe's *Free Press*, he tried once more to excuse the repudiation of Riddell; insisted that Canada had enforced the limited-sanction policy as loyally as any nation; warned the House that the oil sanctions might well have led to war; declared that his Government had never approved those measures and did not believe Canada should take the initiative in "such a pretentious gesture" when other countries would bear the brunt of the resulting war, if it came. He quickly added, however, that if oil sanctions had been "generally supported" in the League, Canada would have enforced them. Canada, in other words, would follow. It would not lead, as Riddell had proposed.

By one of those strokes of lucky coincidence which so often rescued him from a tight corner, a Canadian Press dispatch was handed to King that day as he entered the House. It reported Anthony Eden's statement to the British Parliament a few minutes earlier that real sanctions would produce war in the Mediterranean "and no man can say such a war can be confined to the Mediterranean." With this exhibit in his hand King could prove beyond doubt his assurance that Canada was not running out alone on the League. The rout was general. The League had never been ready to call Mussolini's bluff and did not find out, until too late, the emptiness of that bluff.

Like many others in those days, King's speech is full of retrospective irony. "It would be the height of folly," he said, "to risk an imminent war today in order to avert a hypothetical one tomorrow." A "hypothetical war" when Hitler had entered the Rhineland, torn up the Versailles treaty, and was preparing to burst out of Germany in less than two years! Again, "only doctrinaires would urge risking war to save a formula." The formula being the world's final chance to crush Mussolini and Hitler in their shells.

King's chief purpose, however, was not to give excuses for the past but to make the future look better than it could possibly be. He now completed the shift in foreign policy which he had been approaching gingerly for some time, and rounded the corner so smoothly that few Canadians, besides Dafoe, realized that this was a final retreat from reality.

The League, he said, had misconstrued its purpose. It was regarded by too many people as "an international war office" designed to punish offenders, whereas its true purpose was to conciliate disputes. Its function was "prevention rather than punishment . . . the peaceful remedy of grievances rather than making war upon a country resorting to war."

This view was not new in Canada. King could demonstrate from the record that all Canadian Governments since the World War had tried repeatedly to water down the commitments of the Charter and this, he agreed, was sound. For it was folly to pretend that there was yet an enforcible international law in the world and there could be none while great nations like the United States, Germany, and Japan were not in the League.

Realities must be faced, he said, as he went on to elaborate the current course of utter unreality. All nations operated "on a calculation of immediate interest." (This was true enough but only meant that none saw where its interests lay and all were bent on destroying them.) In such a world, Canada could not commit itself to economic or military force against aggressors. It must decide through Parliament what should be done in circumstances as they arose.

The League could still do a great work in bringing the nations together, in removing grievances, and in striving for "world appeasement" (a word which would not become disreputable for some three years yet). It was a "counsel of despair" to say that war was inevitable and Canada, for its part, would work against that result by the development of world prosperity through increasing international trade. And it would work for these fundamental solutions in cooperation with the League, "that indispensable agency which the conscience of mankind fashioned on the morrow of the greatest international disaster of all time and bequeathed to our own and future generations."

Brave words and meaningless when the League was already dead, an undertaker's futile attempt to paint the white cheeks of a corpse. The undertaker had never been more sincere. He believed what he said because he compelled himself to believe, at least in the conscious half of his mind. The other half was clouded with repressed doubts. He still could not bring himself to face the facts which Dafoe was proclaiming every day, nor could Parliament and the Canadian people. All but a small minority in Canada stood expectantly behind Canute as he ordered the waves to recede.

Looking back on all this folly, few Canadians will find themselves sufficiently without sin to condemn King and his distinguished companions. The present writer does not claim to be among those few.

Reassured in Parliament, King sent a strong delegation to Geneva, headed by his friend Massey, to vote for the end of the farcical sanctions. The general retreat was executed at midsummer, in the final madness of that season, with dispatch and an outward show of order.

So that the world might hear his message of false hope and his new interpretation of the League, King went to Geneva and delivered, on September 29, a short version of his Ottawa speech. He said Canada's attachment to the League—provided it did nothing to preserve the peace by the only possible method of force—was as strong as ever. Canada, however, would not make those commitments without which the League could never be brought back to life. Instead, Canada would emphasize "the mediation and conciliation of the Covenant" and thus "help to transform the collective system from a hope into a reality."

Having thus rejected the chance of reviving the League as an international fireman, King took up a posture of dignity on the other side of the street, along with Baldwin, Chamberlain, Laval, Roosevelt, and the others, to watch the house burn down. But it should never be forgotten that at the moment Canada had no fire department.

Far away in Winnepeg Dafoe read King's Geneva speech and uttered a memorable obituary: "The League of Nations, with assurances of the most distinguished consideration, was ushered out into the darkness by Mr. Mackenzie King."

At the League's funeral King had been only a junior usher. That, as Dafoe agreed, did not make him the murderer. The proper verdict on him, in this phase, was that, refusing to admit the premature demise of his new era, he did not appear to be even a mourner. He continued to whistle cheerfully in the graveyard when the dark already was descending.

24

Under the Shadow

IT HAD GOT OFF TO A BAD START IN THE ETHIOPIAN FIASCO BUT THE
Ministry constructed by King on October 23, 1935, marked the
opening of his greatest days. From then on, he was invincible
and could assure his Party at least three more electoral victories,
outlasting his own life.

Political durability was not the true measurement of the long-lived
regime deposited by the depression which had drowned Bennett.
The new Government had far more than an instinct for survival. Its
test and vindication were four years away. It must fight a war and
meet the postwar depression confidently predicted by all reputable
economists.

Since it was to bear such heavy freight and to alter the politics,
the economics, and the society of Canada more than any predecessor,
the Ministry of 1935 is worth a passing glance.

Of Laurier's Ministers only King remained; of his own first Cabinet
only such veterans as Lapointe, Cardin, and Dandurand. A new
generation had arrived.

Dunning returned poor from exile to re-enter the Finance Department with no chance of replacing King in the visible future but
apparently sure of succeeding him when King voluntarily retired.
That hope was doomed by Dunning's health, already undermined,
and, in any case, would have been imperiled by the entry of James
Garfield Gardiner, as Minister of Agriculture, another Westerner of
even tougher mind, stronger body, and more durable temperament,
who remained a farmer while Dunning became a financier.

Gardiner's eruption into Federal politics meant several things.

It meant that the two former premiers and colleagues of Saskatchewan were locked from the beginning in a struggle to control the
politics of the prairies and thence to seize King's mantle in due time.

It meant that Western agriculture, with all its political power, was entering a new phase wherein the free market would be traded for the hope of security in a market managed by the state.

It meant that the Liberal Party was becoming more and more a coalition of sovereign powers, one of them soon under Gardiner's undisputed control.

It also meant that, with such power in his possession, Gardiner would proceed to manage agricultural policy under his almost exclusive jurisdiction, often in disregard of the Prime Minister and the Cabinet.

Gardiner was formidable enough as a personage, with his four-o'clock-in-the-morning courage, his brutal, battering-ram force in debate, his ingenuity in political maneuver, his complete disregard of historic Liberal principles, his loyal friendships and implacable hatreds, his grim sense of humor, and his boyish charm under the outer disguise of a wooden Indian. He was even more significant as a portent of profound changes in the nature of the Party and of the national economy.

Perhaps sensing that, King watched without alarm and with some secret amusement the fierce contest between his two Saskatchewan Ministers. It demonstrated one of the basic laws of politics—that the disagreements within ruling parties and cabinets usually are wider and deeper than the visible quarrels with the opposition. At all events, as King had foreseen, both the present contestants were certain to destroy themselves as potential party leaders, Dunning by physical collapse, Gardiner by the ferocity of his pursuit.

The third Westerner was not King's own choice but Dafoe's. On election night King had phoned the Winnipeg editor, who was not yet disillusioned by the Ethiopian affair, and invited him to join the Cabinet. Dafoe refused, as he had refused all public office and a title. Who, then, asked King, should represent Manitoba? "Why," said Dafoe, "Crerar, of course!" King had been glad enough to embrace Crerar in 1929 and thus swallow the last vestiges of the Progressive Party. Now he could do without this prickly partner. Grudgingly he took Dafoe's advice and gave Crerar the Interior Department. Advice from that quarter, as usual, proved sound, though exactly nine years later King would regret it, too late.

The Cabinet contained a promising newcomer in young Norman Rogers, as Minister of Labour and King's chosen successor. He had many of King's virtues and few of his faults. He was learned, gentle, courageous, and admired by everybody. Just as he began to make his mark, he died in the line of war duty.

The latest generation also included Charles Gavan Power, a swarthy, handsome young veteran of the first war, who bore its medals and honorable wounds. In many ways Power must be judged the most remarkable as he is surely the most popular politician of his time in Canada.

He had been elected to Parliament while serving overseas in 1917, had been returned ever since then, and could never be defeated in his father's constituency of Quebec South. The child and darling of the Commons, he was beloved by all as no member had been since Laurier. He had courage, oratory, wit, a genius for politics, far greater gifts of administration than anyone yet suspected, and a personal hold on the affections of the House which none of his contemporaries could ever exercise.

Though born at Sillery, brought up among French Canadians and thoroughly attuned to their ways, he was of Irish descent. His unique place in politics was indicated from the start by the fact that French Canada regarded him as one of its surest champions. Its faith, and King's, were not misplaced. Power began as Minister of Pensions and Health. Much larger tasks lay ahead of him—among them the discovery of the next Prime Minister.

An entirely different sort of man had come out of Ontario into the Railways Department. Clarence Decatur Howe was born an American, had long practiced his engineering profession in Canada, and now introduced into politics an engineer's capacity to get things done, a courage which feared nothing because it could not understand the meaning of danger, an impatience with Parliament, an equal ignorance and contempt of political theory, nerves of tempered steel, and probably the most powerful organizing talent Canadian government had ever seen.

Howe began by hating politics and presently found in it the only project large enough for his skill. He began as a conservative accidentally attached to another party and became a modern Liberal, even a rather confused radical. Obviously he would go far, never quite sure where he was going, and presently accomplish an industrial revolution.

Finally, as Minister of National Revenue, King had found in James Lorimer Ilsley—a blue-nose of character and look like the sea rocks of his native Nova Scotia—the ideal man, both for his abilities and limitations, to manage Canada's largest financial and economic adventure in the approaching war.

Of these newcomers none but Rogers really liked King. Howe could get along with anybody, so long as he was left alone to do his work, and was little interested in King's theories or character. Gardiner was soon quarreling almost openly with his chief. Power, utterly loyal, both admired and distrusted the Prime Minister and came to deplore him as the destroyer of real Liberalism. Crerar never admired him and never hid his own feelings. Ilsley deplored him to the point of laughter and tears.

There were no doubts of this sort in the mind of Ian Mackenzie (a Scotsman of erratic language and horrendous Highland accent, concerning whom it was said, after his first speech in Parliament, that he spoke neither of Canada's official languages). Mackenzie was not only King's Minister but his personal mascot and worshiper. This gangling and dashing personage had great native abilities, volcanic energy in debate, and an unequaled knowledge of parliamentary procedure. Unfortunately, he held a powerful prejudice against work and, as King sometimes lamented, was far too close to the notorious Liberal machine in Vancouver. Not a major figure, he could engineer one of the decisive and disastrous acts of King's career.

While perpetually rent by private feud, these men soon settled down to form a team which made all King's former Ministries and most others appear mediocre by comparison. With two essential additions, he would soon be ready to give Canada the ablest Government in its history.

Throughout this period of bungling in foreign affairs, King attacked domestic problems with a sudden burst of energy.

Three weeks after the election he redeemed his first campaign promise by closing a trade agreement with the United States to reduce Canadian and American tariffs. The agreement was far more important for its long-range intent than for its immediate results and represented a drastic change in the high policies of both countries.

Roosevelt had been elected as a traditional low-tariff Democrat. At the expense of smashing the London economic conference of 1933 and repudiating his representatives there, he had abandoned any thought of encouraging imports. Instead, he relied on the magic of N.R.A., deficit spending, and the theory of pump priming under a siege policy of economic self-containment. The patient Cordell Hull, despite his humiliation at London, refused to resign, continued his fight for lower tariffs within the Administration, and finally got his reciprocal trade-treaty legislation passed in 1934. Under it the President could reduce the tariff within certain limits and this Roosevelt was now ready to do, having thought himself around a full circle.

On the Canadian side it turned out, when the documents were published, that Bennett's mind had moved by the same circular route. In 1932 he had forced the whole Commonwealth to raise its tariffs against the world. By the following spring he was visiting

Roosevelt and agreeing to "search for means to increase the exchange of commodities between our two countries."

As such an exchange cut clearly through Bennett's election plan for ending the depression by keeping foreign goods out of Canada, and as it would contradict the whole purpose of the Ottawa Treaties, it was evident that Bennett had experienced second thoughts. Less than a year old, the Empire trade experiment showed cracks. From then on, the retreat from Ottawa continued to the eve of the 1935 election, when Bennett had negotiated and was almost ready to sign a tariff-reducing agreement with Roosevelt.

On taking office, King found that agreement ready to his hand. He promptly signed it with a few amendments. It was Bennett's work, a work denying his original principles but no less valuable for that. Why had he negotiated an agreement and dropped it at the last moment? Because, said King, he could not get his protectionist Party to accept it. He did not dare to admit that the self-containment policy had failed, that the blasting powder of the 1930 election had exploded in his own face. Whereas Roosevelt, a subtler politician, could reverse course overnight while admitting no change.

To understand the ambitious intent of the 1935 agreement appropriated by King from Bennett it is necessary to break the chronology of the larger events now in train and move forward to a little-noted incident in the first days of 1937.

King called one of his rare press conferences in the Speaker's chambers of Parliament. He bounced into the room, obviously well pleased with himself, and pulled from an inside pocket a handwritten letter signed by the President of the United States. The letter began: "My dear Mackenzie." King read no farther than that and hastily thrust the letter back into his pocket. The President, he said, had invited him to Washington. He was going there immediately.

At Washington the two Harvard graduates, who had known each other slightly in college days, began a political collaboration and a curious kind of personal friendship destined to prove one of the most useful of King's works.

The diverse natures of the friends were indicated by their form of address. To Roosevelt, King was always "Mackenzie," a name no one else had ever used but flattering to its owner when it came from that quarter. To King, the older of the two, Roosevelt always remained "Mr. President."

Roosevelt admired King's political talents, somewhat resembling his own, but the Canadian was not the kind of man he relished as a companion. King was too studious, spinsterish, and precious for the lusty inner White House circle. He could never be a Great Guy. For his part, King regarded Roosevelt with public adulation and privately with a mixture of admiration, amazement, skepticism, and some merriment. He thought many of Roosevelt's policies quite crazy, he looked on much of the New Deal as mere political hokum, and he told his confidants that Roosevelt would like to annex Canada. Who, King added, could blame an American President for that?

The White House conference of 1937 was designed to pull the English-speaking peoples together, to ease the world's tensions, and, if possible, prevent a world war. This was to be achieved by the method of expanding trade and prosperity as long preached by Hull. Three nations, the United States, Britain, and Canada, were primarily concerned because their ancient North Atlantic triangle contained the largest segment of the world's trade; and because Canada had binding trade agreements with Britain, there could be no new trade agreement between Canada and the United States, or between Britain and the United States, without a deal embracing all three. King, it was agreed, would go to London to attend the coronation of King George and there act as an intermediary between the United States and Britain.

His mission succeeded. By the reduction of Canada's preferences in the British market and Britain's in Canada, in exchange for a reduction in American tariffs, the three-way trade agreement was slowly negotiated and signed on November 17, 1938. King hailed it as the highest success of Liberal tariff policy to date.

"If," he said, "this Administration were to end tomorrow it would have its honorable place in world history on this score alone—like Canning we have done our indispensable part to call into existence a new world to redress the balance of the old."

The balance, by that time, quivered on a knife's edge and would soon collapse. King, and Roosevelt also, still hoped that even this partial return to economic sanity in a world long maddened by the doctrine of self-containment might bring a return of political sanity as well. "No more important contribution toward a new order of relations," said King, "has been made at this critical period in the affairs of the world."

The trade agreement was indeed a bold and imaginative stroke at the tariffs that strangled the world economy. It came too late by several years to halt the march to war.

King could say of his handiwork that "each of us sleeps more safely in his bed because of the rapprochement between the world's two greatest democracies, a rapprochement which could not have been effected without the assent and co-operation of Canada." It was a false and troubled sleep, soon to be broken.

Whatever the agreement was worth, King had been its essential agent and honest broker. He alone could bring the United States and Britain together because the trade of both was deeply involved in the Canadian market. He had acted, as he told Parliament, the traditional role of Canadian interpreter between the old world and the new. For that brief moment he felt himself to be, as Churchill said of Canada, "a magnet exercising a double attraction, drawing both Great Britain and the United States towards herself and thus drawing them closer to each other . . . the linchpin of peace and world progress."

If there was to be no peace or progress, King could say, after two years of office, that under his reduced tariffs Canada's trade was twice its 1932 volume. He had begun to revive Laurier's reciprocity policy and to reverse the mistake of 1911. He had gained large advantages for the Canadian producer in the American market. He had laid the foundation for the postwar Geneva agreements and staked out in the United States a trading territory which, later on, could save Canada from threatened disaster.

The larger purpose of the 1938 agreement, what King called "a real contribution to world appeasement," must fail—as the debacle of Munich indicated even while the agreement was being closed— but the motives of Roosevelt, Chamberlain, and King in attempting to break the world's economic deadlock were sound and their work was not wasted. After the war the economic task could be resumed when the political objectives of 1938 would be more necessary than ever.

King had repealed Bennett's protectionist policy. More than a tariff reduction was required to repeal the depression. It hung on, a phenomenon recognizing no party line or change of government. Its assistant, the prairie drought, continued year after year. The relief rolls showed only a small decline and even by the end of 1939 totaled 445,565. King soon found himself using Bennett's old plea that the depression was caused by world forces outside Canada's control. This was an obvious fact, strangely overlooked by the Liberal Party in the days of Opposition.

At last, very slowly, the depression began to lift as the dislocations of the world economy were mended, and 1937 was considered a good year by comparison with its immediate predecessors. When Roosevelt announced that he had planned it this way and reduced his deficit spending, this brief spurt subsided, 1938 was another bad year, and King, again using Bennett's excuse of uncontrollable world forces, hesitated, as he told Parliament, to think what conditions would be without the increasing trade built by his tariff reforms.

At least, conditions were sufficiently improved to provide a contrast between the Bennett and King Governments, an unfair contrast, perhaps, since neither could make or cure depressions. Besides, the public mind was better conditioned to hard times. More important, so far as King's political posture was concerned, the public was distracted from the familiar skeleton of poverty at home by the overpowering specter of anarchy abroad. Anarchy would produce war and war in its turn would cure the depression by a general process of suicide. Meanwhile, depression could be borne in this atmosphere of a greater fear. King's position was incomparably easier than Bennett's.

The political tensions lifting, King seemed in no particular hurry to implement the New Liberalism.

The trade treaties were Liberalism but of the oldest sort. The Bank of Canada was nationalized, the Government now had the right to manage the money system "in terms of public need," but so little was the inevitable result imagined then, so little use was made of the new system as a weapon against depression, that Rogers was still attacking in Parliament the whole Keynesian theory of compen-satory spending which he pronounced a failure in the United States. Unemployment insurance, one of the few specific pledges of the Fourteen Points, encountered such constitutional barriers that it could not be effected until 1940.

King might argue that he had made good another pledge by restoring responsible government after Bennett's usurpation. He might say that personal liberty was safe now that the iniquitous Section 98, so long maintained by a Conservative Senate against a Liberal Commons' protest, had been revoked at last.

All this, however, seemed to fall far short of the visions painted by King from the Opposition benches. It hardly looked like *Industry and Humanity*. It did not even look to the public like a New Deal, after Bennett's version had perished in the courts. All in good time. King's delayed New Deal (he never used that phrase) was contained in the banking system and in a series of measures yet to come. In some respects it would go further than Roosevelt's.

Meanwhile, King attacked some of the fundamental problems of a federal system now in grave disrepair. At a conference with the provinces soon after the 1935 election, Lapointe devised a formula by which Canada would take power to amend its own constitution—a project unwisely dropped at the behest of one provincial government and still incomplete—and two years later King set up the Rowell-Sirois Commission to bring the relations between nation and provinces up to date.

While its significance was hardly realized at the time, this became one of King's most solid accomplishments. It resulted in nothing less than an overhaul of Confederation, a better balance in the living standards of all areas, a fairer distribution of national income.

It can be seen, therefore, that King had begun his Ministry with a new confidence and quick results. He was enjoying himself as never before, partly because he was unquestioned master of Party and Parliament, partly because he had found abler colleagues, and partly because he still did not guess how quickly all his plans would be engulfed in the shipwreck of mankind.

Among his special pleasures in this last period of placidity was the coronation of King George VI. With every instinct of history in him he relished the ceremonies of the Abbey, the processions, routs, and balls, still more the friendship of the young monarch and the Queen. The royalist half of his nature had been first aroused by this King's brother long ago. He had approved Edward's abdication, taking Baldwin's respectable view of Mrs. Simpson, and his admiration for royalty had been increased by the accession of George. King was the monarch's first Minister in the second Commonwealth nation, an old hand, an adviser to be trusted. He made himself more than that. He became a familiar of the Royal Family and soon regarded himself as a kind of overseas uncle to the little Princesses.

His attitude toward the palace amused some of King's colleagues. They smirked about it among themselves and wondered how deep it went. They were to find that it went deeper than anybody then supposed.

A Canadian watching the coronation procession from Canada House, in Trafalgar Square, suddenly became aware of the Prime Minister's odd figure when it was removed from its familiar drab serge and elevated to Windsor uniform. Stuffed into gold braid and double-ended hat, King was a Tenniel drawing out of *Alice in Wonderland*, a very caricature of the Frog Footman.

As the round and gleaming face was thrust out of the coach window, as the preposterous hat was waved at the crowds of Canada House, they replied—some of them King's enemies at home—with a hoarse cheer. He might not look it but he was for the moment the incarnate spirit of Canada, and Canada was feeling the tug of history that day. In a grudging fashion the Canadians in London were proud of him. And if King gave the English crowds a quaint impression of his country, the huge and splendid figure of Lapointe seemed to express Canada's true dimensions and strength.

After these ceremonies King attended an Imperial Conference remarkable—apart from the trade negotiations—only for its futility.

He also found time to pursue his spiritualistic researches with obscure mediums so discreetly that even his closest colleagues heard nothing of them. In a tour of western Europe he interviewed a mystic of another sort, with surprising results, to appear in their proper place. Altogether, the trade negotiations, the new friendship with the King and Queen, the communication with the dead, and the interview with Hitler brought him back to Ottawa with a gratifying sense of achievement and a total misconception of events.

Except for the shadow of war, these were congenial days at Laurier House and Kingsmere. The royal jelly had been thoroughly absorbed, the worker had been transformed into the queen and autocrat, whom nobody could challenge.

In this new sense of power, verging at times on smugness, King could even offer condescending advice to his enemies. When Bennett resigned the Conservative leadership and moved with his heartbreak to England (telling Meighen, according to the legend, that he was "going home," to which Meighen is said to have replied: "How I envy you!"), the best substitute the Opposition could find was Dr. R. J. Manion, a fine gentleman in private life, a gallant soldier in war, and in politics a firecracker of brief detonation. The Prime Minister at once invited him to Kingsmere, and Manion, who railed at the Government but could dislike no one, as no one disliked him, was happy to accept.

He was not the first Conservative statesman to pay court to the country squire. Cahan had gone to Kingsmere seeking sympathy in his troubles with Bennett and lesser Opposition members were glad of a word of advice from a wizard of politics. Manion, the apprentice party leader, was eager for any wisdom he could get from his opponent.

King's advice was not important or new—merely that Manion should ration his time, see very few people from day to day, and conserve his strength. It showed, however, that King had come to occupy a position above party and could afford to be generous. Not for long. Within two years he would be ready to destroy Manion as he had destroyed Meighen and Bennett, and with much less effort.

Among his official family King had become increasingly fussy and demanding. More and more he disregarded the convenience of his secretaries and stenographers, summoned them at any hour of the night, and expected unquestioning obedience. A certain secretary was almost dismissed because he failed to attend one of the Prime Minister's occasional departures from Ottawa and to be at the station platform when he returned. On a Western tour, when another secretary allowed one of the juniors to hurry home a day ahead of the official party, King was furious. Saying nothing, he sulked like a child and then acted like a man betrayed.

A robust character like John Pickersgill—the obscure Western heretic who had denounced Liberalism's bankruptcy during the depression and now had become not merely a secretary but the actual manager of the Prime Minister's office—could refuse to tolerate such treatment. Always respectful, he never hesitated to speak his mind about anything, and presently had more influence on his boss than most Cabinet colleagues.

The brilliant Walter Herbert, now helping Norman Lambert to manage the Liberal Federation, could endure for a time a party leader who telephoned at midnight to complain that the proposed menu of a public banquet was unsatisfactory, that peas must be substituted for beans and the whole program reprinted. In the end, he, like so many others, resigned in disgust.

The labor turnover in the Prime Minister's office remained high, but the retiring assistant could usually count on an easier job in the civil service.

Becoming more of a hermit than ever, King sometimes appeared at official functions and there displayed an increasing charm as his career prospered. He had no interest in them as a sex, yet his manners with women, especially older women, were exquisite. He was every woman's idea of the perfect son.

Occasionally he could turn a gallant phrase or utter a witticism good enough to be repeated all over town. As when somebody said at one of his dinners that the ladies' faces matched the flowers and the Prime Minister shot back: "That is expecting too much of the flowers!" Or when, years later, he found himself confronting his enemy George Drew in the box of the latter's father-in-law, Edward Johnson, manager of the Metropolitan Opera, and covered his embarrassment by remarking to Mrs. Drew: "How pleasant to be in your father's house!"

If he was a pleasant social creature when the circumstances required, he was also a loyal citizen of Ottawa, laid out great plans for its beautification, and made sure that on its outskirts, beside his own estate, a noble park was created in the Gatineau forest.

For the moment, but only for the moment, he was taking things rather easy.

As the pressure of hard times somewhat lifted he talked less of social reform and the evils of capitalist society. He had forgotten Senate reform entirely and continued to cram the upper chamber with his friends, converting it into an asylum for tired Liberal politicians.

While he disallowed some of the whimsical monetary legislation of the Alberta Social Credit Government, since he could do so with political safety, he never interfered with the infamous Padlock Law of Quebec, since that would be politically dangerous.

While he could entertain Manion and give grandfatherly advice to the Opposition because it was no threat to him, his hand on the razor was as deft as ever and when he used it against friend or enemy he was always assured, by prior consultation, that he was doing God's mysterious work.

No day passed without reading of the Bible and writing of the diary, which contained many things too intimate and extraordinary (such as descriptions of his dreams and his bodily health) to be printed in full even posthumously. On Sundays the familiar voice was raised in prayer and hymn at the Presbyterian Church.

A casual observer in these times might have thought that King was growing fatigued, perhaps a little careless, and certainly too sure of himself. Those appearances were misleading. For all he had done so far, his real work, his final struggle, his worst and best days were just beginning. The darkening shadow could be ignored or pushed aside no longer.

25

The Simple Peasant

AFTER THE CORONATION AND THE IMPERIAL CONFERENCE OF 1937, in London, King had a long, secret talk with Adolf Hitler in Berlin. What impression Hitler formed of the quiet little Canadian is unknown. The impression which King formed of the Fuehrer was one not only absurd but calamitous. It distorted all King's thinking on the human tragedy now about to open.

Were it not for firsthand evidence one would hesitate to set down his opinion on Hitler and hence his opinion on events as they moved toward their climax. The writer happens to have received that opinion from King's lips a few weeks after it was formed, and before it had to be changed and then publicly denied. Since the occasion of this intelligence offered a sample not only of King's mind but his methods of life at that time, it may be worth recording.

It was typical of his sudden moods that he should invite an obscure newspaperman to dine with him alone at Laurier House and then discuss the business of his Government candidly with a complete outsider. He was in high spirits and good appetite.

The visitor might well be disconcerted by the somber, candle-lighted dining room, the weight of an Irish terrier on his feet, the ghostly portraits on the walls, and the butler emerging suddenly from the shadows and disappearing again without a sound. The room was excessively large for the two men at one end of the long table. King felt no oppression. He ate with relish and talked with abandon.

Looking peculiarly white and tiny in the flicker of the candles, he talked about everything, attacked the four courses with gusto, and enjoyed two or three discreet glasses of white wine. Having returned from a Europe on the verge of anarchy and already embroiled in the Spanish civil war, he seemed to be a man without a care of any sort.

After dinner we entered the tiny oaken elevator. King proudly

showed how it could be operated by a push of a button, explaining
that this machine and most of the household furniture were gifts
from his friend Larkin and others. He added rather naïvely, as the
mechanical box moved slowly upward, that once he had expressed
to Larkin a longing for the farm next to his at Kingsmere and—
would you believe it?—the title to this land had been presented to
him a few days later. It was a wonderful thing, he said, to have
friends.

The usual tour then proceeded through the great upstairs hall
where hung the Queen's offer of a reward for the Rebel, dead or
alive; the strong room where the three-foot scrap books were kept
with their contents of engraved invitations, banquet menus, and
other worthless souvenirs; the sitting room crammed with ghastly
bric-a-brac; the bedroom where King slept in the great brass bed,
with the basket for Pat beside it; then up to the third story and the
famous rookery now the secret center of the Government and the
nation.

Parliament was sitting that night on some important piece of
legislation. The Government was under Opposition attack and the
world was going merrily to hell while King sprawled on a chesterfield before the coal fire, his feet resting on the familiar cougar
skin, and talked steadily until midnight, almost without a pause for
breath and certainly without showing the least sign of worry.

After fourteen years most of that conversation is forgotten. One
remembers, though, the sly, tolerant digs at various public personages, the twinkling eye and quick smile, the compact figure against
the cluttered background of that room, and the lighted portrait of
his mother at his shoulder. When he turned to the state of Europe
and his visit to Hitler, his remarks remained in the visitor's memory.
They were too surprising to be forgotten and became more startling
in retrospect as events of the following year contradicted them.

He said he had found Hitler "a simple sort of peasant," not very
intelligent and no serious danger to anyone. Hitler was obsessed
with the recovery of neighboring territory inhabited by Germans, a
natural feeling. When he had brought these territories into the
Reich, King felt he would be satisfied. Repeating that Hitler was
at heart only a simple peasant, King predicted that he would not
risk a large war. His ambitions were centered entirely in Germany
and the narrow irredentist regions beside it. For this reason King
looked for no early trouble in Europe—this about seven months
before Munich.

Later, it was widely stated that at his meeting with Hitler King
had acted as a kind of unofficial spokesman for Britain, warning the

dictator that if he provoked war, Canada and the whole Commonwealth would stand at Britain's side. There is reason to believe this was true. In our conversation King made no mention of it.

He must have been pretty confident of peace, or the defense policies (which could be better described as nondefense policies) followed almost to the outbreak of war are inexplicable. Otherwise, even though they were generally supported by all parties and the public, nothing could justify King's part in them. If he had felt war was coming he should have insisted on stronger policies or resigned and then, doubtless, returned triumphantly from the wilderness later on as Churchill did. He was not dishonest in his calculation. He was entirely mistaken, and the unfortunate meeting with Hitler was a large private factor in that mistake.

Still, King hedged somewhat against war. His hedges at the time were kept secret. Later they were revealed and intentionally exaggerated to minimize and defend his errors.

The record is complicated, tortuous, and little remembered. It must be recalled briefly if King's policy, or lack of it, is to be understood and Canada's total unreadiness for war explained.

The collapse of the League had confronted King with two stark alternatives, outlined to him in advance by Dafoe, with the little-noted warning that "Down the road, not far away in point of time, will be the world's greatest war, the hyperbolic war, the war that will never stop until the structure of society as we know it will sink into the slime."

On the one hand, since there was no longer the semblance of a world authority capable of enforcing peace, Canada could throw in its lot with the Commonwealth in some sort of joint defense plan entailing those very commitments that King and the Canadian people had always rejected. As Dafoe had predicted, the Conservative Party now accepted this alternative. It repudiated the theory of the Hamilton Speech and returned to Meighen's former thesis of "Ready, aye, ready," expressing the real instincts of its author. In the summer of 1936 Bennett was urging the Commonwealth to take up the task of defense where the League had laid it down. A substantial element of his Party had never believed much in the League anyway and was rather glad to see it dead so that its corpse could be replaced by the living champion of Commonwealth consolidation. This was logical enough. It had the defect of being politically impossible and militarily quite inadequate.

As a second alternative, Canada could pursue the logic of its isolationism by refusing commitments to League or Commonwealth and arming itself.

It never occurred to King for a moment to accept the first alternative, for he knew what it meant. It simply meant, as Dafoe wrote,
"The consolidation of the Commonwealth in a centralized militaristic
Empire with common policies made in London [however this might
be disguised by some formula of consultation] and under direction
from a centre—London again."

The second logical alternative of a rearmed Canada likewise was
rejected. King found a third which had no logic and nothing to
commend it, except perhaps the assumption that war was impossible.
He refused both commitments and armaments, thus falling between
the two stools of the League and the Commonwealth.

With war under way a little later, he could boast that he had
foreseen it, at least as a possibility, and had prepared Canada
accordingly. That claim is denied by the Government's prewar
defense expenditures. In 1935–36 they amounted to the pitiful sum
of seventeen millions; in 1936–37, twenty-three millions; in 1937–38,
thirty-three millions; in the spring of 1939, four months before the
avalanche, they had reached sixty-four millions. They would have
been much less if King had not fought for the military estimates
almost alone in his Cabinet, at the cost of serious political damage
in Quebec. As a result of these foolish economies, Canada entered
the war virtually defenseless, not only by King's leadership, or lack
of it, but by general consent of Parliament and people.

All this was an ostrich policy, or no policy at all, yet it had been
laid down at Chanak, confirmed in Ethiopia, construed in sweetness
and light at Geneva. What had happened to King was really very
simple. He had continued to use the hand of the physician in a
world now controlled by pugilists and not by simple peasants. His
mistake was shared more or less by every free government and
people. Considering their immediate exposure to the storm, the
European statesmen were more culpable than he. Considering their
power and responsibility, the American statesmen must accept equal
blame. King's share cannot be denied on that account.

Having relied for seventeen years on the League, without effectively supporting it, having escaped hurriedly from its obligations
through the back door of Ethiopia, and being confronted, on the
League's death, with the first defense issue since 1914, Canada
pulled down the blinds and hid under the bed. For this, King must
be charged with major responsibility.

He had been deceived by the peasant of Berlin and still more by
horror of war, which made him refuse to admit its approach, but he
began to erect new hedges against it on the foundation of the first
Canadian-American defense agreement. On his visit to Washington

in 1937 he discussed with Roosevelt the possibility of joint planning between the two neighboring nations. Roosevelt at once agreed. So secretly that the first published report of them greatly embarrassed the Government, technical discussions were begun by Canadian and American staff officers.

Not long afterward such a practical arrangement would appear obviously desirable in both countries. At that time the news that Canada was collaborating with its neighbor even on paper alarmed the Canadian imperialists, who saw a betrayal of the Commonwealth, and the isolationists, who feared that Canada might involve itself in American wars.

In 1937, when King first broached the subject, Roosevelt delivered his famous speech proposing the "quarantine" of aggressors. He was slapped down so hard by public and press that he abandoned the attempt to arouse the nation and, in the opinion of Cordell Hull, set back the cause of internationalism indefinitely by going too far, too soon.

In Canada, Woodsworth asked Parliament to resolve that "in the event 'of war Canada should remain strictly neutral regardless of who the belligerents may be."

Such was the state of North American opinion and it alone can explain, if it does not justify, King's or Roosevelt's evasions.

The first White House defense conference did not seem effective enough at the time to arouse either imperialist or isolationist. Actually, it proved to be one of the most effective day's work King had yet performed. From it in due course evolved the Ogdensburg Agreement and full partnership in defense, both military and economic. The friendship with Roosevelt was beginning to pay off, though its dividends were yet invisible and had to be withheld from a public not ready yet to appreciate them.

King had rejected Woodsworth's proposed neutrality, he would commit himself neither to war nor to abstention from war, reiterating endlessly that Parliament would decide the issue in the light of prevailing conditions. From the secret Washington conference he carried the same view to the Imperial Conference in London.

There he found strong elements in the Conservative Party and press reviving all those theories of centralized Commonwealth defense and single-voice foreign policy which he had fought off in 1923. They had no more effect on him now than before. The attempt to change his mind was a complete failure.

"Those who looked to the Conference to devise and formulate a joint imperial policy on foreign affairs, defence or trade will find nothing to fulfill their expectations," he reported to the Canadian people. A conference, he emphasized, was not a cabinet, "least of all an Imperial Cabinet" as the centralizers of London had repeatedly tried to make it.

Hence, as its formal report said, the Conference had made "no attempt" to "formulate commitments." With a straight face, however, it had resolved to strengthen the League, now in an advanced state of rigor mortis. At the same time, said King, "it was made clear . . . that Canada was not committed to joining in any Imperial or any League military undertakings and, equally, that there was no commitment against such participation." The first military duty of each Commonwealth member was to arrange its own defense as it saw fit.

Even this duty was neglected by Canada. King saw Hitler, returned to Canada, and did little to secure Canada's defenses.

His attitude was indicated in his radio report to the Canadian people on July 19 when he said that his tour had "immeasurably deepened" his two convictions that "how terrible a thing is hate and—how necessary to the cure of our ills is an attitude of good will."

And then, showing how little the physician yet understood the pugilists of Europe, he added the almost unbelievable statement that "despite every appearance to the contrary, I believe the nations of Europe have a better understanding of each other's problems today than they had for some years past. Moreover, despite all appearances, they are prepared, I believe, in an effort to work out a solution, to co-operate to a greater degree than has been the case for a long time. It is going to take time—possibly a long time—to complete the transition through which all countries are passing, in the readjustments which are being made in the existing social order. But that they can be made without adding widespread international conflict to the difficulties all have to face, I have not the least doubt."

No doubt about continued world peace—this in the midsummer of 1937 when the Spanish civil war was providing the overture to Hitler's *Götterdämmerung*, when Japan was setting out to conquer all China and Germany's seizure of Austria already was planned.

King had come back to Canada completely deluded by the Chamberlains of Britain, the gravediggers of France, and such German information as Hitler himself, von Neurath, Göring, and Hess had given him. Altogether, the 1937 tour was the most unfortunate King had ever made.

He evidently knew that himself by the following spring. In March, 1938, Hitler marched into Vienna. The mask had fallen from the face of the simple peasant and the scales from King's eyes.

In his report to Parliament on May 24, King was blinking in the first lightning flash of Armageddon. All the optimism of the previous summer had evaporated and all the brave words had to be eaten.

While it was never his habit to admit any change in his mind, this speech was actually a complete confession of the mistake begun in the first days of office and continued until now, the false diagnosis of the deluded physician who saw at last that he was confronted not by normal men but lunatics.

At the beginning, he confessed that "we look out upon a disturbed and seemingly chaotic world. Bitter and destructive wars are being waged on two continents. Force is openly glorified. Solemn pledges are disregarded. Armaments are mounting to fantastic heights." Why, he asked Parliament and himself, with an inner pain never shown before, "within twenty years after a war to end war is the war spirit so strong in many quarters? Why, after a war to make the world safe for democracy, has dictatorship attained such acceptance and momentum?"

To answer his question he launched into a long and complex analysis of the world's descent from 1918 onward, with the conclusion that "it is a dark outlook, but not one that calls for despair," yet it "may be years before freedom and tolerance revive."

Then came a vigorous defense of Canada's foreign policy. It could not be "a spectacular, head-line policy." It must be based on Canada's actual situation, its geographical location, "the racial composition of its people," its economic development and its own "internal preoccupations and necessities."

That it was still primarily an isolationist policy was indicated by his next remark. Canada was not "inclined to organize or join in crusades in other continents," though "we cannot be indifferent to the fate of democratic institutions, the suffering of unfortunate minorities elsewhere."

"But," he emphasized in a significant passage, "we must keep a sense of perspective. Resolutions or speeches on affairs in Austria or Spain or San Domingo may afford an emotional outlet but they do not give our country any power to shape the destiny of other peoples. . . . We are not asking and will not receive any help from outside in meeting these difficulties [at home] and we are unlikely to have any surplus of statesmanship or good fortune to bestow elsewhere. . . . It is equally unlikely that at the moment, with the world as it is today, any country will single out Canada for attack." On the other hand, Canada must "be prepared to meet any situation which may arise."

He went on to defend Canada's record in the League, to which he was still devoted, so long as it regarded itself as a conciliator and not as a policeman. His words sounded like a memorial service. So far as Canada was concerned this speech could be taken as a legal presumption of the League's death.

There followed an elaborate recapitulation of his lifelong argument against advance commitments to Britain or the League and the promise that Canada's position in any war would be decided by Parliament when the time came, not before, since no one could foresee the circumstances of such a war and "many 'inevitable' wars have never happened."

Moreover—here he was approaching gingerly the motives that governed him throughout this deepening twilight—"to force an issue like this upon the country would bring out deep and in some cases fundamental differences of opinion, would lead to a further strain upon the unity of a country already strained by economic depression and other consequences of the last war and its aftermath."

In plain terms, an advance commitment now would be rejected by French Canada and tear the nation apart. "To invite this risk on a hypothetical question would be as great a disservice to Canada as any government could render."

He agreed, however, that his policy was "not wholly satisfactory, not free from difficulties, not a completely logical position . . . not an ideal solution." It was "only the best of the available solutions" because the Commonwealth nations had worked out a satisfactory relationship in peacetime but had "not yet worked out a completely logical solution of the position in wartime."

King's own position on the crisis now confronting the world also was in evolution, as the final passage of that speech showed. Refusing to make any predictions, he said there were two schools of thought. One held that "Armageddon has already come" and that "the forces of light and darkness are irrevocably swinging into battle-line for the final test of destiny." The other school replied that, while the situation was dangerous, yet "to insist that the policy of dividing Europe or the world into two antagonistic camps, organizing a holy alliance against Fascism, would be still more dangerous and is neither possible nor necessary. . . . The wiser policy, it is urged, is to try to bring all Europe back to sanity . . . to seek to adjust each specific difficulty in turn."

Hastily he repeated that these were not necessarily his views, merely the views now contending in Europe. It was clear to the House, however, that he stood wholly for the policy now becoming known as "appeasement." It was equally clear in his concluding paragraph that he still stood for Canadian isolation, so long as that was possible, for the development of Canadian democracy, a good society, and friendship with everybody. Such was "the task that lies at our hands, our Canadian task."

Apart from the failure in defense, King's policies and predictions can be seen in retrospect as almost comically unrealistic. However, the circumstances of 1938 must be remembered. Britain and France were appeasing Hitler and already moving toward Munich, now four months off. The United States was neutral by the binding law of its Congress. Canada was in no position to stem the downward spiral even if it had wished to. The clear fact was that it had no such wish if any act of intervention would cost money or risk. The nation, except for a minority which found no audible voice save Dafoe's, was as isolationist and unrealistic as its leader. If King was wrong, he was expressing the nation's will.

That, of course, does not excuse him for being wrong, but the theory that he knew better and misled the people merely to hold their votes will not stand examination on the public or the private record. He did not know better. He had never been more sincere than in the long error now rushing to its appointed end.

At home and abroad he shared some eminent company. Certainly there were very few Canadians of that time equipped to throw the first stone.

26

The Bridge Builders

WITHIN THREE MONTHS OF KING'S SPRING REPORT TO PARLIAMENT
came the first breach in the no-commitments policy. It was
well contrived to hide its significance.

On August 18, 1938, as Hitler was preparing to annex the Sudeten-
land, as Europe at last faced the unmasked peasant and the spectacle
of imminent war, King and Roosevelt met to dedicate the Thousand
Islands International Bridge.

The pleasant ceremonies had a somber purpose which neither of
the two participants was yet able to announce by more than guarded
intimations. Even these were sufficient to show that both statesmen
were giving commitments beyond the knowledge of their legisla-
tures.

At nearby Queens University, in Kingston, Roosevelt returned
gingerly to the "quarantine" policy and enunciated the United
States' first peacetime military alliance with a foreign nation. While
compelled to maintain the American policy of strict neutrality, in
the struggle now openly under way in Europe, he began his slow
education of the American public, which would not succeed until
the final lesson of Pearl Harbor, with this statement:

"We cannot prevent our people from having an opinion in regard
to wanton brutality, in regard to undemocratic regimentation, in
regard to misery inflicted on helpless peoples, or in regard to viola-
tion of accepted individual rights."

That was the public end of Roosevelt's own neutrality. Cautiously
he warned his own people that they no longer occupied a "far away
continent to which the eddies of controversies beyond the seas
could bring no interest and no harm" and had become "vital factors
in world peace whether we choose or not," but for the neutralists he
quickly added the comforting thought—and he may have believed
it in part of his own complex nature—that if all the hopes of peace

were disappointed, "we can assure each other that this hemisphere at least shall remain a strong citadel wherein civilization can flourish unimpaired."

A vain hope, soon to be abandoned. If he could not offer to a tottering Europe more than sympathy, he immediately placed Canada in quite another category with one of those casual and masterly digressions of which his foreign policy was made: "The Dominion of Canada is part of the sisterhood of the British Empire. I give you assurance that the people of the United States will not stand idly by if domination of Canadian soil is threatened by any other empire."

This meant, if it meant anything, that the United States would defend Canada against any attack. This had long been implicit in the Monroe Doctrine and in North American geography. On the apparent eve of world war, it was heartening for Canadians to hear an explicit guarantee.

The promise called for reciprocation. After his private conversations with Roosevelt, King was ready to give the obvious reply two days later at Woodbridge, Ontario: "We, too, have our obligations as a good friendly neighbor, and one of them is to see that, at our own instance, our country is made as immune from attack or possible invasion as we can reasonably be expected to make it, and that, should the occasion ever arise, enemy forces should not be able to pursue their way, either by land, sea or air to the United States, across Canadian territory."

Without a word on paper, any consultation with Congress or Parliament, the partnership of Roosevelt and King had signed a joint defense contract. Against Roosevelt's fear of the American isolationists, and King's double fear of the Canadian imperialists, who thought that any overtures to the United States were somehow a betrayal of Britain, and of the French Canadians, who were more isolationist than the Americans, the declarations of Kingston and Woodbridge went as far as either statesman dared to go.

It was perhaps far enough for the moment. In two years almost to the day the alliance could be written into formal terms, again without the knowledge of either legislature.

From now on King's no-commitments policy could be maintained in theory. In fact it had gone by the board with the physician's old illusions. The new commitments were confined entirely to North America. They expressed King's unaltered isolationism, the old force of geography overcoming the force of history, which perpetually drew him, and most Canadians, toward Europe.

The declarations of Kingston and Woodbridge proved vague and

isolationist enough to satisfy both peoples, then at the lowest ebb
of their isolation. In King the struggle between geography and history was only beginning.

Also, a new challenge to his mastery of Canada had appeared
quietly on an onion farm not far from the newly dedicated bridge.
There, as President and Prime Minister were exchanging their first
vows, a young Liberal politician, full of disordered talents and self-
destroying hatred, ostentatiously busied himself with his onions
when, as Premier of Ontario, he should have attended the bridge
ceremonies.

Mitchell Hepburn had thus chosen, with a crude and typical
gesture, to announce his blood feud with King and his determination to capture the Liberal Party.

At the time, he appeared to be a formidable challenger. He was
popular, gay, and witty. He lived lavishly, surrounded by a court of
sycophants, bodyguards, traveling troubadours, and jesters. He
dressed and behaved like a city slicker yet talked the cracker-barrel
language of the Ontario country store and seemed to possess the raw
stuff of Canada which King always lacked. And if he could not replace King, perhaps he could destroy him. That was his obsession.
Like many larger men afflicted by a kind of native Canadian death-
wish, Hepburn was assuring not King's downfall but his own.

For the present, however, the struggle between the onion patch
and the sleepy estate at Kingsmere—the gaudy philosopher of the
cracker barrel versus the scholar of the library—looked serious to the
Liberal managers. It might prove much more than the personal
quarrel of two Liberals who were as unlike in their views and characters as men could be. It might split the Party. Worse, it might split
the nation at the moment of war.

King publicly ignored the onion patch, treated Hepburn with
elaborate courtesy, and patiently awaited the opportunity to sever
his throat as he had severed so many others, much tougher. Unknow-
ingly, in his clumsy attempt to unhorse his enemy, Hepburn was
providing King with the very opportunity he needed to consolidate
himself and the nation. That was two years off.

A month after his meeting with Roosevelt, King was plunged into
the worst hours of his life so far. Laid up at Kingsmere with sciatica,
his first real illness, he watched the climax of appeasement, the flight
of Chamberlain to Berchtesgaden and Godesberg, the final surrender
of Munich, and the last convulsive death-dance of Europe.

He watched it so secretly that, as he told this writer, he did not
dare to let his Cabinet colleagues or even his secretaries read the
coded cables from London. He said that, in his brass bed, wracked

with pain, he had decoded the messages himself. This was one of his frequent flights of imagination. He knew nothing of codes and could not have deciphered Chamberlain's communications, but certainly none of them reached the Cabinet.

Such was King's control of Government and nation, such the numbed state of his colleagues, that he could take foreign policy into his own hands and direct it as he pleased. He doubtless talked to Lapointe and to Skelton, the operating head of the External Affairs Department, who was saying that Czechoslovakia was not worth the life of a single Canadian soldier. It can be said on the authority of Ministers who attended the Cabinet in these hours that it never discussed the European crisis. Two Ministers raised the question in council. No answer came from Kingsmere.

Government, when the nation quivered on the knife edge of war, had moved from the East Block to King's bedroom in the country—a situation almost incredible and probably unique in any parliamentary state, to be explained only by King's equal power and fear.

He could not trust his colleagues, he lay prostrate among his cables, but his foreign policy, the foreign policy of his own private making, was perfectly clear in his mind. He stood unreservedly behind Chamberlain and appeasement. As Dafoe muttered out in Winnipeg, where he was watching the uncoded newspaper dispatches and giving them a very different interpretation, King had become "an appeaser of Appeaserville" and a convinced "Municheer."

Recovering from the first shock of the news and from his illness, King returned to Cabinet and indicated the policy he had laid down alone. On September 17, in a public statement, he declared that the Government "have been giving unremitting consideration to the European situation." This was literally untrue unless the Prime Minister could be considered the entire Government, as indeed he was in foreign affairs. The British Government, King went on, had undertaken the task of European mediation "with a courage and vision which I have stated the people of Canada unanimously appreciate." The Canadian Government, he added, "are examining all possible contingencies" (news, this, to the Cabinet) and would summon Parliament "if occasion arises" but "meanwhile we do not consider in the light of all the circumstances known to us, that public controversy as to action in hypothetical contingencies would serve the interest of peace or of Canadian or Commonwealth unity."

The crisis, in short, was too serious to talk about, even in the Cabinet chamber. The Canadian people, dazed and stupefied by a situation for which King had never prepared them or himself, made no protest. Most of them, even many of his political enemies, were glad to let the sick man wrestle with forces beyond their comprehension. He was quite right in saying that the nation as a whole was behind him, Chamberlain, and appeasement.

On September 27, King received the cabled text of Chamberlain's speech that day, two days before the flight to Munich. However much Britain might sympathize with Czechoslovakia, said Chamberlain, "we cannot . . . undertake to involve the whole British Empire in war simply on that account. . . . War is a fearful thing and we must be very clear, before we embark on it, that it is really very great issues that are at stake and that we should risk everything in their defence."

King instantly endorsed those sentiments. His Government, he said, "is in complete accord with the statement Mr. Chamberlain has made to the world today." While preparations were being made for any contingency and for a session of Parliament if Chamberlain's mediation should fail, yet "for our country to keep united is all-important" and "to this end, in whatever we say or do, we must seek to avoid creating controversies and divisions that might seriously impair effective and concerted action when Parliament meets."

In plainer terms, both Government and public must keep their lips sealed lest a single word shatter the last chance of peace.

Those were terrible hours for King, much more terrible in their suspense than the hours of war when the die had been cast; moments made especially terrible by his private estimate of Canadian opinion, his belief that the nation was not morally ready for war and, in Quebec's present humor, might fly apart at the first blow.

If there was to be war, he needed more time to prepare the nation for it. If lack of preparation was his own fault, the state of the nation, both military and spiritual, could not be denied. Canada, like its neighbor and the democratic states of Europe, was not ready. The nation's reaction, when the blow fell just one year later, seems to indicate that King in 1938 underestimated its intelligence and its courage.

On the eve of Munich, King had not quite lost faith in his original diagnosis of the diseased mind now engulfing Europe in its fantasies.

He remembered, at this critical hour, a chance remark of Hitler's to him a year earlier. Hitler had said it was impossible to think clearly in Berlin. Only in his Bavarian eyrie could he escape the pressures and conflicts of his advisers. King had replied that he found the same escape in Kingsmere. Now, when Hitler was beset by other lunatics at his capital, King sat down and wrote him a personal message which Hitler alone would understand. Hitler, King urged, should get out of Berlin.

That advice, if it was ever read, must have made Hitler smile.

Thus King watched with agony of body and mind the flight of Chamberlain to Munich. When the first news of peace-by-surrender reached him on September 29, he was ecstatic and dashed off a cable to Chamberlain. The message would look exceedingly queer not long hence.

"The heart of Canada," he said, "is rejoicing tonight at the success which has crowned your unremitting efforts to peace. . . . My colleagues in the Government join with me in unbounded admiration of the service you have rendered mankind. Your achievements in the past month alone will ensure you an abiding and illustrious place among the great conciliators. . . . On the very brink of chaos, with passions flaming and armies marching, the voice of reason has found a way out of the conflict. . . . A turning point in the world's history will be reached if, as we hope, tonight's agreement means a halt to the mad race of arms and a new start in building the partnership of all peoples. May you have health and strength to carry your great work to its completion."

Nearly all Canada agreed with that sigh of relief from the depths of King's soul. Munich satisfied the imperialist since it was the work of a British Prime Minister, and the isolationist who grasped at any straw to avoid war.

Only one clear voice was raised against the general thanksgiving. While King in his tiny handwriting composed his message to Chamberlain, Dafoe sat down with his stub of a pencil and scrawled his most famous editorial, headed: "What's the Cheering For?" The warning that the fake peace of Munich could not last was drowned in the nation's cheers and King's brief ecstasy.

Momentarily, if not heroic himself, King basked in the heroic light of Chamberlain. Dafoe was cut by old friends in the Manitoba Club and lost thousands of subscribers to his paper. Eleven months only would be required to show which of the two great Canadian Liberals was right.

Munich came to King like a reprieve to a condemned man. He felt that relief far more deeply than the Canadian people because he knew better than they, or the professional soldiers, what war would mean. His congratulations to Chamberlain, always to be quoted against him thereafter, were completely honest. He believed in Munich as profoundly as did its architect.

It seemed to confirm his diagnosis of Hitler, the peasant who only wanted to recover the lost German populations. It might not assure permanent peace but it provided the precious time in which peace might be negotiated or, at worst, in which the free nations might prepare.

Above all, this delay, should it prove to be nothing more, might give the Canadian people the chance to clarify their minds, find unity, and avoid the total smash-up which had preyed upon King's mind since 1917.

Never for a moment, as the later record would show, did King regard Munich as anything but a stopgap, a mere incident in a huge, historic process of readjustment. Of this even war would be an incident also. He seized Munich only as a possible chance not to avoid this readjustment but to keep it from reeling into general anarchy.

Whether he was right or wrong about Munich, only a very wise or very foolish man would care to say yet. Under his public jubilation we do not know his secret doubts; and whether the free world could have fought better in 1938 (when Russia was supposed to be a reliable ally, assuring two fronts against Germany) than in 1939 is one of those might-have-beens which, intriguing to the later historian, are of but little use to the current statesman.

At any rate, though Munich seemed to provide a breathing spell of peace, it ended King's peace of mind. From then on he was a changed man. While the distraction of the world crisis had turned the nation's eyes from its own troubles, almost blotted out the depression, and thus eased the political tensions at home, the cosy life of Laurier House and Kingsmere was ended for good. All the great dreams of social progress, all the bold hopes of *Industry and Humanity* looked irrelevant under the shadow of a world which might not plunge into war but certainly was heading for a period of long and desperate strain—no climate for the reformer.

27

The Shadows Lengthen

THE DRUGGED PEACE OF MUNICH MOVED INTO THE TRANCE OF winter and still held through the first false Canadian thaw. In January, King intimated his serious concern to Parliament, adding significantly that when Britain was at war, Canada was at war. After that, his spirits seemed to rise somewhat. In the early days of March, when Hitler was making gestures at the remaining provinces of Czechoslovakia but had not moved, King assured a worried Parliament and people that the world situation appeared easier. He repeated that assurance on March 7, with the warning, however, that the crisis was by no means over.

He had hardly finished speaking when Hitler devoured the rest of Czechoslovakia, throwing a small southern crumb to the jackal of Hungary.

King was crushed by that news, for he understood its meaning. Munich had been destroyed within six months. Hitler would not keep even the one-sided bargains extorted by blackmail. The bitterness of Chamberlain, on finding that Hitler was no gentleman and would break his personal word to a Prime Minister of Britain, was echoed in the heart of King, who also had found that he had completely misjudged the enemy.

When King faced Parliament on March 20, his simple peasant had turned into an insatiable conqueror. Fortunately, Parliament did not know how wrong his judgment had been. His record could be presented with some look of order and consistency.

He said little that day. The news was too incredible and shocking to be fully assessed. Moreover, he did not know the policy of the British Government. Actually, by the anguished confession of Chamberlain in his latest speech, it had none. All King could tell Parliament was that his Government was ready for anything (as assuredly it was not), would call Parliament if the need arose, and then present a policy when the facts were clear.

This speech contained, however, the intimation of the inevitable policy. "If," King said, "there were a prospect of an aggressor launching an attack on Britain, with bombers raining death on London, I have no doubt what the decision of the Canadian people and Parliament would be. We would regard it as an act of aggression, menacing freedom in all parts of the British Commonwealth. If it were a case . . . of a dispute over trade or prestige in some far corner of the world that would raise quite different considerations."

There was "still no reason to despair of peace," and he would sacrifice anything for it except "the liberty which we enjoy and which we will never surrender."

No surrender of liberty, and to liberty the survival of Britain was essential. The noncommitment theory could be maintained in words but had now become so transparently thin as to deceive nobody. In this speech King had given the commitment. It was a commitment to fight if Britain were endangered.

This was plain enough for Britain to understand. It was intentionally vague enough to satisfy English-speaking Canada and to warn French Canada that the nation could not escape a general war. All this might seem mere wobbling and evasion. It was in reality the first step in a considered campaign to prepare Canada for war.

The next step was taken ten days later, just twenty-four hours before Chamberlain found a policy at last, drew a line, and guaranteed that Britain would fight for Poland. On March 30, King delivered perhaps the most remarkable speech of his life.

It was remarkable for its sudden change in style and pace—the usual convolutions shortened into stiff, brisk sentences, the chaotic events since Munich marshaled in quick, vivid procession like a well-directed documentary film. Skelton had written that speech.

In content it was all King and stripped King's mind naked as it had never been before. It was the full portrait of a man who had emerged from an imaginary world after sixty-five years and now looked in horror at the real world and far beyond, as few other statesmen had yet looked, into the world of our time. He looked, he understood, he knew, but, at this moment, he could not quite face the ultimate horror.

He began by defending Munich without any attempt to evade his small part in it. Chamberlain had "made emphatically the right choice in striving to prevent the outbreak of war." Czechoslovakia could not have been saved anyway and the attempt to save it would have devastated Europe. If Canada had made threats in the uncertain moments of Munich it might have destroyed Chamberlain's chances of mediation, since he would have been suspected by Hitler of promising peace when he meant war. And while the Canadian

Government was accused of lagging timidly behind the other Dominions in bellicosity, the record showed that none had gone an inch further than Canada.

Again, it was said that war had only been postponed by surrender at Munich but "it must have taken a good deal of confidence in one's powers of guessing the future to be sufficiently certain of what might happen in 1940 to have been ready to plunge the world into war in 1938." Then a last, rather despairing hope of avoiding the inevitable: "Most inevitable wars have not happened." The same sentence contained the first intimation of the inward torment of a man who was looking beyond war and victory: "And of those that happened the ultimate consequences were usually most unexpected." Here he paused suddenly to utter a cry wrung from the depths of his soul and expressing its deepest Christian conviction: "War would settle nothing, prove nothing, help nothing!"

His words might be interpreted in the spring of 1939 as cowardice, stupidity, or mere political maneuver. A dozen years later, in the face of an ally transformed into a new and daunting enemy, this prophecy would wear a different aspect.

Parliament beheld that day a little man, pale, wracked, and uncertain, no hero when the times cried out for heroism, but at least it was listening to a scholar and a thinker who understood the meaning of events if he could not direct them.

The thoughtful men of Parliament, and especially the Cabinet Ministers around him, wondered if such a man, crying out against war as certain to settle, prove, and help nothing, could lead a nation if that war came. The thoughtless could see no signs of leadership. Very few in that House and perhaps none in the nation realized that King was now launching his greatest feat of leadership, was preparing to make himself the most unlikely but the greatest war leader the nation had ever known.

He was beginning in his queer, obscure, and deadly fashion to take a divided nation into war, united as no other living Canadian could hope to unite it.

How this could be done he was not yet sure. He was groping for common ground between the two Canadian races. He was educating each in the opinions of the other. He was trying to convince Quebec, on the one hand, that war could not exempt Canada, and the English-speaking Canadians, on the other, that Quebec could not be coerced without smashing the nation and its chance of victory. He was fumbling for a point of agreement to avoid the tragedy of 1917, which had made him Prime Minister in the first place but which now reappeared and threatened to undo him and all his works.

This, to be sure, was not heroism. As the results would show, it was statesmanship, or at least management of a diverse nation such as neither Borden nor Laurier had achieved in the same Canadian crisis.

Hence for English-speaking Canadians the assurance that Canada would never abandon Britain under fire. Hence King's flat refusal to commit himself to neutrality, as urged by Woodsworth. Hence also his rejection of a proposed statute stating Canada's right to neutrality, for such legal quibbling, he said, would split the nation when unity was more necessary than ever before.

To the isolationists of Quebec he intimated that "we must to a greater or less extent choose between keeping our own house in order and trying to save Europe and Asia." In any case, the war, if it came, would not be a repetition of 1914. "The days of great expeditionary forces, of infantry crossing the oceans, are not likely to recur."

Two years ago, he recalled, he had said that it was "extremely doubtful if any of the British Dominions would ever send another expeditionary force to Europe."

That opinion still stood—less than a year before the first Canadian division would be in England.

"One political fact," he said, "is equally clear: In a war to save the liberty of others, and thus our own, we should not sacrifice our own liberty or our own unity."

Then came the outright commitment to Quebec. These twenty words, lying like a long fuse to a powder barrel, would produce the last and almost fatal explosion of King's career: "The present Government believes that conscription of men for overseas service would not be a necessary or effective step. Let me say that so long as this Government may be in power, no such measure will be enacted."

It would be said later that he regretted this solemn pledge. He never regretted it. Without it, he believed until his dying day, he could never have led the nation into war, except as two weak and quarreling fragments.

The three purposes of the speech had now been served—the Canadian people had been told candidly that war might break out at any moment; the English-speaking people knew that Canada would stand by Britain; and the French had been given a guarantee against conscription which, in a way that no outsider could understand, represented for them subordination and the bitter bread of English conquest.

The course was plotted. Canada would fight if it had to but within its means, both material and spiritual, probably without an expeditionary force and certainly without a military draft.

It was all very well to articulate the instincts of a divided and baffled people whose will had not yet jelled, and could not yet be foreseen, to lay the course of compromise, to seek the middle ground acceptable to both races. Had King found it? He could not be sure. He was tortured, not, as his enemies supposed, by the risk of losing his own political skin—the thing before him had grown too big for that—but by the thought of losing at one stroke all the work of his life, of Laurier's, of every leader back to the Rebel who had tried to make one nation in Canada.

He was horrified of war itself abroad and of another 1917, or worse, at home, and in his horror he blurted out the most famous sentence that ever passed his lips: "The idea that every twenty years this country should automatically and as a matter of course take part in a war overseas for democracy or self-determination of other small nations, that a country which has all it can do to run itself should feel called upon to save, periodically, a continent that cannot run itself, and to these ends risks the lives of its people, risks bankruptcy and political disunion, seems to many a nightmare and sheer madness."

There was the old struggle of geography against history, now approaching its climax. There was the isolationism, constantly assailed by the call of blood and ancient ties, but never quite subdued so long as he lived. There also was the ultimate pessimism to be disguised to others and himself from now on but never extinguished.

In the last few minutes of that long and aching speech he tried again to convince himself and Parliament that all hope was not quite lost. He deplored the prophecies of "inevitable war," the talk of "a return to the dark ages," and "a fatalist and defeatist mood." The world did not face a breakdown of its civilization, only a period of "profound readjustments both domestic and international," for "we are living in one of those decisive periods of human history when new forces gather momentum and break through the crust of custom, when new tendencies develop with startling speed." This mechanical and economic revolution everywhere "should be viewed as opportunities, not as calamities. Any disturbances involved may be growing pains, not signs of decay."

He closed with his testament to democracy, now in travail: "We cannot hope to maintain democratic institutions unless we are ready to refrain from the temptations to intolerance, to cheap cynicism and indiscriminate criticism and from regarding the state simply as something to be squeezed."

Viewed in the perspective of thirteen years, this speech is seen to contain more wisdom than the nation was then able to grasp. King had seen the threatened war as entirely different militarily from its predecessor. He had seen it not as an accident or a personal conspiracy but as the breaking of revolutionary tides from the depths of history, as the failure of mankind to consummate its revolution peacefully, and as a process which would not end with the fighting but would go on and on, incalculably, to new adventures, new dangers, and perhaps new wars. War would settle nothing, prove nothing, help nothing. The physician's cry was despairing. Who in this atomic age, not then dreamed of, will say that it was untrue?

From that day onward, all King's youthful hopes, his whole vision of a new and better world seemed lost for his time. Others might see that world. He could not hope to live long enough. Sometimes before he died he could persuade himself that the miraculous had happened, that the war was establishing a permanent peace, that the revolution could proceed in good order to its consummation. Never for a moment would he imagine, as so many old-time Liberals did, that the past could be reborn, the classic age recovered, or anything recognizable as normality restored. Until he died, the dark man was never far from his side.

As the spring came late at last, as the snow melted on the rock of Quebec, and still the world enjoyed peace of a sort, King had other visitors to entertain.

28

The Awakening

O N THE MORNING OF MAY 17, 1939, THE FRENCH CANADIAN PEOPLE repaired to the rock of Quebec where their life had begun. They covered the forgotten site of Champlain's Habitation, clung to Wolfe's trail from the Anse au Foulon, and spread across the Plains of Abraham. A race which had been conquered on this spot and remained forever unconquerable awaited its sovereign, who was the symbol of its defeat, its victory, and its sovereignty. From the river, this multitude, in gay holiday dress, looked like a gush of spring wildflowers. The King's first glimpse of Quebec revealed the perpetual crop of the Laurentian soil.

The figure of a young man in the admiral's uniform of the British Navy appeared at the rail of the liner as she neared the shore. The wife beside him had the soft, pink beauty of an English spring.

The Prime Minister and Lapointe stood together, bolt upright, on the wharf. In their identical Windsor garb of cocked hat and gold braid they reminded the observer inevitably of a tiny Tweedledum and giant Tweedledee.

From that hour onward, across the continent and back, until they sailed for home, the royal visitors were seldom out of King's sight. He treated them almost as his own children. He changed from Windsor uniform to evening dress, to morning coat, to country tweeds, in exhausting sartorial sequence. He fussed over every detail of the tour. Eager to be seen and photographed in the royal presence, he leaped from the moving train at a western station and would have fallen on the platform, perhaps injured himself, if a Mounted Policeman had not caught him in his arms.

Those were weeks when every drop of King's royalist blood tingled, when history thrust geography from his mind and he basked in a warm, sweet nostalgia. The Canadian springtime, the burgeoning earth, the cheering crowds, and the trusting young visitors who placed themselves entirely in his keeping gave King a month of rapture. Bliss it was in those days to be alive, but to be the sovereign's first adviser and the unofficial uncle of the Royal Family was very heaven.

No one who saw the Rebel's grandson as the loving guardian of his King and Queen, and at every hamlet along the way the crowds of Canada cheering the regal procession, could doubt the nation's course should war come to England. If the tour was designed to test that sentiment and to strengthen it, the results were conclusive. Canada's long isolationism, and King's, melted by the hour. As he admitted later, King had questioned two years before whether Canada would go into a European war under any conditions, and certainly he would have been unready to lead it. For him, for the nation, such questions were fully settled by this midsummer.

It was none too soon. The visitors had hardly left, and Parliament returned home expecting nothing more serious than the congenial sham battle of a general election, when the old specter returned after brief vacation. By the end of July, King faced "nightmare and sheer madness" on the march.

The thought of Canada fighting again in Europe was still nightmarish but it no longer appeared mad, for it had at least the final sanity of the inevitable. And when Germany's treaty with Russia was announced on August 21, King's no-commitment policy was dead.

As events moved at a gallop, the pedestrian of Ottawa strove desperately to keep up with them. Distinguished visitors from Britain continued to assure the Canadian people that talk of war was newspaper hysteria. Lord Beaverbrook remarked that his presence in Canada showed what he thought of these absurd rumors. King was not deceived but he was torn between his emotions and his reason. As strongly as he had resisted the thought of war he embraced it now, with one side of his mind, as unavoidable, while to the other it was still unthinkable.

At ten o'clock on the night of August 22, when he was about to board a train for Toronto to attend the funeral of a friend, King was handed a cable from London. The British Parliament had been summoned. As he hesitated to cancel his trip a second secret message arrived from Chamberlain warning him that the worst seemed likely to occur.

King decided to remain in Ottawa. He called Manion in Toronto, and as clearly as he dared on the wire, told him the facts. The same message was telephoned to Woodsworth in Vancouver and to John Blackmore, of the Social Credit Party, in Cardston.

The next day King proclaimed the War Measures Act, announced

that Parliament would be summoned if the peace was broken, and
assured the nation that the Government was ready for "any emergency."

On August 25 the Governmer.. called for army volunteers, while
King, in a last despairing gesture, cabled to Hitler and Mussolini
that "force is not a substitute for reason," to which the Italian dictator replied unblushingly that he was sparing "no effort to safeguard the peace of the world." The simple peasant of 1937 did not
bother to answer.

At one o'clock on the morning of September 1, the Canadian Press
telephoned Pickersgill, one of King's secretaries, to report that the
German armies had crossed the Polish frontier. Pickersgill was living
with Norman Robertson, of the External Affairs Department, and
the two of them followed the press reports through that night of
waiting. They decided that it was useless to rouse their chief, for he
could do nothing. At six o'clock they telephoned Skelton, who called
Kingsmere and got the Prime Minister out of bed. King received the
news in silence.

What could he say? The illusions of his lifetime were broken. His
philosophy of conciliation had never faced the necessity of force
when conciliation fails. Now that extreme dilemma could be escaped
no longer.

King dressed and ate a leisurely breakfast. Years of war stretched
ahead. The thing was too big for haste or excitement. He made up
his mind then, as he said afterward, that no single man could alter
the process now in train, could win the war or lose it.

At that moment a new career began, the last career he had wished
or foreseen. The man of peace must become a man of war. The lifelong conciliator must use force. The apostle of humanity must shed
blood. From those first hours he drilled himself in the conviction
that the war must and would be won. It was fortunate, in the succeeding months, that he could convince himself of anything.

King motored to town, entered his office as calmly as if this were a
day of routine business, and summoned Parliament for September 7
to authorize "effective co-operation by Canada by the side of Great
Britain, if Great Britain should be engaged in war in the effort to
resist aggression." His summons, deliberately vague, buried the
corpse of noncommitments for good and with it the hopes of his
sixty-five years.

For all practical purposes the nation was at war already. The
Government was committed to fight and Parliament would sustain
it. When Britain and France made their formal declarations on
September 3, Canada remained technically neutral, but King used

the radio to redeclare the Government's policy "in a struggle between the pagan conception . . . and a civilization based upon the
Christian conception of the brotherhood of man."

Parliament, he repeated, must decide—that much was left of the
old formula and it was important to King and the nation. He could
not deflect the torrent of events by a hair's breadth. He could establish Canada's right to make its own decision as a sovereign state
independent of Britain. The national status which had been his chief
lifework must be given final confirmation in the test of war.

In the twilight period of technical neutrality King was called to
his private telephone. The voice of Roosevelt in Washington asked
him if Canada was at war. King replied that it was not. Turning to
his own advisers in the White House, Roosevelt exclaimed: "You see,
I was right!" Being legally neutral, Canada could receive American
war supplies despite the Neutrality Act, which forbade such ship-
ments to belligerents.

During the next week the United States rushed across the border
what munitions it had to spare, including some airplanes invaluable
for training purposes in times when any plane or the oldest gun was
worth a hundred later on. Another interim dividend had been paid
on the Roosevelt-King friendship, and Roosevelt's neutrality had
become technical also.

Unknown to the public or even to the Cabinet, King was engaged
in another struggle with neutrality under the most wrenching personal strains of his career. Skelton, his trusted adviser on foreign
affairs from the beginning, insisted with all the power of his experience and integrity that Canada must remain neutral.

As King told that story in his last days, Skelton argued that the
surrenders and the hypocrisy of appeasement, from Ethiopia onward,
had undermined all the moral purposes for which the war ostensibly
was to be fought. Since no moral question was involved, Canada,
like Ireland, should keep out. Being a North American nation, it
might exercise some mediation in the course of a conflict morally
chaotic.

It was easy for King to reject this advice. He grieved to see as
great a man as Skelton so broken by frustration and despair. According to his own account, King told Skelton bluntly that his counsel,
whatever else might be said of it, was impossible. Apart from all
other considerations, any Canadian government which attempted
neutrality would be swept out of office by public indignation within
a week. Canada, said King, "must go in with everything it has."

He had no intention of compromising with Skelton. He could not
bear to break their old friendship by accepting Skelton's resignation.

So for two days, with only Lapointe privy to their secret, King and Skelton wrestled with their consciences, in perfect amity and insoluble disagreement. At the end of the second day, Skelton, who could never be ordered, was at last persuaded. After the travail of that lonely and honorable decision he never wavered again. In Ottawa there was no more thought of neutrality. But it survived elsewhere and must soon confront King with another and worse trial.

On September 7, King met a Parliament whose mind was fully made up. It was a little puzzled to hear in the Speech from the Throne only that the Government desired power to defend Canada and to co-operate in the effort to "resist further aggression." The opening formalities were observed, the tribute paid to dead members, the usual reports filed, the committees appointed without a word of war. Next day, King left no doubt of his meaning—the adoption of the Address in reply to the throne speech would be followed instantly by a war declaration.

·Coming from the conciliator, the appeaser, the man of peace, King's war speech of September 8 must be considered the most important he ever made. In form, wording, and style it was one of the worst.

Physically he was tired that day after the struggle with Skelton and the office work of a Government actually at war. His face was pale, his hand shook a little, and his shoulders twitched. Not trusting himself to speak without it, he read from a rambling and unwieldy manuscript, hastily thrown together without shape or order, yet minutely edited in every word. Parliament awaited a trumpet blast. From King it received a lawyer's brief.

·Canada, on September 8, presented a picture curious and deceptive—the lusty young nation, heir to three centuries of battle on Indian frontier and foreign field; the pale and bookish little man who proposed to lead it in the final adventure. Could this flabby scholar, this student of political theory, this mere manager of practical politics change his entire nature overnight and become a warrior of the Canadian breed? Could the tiny creature now standing nervously by his desk stand in the path of Armageddon? Many men in Parliament and most of the nation doubted it.

Parliament and nation thought they knew King. They knew only one side of him and forgot that the old Rebel had been a tiny creature, too. The larger side had yet to appear and did not appear that day. King had yet to discover that other side of himself. He, Parliament, and nation must sound his full depths together.

Though this bumbling and lamentable speech did not indicate it, the change from the prophet of peace to the man of war already was under way. Having accepted the inevitable and emerged from the enervating weeks of suspense into the cold climate of action, King had begun to feel a new exhilaration.

In his own bloodless fashion he had always been a fighting man— the first fact of his nature, the last to be discovered by his people. As he stood before a silent and skeptical House he knew that this was not the kind of fighting he had expected or prepared for. The mission he must perform was the very opposite of all his plans. After his sane works of peace he must grapple with the nightmare and the madness.

His ego, at least, was equal to the challenge. He had demonstrated his mastery of Canada in peace. All that must fail and be forgotten on the record unless he could establish his mastery in war. Now he must exceed all his predecessors as the double master. He had the will to perform his task, the health, the vigor, the essential and encompassing armor of personal vanity in which no doubts must find an entering chink.

Of that the House had no doubts either. Even King's enemies knew that he possessed a full, a godlike confidence in himself. Had he the capacity to match it? Technically he had not. He knew nothing of war. He had never worn a uniform or carried a rifle.

In his estimate, that was of no importance, for he saw war in the round, as a political process far larger and more intricate than its physical weapons. Especially for Canada it was a political process. If it was mismanaged, the two Canadian races would fly apart, the weapons would break, the armies would falter. Other men could build the weapons and lead the armies in battle. His battle was of a different and more dangerous sort. If he failed, the nation itself might be destroyed.

In part from vanity, in part from cold calculation, he knew, or thought he knew, like Pitt a hundred and eighty years before, that a divided nation must be saved from its own division, that he alone could save it.

A rash presumption it might seem to Parliament and nation. Yet the political calculation was a solid as the vanity. No other English-speaking statesman could hope to hold, as he already held, the confidence of French Canada. No French Canadian leader would be accepted for a moment outside Quebec.

The successor of Laurier had even greater assets for this trial than his spiritual parent, was in a stronger position than Borden in the first war. King was not attached to one side or the other in the ceaseless contest of the two races, now entering a new and perhaps a disruptive phase. His years of compromise, mediation, and often cynical expediency, intended for another purpose, now served him and the nation well. In the crisis King was better prepared, without intention, than any other man. All the contradictions of his work and of his nature merged in the final contradiction of the peacemaker transformed into the civilian warrior.

Like a general whose forces are outnumbered by a powerful enemy, he was planning every move in the battle of politics with a clear reckoning of his own weakness, knowing above all that he needed time to build strength. For the moment it must be a Fabian strategy until he could persuade French Canada into a war for which it was not yet ready. In his judgment everything depended on that.

Hence this twisted and sinuous speech, this wriggling between forces not yet calculable, this deliberate buying of time. And hence, to all those who miscalculated King, this spectacle of a virile young people led by a weak old man.

That false impression was exaggerated by the confused introduction to King's speech, the endless citation of documents, the fussy recital of details that no one cared to hear. Even as a lawyer's brief the job was botched by the nerve-strain of its author. As he confessed, "I never dreamed that the day would come when, after spending a lifetime in a continuous effort to promote and preserve peace . . . it should fall to my lot to be the one to lead this Dominion of Canada into a great war, but that responsibility I assume with a sense of being true to the very blood that is in my veins. I assume it in defence of freedom."

Then, in another random stroke, he promised to treat all war profiteers as creatures of "the underworld" and warned any of his followers seeking political patronage to "keep away from me for I will never listen to you." Those were large promises. They were made good as in no former war.

Next came a strange public examination of his own conscience to justify the doctrine of force evaded in his philosophy: "I am inclined to agree . . . that force has never accomplished anything—and yet I am not so sure of that. I believe that force does not fundamentally change a situation and that the only thing that in the end will change a situation is persuasion. You can persuade men; you can convert them, but there have been times . . . when if force had not been opposed by force, there would have been no Christianity left to defend." Force was accepted with horror but his conscience was clear.

He was clear also on Canada's freedom to choose for itself, as he had always insisted. If it went to war it would act "voluntarily, not because of any colonial or inferior status vis à vis Great Britain but because of an equality of status." The work which Macdonald, Laurier, and Borden had begun, which King had carried forward since 1923, was now to be vindicated, just as his isolationism already was discredited.

Until the dinner hour and through most of the evening, King continued his endless digressions into the history of the last five years. He read pages of telegrams, public documents, and orders-in-council into the record as if the sheer volume of exhibits could prove his case, as if Canada needed any proof that it must fight. He proved over and over again that he had made no advance commitments to Britain, as if he or anyone could alter the commitment of history. He feebly defended his inadequate preparations for war on the ground that he had given the fighting services all the money Parliament would vote, as if his Government had ever sought more.

By slow circular movement he began at last to creep up on the real purpose of his speech and on the real problem of Canada at war. He would not yet commit himself for or against an expeditionary force in Europe but the commitment against conscription for overseas service was given without reservation, as the only basis of racial unity: "No such measure will be introduced by the present Administration." In those words King offered French Canada the guarantee without which it would not accept the war. Was it enough?

The question would be raised and answered, not without agony and tears, before the first snow fell on the rock of Quebec. By those same words, chosen to placate the two Canadian races, King had planted a bomb to explode within his Cabinet five years hence. His greatest crisis would take time to develop. Invisibly, it had begun.

This he could not surmise but he saw further than many experienced soldiers. Remembering the face of Hitler, which had so deceived him, King cried: "Where is he creeping to?" He was creeping into the northern communities that proposed to be neutral. If they would not fight, if Britain and France went down, all the neutrals would go down, too, and "the whole business of isolation" even in America "will prove to have been a myth . . . there will in time be no freedom on this continent. Life will not be worth living."

This on the eve of the phony war. King never doubted from the beginning that the war would be long and cover the earth. He had escaped from his own myth of isolation. As nearly as he confessed anything, this was a public confession of his errors.

The speech trickled to its end at last in an ooze of borrowed sentiment. As the last exhibits of the legal brief, the fourteen stanzas and seventy lines of Lowell's poem "The Present Crisis" were read laboriously into the record. Plastered like sweet frosting on the dry substance of that speech, they had a cloying flavor. If dry, the substance was solid. Canada was going into the war with all its strength, of its own will for its own survival.

As King slumped into his chair, exhausted, a gray and tragic figure rose on the other side of the House.

Woodsworth, the saint, knew that he had reached the hour of his martyrdom in politics. Like King, he had refused to face in his philosophy the dilemma of force. Unlike King, he could not and would not accept force when the alternative was destruction. The prophet of peace refused to vote for war.

This man had left the church. He was still a Christian, and war, he cried, was the "absolute negation" of Christianity. Being himself more Christian than the church, and closer to the spirit of Christ than any Canadian in politics, he looked with loathing upon the slaughter of innocents throughout the world. He was driven away from the world and back to the isolation of North America, where "there may at least be the seeds left from which we can try to start a new civilization along better lines" after the general suicide.

The same sort of choice had faced many saints. For Woodsworth it was peculiarly agonizing. Other saints could abandon this world as insignificant and turn toward another. Woodsworth's work had been in this world, his whole life of labor, poverty, and daily suffering had been devoted to the salvation of human beings here and now, and it had all been in vain.

The House, as it watched a man going to the stake as surely as Jogues or Brébeuf, could see the world's anguish carved deep on this worn face.

None, perhaps, could read it as well as King, who watched with anguish and doubts of his own. He had warned the House to respect Woodsworth. He had called Woodsworth, his opponent, "an ornament to any parliament." He had pleaded with him, as one Christian to another, to consider where the doctrine of nonviolence would lead when violence threatened to exterminate Christianity altogether. All in vain.

Looking straight at King, Woodsworth refused to surrender his principles. The House was silent. It was witnessing a personal tragedy within the larger tragedy of the times and it listened in decent respect to one whom it knew to be nobly wrong. But when Woodsworth cried out that he would be proud of his own sons if they refused to enlist and faced a concentration camp or a firing squad for their convictions, a member in the Conservative back benches shouted "Shame!" No one joined him in casting the first stone.

As Woodsworth sat down, alone and defiant, he had broken with his own Party, he had thrown away his leadership of the Left in Canada, he had deliberately jettisoned his career in politics, and he was the most revered member of the Parliament which rejected him. His tragedy and triumph were now complete. They had been ordered from the beginning. In the jungle of these times the path of the saint leads inevitably to the stake. With one side of his diverse nature King must have envied Woodsworth his martrydom.

On the following day a practical politician replaced the saint as the leader of the Left. Through no wish of his own and with a visible pang at separating from the man he had followed and loved, M. J. Coldwell announced the C.C.F. policy in favor of the war.

Coldwell, if not a saint, was a man of high intelligence, deep culture, and a private life of pain and nobility. He revealed his stature in taking leave of his old leader and supporting a Government whose social philosophy he abhorred, whose foreign policy he could not refuse to accept. For Coldwell saw that if the war resulted from the bungling of capitalists, it could not be lost without destroying all the hopes of Socialism. The brave new world of the C.C.F. would be postponed indefinitely by war. Defeat would doom it for all imaginable time.

The C.C.F. repudiated neutrality. It, too, had its agony and doubt and Coldwell tried to dissolve them by an impossible compromise. The C.C.F. policy, which he now read, declared that "Canada should be prepared to defend her own shores, but her assistance overseas should be limited to economic aid and must not include conscription of man power or the sending of any expeditionary force."

Such a futile straddle lacked the grandeur of Woodsworth's act of faith and, on the other hand, any practical use in a war far larger than the C.C.F. could or would admit. It was the pitiful gesture, midway between Woodsworth's neutrality and total war, of puzzled men who had suddenly realized that their mild, reforming socialism had been living in a dream. In the torture of that discovery they gibbered and postured on the brink of the pit.

King also had lost his dreams. There was no time to regret them. Once embarked on the nightmare, his immediate concern was to carry the whole House and nation with him; above all, to prevent any break among the French Canadian members and thus in the vital tissue of the state.

The break came, but was too small to matter. Maxime Raymond, a sincere French Canadian who could never become a total Canadian, denounced all wars as contests of interests, not of ideologies (strange words today when Raymond's church confronts Communism). Since Canada's interests were not involved in this war, Raymond was against it, for it would "ruin" Canada.

Here was a voice out of the depths of the French Canadian nature. Had that nature grown beyond old bounds, had it learned, as King himself had learned, that there was no isolation for anyone?

Raymond had not learned. He still stood where King had stood before the nightmare and he hurled all King's old isolationist speeches at their maker. These were pinpricks, no more. The importance of Raymond on this occasion lay in his clear warning that war, whatever the Government might promise, would mean conscription. Quebec would never accept it. The final crisis, five years hence, was implicit in Raymond's speech and explicit in that of Liguori Lacombe, who moved a motion directly opposing Canada's participation in the war.

Like the C.C.F., the two lonely isolationists of Quebec were making gestures only, and they knew it. The real voice of French Canada poured out in the organ tones of Lapointe.

That great man had faced his own ordeal and grown with it. And what a growth! The peasant who had come to Parliament without a word of English had made that alien tongue his own. The son of the narrow Quebec earth had seen the vision of the greater Canada and inherited as well the legacy of the old world. The isolationist who had repealed the oil sanctions because Ethiopia was not worth the life of a single Canadian knew now that his hour and the hour of his people had come. Knew also that on him more than on any man the outcome of that hour must depend.

Parliament and nation beheld here the indigenous and authentic product of a people who had first seized Canada from the wilderness, who had clung to it and would never abandon it, who had loved it longer and better than any Canadians. And all the instincts of this race, all its leaders from Champlain to Laurier, spoke now through their heir and vindicator, but in larger accents, with wider vision.

The House listened and King sat transfixed beside a greater human creature as Lapointe, with massive shoulders heaving, huge hands clenched, and dark face contorted, proved that in him the conquered race had conquered itself. That was the true meaning of Lapointe in his hour. Others might quail. He looked into the pit unblinking.

It was not quite his finest speech, there was a finer to follow, but Lapointe used it, as no other man could, to speak in an alien tongue for his people to the other Canadian race, and then to speak to his people for the majority of Canadians. The minority, whom the

s

majority might not understand, but without whom the nation could not survive, had found a voice understandable to Canadians of every tongue. Incarnate in this man the two souls of Canada were striving toward elemental fusion.

As a lawyer, Lapointe argued that neutrality was impossible in law. As a statesman, he pronounced it impossible in practice. As a practical politician, he affirmed that no government could live if it attempted to resist an overseas expeditionary force.

So much for his own people. He turned as their leader to the rest of Canada: "Sons of one country, brothers in one family, for the future of Canada is it not imperative that no section of Canada, no race, no creed, should inflict upon the other sections, the other races or the other creeds incurable wounds which might destroy our country forever?" If unity would be shattered by neutrality, it would be shattered as completely by the other extreme of conscription for overseas service. That French Canadians would never, never accept.

For himself and all the Quebec Ministers he gave the solemn undertaking that they would never be members of a government which attempted to enforce conscription. Looking hard at the Opposition, Lapointe asked: "Is that clear enough?" His question must be answered five years hence when Lapointe would not be alive to answer it. Power was silent that day. He would answer in due time with honor.

No party denied Lapointe's proposition that conscription would split the nation, that no French Canadian would sit in a conscriptionist government, that the agitators for conscription were really agitating against a concerted war effort. Even this proposition would not satisfy some elements in Quebec and no one knew it as well as Lapointe. He could not convince them, but "I disdain them! They will not deter me from the path of duty, as God gives me the light to see it. I will protect them against themselves!"

In those words he had pronounced the certain verdict of history on his work—by evoking the best side of its nature, he had protected Quebec against itself.

"I have been told," he concluded, "that my present stand means my political death. Well, at least it would not be a dishonorable end and I am ready to make sacrifices for the sake of being right. But let me assure you . . . that if only I can keep my physical strength, fall I shall not; and my friends shall not fall either."

He had the strength to make good that guaranty and no more. The God he trusted had left him time to complete this one task only. It was enough for a single lifetime.

Also, there was more unconscious logic in the performance of the task, thus far, than most of his friends and enemies yet realized. Lapointe, it was said, had bungled the Ethiopian crisis as King's agent. If this was true it was equally true that by his action then he had made his action now politically possible. In the case of Ethiopia, and in all the years of isolationism, the Government had proved to Quebec that it would never enter any war which could be avoided, even by retreat and humiliation if necessary. Now Quebec could not doubt the necessity of war when Lapointe and his French Canadian colleagues accepted it. Their bona fides in this respect had been established beyond question. In the view of their people they entered the court with clean hands. That fact was vital and perhaps decisive in the dangerous events immediately following.

In Quebec City, a crisp gentleman of the law, knowing little of politics or politicians, read Lapointe's speech in the papers with approval. Of all Canadians, Louis St. Laurent was the last to suppose that he must shortly take up the torch dropped from Lapointe's tired hand.

King, then, was in complete control of Parliament and nation, with no reservation on their energies in the war except the no-conscription pledge. The Conservatives, through the gallant Manion, and through Stevens, in a chivalrous speech (Customs scandals, price-spreads, and all old feuds forgotten) had pledged their complete co-operation to the Government. The C.C.F. had made its own reservations, so impractical as to be soon forgotten. Woodsworth and two Quebec members only were against the war.

Even at that early hour, however, the first rumble of racial collision could be heard in the voice of J. E. Lawson, a Conservative of the old school, who needed only one paragraph to say that he did not subscribe to the no-conscription policy. Many others in Canada, sharing his view, were willing to keep silent for the time being. For the time being only.

The Lacombe motion of neutrality was rejected and the main motion, which meant war, was passed without a recorded vote, only Woodsworth rising to express his objection. The Prime Minister left the House to advise the King of Canada to declare war on Canada's behalf.

On Saturday night the cables went to London. No reply was received on Sunday morning. As the day dragged on, King waited impatiently at Laurier House for word that Canada was at war. He tried to reach London by telephone and could not get through. He went to bed, still waiting.

What had happened in London? Had all his messages gone astray? Had the Germans tampered with the telephone and cable? Would he face Parliament and the world on Monday, empty-handed and ridiculous? He lay awake until dawn. During the rest of the war there would be only one more sleepless night.

At 6 A.M. the telephone rang at King's bedside. The delayed message from London had arrived. The King of Canada had declared war on September 10. His Prime Minister at last could sleep, with the knowledge that a sovereign nation had made its own decision.

The decision was not quite unanimous. A French Canadian of smaller stature and large ambition even now was preparing to challenge Parliament's right to vote for the people. The final struggle of Lapointe's life was only a month away. And in English-speaking Canada King faced a movement, not yet organized, but strongly backed, to oust him, erect a coalition government, defeat Lapointe in Quebec, and divide the nation before it could begin to fight.

29

Victory at Home

CANADA HAD BEEN IN THE WAR BARELY A FORTNIGHT WHEN Premier Duplessis undertook to lead Quebec out of it.

The motives of this crafty, volatile, and likable personage were not deep-seated. He was no mystical evangelist of racial dogma like Bourassa, nor a Raymond driven to impossible courses by high principles. He was a practical politician out to win another election and to smash the Grits in Ottawa. If he smashed Canada in the process, that was an unavoidable inconvenience, a casualty of war.

In dissolving his provincial legislature Duplessis demanded a new mandate for Quebec's "autonomy." That might mean anything or nothing.

What it meant to Duplessis—apart from his own victory—was never clear, probably not even in his own mind. For the moment, clarity was the last thing he wanted.

At least it meant that the Provincial Government assumed the right to veto the war plans of the Federal Government in Quebec and make a travesty of the constitution.

To Lapointe it meant that a third of the nation would declare its neutrality for all practical purposes, isolate itself from reality, undo all the work of Lafontaine, Cartier, Laurier, and of Lapointe himself. In winning a Pyrrhic election Duplessis would ignite the hatred of the Canadian majority and damage his own race for generations. In Lapointe's speech to Parliament, the divided Canadian soul had seemed to fuse in a single substance. Must the fusion dissolve again, must the substance break even before it felt the real shocks of war?

To King, a victory for Duplessis meant the disruption of any national war effort and might mean the disruption of the nation itself in a consuming fury between the two races.

To Britain, as would be clear within eight months, the decision of

261

Quebec to increase or shatter the strength of Canada must mean hardly less than life or death.

To Chubby Power, who would have to manage the politics of this crisis, it meant the most difficult, dangerous, and doubtful election he had ever fought.

In retrospect it may be considered the most important election in modern Canadian history. A nation frantically attempting to prepare for war was required overnight to confront as well the oldest problem of its life and prove to itself and the world whether it was a nation or not.

Lapointe's advice to King was immediate and unequivocal— Duplessis must be defeated by all the power of the Federal Government. The election was chancy, nothing better than a gamble. It might be lost in any case but it must not be lost by default. Everything Lapointe had done in thirty-five years of politics would be put to the hazard, win or lose. On a contest with a small-bore local politician, the French Canadian giant proposed to stake his political life and the future of his people.

Power, a man of deep and sensitive feeling, usually hidden under a mask of raillery, gave the same advice. He knew, for he never deceived himself, the nature of the gamble and the odds against success. "If Duplessis wins," he told King, "the war is over, so far as Quebec is concerned."

King's theory of war leadership, his self-chosen mission as the only statesman who could unite the nation and make possible the victory of the soldiers in the field, thus was challenged at the outset. Because he saw the dangers in English-speaking Canada better than the French Canadians, King hesitated at first to meet Duplessis frontally. He would have preferred conciliation and compromise, a purchase of time while Quebec opinion was educated, if that were possible.

Impossible, said Lapointe and Power. In dissolving his legislature Duplessis had asked his voters to give a no-confidence vote in the Quebec members of the Federal Government for their support of the war. That, said Duplessis, was the central issue of the election. Lapointe and his colleagues replied that if Quebec voted no-confidence in them they would be forced to resign. King insisted privately that he would not accept their resignations under any conditions. Actually, in the event of Duplessis' re-election, King could not have prevented the retirement of all the Quebec Ministers, the wreck of the Government and of national unity before the war was well under way.

Reluctantly, King agreed to fight Duplessis in the open. And so Lapointe, the peasant who had come to Ottawa without a word of

English, went home to tell his people that their destiny lay within the larger Canada which he had discovered for himself. This was one of the noblest acts of statesmanship, of human courage, and of political genius on our Canadian record. No other Canadian could undertake Lapointe's mission in his finest hour.

Cardin's finest hour also had struck. That strange man might be confused in his motives between patriotism and ambition, between his love of his own land and his hatred of English domination. He might hesitate to quarrel with Duplessis. Once the break was made, he threw into the campaign all his magnificent gifts of oratory, energy, and organization. In one respect he was perhaps more effective among his people than Lapointe because, being the most nationalistic of the French Canadian Ministers, he was the least suspect of mere sentimental sympathy with Britain. Later on, his work would be obscured by his part in the final crisis of race. The nation owes his memory a large debt for his gallant part in the perilous struggle of 1939.

Quebec was aloof. Power, on whose shoulders fell the whole job of organizing the campaign, raising the money, and pulling the strings in the constituencies, reported that the fight was going badly. He could not foresee the vote. He could not even raise funds to get the vote out.

At Ottawa, King watched anxiously, for on that vote everything hung. Never knowing or pretending to know the French mind, distrusting the Church, baffled by the power of Duplessis, a mere adventurer as he thought, King wisely refused to intervene. Lapointe and Power were on their own. They seemed to be failing.

Then suddenly, almost overnight, the tide turned.

Lapointe and Power had been met at first with sullen opposition and angry heckling. They had refused to give an inch, to conciliate their enemies, to discuss anything but the war and Quebec's duty and interest in it. Now Quebec began to listen.

It heard from Lapointe a passion of oratory which Laurier had never excelled. It saw a towering black figure whose soul was poured nakedly into his pleading, whose outstretched arms seemed to embrace the province and the nation, whose face was knotted in pain, whose eyes often gushed tears. Soon the audiences in the cities and the little towns were crying with him. He had touched an ultimate stratum of French Canadian feeling which the pinpricks of Duplessis could never penetrate.

Power at last saw that and knew the fight was won.

On election night Adelard Godbout, the Liberal leader, had 69 seats in a legislature of 86. Quebec had declared against "autonomy" and had voted itself into the war. Duplessis had lost and the team of Lapointe, Power, and Cardin had won the great gamble.

Looking at the popular vote—a small Liberal majority of 53 per cent—King knew that only one watershed had been crossed. There might be others. In the election, Lapointe, Power, and Cardin had promised to resign rather than accept overseas conscription. If that issue were ever raised, King concluded, Quebec's present decision would be reversed and all these gains lost. His no-conscription policy, therefore, had been vindicated by a vote which was at once a victory and a warning in the first days of the war. Any other policy would convulse the nation and make the war unmanageable.

So thought Lapointe, Power, Cardin, and the others. They underestimated Quebec. Also, they had overlooked the crisp lawyer, with keen, terrier face, of whom the Canadian people had yet to hear. St. Laurent had watched the struggle in silence, still knew little of politics and politicians and took little interest in them, but he was learning. He would have been surprised to hear that he was to be the legatee of this election and the national crisis temporarily buried in it.

King had little time even to watch events in Quebec. Apart from any long-range planning, the physical business of organizing a nation for war kept the Cabinet in almost continuous session. The easy days at Laurier House had gone and seemed unlikely to return. In the hive of Ottawa, now aswarm, the Queen Bee had retraced the normal life circle and become a worker again.

His first concern was to reorganize the Cabinet for the long pull ahead.

After the outbreak of war he had moved Ian Mackenzie, whom he liked but considered inadequate, out of the Defence Department, where the unhappy Bren-gun contract already had involved the Government in serious trouble and an interminable investigation, to the political profit of a rising Conservative politician, George Drew. The administration of Defence, the second job in the Government, was given to young Norman Rogers, King's chosen heir.

Dunning had resigned in the summer, exasperated to the point of tears by the attrition of that explosive atom, Gardiner, broken in health by overwork, and now out of politics (where he had missed the great prize by a hair's breadth) to begin a second career in business. In his place at the Finance Department King placed Colonel Ralston, the old soldier with the big chin to match the big heart. He had closed his opulent legal practice in the first hours of the war and hurried to Ottawa "to do any job, even if it's only Clarence Howe's messenger boy." With Ralston, King had imported ability, character, and trouble, all of the highest order.

Howe, with a capacity to match his boundless optimism, was to manage all war production and in the course of his duties was soon, half frozen, pulling an oar in a lifeboat on the North Atlantic. Rescued an hour this side of death by exposure, and then living for a week on hardtack and Scotch whisky, he demonstrated in this and many subsequent storms that he was unsinkable.

Power, untried in a major department, took over the Air Force in the following spring and performed one of the largest single tasks of the war.

Angus Macdonald was drafted from the premiership of Nova Scotia a few months later to give Canada a Navy and the Cabinet a philosopher of politics.

Because of his experience in the first war Crerar was appointed to the all-powerful Cabinet War Committee as a kind of watchdog and immediately was dispatched to Europe for a close-up look at the phony war. At the Admiralty he roused Churchill from an afternoon nap and heard from his old friend, over a discreet drink, that the war would be long and hard "and we shall suffer but the Germans will suffer more." What Crerar saw of the politicians in Paris prepared his mind for the news of next May.

Something much deeper and longer-lasting than Cabinet reorganization was now under way in Ottawa. The effective power of the state had long been oozing out of Parliament into the executive. Under the emergency of war this transfer became almost complete. Now power was oozing from the executive into the anonymous ranks of the civil service. Without public notice Canada's first real brain trust was emerging to grow at mushroom speed and to proliferate into every corner of the public domain.

This was necessary and inevitable. The technical side of war, military and economic, was a problem for experts. In the pinch Canada discovered that it already possessed an upper echelon of civil servants as able as any in the world. Without them the mobilization now beginning could never be completed.

At the Bank of Canada the brain of the deceptively austere Governor, Graham Towers, was commonly accounted the most remarkable invention in mechanics since the wheel. With him as deputy was a burly Scot, Donald Gordon, who had started life as a newsboy, would soon manage most of the national economy and move on to the C.N.R. The Government's finances were safe in the hands of Dr. Clifford Clark, a round cherub with a will of cold steel and the soul of a crusader. When the Government imported the quiet, homespun, W. A. Mackintosh as a general economic handy man and such brilliant recruits as Kenneth Taylor, Robert Bryce, John Deutch, and a galaxy of others then unknown, it was technically equipped as no other Canadian government had ever been to manage the economic side of war.

In External Affairs, the control room of the expanding power-house, the science of government held no more competent practitioners than Lester Pearson, who had yet to master his later profession of politics; Hume Wrong, whose mind worked like a flawless and flashing machine; Norman Robertson, an unfailing inventor of solutions for insoluble problems; Arnold Heeney, Escott Reid, and a younger generation of unsuspected talent, now nearing the top.

Howe, temperamentally a lone wolf, ran his own show from the start. The Cabinet seldom knew what he was doing and no one, probably not Howe himself, how he did it. His method, like King's, was to appoint good men and leave them alone; to drive himself sixteen hours a day; and, as he told a friend in the worst days of the war when everything seemed lost, to refuse to consider for a single moment the possibility of defeat.

His corps of industrial managers, controllers, technicians, invisible men, and other birds of swift passage flitted silently through the capital with brief case and frozen look, or roosted in the superior barracks of the Chateau Laurier month after month, year after year, with little pay, heavy personal sacrifice, and no public recognition.

As much as King's constitutional procedures, this extraordinary human engine of administration showed that Canada was managing its own war. In the first war it had been an auxiliary, mainly supplying soldiers and raw materials. Now it was a principal, able to supply almost any product from radar to airplanes. As Howe soon proved, to the surprise of most Canadians, Canada had grown into a major industrial power.

While the wartime administrative machine would be dismantled at the end of the emergency, the permanent civil service would remain and quietly shift the center of gravity in the Canadian system.

In the past, a new minister entered a department generally knowing far less than his officials and, if wise, was glad to accept their guidance. They were always more powerful than the public imagined. Now their power reached a new level. Operating collectively in large affairs, the Cabinet's chief advisers became almost a second Cabinet, at times more potent than the first. A managerial revolution was under way and could never be repealed.

The managers varied in temperament, they often disagreed among themselves and with the Cabinet, but they had in common their ability, their knowledge, their devotion to the public service, and their quiet enjoyment of power, in which they were mainly paid (for few of them got adequate pay in money).

The centralization of the state in the Cabinet, the delegation of its authority to the War Committee, the deluge of orders-in-council which the Cabinet could not begin to read, the teeming regulations which only a few officials understood, and the steady rise of the expert all combined to undermine Parliament, especially when the Opposition had reached its lowest point of impotence. Ideas and policies no longer traveled upward from Parliament but downward from officials to the Cabinet and then to the House of Commons for cursory approval. Parliament in wartime held little more than a watching brief with a right of criticism and the final prerogative of death sentence against the Government, and that it did not intend to use except in a supreme crisis. Such a crisis was five years away.

The elevation of the executive, the emergence of the official, and the decline of Parliament were part of the price democracy must pay for total war. The question which students of government asked themselves then and are still asking is whether the damage to Parliament was temporary or permanent, whether it was accidental or the issue of forces long under way in a changing society and only speeded up by the necessities of war.

It is still too early to answer those questions. Whatever may be said about Parliament, there can be no doubt that in a brain trust of these proportions a new estate of the realm was born. It must be an essential tool of government in the welfare society now in an advanced stage of gestation. Wartime Ottawa, with government in control of everything, was the chart, maybe the embryo, of a new kind of Canadian life.

Since King had been working toward some such end all his life, he watched the shift of power without alarm. It had been implicit in his social philosophy since his early days when he, as a representative of the state, had intervened in labor disputes and later had proposed to make the public, through the state, a third partner in the economy.

He was meticulous in his outward deference to Parliament. He regarded it both as an index of political pressures, his main concern, and as an instrument to reconcile them. He was so well established as head of the state above party division, and in wartime given such broad authority by emergency legislation, that he could largely control Cabinet, brain trust, Parliament, and nation. No Canadian had ever exercised such power since 1867 and no one knew so well how to conceal it.

Professor Lower thinks that King, a child of Parliament, already was growing tired of his parent. Tired he may have been but he was always terrified of Parliament because he understood its latent instinct of rebellion and its ultimate death sentence, which was to come uncomfortably close to him later on. In moments of crisis the child always returned in haste to the parent. At the first breath of trouble his instant impulse was to summon Parliament and contrive to appear not as its controller but its agent.

"In reality," says Lower, "few prime ministers have left less to Parliament." None had stood in greater awe of it.

While a new philosophy of government had taken root in the depression and grew steadily during the war, King's technique of management was unchanged. He refused to interfere in departmental matters until they touched on high policy. He treated his colleagues with a respect he did not always feel. He was courteous to the experts and never overawed by them because he regarded himself as the best-trained expert of the lot.

He was the brain trust's chief creator. Unlike some Cabinet Ministers, he was never its stooge. He allowed the innumerable interdepartmental committees to study every aspect of a problem, he watched the trust beat its brain out against some stone wall, and then he took its recommendations, weighed them against the facts of practical politics, decided how much of them the nation would accept, and usually devised a compromise seldom satisfactory to anybody but tolerated by all.

He refused to excite himself over anything of importance. While he continued to fume over trifles, the big problems were never allowed to interrupt his long night's sleep, his leisurely breakfast, his daily consultation with the Bible, his late arrival at the office, his methodical hours of work. He dared not worry lest it imperil his physical health, a vital weapon of war. Others would exhaust themselves and collapse, as many did. The nation could not afford to waste a fragment of his energy.

It was husbanded as never before in an office smoothly managed by Walter Turnbull. King had borrowed Pickersgill from External Affairs for minor duties. Soon he was leaning heavily on an assistant with the rare qualities of independent mind and no fear of expressing it to anybody. In everyone else, King liked subservience. From his brilliant factotum he received, and liked, a candor often brutal. The prairie professor who had seen the Liberal Party dying in the 'thirties now watched its reincarnation.

King's first direct intervention into the Allied strategy occurred on September 26, just as the Quebec crisis was appearing. On that day he received a cable from Chamberlain proposing that the Commonwealth train its air crews in Canada. The training scheme, Chamberlain believed, would probably prove the largest factor in the final victory.

This project revived some bitter memories. In 1938, Britain had asked for the right to train pilots in Canada, under its own control, and King had countered with an offer to train British pilots in Canadian establishments. All military establishments in Canada, he said, must be under Canadian control. The Conservative Party had made much of his refusal and Bennett had denounced it in a passionate philippic as disloyalty to "the old partner." King was ready in 1939 to undertake the largest air-training scheme ever attempted anywhere. As before, he would not share its control with any other nation.

When Chamberlain's delegates reached Ottawa, they had different ideas. Canadian boys, as well as those from Britain, were to be trained for the Royal Air Force and in it their identity would be submerged.

King knew nothing of air power, he had never been in an airplane, but he knew all about the power of Canadian nationalism and his own. From the start of the negotiations he insisted that every Canadian airman must wear an identifying mark and that, as soon as possible, all Canadians must be mustered in distinct units of their own.

The British threw up their hands. They appreciated his sentiments, but King's plan, for technical reasons, was impossible. Impossible or not, said King, it must be followed or there would be no plan at all.

For weeks he let the technicians wrangle until the whole project was about to collapse and with it, perhaps, the chance of winning the war. At the last minute, in fact at one o'clock in the morning—Governor General Tweedsmuir having been roused from his bed to plead with London—the British agreed, as King expected.

Canada had thereby accepted one of the chief responsibilities of the war, Ralston had accepted costs apparently beyond his ability to pay, Power was soon to tackle an impossible job, and King had assumed, in practical affairs as in constitutional trappings, the position of an independent and major belligerent.

Canada's part in the military struggle cannot be told here. That is another story certain to fill a library of books. It began with the mobilization of a reserve force on September 1 and the formation of the first division and its dispatch to Britain at the end of the year. The theory of the previous spring, that the day of overseas expeditions was over, did not survive four months of war.

General A. G. L. McNaughton was given command of the first

division and the others added to it later. He had been a brilliant artilleryman of the first war, a scientist in peacetime, a patriot and something of a dreamer. He had yet to become a politician and a human sacrifice to King's purposes.

The work of the autumn was satisfactory to King as far as it went, it might satisfy the soldiers and the industrialists, but he knew it lacked a solid foundation in politics. His present Government was four years old, an election was overdue, and while Quebec had been won by Lapointe and Power, trouble was brewing on the other flank. The Government could not succeed in the management of the war if it did not re-establish itself, beyond possible challenge. It must extinguish the latest cabals and discontents by securing a new mandate from the people. Either it or some other government must fight the war with the whole nation behind it.

What possible excuse could be given to the public for an early election? Foolishly, as he now thought, King had promised Manion not to dissolve Parliament before it met again. He would not break the promise. In any case, how in common decency could a new mandate be asked when the Government had a large parliamentary majority? And could the Government be sure of winning? As usual, King's enemies supplied the desired answer.

30

The Old Actor

THE WORLD DROWSED THROUGH THE AUTUMN AND WINTER IN THE stupefaction of the phony war. Hitler paused on the borders of France. Russia bought him off on the east with the Danegeld of strategic materials. The Chamberlain Government of Britain rearmed at leisure while in the Admiralty an impatient man awaited his chance. Sumner Welles dragged himself through the capitals of Europe as Roosevelt's agent, in futile attempt to suppress the approaching eruption. Colonel Charles Lindbergh, an aviator turned statesman, informed Canadians that they could not be permitted to drag his country into foreign broils "simply because they prefer the Crown of England to American independence." In Ottawa, King panted in a fog of suspense and chafed for an election which alone could end it.

The eccentric onion-grower of Ontario had not been touched by the general paralysis. Hepburn's restless energy was now devoted to the high purpose of destroying King. In this feud King's silence only increased the fury of his enemy. Expecting King's power to collapse under the first shocks of war, Hepburn had been somewhat chastened by the Liberal victory in Quebec. Not for long.

On January 17, he was observed from the galleries of the Ontario Legislature hastily scribbling on a scrap of paper. He was writing, as he thought, the political death warrant of King. It was his own.

Leaping to his feet, Hepburn read his motion. It regretted that King's Government "has made so little effort to prosecute Canada's duty in the war in the vigorous manner the people of Canada desire to see."

The Conservatives under Drew were quick to see a good thing. They rallied to the support of a Liberal Premier who was undertaking to wreck his Party in Ottawa. The motion of condemnation was passed with a whoop.

King said nothing. In Richmond, Virginia, his sagacious organizer, Norman Lambert, paused on a holiday trip, read the news from Toronto in a brief newspaper paragraph, remarked to his companion, "There's your election," and hurried to Ottawa.

The immediate purpose of the Ontario revolution was to unhorse King. What Hepburn saw beyond that was not revealed to his supporters. Perhaps he did not know. King's fall would probably mean at least a national government of some sort with Hepburn its actual master, visible or invisible.

In King's judgment it would also mean the final schism of the two races and national chaos.

Hepburn might seem to be manipulating merely an excited provincial legislature. Whether he knew it or not—and beyond the onion patch and cracker barrel of local politics he knew little—the verdict of condemnation on the national Government struck deep into the stuff of Canada. It appealed to that large minority of Canadians who still felt instinctively the imperialism, the colonialism, and the passionate loyalty to Britain which had built Upper Canada in the beginning. By strange convolution, as King thought, the spirit of the Family Compact had leaped a century and installed itself in the onion patch, the cracker barrel, and a lavish Toronto hotel suite. In Hepburn the Simcoes, Bond Heads, Maitlands, and Colbornes had bred a curious posterity. Like his spiritual ancestors, Hepburn, in King's judgment, could split Canada.

By striking now, King might not only crush Hepburn but forestall the split. He had suppressed Duplessis in French Canada. If he could suppress Hepburn in Ontario he would give national politics a new balance, his Government another sure tenure of office, free of distraction, to fight the war. Against the repetition of the old contest with the rulers of Toronto, the Rebel's grandson sharpened his pike.

When Lambert reached Ottawa he alone was told King's plan, but not its timing. It was cold-blooded, diabolical, and risky. Lambert prepared accordingly.

Power, who understood the two Canadian races and saw the present issue as it affected each, advised King on January 21 to dissolve the Parliament, called to meet four days later. Some of his colleagues took the respectable view that, having promised Manion another parliamentary session before dissolution, King must conduct a session even if it was brief. King's mind already was made up and he let the Cabinet argue.

When the Liberal members reached Ottawa, they seemed opposed to an early election. King reminded his caucus bluntly that he was trying to assure it four years instead of four months of power. At noon on the day of the formal opening, he told the Cabinet what he intended to do before nightfall—a make-or-break strategy of sudden assault and this time no pause at the barricades of York.

The Cabinet's secret had been well kept for once. The Press Gallery, refused the usual advance copy of the Speech from the Throne, suspected nothing. When King bounced into the House at twenty-two minutes past three he smiled wanly at his followers' applause. His anger was masked by a passive face, his pike well hidden. Even when the Speech from the Throne announced "an immediate appeal to the country," it was assumed that the election would be delayed for some weeks until Parliament had finished its urgent business.

King maintained that impression by conducting a solemn masquerade. One by one he escorted four newly-elected Liberal members, including Ralston, to the Speaker's dais and formally introduced them to Parliament. Manion was permitted to do the same for his latest supporter. Lastly, a bewildered and venerable minister of the Gospel from Saskatoon beamed on the chamber in Christian charity a few minutes before the flood carried him forever into limbo.

Like an old trouper, a trained character man, King answered all his cues without a slip. He shook the hands of the new members and wished them a happy life in Parliament as he prepared to strike them down. He was playing it straight, knowing it was pure farce.

When he rose in his place, his fingers fiddling nervously with the black ribbon of his eyeglasses, a lock of hair sprawling over his forehead, he appeared, as he always did in his deadlier moments, like a rather harassed professor addressing a class of freshmen.

As usual, he began with a recitation of documents and old speeches, recalled his promise to Manion that Parliament would meet again before another election, and then mentioned, quite casually, that the Legislature of Ontario had passed a certain resolution. He fumbled in his red brief case, produced a paper, and read the resolution in full.

Now his mild tone changed, the voice turned harsh, the actor switched in the middle of a sentence from farce to melodrama with overtones of tragedy. These Manion at last perceived and his face flushed scarlet at the discovery. He started to scrawl notes feverishly on his desk. The point of the pike was visible and aimed plainly in his direction. Like larger Opposition leaders before him, Manion knew he was already half impaled.

The final thrust was quick and brutal. King said he could not fight a war and the Hepburn-Drew campaign of vilification at the same time. The Government's capacity had been challenged by the largest

T

Legislature in the country, the hustings rang with the cry of "King must go," and he proposed to let the people decide between him and his slanderers.

The pike aimed at Manion was about to strike down Parliament itself. The whole House gasped. The Conservative members faced an election for which they were totally unprepared. The Liberals, who had come to Ottawa expecting a session and a full indemnity, looked at one another with a wild surmise, realizing that they must go home, unpaid, and convince a doubtful electorate. With fists raised, starched white cuffs flashing through the air, the Prime Minister was now waving openly his old and tried weapon, the pike of dissolution. Then, as unexpectedly as he had begun, he moved an adjournment and sat down.

Manion was on his feet, purple with anger and bewilderment. King remarked mildly that his motion to adjourn was not debatable. This was too brutal altogether. After a moment's pause, King added that, of course, if the House wished to hear him, Manion could speak.

Poor Manion had come with a speech carefully contrived for quite another situation. He threw it aside and, with the sound of exploding firecrackers which always marked his passage through politics, denounced King for insulting Parliament, gagging the people's representatives, sneering at the traditions of the British Empire, playing a low trick on the constitution, and proving himself "unfit to govern."

That was precisely what King had wanted. The impalement was complete. For if Manion thought the Government unfit to govern, then, said King, it was high time that the people decided the question. The Hepburn-Drew resolution had been a weak peg on which to hang an election. Manion had provided the perfect excuse by challenging the Government's right to office.

Unaware that he had played straight into his enemy's hands, Manion fairly danced with anger and predicted the Government's ruin at the polls, while King sipped a glass of water and looked thoughtfully at the ceiling.

Now Woodsworth, whom King respected but no longer feared, jumped up to protest the slaughter of Parliament, the Government's virtual conscription of the unemployed, the decline of free speech, the appearance of a dictatorship, and the silent fear gripping the country.

King was not shaken. He had memorized the closing lines of his tour de farce and recited them with horrendous denouement—in the light of this afternoon's discussion he would meet his colleagues immediately and decide what "is best to do with respect to further proceedings of this Parliament."

The members went to dinner upstairs, not knowing whether they were still members or not. By seven o'clock they were not. As he had intended from the beginning, King had gone to Rideau Hall and advised the Governor-General to dissolve Parliament on the instant. The Governor, doubtless with wry memories of Byng, duly signed the document. In 1926 King had denounced Meighen for just such a dissolution without ceremony or warning. Now King had done the same thing precisely. His ends must excuse his means. Unlike Meighen, he had a war to fight and needed the whole nation behind him.

Strangely enough, King was not sure at first of winning the election. The country was restive, dissatisfied with the progress of the war, ignorant of the blow to fall within three months. Almost half of Quebec had voted for Duplessis. The Hepburn-Drew axis might well control Ontario.

Still stranger, Manion thought he could win if he compromised enough to penetrate Quebec, where he expected twenty seats. But when he opened his campaign in Brockville no one could doubt the outcome.

He drove through a snowstorm that night like good old Doc Manion, the family physician, coming to attend the latest accouchement, he began by earnestly denying that he abused his wife, he announced that he was as much opposed to conscription as King, and he proposed to establish a National Government and win the war.

Who could dislike the handsome family doctor? Here was a reliable practitioner, who could deliver a baby. Few people who heard him in Brockville and elsewhere could imagine him delivering a victory at home or abroad. The baby was dead at birth.

Manion appealed to Quebec on King's no-conscription policy but it was Lapointe whom Quebec trusted. Already, Manion had antagonized the conscriptionists of his own Party, now only awaiting the chance to fight King's policy openly, and many other Conservatives who resented the disappearance of their ancient name and Manion's new disguise as the leader of a National Government Party. He was thrown back on the claim that, with little experience in government, he could manage the war better than King, and on the charge that King, its professed child, had murdered Parliament in callous patricide.

This last was a fair argument, disturbing to many thoughtful Canadians, among them Lower, who wrote that King had provided "a road to any future Prime Minister looking for an excuse to dispense with Parliament." Manion was not the man to argue such an issue. King, in opposite circumstances, would have used it (as he had done in 1926) with devastating effect. In any case, the nation was not much interested in Parliament, the instrument of democracy. It was watching democracy in its death throes across the plains of Europe.

In the election campaign, King took a high line, refused to wrangle with Manion, warned the people that the next Government would have the power of life and death over the nation's future, predicted staggering shocks just ahead, asserted that they could be met only by a unified people, and asked them who was best equipped by experience and proved strength to assure that unity.

He did not need to extend himself. The firecracker soon turned into a damp squib. The National Government Party was obviously as phony as the war. Everybody liked and admired Manion as a man and a patriot. Long before the polls closed, the nation showed that it could never trust him as its leader.

So the vote proved. On the night of March 26, King had 178 seats, seven more than in the 1935 election, the largest majority since Confederation, a solid Quebec (58 seats), the mandate he had asked, and, for the time being anyway, the unity he required.

Meighen, Bennett, Manion, Duplessis, Hepburn—the string of scalps at King's belt was still growing and still not complete.

Something more fundamental than Meighen's ill luck, Bennett's depression, and Manion's stillborn baby had happened to the Conservative Party. The elevation of such a gallant but incompetent leader as Manion represented the Party's decline. Its ancient womb no longer was bearing great men. Its sterility followed perforce the abandonment of Conservative principles. After Bennett's New Deal it could no longer call itself a Conservative Party. It had tried to outbid the Liberals on the Left and it had failed. It dared not move to its own historic position on the Right. In the middle, King's juggernaut left it no room. It had decided to take the cash and let the credit go. With the election of 1940 it had exhausted its credit.

No one knew that better than Meighen. The lonely eagle, from the high perch of the Senate, was getting ready for his last flight to save Conservatism from bankruptcy.

All these were trivial matters in the spring of 1940. They would be little noted nor long remembered in the descent of the avalanche.

31

The Black Springtime

IN APRIL, KING WENT TO VIRGINIA FOR A REST. IT WAS A BUSMAN'S
holiday. He stopped at Washington for a long talk with Roosevelt and together they made large plans to be communicated to
the public four months later. Neither knew then how essential these
plans would prove, for neither knew that the world's foundations
were about to crack.

More important than specific preparations was the growing intimacy of the President and the Prime Minister. While Canada had
long regarded itself as the interpreter between the United States and
Britain or, as Churchill said, "the linchpin of world peace," King
undertook to play that role as no predecessor had played it. He liked
and admired Roosevelt as a person. Knowing that Roosevelt was the
most decisive figure in the free world, and for Canada an essential
friend, King deliberately cultivated him as a statesman. With
Churchill, for similar reasons, he did the same.

A bizarre and ill-assorted triumvirate was beginning to take shape.
Publicly it was King's misfortune, by the accident of war, to be
matched on either side by a spectacular personage who outshone
him. The third partner must remain silent. His position was fixed by
the dimensions of his nation. But he was not a minor partner. He had
a far larger effect on the other two than the public ever guessed.

King preferred to leave his people ignorant of his influence in
Washington and London. He knew his public place and kept it,
content to remain a shadow behind the growing bulk of the two
colossi. Few men outside his own country had a more profound
effect on Churchill. No foreigner, except Churchill himself, had an
equal effect on Roosevelt.

In King, Roosevelt found an unprejudiced consultant to whom he
could talk freely as he could not talk to most of his colleagues. The
Canadian understood the United States and brought a fresh outside

view to world problems. He was an older and more experienced politician and, of course, he had a way with him. Presently Roosevelt was telling King things he dared not tell his Cabinet. From the spring of 1940 onward, everything of the least concern to Canada that Roosevelt knew was passed on automatically to King by conversation, letter, or telephone. King kept Roosevelt's confidences. They were not shared with the Canadian Cabinet but they were invaluable in forming King's own decisions. He was sitting in, even though not physically present, on the largest Allied decisions of the war.

On returning from one of his Washington visits, King remarked to a friend that of course Roosevelt would like to annex Canada. "I would, too, if I were President," he added with a chuckle. Such notions, detected at the back of Roosevelt's mind, did not disturb King in the least. They were not practical politics and could be ignored.

With Churchill, King's experience was quite different. He had begun by underestimating Churchill as he may have overestimated Roosevelt. The young Churchill, fresh from his South African adventure, had come on a lecture tour to Canada, and King, who had matured earlier, considered him an arrogant pup. When King reached England in 1908 he was told that he must meet Churchill, the glamour boy of British politics. "Anybody but Churchill," said King. "I've met him and he's the last man in England I want to see." However, when he received a handwritten luncheon invitation from Churchill, he could not refuse it.

Churchill greeted him with a boyish grin. "We met in Canada four years ago, I think. I did make a frightful ass of myself on that trip, didn't I?"

King gave his host a hard look. "Well, Mr. Churchill," he said, "there were many Canadians who thought so. I was one of them."

From then on they were good friends. It would be thirty years, however, before they knew each other or tried the depths of their friendship. Churchill and England began to draw heavily on it in the black springtime of 1940.

The dikes of Europe broke on May 10. In London, Churchill improvised the victorious defeat of Dunkirk and pleaded with the United States and Canada for aid. In Paris, Reynaud beseeched Roosevelt for "clouds of airplanes." In a sweltering Washington, Roosevelt, his shirt limp with sweat, sat helplessly in his chair with a gray face of agony, the prisoner of the Neutrality Act and his people's blindness. In Ottawa, watching the flood rise daily, King observed with alarm the sudden friction between the two other partners.

How King intervened between them, cooling Churchill, who was pressing Roosevelt too hard, encouraging Roosevelt to do his utmost for Churchill, perhaps will never be known in detail. Some of the work of the honest broker between old world and new is on the record. To his last days King treasured nothing more than Churchill's cables humbly testifying to that work which, though the most secret, may well have been the most important King ever did. Until now, as he confessed, Churchill had not grasped his friend's capacities. Britain would need them before autumn.

The May days of disaster put King's private system of life to the test. He had resolved not to sap his strength by worry, to do his best and sleep well every night. Probably he was one of the few chiefs of state who slept serenely through the fall of France. London and Washington were in chaos and in Ottawa wild men of every sort screamed at King's keyhole. They never got beyond it.

If King felt the full impact of the blow, if he understood what had happened and what now seemed likely to happen, he refused to admit it, even to himself. Whatever else may be said about it, this was an extraordinary feat of self-control or self-delusion. The nerves under the flabby flesh were of the finest steel.

Other men, with weaker nerves or warmer hearts, could not control or delude themselves so conveniently. Lapointe, hearing the call of his French blood, had grown suddenly old and ill. To him the fall of France was as a wound to his own body. Like most French Canadians, he had grown up with little feeling for the France which had abandoned his race in 1759, but frequently visiting the old land and making friends there, he had come to feel its ancient glory as a personal possession. Its ruin overwhelmed him.

When his friends, Pétain and Weygand, wrote him, imploring the aid of Canada, Lapointe cried like a child. He was tortured with self-accusation for his part in the Ethiopian fiasco, the beginning of all the present miseries. Over and over again he read the record of those times, seeking some justification for himself and realizing, too late, where the policy of isolation had led.

For Lapointe the ledger was balanced, and more than balanced, by his victory over isolation in Quebec and in himself. There were others who shared his pangs of conscience and some who now believed, on the day of Pétain's surrender, that all was lost.

The thing was too big for talk. In Ottawa it was a time of ceaseless talk about the business of the day, in which despairing men could find some relief, but of silence on the single question felt too deeply for utterance.

Could Britain hold? Must Canada join the United States in a

military fortress permanently under siege? Were Canada's three centuries of life now closing? Was this the end of freedom in the world?

Such thoughts, seldom spoken in Ottawa, were written on many
faces. Not on King's. His colleagues noted a certain pallor, a wish to
be alone, but his inward faith or his ego, or a combination of both,
was sufficient to still all regrets for his past, all doubts about the
future, and to leave him free for the work at hand.

It was the greatest work that Canada had performed in its three
hundred years and its proportions have not been grasped even today.

Until Hitler marched to the Channel, Britain had planned a well-
ordered and leisurely war. Canada was to supply raw materials, airmen, and naval patrols. Britain's factories would equip all its own
forces and Canada's as well. Now, under the blitz and the threat of
invasion, Britain saw all its plans in ruins. It was for Canada to equip
its own forces, to supply equipment to Britain, and to carry the
gigantic air-training program alone.

For Canada the war began in the spring of 1940 when all previous
planning was scrapped overnight. It suddenly dawned upon the
Government in Ottawa that the future of mankind might hang, for
the time being, on eleven and a half million Canadians. As was their
nature, they took it calmly. And in Ottawa they found a Government
calmly prepared to produce a miracle.

It fell into three categories.

For eight months Howe had fretted under the repression of his
war industries. Britain did not want them expanded, because its own
industries could do the job alone. Howe finally told Parliament the
shocking truth that British manufacturers had refused him blueprints, designs, and secret processes lest they lose their profitable
business. With the arrival of disaster and then of Churchill, all that
was changed. Howe was expected to build in a few months what,
under the best of conditions, should take years. By his own miracle,
Howe, who thought nothing of such things, made himself one of
the nation's immortals.

In Ilsley, King had found Howe's equal in the management of
finance, the counterpart of the economic revolution now beginning.
An air accident had put Ilsley where he belonged. On June 10, young
Rogers, like one of his soldiers, was killed in the line of duty. Ralston
took his place in the Defence Department and became an immortal
in his turn. Ilsley was promoted from National Revenue to Finance
and undertook unthinkable war costs with such taxes as no Canadian
had ever dreamed of. Presently, half of every earned dollar in
Canada was going to government and even that paid only half the
cost of war.

The third problem, manpower, was the key to everything, in the armed services, in industry, in finance and in politics. That problem had been mishandled. While General McNaughton had recommended against too big an army at the expense of industrial production, public pressure had forced the Government to build up armed forces that it could afford before Dunkirk but, as it thought then, it could not afford when it was called upon to expand industry and, on its own resources, to carry the whole air-training plan. The various items of the program, taken over piecemeal, apparently added up to a total beyond the nation's capacity.

The collapse of an orderly plan, as outlined in the previous autumn, was the price of Europe's collapse in the spring. The commitments had been given by Canada and somehow must be made good.

The immediate concern was the air-training scheme. Britain no longer could supply even the essential training planes, needed now to fight in the blitz. A cargo of them bound for Canada was turned back to Britain in mid-Atlantic. On Power and Howe fell the responsibility of carrying through a project large enough to tax Britain and Canada together, of completing in six months airfields and other installations supposed to take two years. Canada was on its own. Lacking planes, fields, and everything else, Canada did not reduce the training plan. Instead, it was vastly expanded.

Even the construction of the C.P.R. did not approach the daring of Canada's undertaking in the summer of 1940. It was less an act of mobilization than an act of faith by a handful of people prepared for it by their lonely conquest of half a continent. And it was one of the chief ingredients of the Allies' victory.

The nation's resources already seemed spread far too thin. Those resources in materials, skills, productive power, and, above all, in spirit, had been grossly underestimated. Now the Government began to reassess them.

At midsummer Parliament passed the National Resources Mobilization Act to conscript men for home defense. They were to be trained for one month only but this was extended in the following spring to four months and then to the duration of the war.

If the war were to last long, the end of this process could be foreseen. By canceling one clause in the new law, Parliament could apply conscription to overseas service. If King did not admit it, even to himself, the practical politicians of Quebec knew that once the law was passed the conscription crisis would follow. It was only a question of time.

Quebec accepted conscription in Canada with no public objection, except on the part of that genial gargoyle, Mayor Camillien Houde, of Montreal, who urged his people not to accept the national registration now under way. Lapointe clapped his fellow French Canadian into an internment camp. If conscription was limited to Canada it was to be enforced to the letter.

All this passed off much more smoothly than anyone could have expected a year before. In the summer of 1940, the shock of Europe's fall and the siege of Britain had made Canadians eager to do anything the Government asked and angry because they were not asked to do more. The Government was not ahead of the public, but behind it. The real heroes in this period of unbroken disaster were not the men in power at Ottawa but the ordinary folk of Canada.

Ralston's brutal taxes were accepted without a· whimper. When Ilsley brought down the next budget, R. B. Hanson, successor to Manion as Opposition leader, threw up his hands in horror and looked, in his squirming rotundity, like a stranded whale. Hanson, the true-blue Tory of New Brunswick, was a patriot before he was a politician. He and the nation soon thought the Government was not doing or spending enough.

Ilsley knew, as Hanson and the nation did not, that the Government was planning to do far more than its financial resources could possibly permit. The North Atlantic triangle of trade, Canada's ancient economic foundation, was broken beyond repair. Canada could not earn dollars in Britain, yet needed more dollars than ever to pay for its American imports. Despite the superb management of the Foreign Exchange Control Board, Canada was rushing into a dollar crisis. If it was not solved, it would wreck the economy and the whole war program. There was no chart for such waters. King was steering blind. Without the help of his friend in Washington, shipwreck was certain before long.

On Friday afternoon, August 16, the telephone rang at Kingsmere and King answered it himself. Washington was on the wire.

"What are you doing this week end?" Roosevelt asked.

"I'm at your disposal," said King.

Roosevelt suggested that they meet next day at Ogdensburg, New York.

Ogdensburg on the St. Lawrence was a happy choice for a meeting between two neighbors who were about to become allies. In the War of 1812 the Canadians had sacked Ogdensburg and the Americans retaliated by burning Elizabethtown. The two men sitting in the President's railway car finally expunged that dismal record, consummated their discussions of the last two years, and announced that their countries had entered into a permanent agreement of joint defense.

In times like these, history was made fast. Without a word in Congress, with only a brief conversation on a railway siding, the United States had signed its first military alliance with a nation of the Commonwealth. Without a word in Parliament, Canada had bound itself to stand with its neighbor in the defense of North America.

The Ogdensburg agreement was hurriedly scribbled by Roosevelt on the back of an envelope. Joint defense had been so long accepted between the two friends that they required only a few minutes to frame it in a binding contract.

The secret purpose of their meeting, which lasted from dinnertime until two in the morning, reached far beyond America. Roosevelt was proposing to rescue Britain, so far as that lay in his power, with a gift of fifty destroyers. Under the American Constitution and the Neutrality Act it was a tricky business, even for Roosevelt. He could manage the Constitution and the Congress, but he could not manage Churchill. That was why he had called in King.

In exchange for the destroyers, the United States must have American bases on British territory in Newfoundland and the West Indies. It was for the honest Canadian broker to make sure that the British accepted the deal.

King hurried back to Ottawa to explain to his friend in London that Roosevelt could not give away the destroyers without the *quid pro quo* of the bases. These the British were not eager to grant.

In smoothing the way for the deal, King probably exercised a greater influence on world events than any Canadian Prime Minister before him. For in his mind, and doubtless in Roosevelt's, the United States had by-passed the Neutrality Act, had made a fiction of neutrality, had committed itself to the survival of Britain. Its decisive intervention had begun in a St. Lawrence town where Britain and the United States had once waged an absurd war.

Speaking in Parliament of the joint defense agreement, King said that "Canada, in liaison between the British Commonwealth and the United States, is fulfilling a manifest destiny." In this friendly theft of Manifest Destiny from the Americans, who had used it in a directly opposite sense, King did not tell Parliament all he had done at Ogdensburg, though he soon produced the honest broker's commission in the form of six American destroyers for Canada.

The secrecy of the deal in its early stages and the delicate political ramifications in Washington forced King to silence when his enemies completely misconstrued his work.

Hanson, with the best of intentions, attacked the Ogdensburg

defense agreement as mere window-dressing, a stunt to re-elect
Roosevelt, a threat to the British connection in Canada. King, he
said, was always turning away from Britain and toward the United
States.

The canard of King's Americanism, his disloyalty to Britain, was
worn out by now, yet Hanson still believed it. The dear old patriot,
the stranded whale, could not see that in the defense agreement the
United States had not drawn Canada further into its orbit; Canada
had been drawing the United States toward the Commonwealth.
And by the destroyer deal (King's participation being still secret)
the United States was being drawn irresistibly into the European
war.

Hanson could be forgiven for misunderstanding. To men like him,
King remained at bottom an isolationist, a pro-American, an anticonscriptionist, a lukewarm friend of Britain. In August of 1940,
when Britain seemed to be sinking under the blitz, King's actions at
Ogdensburg appeared to be a retreat into America and into defeat-
ism, not an advance into Europe and victory.

It was doubtless true that, while bringing Roosevelt and Churchill
together, King regarded the defense agreement as a final insurance
policy if Britain went under. As the Prime Minister of Canada he
would have been mad and treasonable to refuse it under the conditions of that summer.

Meighen, knowing more than Hanson and having ample time to
think the matter over, was denouncing Ogdensburg as late as November. As usual, his genius for the perfect phrase betrayed him. He
called Ogdensburg "Twilight twitterings!" and condemned the defense agreement as a worthless side-issue, distracting Canada from
its real task in Britain and from its only real defense, the British
Navy.

The aberration of the Hamilton Speech now forgotten, Meighen
was again "ready, aye, ready" to do his duty. It involved the destruction of King, as Meighen thought, eighteen months hence.

Happily for Canada, for the United States, and especially for
Britain, King and not Meighen had been at Ogdensburg that August
day. Hanson at least had served his purpose. By expressing a real
body of alarm in Canada he had compelled the Government to explain the positive results of Ogdensburg, which to many had seemed
at first to be purely negative. Such critics were reassured by Churchill's cable thanking King for "promoting a harmony of sentiment
throughout the New World. . . . This deep understanding will be
a dominant factor in the rescue of Europe from a relapse into the
Dark Ages."

Meighen remained unconvinced by Churchill and continued to believe that King was betraying Canada and Britain. Like Cato's, his chant was unchanged. King must be destroyed.

Ogdensburg had dealt with military problems. It had not touched the economic problem undermining Canada's contribution to the war. Ilsley found himself rushing toward a dollar crisis and national bankruptcy.

Roosevelt and Churchill were pondering the ideals of the Atlantic Charter, to be framed at sea in the summer of 1941. The senior partners of London and Washington could not affront their other friends by publicly favoring a Canadian, so King would not be invited to the Atlantic meeting. Anonymity was part of the price he must pay for his role of interpreter and conciliator, even if the new Charter was to be a brief statement of his own ideals.

All this he well understood. What concerned him was the immediate case of Canada's dollar shortage. Would the United States make good the brave words soon to be written into the Charter? Would the military aggreement of Ogdensburg extend to economic co-operation? By the end of 1940, that was King's main anxiety and so far Roosevelt had not grasped it.

Meanwhile, as the daylight Battle of Britain dragged into the winter of the night blitz, as Britain held under fire, as Hitler abandoned his thought of crossing the Channel and began to turn eastward to devour his ally, King ignored Meighen, and found time to deal with his other old enemy, Bennett.

Now idle in the House of Lords, Bennett's large and restless energies sought release in some war job. He appealed to Churchill, who asked King to suggest some useful employment. With quiet glee, King replied that Bennett was now a British resident and Churchill's problem. King never forgot and seldom forgave.

32

A Grand Sunday in April

S INCE IT BROUGHT RUSSIA AND THE UNITED STATES INTO THE WAR,
the year 1941 may be considered the crossroads of our times.
For King it was a comparatively easy year until its last month,
when it ended in private terror.

Throughout the world at large, things were going badly. In
Ottawa, however, the Government seemed to be on top of its immediate problems, except for the dollar shortage. Howe's industrial
machine was getting into full production. There was no scarcity of
manpower for the armed services and, with the army locked in
Britain, few casualties. Power's air-training scheme had miraculously
crossed its hump. The Canadian Navy bore its full share in the Battle
of the Atlantic.

King used this deceptive lull to deal with the findings of the
Rowell-Sirois Commission which, after three years of work, had
produced possibly the most significant Canadian state document
since the Durham Report.

Briefly, it proposed that the Federal Government take over the
provincial debts; that it make flexible grants to provinces on a basis
of need in order to establish a minimum level of public services
everyhere; that provincial borrowings be governed by a central
authority; and that the provinces surrender the whole field of corporation and personal income taxes and succession duties to the Federal
Government.

This, of course, would mean an organic overhaul of the Canadian
federal system with a large measure of centralization, so far as finance
was concerned, in Ottawa. The Federal Government then would
have the means, as it hoped, to preserve the national economy from
the fluctuations of inflation and depression. The Commission's plan—
accompanied by the largest survey of the Canadian economy ever

made—was designed to bolster the weak provinces and it naturally antagonized the strong.

When King called a conference of the provincial governments he was confronted by an interesting trio of objectors.

Hepburn refused to surrender Ontario's preferred position in Confederation and, smarting from his defeat a year earlier, eagerly seized the opportunity to harpoon the Federal Government.

He was joined by Thomas Dufferin Pattullo, of British Columbia, a loyal Liberal, but a provincialist who would never give up his taxing powers, and William Aberhart, of Alberta, who never understood his doctrine of Social Credit, but insisted on retaining his right to enforce it.

These three would not agree even to discuss the Commission's plan because, in their view, it must destroy provincial sovereignty. The weaker provinces, unable to finance themselves adequately and eager for federal grants, generally embraced the report. Under Godbout, Quebec, the fourth "have" province, was ready to discuss a settlement but its final agreement was doubtful.

The stone-wall objection of three provinces made a settlement clearly impossible. King retired to consult his colleagues and returned a few minutes later to dissolve the conference. The problem could not be left there. Somehow, for the war period at least, the Federal Government must have control of the nation's chief revenue sources. It managed to secure them by *ad hoc* arrangements which, after repeated changes and without the postwar participation of Ontario and Quebec, have continued to this day. All this fell far short of the Commission's well-balanced plan but it has produced a transfer of wealth from the rich provinces to the poor and assured a minimum standard of government, as the Commission desired.

In the depths of war, few people paused to note that the federal system had been changed organically and doubtless permanently. King never reminded the public of that fact. He avoided clear targets for his enemies to shoot at, labels that might prove embarrassing, and fixed formulas likely to restrict his elbow room.

Lately he had been pondering the postwar society. In March he welcomed Wendell Willkie to Toronto and announced his own long thoughts on the future. If, he said, the new world order "is not already on its way before the war is over we may look for it in vain."

He had never spoken truer words. The question raised in the spring of 1941 was to be answered by the spring of 1945. The answer, as he read it, was in the negative.

By April, Canada could endure the dollar hemorrhage no longer. Experts of the Finance Department had vainly tried to secure some form of assistance from their opposite numbers in Washington. Within the American law there appeared to be no way of saving the northern defense partner from a foreign-exchange disaster bound to impair, perhaps fatally, its ability to fight overseas or defend itself and North America.

King listened impatiently to the experts who had returned empty-handed from Washington. He was an economist himself, as he often reminded his advisers, and he saw, as they did not, that this was essentially a political problem, to be solved by politicians.

It was solved in half an hour by the two foremost politicians of America.

At Hyde Park, King did not attempt to explain the economics of the Canadian crisis to Roosevelt. As they drove about the estate in his queer little hand-manipulated car, the President admitted that he could never get his mind around the intricacies of foreign exchange.

King therefore told his old friend simply that Canada was about to go broke unless it could earn more American dollars. The United States could postpone the debacle by forcing Canada to liquidate its last reserves of gold and what assets it still held in the United States, but only for a little while.

What would be the result? Canada would turn upon its neighbor in the anger of a people who were fighting a war for the defense of America as a whole and were now crippled by their neutral partner for the sake of an economic formula. Even if the United States lent Canada money, the sense of charity would rankle. The Americans would seem to be driving a callous bargain, to be demanding a safe investment instead of supporting their ally.

At the wheel of his car, with the familiar cigarette holder uptilted from his lips, Roosevelt listened. He might not understand foreign exchange but he understood people. He said he was shocked at any possibility of a rift in the friendship of the good neighbors. How could the thing be fixed?

Quite easily, said King, and he pulled out of his well-stocked hat the rabbit of the Hyde Park Declaration. Let the United States buy from Canada roughly as much as Canada bought from the United States. Let the United States pay Canada in American dollars for materials that would be supplied to Britain under the Lend-Lease formula. Let the United States use Canada's productive machinery to support Britain and, in the process, provide Canada with dollars needed for its own support. In other words, let the economies of the two North American nations be geared together for defense purposes.

That, said Roosevelt, was a "swell" idea. Returning to his house, the two politicians applied a political solution to an economic problem too big for the economists and jotted down their thoughts on a slip of paper. To this Hyde Park Declaration Roosevelt scrawled his famous postscript: "Done by Mackenzie and F.D.R. on a grand Sunday in April." It was a good Sabbath's work.

In operation, the Declaration proved technically difficult. The technicalities could be left to the technicians. When they raised detailed objections in Washington, King telephoned Roosevelt. He thundered at his advisers: "This is what I want done! Don't tell me why it can't be done, just do it!" It was done.

To the end of the war, Canada had the dollars it needed and used them to nourish a war effort beyond the imagination of the men who had integrated two national economies while taking the air in a flivver. The integration was designed to continue for the war only. After the scribblings of Hyde Park had been rewritten into a formal postwar agreement, they became a basic policy for another struggle against another enemy.

King thought well of his Hyde Park week end. A few days later, sitting in his comfortable little cubbyhole outside the House of Commons with a cup of tea in hand, he laughed mischievously at the agonies of his experts and at his own easy solution. He had taught Roosevelt a few simple lessons in economics.

It was often forgotten, he remarked, in a pardonable mood of self-esteem, that he was an economist himself, a much better one, so far as studies, degrees, and experience were concerned, than any of the bright young men in the Finance Department and the Bank of Canada.

After all, he added, with a modest gesture of a hand which held a biscuit, he had the highest degrees in economics that Harvard could give him and, in fact, had taught economics there before the current crop of economists had left school.

He was asked by his interviewer if he liked Roosevelt personally. "I certainly do!" he exclaimed enthusiastically and went on to say that Roosevelt had magnificent courage, optimism, a flair for comradeship, a broad sweep.

The most important contribution King had ever made to the world so far, he suggested, was the healing of the friction between Roosevelt and Churchill in 1940 when Churchill had pressed too hard for aid beyond Roosevelt's power to grant. That situation had been bad, very bad—a head-on collision.

He pulled from his pocket a wallet, fastened with silver clasps, and extracted Churchill's three cables thanking him for his intervention. In his grandest manner Churchill indicated his contrition for earlier slights to King. Churchill had not realized in the beginning, he confessed, the abilities of King, his wise judgment, his capacity to interpret the old world to the new and vice versa. These cables were too precious to be placed in the official files. They were thrust back into the wallet and the wallet into King's inner pocket, for publication in his autobiography.

He seemed to feel an almost boyish pride in Roosevelt's confidence. The President, he intimated by dark hints and a glint of the eye, had told him his secret plans, certain to stagger the world, secrets that Roosevelt did not share with his own Cabinet. All, said King, would appear in the immediate future on the broad bosom of the Atlantic, as they did.

(What neither of the two friends could anticipate in the spring was that, on December 7, the Japanese would rescue Roosevelt from his imprisonment in American neutrality, take his country into the war, and permit much larger measures on the Atlantic and elsewhere.)

In a mood of candor and communication, King went on to condemn the theory of a National Government, still popular in some Conservative circles, despite its defeat in the 1940 election. His own Government, he said, was completely "national" in representing the majority of the people, the parliamentary system was preserved with a critical Opposition to watch the Government, and, in any case, the nation should come through the war with an alternative government available in the Conservative Party.

He intimated, however, that he had tried to introduce into the Cabinet a few men who were not Liberals, for war service only, among them J. M. Macdonnell (not yet an active Conservative politician), J. W. McConnell, the Montreal industrialist and publisher, and Tom Moore, the labor leader. All had refused for one reason or another. King admitted regretfully that he saw no Conservative politicians who would add any strength to the Cabinet. There was nothing in the Opposition party "worth having." Meighen? That gentleman, King replied, had done only harm at every opportunity.

On the whole, he believed, Canada's war was going well. He held up his left hand and ticked off the important points on his fingers: The nation had gone into the war united and continued so. There had not been a single hard word between the British and Canadian Governments, whereas in the first war the two had often disagreed violently. The Canadian Defence Department was co-operating perfectly with the British War Office, whereas in the first war Kitchener and Sam Hughes had been like dog and cat. The Canadian war effort was much larger, proportionately, than last time.

Maybe, he concluded, it was just as well that the Canadian people had not realized so far how vast their commitments were, lest the task appear too great to be borne. It was only amusing to hear the Conservative complaint that we were not doing enough. It would soon be found that we were doing all we could do and far more than we could complete without heavy new sacrifices.

33

The Commander-in-Chief

THROUGHOUT THE PARLIAMENTARY SESSION OF 1941, KING WAS increasingly enraged by the slurs that a few irresponsible American politicians were heaping upon Canada for their own purposes. The time had come, he concluded, to tell the American people how Canada was fighting its war.

At New York on June 17—his words carried across the nation by radio—he declared that Canada had entered the war not for others but to save itself—an oblique reminder of the United States' own dangerous position. Knowing Roosevelt's mind, he spoke as one who already regarded the United States as an active ally (as it already was in fact) and only awaited its formal entry into the war. Perhaps only a Canadian could have spoken so bluntly without offense.

With ill-concealed anger he went on to deny the Congressional slander that Canada had demanded "cash on the barrelhead" for all its aid to Britain while the United States was asked to give away its lend-lease goods for nothing. Canada, he said, was giving its treasure and offering the lives of its sons freely not only to Britain but to the "common cause of freedom."

To answer another canard, popular in Washington, he added: "Don't let any one dare to tell you that French-speaking Canada is not on the side of freedom in this war. The union of the children of New France and their English-speaking brothers which fashioned the Canadian nation remains unbroken and will always so remain."

His figures on Canada's war effort were unanswerable, especially when he calculated them in equivalent American terms and politely showed the United States how far it lagged behind in the ability to defend itself.

That was the end of the cash-on-the-barrelhead libel. Roosevelt, who had encouraged King to speak out, was delighted.

By this time a deep change could be noted in King. He had

entered the war as a statesman, remote from the military side of the struggle and terrified by its effects on the brittle unity of Canada. Now he felt like a soldier in the line.

He was obsessed with the grand strategy of the war, learned from Churchill and Roosevelt, and his judgment of it proved better than that of many professional soldiers. Moreover, he had come to feel a burning pride in the Canadian armed services, was outraged by the slightest reflection on them, and liked to think of himself as their real commander-in-chief, which, actually, he was. The cold scholar was alight with a martial fire and fighting mad at enemies abroad and at home.

Among the potential foreign enemies he included Russia. In the spring he had drafted a speech which affirmed that Germany and Russia intended jointly to possess the world. His advisers dissuaded him from a statement so provocative when Russia might turn out to be a friend after all. Reluctantly King abandoned his speech. It was a narrow escape a few weeks before Russia was driven by Hitler into the Grand Alliance. King's original opinion of Russian policy was premature by only a few years.

After his New York speech, he hurried across Canada to stimulate recruiting. At Winnipeg, on July 10, he reminded the nation that it had 300,000 men in the active Army, Navy, and Air Force, 170,000 in the Reserve Army, with two divisions of infantry in Britain, two more divisions about to go there, and garrisons in the West Indies and Newfoundland. He predicted, accurately, a vast expansion of the war and warned the Allies not to count on Russia's winning it alone.

Then, more frankly than ever before, he told Canadians how he construed his own war leadership: "My duty, as I see it, is to seek above all else to preserve national unity, for on the maintenance of national unity all else depends."

Coming to the heart of his own problem, he said: "I believe my efforts have encouraged and assisted others who have been engaged in the recruiting campaign. I believe, or at least I hope, that in connection with the present recruiting campaign they have served to remove any excuse for raising in Canada the issue of conscription for overseas service."

He had been condemned, he said, for not going before this to the battlefront in Britain. If he had gone, his critics would have taken advantage of his absence to force the conscription issue "into the arena of party strife," and "how dire the consequences to our national unity might have proved none can say."

He could not suppress the issue. It would be in the political arena before the end of the year. By August 19, however, he felt able to leave Canada and boarded an airplane for the first time. The bomber carrying him from Montreal to England, via Newfoundland, was noisy, uncomfortable, and cold, but it had been equipped with a cot for its distinguished passenger. Bundled in a flying suit, he slept through most of the journey. In those days a transatlantic flight was an adventure which King certainly did not relish but, having undertaken it, he worried no more. The legend that he was a physical coward was one of the most absurd among the many contrived against him by his enemies.

Though some of Canada's fighting men, now restive in their long and dreary defense of Britain, may have regarded him as a sissy, the dismal incident which spoiled his first visit to the troops in the south of England was generally exaggerated and misunderstood at the time. As usual, King was late for his appointment. The soldiers had been standing in line for an hour in an icy rain. When King arrived at the reviewing stand, he was greeted with unseemly boos.

The Conservative politicians at home chuckled at this affront, and the Opposition press insinuated that it expressed the soldiers' hostility to the no-conscription policy. In the opinion of King and his entourage it had nothing to do with conscription. The soldiers were cold, wet, and impatient, but they were not thinking of politics, and conscription, when the Canadian army had plenty of manpower and no place to use it, was not an issue. For keeping the troops waiting, an inexcusable discourtesy, King got what he deserved and knew it. Such, at least, was his own interpretation of his first unfortunate venture into the military side of war. He treated the affair lightly and quickly forgot it. His enemies did not forget.

After conferences with the leaders of the Commonwealth and a renewal of his friendship with the Royal Faimly, King went to the Mansion House with Churchill and there, in one of his finest speeches, paid his tribute to the noble ruins of London, "whose very name reverberates around the world like the sound waves of a great bell, calling together all who love and cherish freedom."

The speech showed that King had felt the devastation of London as a personal hurt. The spectacle of the broken Parliament buildings had aroused in him, as nothing had done before, the sense of history, the subconscious love of the British heritage and its parliamentary institutions, which had always struggled with his nationalism in the perpetual schism of the Canadian nature. The history man in him spoke above the man of geography when he told Britain that "we will be with you to the end."

The notion that King was lukewarm toward Britain had always

been untrue. Those who walked with him through the shattered London streets and listened to him at the Mansion House knew that no Canadian Prime Minister had ever felt Britain deeper in his heart.

Churchill at least understood that. He grasped the Mansion House occasion to put on public record what he had already told King in private. He called King the statesman who had maintained Canada as the "link which, spanning the oceans, brings the continents into their true relation and will prevent, in future generations, a division between the proud and once happy nations of Europe and the great countries which have come into existence in the New World."

Such a tribute from such a man was heady wine for any Canadian, but King had other business which would have scandalized some of those who saw only the public man at the Mansion House.

As on all his visits to England, he slipped away to visit his psychic advisers and establish contact with his mother. His questions and the answers from the spirit world were usually scrawled rapidly on foolscap pages by the medium. King kept the original notes, had them secretly transcribed, and sent copies to the medium with his own comments to prove the accuracy of the communications.

What would the Canadian people have thought of their leader if they had known that he consulted the dead in the midst of a war among the living? The breach of his secret probably would have ruined his public career. The few who knew it had long been bound in a conspiracy of silence, never to be broken until his death, and then only by his spiritualistic counselors.

Some of his intimates regarded his seances as a harmless fad. Some understood that in his mind the other world had become as real as this one and more important. Therein lay his capacity to meet with composure all the larger shocks of life here and now. They mattered little when he had the promise of the life to come. Against this background of assured eternity only small things generally disturbed him.

The servants who placed him upon the returning bomber could hardly lift his bulging Gladstone bag. It had been light on the outward flight. Now two men were required to put it aboard the plane. What sort of confidential documents could it contain? It contained a collection of broken stones from the bombed British House of Commons.

How King had acquired them he never told anyone. The sentimental builder of Kingsmere was adding a final precious relic to his structure of synthetic ruins. A fragment of British history was to

stand forever on the hill above Ottawa. Unhappily, the architect
never got around to using his English stones. At his death they were
still lying in a shed and probably remain there yet. It seems a pity.

Arrived in Ottawa, King was confronted again by the experts of
the Finance Department and the Bank of Canada, to announce that
the national economy, which had plenty of American dollars and
seemed to be surmounting the heavy weather of inflation, was
approaching shipwreck. The swollen wages of wartime, even when
tapped by ferocious taxes, were bidding up prices. An inflationary
explosion was not far off.

The experts had relied on the indirect fiscal safeguards of taxation, the borrowing of real savings, and credit policy. They knew
what direct wage and price controls would mean, an almost impossible task of administration, and, in fact, virtually total state control
of the economy. But if King did not wish to see the economy explode
and sink, carrying the war program with it, the last desperate measure must be taken.

At first King objected. Reminding his advisers again that he, too,
was an economist, he pronounced total price and wage control
impossible to enforce. Partial controls might work, were already
working in certain commodities. A horizontal ceiling, as now demanded by the experts, especially by Towers and the Bank, would
soon be smashed outright or submerged by a black market.

For many days the struggle continued in the experts' committees
and in the Cabinet. In the end, King, not entirely convinced, agreed
to make the experiment. Now that he had accepted a policy unwill-
ingly, he announced it to the people by radio as his own.

Prices and wages were frozen. Canada once more was pioneering
in unmapped territory and its allies watched it with an interested
skepticism. Roosevelt's experts, who faced the same inflationary
problem, dismissed the Canadian experiment as unworkable. After
observing the weighty figure of Donald Gordon astride the ceiling
and the price index steady beneath him, they changed their minds
and hastily adopted the Canadian system.

It was Gordon who made it work, almost to the point of his own
physical collapse, but it was Ilsley, finally passing that point, who
kept the economy afloat by a prodigy of finance as remarkable in its
way as the more spectacular works of Ralston, Power, Macdonald,
and Howe.

This was no time to talk of such things when the nation could not
afford the luxury of doubt, but the experts who had built the ceiling
knew already that it was thin, fragile, and temporary. With luck it
might last through the war though it had not suppressed, had merely

postponed, inflation. For Ilsley could not finance the war entirely out of sound money. He was quietly manufacturing what he could not collect in taxes or borrow from savings. This extra money must flood the market in due time and smash the ceiling.

King doubtless knew that, too. At the moment he had more urgent matters on his mind.

In October he visited Roosevelt again and returned to Ottawa, deeply depressed. Some two weeks before the attack on Pearl Harbor he told this writer that war with Japan was certain. And looking through his office window to the westward, as if he could visualize, beyond the Ottawa's peaceful curves, the defenseless shape of Asia, he added that the Japanese war would spread far.

How he could be so sure of these events when the United States and Japan were still negotiating for peace he did not indicate. His prognosis may have come from Roosevelt. Perhaps his friend Hull had told him of the coded messages from Tokyo to the Japanese negotiators which the Americans had deciphered. In any case, he was convinced in advance that the whole face of the war would soon be changed, with dangerous consequences to Canada. These he was now trying to calculate.

They were complicated by a new factor more disturbing to him than war itself.

After the retirement of the patriotic Manion into a war job, Senator Meighen had looked around for a new Conservative leader and looked in vain. His duty, as he saw it, was obvious. He must revive his Party and rescue the nation's war from King's bungling management, with the enforcement of overseas conscription.

Accordingly, he resigned from the safe haven of the Senate and presented himself as a candidate for the House of Commons. By the approval of the Party caucus and without the usual convention he had resumed his old leadership.

To King this implied several things, all bad.

He saw at once that in Meighen the conscription issue was emerging, could not longer be put aside, and, one way or another, must be faced. Meighen was wrong. He could not be discounted. This was no pipsqueak from the onion district nor a French Canadian ward boss. King had always disliked Meighen. Now he detested and feared him to the edge of absurdity.

As he said that day, if Meighen entered the Commons life would be "insupportable." He remembered the old race of the tortoise and the hare. Once again the unthinkable seemed likely to happen. The forgotten hare was making a last attempt to catch up to the comfortable tortoise.

Pacing his office, as in a cage, King repeated that the thing was insupportable. Meighen represented the most reactionary and disruptive elements in Canadian life, and if they now drove a wedge into the unity of the nation, well—he threw up his hands in desperation.

Then, pounding his desk in a rage almost irrational, this most rational of men asked what the return of Meighen to politics meant. It meant nothing less than the beginning of Fascism in Canada.

Why Fascism? One did not venture to ask that question of the Prime Minister in his present humor.

He rose again from his chair, walked about the room, and, raising a clenched fist, uttered a curious pronouncement: "The people, mark my words, will have their rights!"

This childish outburst, so unlike King, seemed meaningless and inane, but its meaning was very simple. King could not tolerate Meighen's presence as a man near him in Parliament. He could not manage the war with Meighen's presence as a statesman and as a conscriptionist. At all costs, the threat of York South must be crushed in the egg. To which end the necessary steps already were being taken.

In the midst of these distractions, King and Canada suffered a grievous wound. King visited Lapointe in a Montreal hospital on November 19 and saw that his closest colleague was dying. The two friends said their last farewell, both aware that the old and fruitful partnership was finished.

The end came on November 26. The tribune of the French Canadian race did not live to see the victory to which he had given, in his own fashion, the last full measure of devotion, nor, mercifully, the racial crisis which he had struggled to avert.

When Lapointe was buried, his fame was safe among the greatest French Canadians, from Champlain onward. Who could replace him? King and nation had lost not only a statesman of genius but the one man apparently able to hold his people in unity with the Canadian majority through the hard days now beginning. There were other able French Canadians but, it seemed, no successor to Lapointe.

After parting with Lapointe on his deathbed, King had gone to St. Lin to open Laurier's birthplace as a national shrine. There he met Godbout, told him of Lapointe's approaching death, and invited him into the Cabinet as the recognized Quebec spokesman. Godbout asked time to consider. He met King again at Lapointe's funeral on November 29 and again was pressed to occupy the vacant chair. He gave no definite answer and evidently was not favorable.

This was a bitter disappointment. Returning from the funeral, King despaired.

A group of Ministers on the train listened patiently to his vain speculations. At last Power suggested St. Laurent. The name seemed to strike no spark in King's mind. He had seen little of St. Laurent and knew him only as a distinguished and rather chilly lawyer, while St. Laurent hardly knew King at all and knew, as he said, nothing of politics. He had taken so little interest in politics that in 1926 Meighen had approached him indirectly to join the short-lived Conservative Ministry and had been surprised, apparently, to learn that St. Laurent was a Liberal.

King noted St. Laurent's name, without enthusiasm. He consulted Cardin, who warmly approved. St. Laurent in his inexperience could hardly challenge Cardin's control of the Liberal Party in Quebec. King continued to hope that Godbout would change his mind and enter the Government. When Godbout finally refused on December 4, King telephoned St. Laurent at his home in Quebec that same evening.

St. Laurent returned to his dinner table and told his wife that the Prime Minister wished to see him in Ottawa. She guessed at once what that meant and implored her husband to stay out of politics. Such was St. Laurent's intention as he left for Ottawa next day.

In the evening he telephoned Mrs. St. Laurent. She asked how he had impressed King. "Too well, I fear," said St. Laurent in a glum voice.

He returned home to think over King's offer. Only because he was being conscripted for war service he could not refuse. He telephoned his acceptance to King on the ninth and was sworn in as Minister of Justice the following day, with the promise that he would be released at the end of the war.

For a man of St. Laurent's talents there could be no such release. Lapointe's and King's successor had been found in the most unlikely place. Also, for the first time St. Laurent found himself. He had lived fifty-nine years before entering the one element in which all his unsuspected capacities could flourish. The meeting was late but the man and the occasion had met as if by prior appointment.

In the last days of 1941, King realized that he would need his untried lieutenant before spring as he had seldom needed even Lapointe. Could St. Laurent face the approaching crisis? Would French Canada follow him?

King began to feel easier about these questions after watching the quiet little man with the terrier face, the bright black eyes, and the crisp speech, in Lapointe's place at the Cabinet table.

When the Japanese struck at Pearl Harbor on December 7, King was surprised only by the point of the attack. As he had predicted, the war now circled the world. He called the Cabinet together that same night and, without waiting for Parliament to meet, advised King George by cable to declare that Canada was at war with Japan. At 7:10 next morning the royal approval reached Ottawa. King immediately announced it by radio to the Canadian people.

From its first hours Canada was actively engaged in the new war. At the urgent request of the British Government (which, on October 26, considered "war in the Far East unlikely at present") two Canadian battalions had been sent to Hong Kong and there, hopelessly outnumbered, were soon slaughtered or captured by the first sweep of the Japanese wave to the southward.

King had gone to Washington on Christmas day to meet Roosevelt and Churchill. Next morning he heard the news of Hong Kong's surrender and knew that it meant grave trouble for his Government. It could wait. On December 27 he returned to Ottawa with Churchill, who was given his first close-up view of Canada's war administration.

In disrupting Asia, the Japanese had cemented the English-speaking world. With Hitler's help in Russia, they had built the strongest military alliance in history. At the Christmas meeting in Washington they had perfected the partnership of Roosevelt, Churchill, and King.

Of the three, only King had to face serious enemies at home. On November 12 he had reaffirmed his determination never to break his pledge and impose overseas conscription without consulting the people. That night Meighen announced that he had accepted the Conservative Party leadership on a policy of "compulsory selective service over the whole field of war." On the unlikely battlefield of York South, where Meighen sought election to Parliament, his ultimate struggle to reverse the past and extinguish King had opened. It must extinguish one or the other.

Now that the United States had entered the war, York South was a small matter to the world at large. To King, despite his joy at the Americans' arrival, Meighen was a challenge to imperil, as he thought, everything he had accomplished in the last twenty years.

34

The Crisis, First Stage

THE 1942 SESSION OF PARLIAMENT IMMEDIATELY CONFRONTED what may now be given the capital letters of a major historic event and called The Crisis. It was the first stage only.

In York South, Meighen had come out flatly for overseas conscription. In Parliament, his followers were prepared to unseat King if they could and establish some kind of national conscriptionist government. To have any chance of success they must first elect Meighen, with a mandate for conscription, to lead them.

King must deal with two enemies, Meighen himself and the rising conscriptionist sentiment of English-speaking Canada which he represented.

To assure Meighen's defeat in York South the Liberals resorted to a stratagem. After Hepburn had publicly endorsed Meighen, the Ontario Liberals refused to nominate their own candidate and thus split the anti-Government vote. Instead, they threw their support to J. W. Noseworthy of the C.C.F. Even with this disagreeable bargain to protect him, King was beside himself with hatred of Meighen, concern for his own safety, and terror for the nation. The days of the York South by-election were some of the darkest in his life.

By luck and good management, Meighen could be quickly dispatched at the polls and removed forever. The growing anger of English-speaking Canadians against a military-service law which seemed designed solely to protect French Canadians, which was conscripting a large Army to serve unnecessarily at home, which was frankly based on political considerations and disregarded equity altogether—this, as King now realized, was a force certain to outlast Meighen. It could crush the Government and split the nation. Even King had yet to measure the dimensions of this force and would comprehend them only an inch this side of his own downfall.

The attack on Pearl Harbor, Japan's engorgement of southern Asia, and its occupation of the Aleutian Islands had instantly changed the military balance of the world. In Canada it compelled new measures of self-defense against a Japanese attack, perhaps even an invasion. On the night of Pearl Harbor, Japanese naval forces were off Alaska, a task force actually bound for Kiska was believed to be heading for Vancouver Island. Vancouver and Victoria were blacked out and the pathetic little air force at Patricia Bay prepared to commit suicide against overpowering odds.

In one sense, the necessity of defending Canada eased King's position in politics, for it justified the retention of a conscripted "Zombie" army at home. For both military and political reasons he repeatedly emphasized the danger of Japanese attack, acceded to the demands of a frightened British Columbia Government, and transported all Japanese residents from the Pacific Coast to the interior, moved more of the home defense Army into British Columbia, and, at secret meeting with his military chiefs, asked their opinion about the safety of Alaska. He was told that Alaska could easily be taken by two Japanese divisions.

About the same time, Fiorello La Guardia, American chairman of the joint Canadian-American defense board, was pounding Roosevelt's desk and demanding more air power in the Alaska bases.

While the eyes of Canada were momentarily diverted from Europe to the Pacific Coast, this provided only a brief lull in The Crisis. Meighen had brought it into the open as a straight party issue but it had long been planted by the Government itself in the big army program of 1941.

Crerar and others had warned the Cabinet that Ralston's plans eventually would involve overseas conscription if the Army was to fight in Europe. This the military command repeatedly denied, assuring King that it could secure all the men it needed by voluntary recruitment.

King had regarded the army plan as too big, always blamed Ralston for surrendering to his generals, but believed that conscription could be avoided.

Ralston had told his friends in 1941 that King would never consent to conscription even when it became necessary, as it probably would. Yet Ralston felt that King could win another election on an anti-conscription policy. "King," he said, rather wistfully, "is certain about it and King is always right."

At a Cabinet wrangle over the manpower problem on December 4, 1941, King told his colleagues impatiently that if there was to be conscription, someone else could lead the Government, for he would not. He had warned Churchill of the approaching Crisis and Churchill, he said, had earnestly deplored any such breach in the unity of the Canadian people. For the present, Ralston and all the Cabinet were prepared to go along with their leader, since there was no lack of army recruits.

The Cabinet was still solid, Meighen might be buried in the ballot boxes of York South, but somehow the rising anger of English-speaking Canada must be appeased. King had saved national unity, as he believed, in anticonscriptionist Quebec. Now it could be broken by the conscriptionists of the other provinces. The time had come for a new compromise between the two races. King produced it when Parliament opened on January 22. In the long line of rabbits pulled from his fertile hat, this was perhaps the most ingenious of all.

The Government, said the Speech from the Throne, had given a solemn commitment never to impose overseas conscription. Now that the nation's material resources and manpower must be mobilized for "a total national effort," the Government must be released from its original promise. Only the people could release it and the people would decide by plebiscite.

The first purpose of the plebiscite was obvious enough. It was designed to defeat Meighen by taking the conscription issue out of his hands and referring it to the voters, and, at the same time, to satisfy English-speaking Canada that the Government was prepared to impose conscription if it should ever be necessary. Many people supposed, however, that King had some deeper purpose, that he already knew what he was going to do about The Crisis when it finally arrived. In fact, the plebiscite, so far as he was concerned, was designed only to buy time in the hope that The Crisis would never arrive.

As will be shown by firsthand evidence in its proper place, King at this point, and for nearly three years more, had no intention of en-forcing overseas conscription under any conditions. The plebiscite had no military significance for him. It was solely political, calcu-lated at once to save his Government from rupture and the nation from a racial schism.

As he expected, the first public reaction to the plebiscite was be-wilderment, anger, and humiliation. The Quebec politicians saw it as the entering wedge of conscription. Despite King's assurances to the contrary, they were right. Much of English-speaking Canada saw it as a spineless attempt by the Government to dodge its clear responsibility. Hepburn emerged momentarily to denounce it as "dastardly, contemptible and cowardly," and Premier John Bracken, of Manitoba (who had not yet discovered that he was a Conserva-tive), called it "this crowning indignity."

In York South, Meighen used his full arsenal of adjectives. In Parliament, Hanson, who now looked more like a fighting Opposition leader than a stranded whale, paraphrased Churchill to observe that "verily never were so many humiliated by so few" and moved a want-of-confidence motion in favor of total conscription forthwith.

The Conservative strategy was fully revealed when Hanson declared that there could be no national unity except under a national government. The Conservatives had no chance of winning an election, because King would not call one, but they hoped for a coalition which would include them. This was Manion's program of 1940 with one vital difference. Manion's national government would accept King's no-conscription policy. Meighen's would force conscription on the Liberals.

King was ready for Hanson's want-of-confidence motion. In one of his longest speeches, filled with intentional confusion, he argued that Canada's war plans would strain it to the limit, that they must not be judged by one single aspect, the use of overseas conscription, which was irrelevant when the army was finding all the volunteers it needed.

Wherever it was needed, for home defense, in industry, and in finance, conscription had already been applied. Overseas conscription had been avoided to maintain national unity, and all parties, including the Conservatives, had supported that policy in the last election. Only now was overseas conscription raised as a political issue by Meighen, and the "political skies have become so overcast with controversy promoted by high-pressure methods and highly-financed publicity that the nature and extent of Canada's war effort is not only being obscured but is in danger of being seriously impaired."

Still, in this, the greatest crisis of the world's history, the Government, said King, must be free to meet any emergency, it must not be restricted by its early pledge against conscription. The people could not make military decisions when they lacked the secret military facts. They could only give the Government freedom to act in the light of those facts, which only the Government knew. In asking for freedom the Government was "not shirking responsibility but . . . asking for full responsibility."

As for the Conservative demand that the no-conscription pledge be disregarded, "I do not propose to erect bad faith and the broken pledge into a principle of action . . . to sell my birthright for their mess of pottage" and destroy the people's confidence in him, in the Government, and in the nation's political institutions "for all time."

Therefore, the people would be asked to answer a simple question at the polls. The simple question, written in King's worst style of sprawling participles but as sound in politics as it was weak in construction, would be as follows: "Are you in favor of releasing the Government from any obligation arising out of any past commitments restricting the methods of raising men for military service?"

The voter who could wade through the labyrinth of that sentence should be able to see that it did not provide a vote on conscription. As King repeated over and over again during the next five months of debate, the electorate was asked only to free the Government's hands for conscription or no conscription, as military conditions demanded.

While the Commons wrangled over the plebiscite, the Conservatives attacked the Government for evading its duty, some Quebec Liberals attacked it for even contemplating conscription, and Jean Francois Pouliot, an aging sprite, demanded the resignation of Ralston as the head of a conscriptionist conspiracy. King's eye was not on Parliament but on York South.

When the ballots were counted on February 9 and Noseworthy received 16,408 votes to Meighen's 11,952, it was a night of ecstasy at Laurier House. The Liberals had not won, yet to King the defeat of Meighen was the sweetest victory he had ever known. In Winnipeg, Dafoe read the returns from York South and muttered Meighen's political obituary: "Mighty Casey had struck out."

So he had. After three strikes, in 1921, 1925, and 1926, and a fourth in York South, there could be no more. Meighen had reached his end as a political power in Canada.

No, not quite the end. He still had power to arrange the appointment of a successor and, as usual in all his political decisions, to make the worst choice. But the tortoise had finally won the race of twenty-three years. For Meighen, perhaps for the nation, it finished in tragedy, the tragedy of a great man who had every quality of greatness except an understanding of the Canadian people.

Anyone who talked to King at this time saw his unutterable relief at Meighen's disappearance. Turning the palm of his hand down in a gesture of distaste, he described Meighen as "an unbearable type of man." He said he had been approached some time before by Hanson with an interesting suggestion. Hanson had proposed that he and Meighen be taken into the Government and then there would be no trouble between the two parties. When King had refused this offer, the Conservatives had begun their present attack.

Actually, King added, there was no future for the Conservative Party. The real opposition of the future would come from "radical parties." He showed no alarm at that prospect.

The war, he remarked, was going badly everywhere. As soon as

x

the Japanese were ready they probably would attack Alaska and the Pacific Coast of Canada. The danger to Canadian soil was very great. Once the public realized that danger, the agitation for conscription to send more men to Europe, where there was yet no serious fighting, would peter out. He was wrong on both scores. There was no attack on the Pacific Coast and conscription would threaten to cleave his Cabinet within four months.

At this same time, while Parliament debated the plebiscite, another portent of The Crisis appeared in the person of General McNaughton, home from England for a brief visit. He returned bitterly critical of the British War Office, of the Canadian Government, and of Ralston.

At a famous dinner party in Toronto he expressed his criticism of Ralston with candor, supposing himself to be among trustworthy friends. Unless Ralston left him alone to manage the details of Army administration, McNaughton was ready to resign. Under Ralston's continual interference, he said, the Army organization was in danger of a breakdown. McNaughton, however, was not suggesting conscription. He was opposed to it and in the end was fated to perish politically for his opposition.

McNaughton's confidential chat in Toronto was fully reported in Ottawa before morning. His statements did not anger so much as they wounded Ralston. He had been loyal to McNaughton and was his champion before the Canadian and British Governments—a champion whom McNaughton would soon need.

Ralston at once telephoned King and offered his resignation if King shared McNaughton's feelings. King rejected the offer, praised Ralston, and smoothed over the dispute. Ralston then confronted McNaughton and asked him if the Toronto reports were true. McNaughton, equally frank, repeated his criticisms and the two men, having reached a full understanding, parted friends.

That was to be only the first act of their personal drama. The denouement for both of them would be reached in three more years.

Meanwhile, the Conservative professionals were staring hard at McNaughton. Here was a man who already had captured the imagination of the Canadian people, who mixed a deep military and scientific knowledge with a fine homespun simplicity, who seemed to possess the mystique of leadership lacking in King, whose grizzled face and faraway look seemed to represent the inner spirit of the nation. Perhaps he could be made the leader of a national war government.

There is no reason to suppose that McNaughton was yet thinking of politics, though the Conservative politicians certainly were thinking of him. Angus Macdonald, a Celt of subtle intuitions, already was predicting to his intimates that King would yet dismiss Ralston and replace him with McNaughton. It was a wild guess in 1942. Like many of Macdonald's guesses, this one happened to be true. It had not yet occurred to King.

In Parliament, the defeat of Meighen had shattered the Conservative Party's hopes of unseating King or even of modifying his policy. The attack on the plebiscite continued sporadically until March 4, when Pouliot's move to cancel it received only 13 votes, all French Canadian except those of T. L. Church and R. H. McGregor, Conservatives who considered the plebiscite a farce. So did Hanson and the rest of the Conservative Party but they supported it since they could get nothing better from the Government. By opposite reasoning most of the French Canadian Liberal members took the same view. For the Conservatives the plebiscite was a possible road to conscription. For the French Canadians it was a method of avoiding conscription. Neither side had much real hope when the plebiscite was called for April 27.

Liberals and Conservatives co-operated loyally in urging the people to vote "yes."

In a series of powerful broadcasts King reduced the complex arguments of Parliament to the simple terms of the radio. Canada, he said, must make clear to the world, especially to the United States, that it was ready to help its allies without any restriction on its energies. The false impression that Canada was not making an all-out effort, merely because conscription had not been enforced in a single phase of the war program, must be removed. The Government must be given a free hand to do whatever must be done in a new and grave situation which had engulfed half the world and endangered Canadian soil.

Hanson, while sure it would never be used, asked the people to give the Government power to fight a total war.

Cardin threw all his influence and his unequaled oratory into the campaign. He did not expect a "yes" majority in Quebec but he hoped for something like an even split. He told the French Canadian people (of whom he now considered himself the leader) that a "yes" vote did not mean conscription, or how could he, irrevocably pledged against conscription, vote to free the Government's hands? Quebec could trust King and him. Toward the end of the campaign, however, Cardin saw that he was losing. He returned to Ottawa in deepest pessimism, for he saw Quebec slipping out of his hands. There was one last chance to retrieve it and he was now pondering that chance.

The results of the plebiscite surprised no one. A total of 2,945,514 Canadians voted "yes" and 1,643,000 "no." In the English-speaking provinces the affirmative majority was 2,569,326 to 649,343. Quebec spoke in the negative by 993,663 to 376,188.

The ancient division of race was never written more vividly than on those ballots. They confirmed King in his judgment that conscription would shatter Canada and its ability to fight the war. He had re-assured, if he had not satisfied, the other provinces but, for the first time, he had been rejected by Quebec, on which his whole career, past, present, and future, depended.

The Quebec vote was a cruel disappointment after Cardin's early optimism. Nevertheless, the will of the national majority must be obeyed. The Government immediately introduced Bill 80, to remove Clause 3 in the National Resources Mobilization Act and make the power of conscription unlimited. With Bill 80, a notable landmark in Canadian history, The Crisis now moved into a phase far more dangerous than King had expected.

It was quickly proclaimed in Cardin's resignation. That strange little man, so calm on the outside, so riven in spirit by racial distrust and personal vanity, had just learned from his doctors that he must soon follow Lapointe. He was now making a last supreme effort to grasp Lapointe's mantle and Laurier's before the end. By opposing the conscription law he hoped to make himself the accepted master of his race.

His sincerity in believing that conscription would damage Con-federation irreparably cannot be doubted and was shared by greater men than he, including King. His motives were a mixture of patriot-ism and ambition, the usual state of any practicing politician. And the results of his retirement, as King knew, might be fatal for the Liberal Party.

Cardin's letter of resignation, delivered to King by messenger, said that there was no need for Bill 80, a measure "containing the prin-ciple of compulsory service for overseas." The new legislation con-tradicted the guarantees he had given his people in asking them to vote "yes."

The meaning of this statement was obvious and Quebec under-stood it—the French Canadian race was betrayed by King, whom it had trusted.

King wrote a hasty reply. There had been, he told Cardin, no change in Government policy, only the removal of a restriction on the Government's power to defend the nation. With this assurance, would Cardin not withdraw his resignation? Cardin would not. He replied in a courteous note rejecting King's invitation. The correspondence was friendly and correct on both sides, but, as both knew, this was war between them. It must decide whether Quebec was with King or with Cardin.

King moved first. On June 10, with every art of persuasion, with all the authority which his long leadership had given him and with hours of repetitive argument, he assured Parliament that the "yes" vote in the plebiscite had not been a vote for conscription because conscription had never been submitted to the voters.

Like himself, Hanson and Coldwell had construed the plebiscite only as a method of freeing the Government's hand. Cardin was right in saying that nothing had happened since the plebiscite to make conscription necessary, and the Government did not intend to impose it. However, war changed suddenly and no one could foresee the necessities of the future. In his most celebrated phrase (taken from an editorial in the Toronto *Star*) King described the Government's unchanged policy as "not necessarily conscription but conscription if necessary."

No other policy could possibly keep the nation united and in this hour of test he could not conceive that Canada would permit a wholly false issue to destroy unity achieved by a century of labor and understanding. He pleaded with Parliament to realize that the question before it was the most critical that any Canadian Parliament had ever faced, that an extreme policy on one side or the other might injure the nation beyond repair.

With figures probably surprising to most Canadians and certainly surprising to the world, King insisted that Canada already was embarked on war to the limit of its resources. Ralston had asked for 100,000 volunteer soldiers in the next fifteen months to fight anywhere and in five months he had recruited 50,000. The overseas Army was getting all the men it needed without conscription. Ralston himself—who could doubt that warrior's will to war?—had said in Parliament that he had faith in the voluntary system and preferred it to conscription.

There were 500,000 men in the armed forces, volunteers for service anywhere, 600,000 men and women in war industry, and, as Ilsley had said in his budget speech, the expansion now planned on all sides, military and civilian, would tax the nation's resources to the absolute limit. Conscription would add nothing to this strength.

As for the "Zombie" army of 30,000 conscripted for service in Canada (the hardest aspect of Government policy to defend), King warned the House that these men might soon be required to defend Canadian soil from attack or even invasion "at any moment from across the Pacific."

It was a diffuse and clumsy speech but effective both in Quebec and in English-speaking Canada.

Cardin held his peace.

Hanson replied bluntly that, as the plebiscite vote had showed, "we have . . . not complete national unity" and there was no use in pretending otherwise. Why flinch from that fact? Why avoid an essential policy to defend a fiction? Then, rising to a stature not expected in him, Hanson appealed earnestly, almost with tears, to the French Canadian members to think what they were doing, to prevent the isolation of their race from their fellow countrymen. After this effort Hanson ended where he had begun, in complete cynicism. This Government, he said, had no intention of using conscription anyway.

So raged the battle of Parliament while The Crisis had moved into the Cabinet and threatened to wreck it. In all his experience King had never faced a revolt of this sort. It was only an introduction to the larger revolt ahead of him.

The First Crisis, as the events of 1942 may properly be called, seemed to rise out of a trivial technicality and would have been insignificant if the technicality had not represented a fundamental clash of personalities, principles, and historic forces in Canadian life.

On one side stood King, who was determined never to enforce conscription. On the other, Ralston, who would not enforce it now but was determined to use it, regardless of consequences, if it ever became necessary.

King controlled a majority of his Cabinet and Party and, on this issue, would certainly control French Canada. Around Ralston a hard core of potential conscriptionist Ministers already was forming —Crerar, Macdonald, Ilsley, probably Howe, and some younger men like Gibson and Mulock. Even more dangerous to King was the obvious fact that a majority in English-speaking Canada, including the whole Conservative Party, would back the Cabinet rebels if the Government broke up. The makings of a conscriptionist national government under Ralston already were available.

Ralston differed from King and most statesman of first rank in his total lack of personal ambition. He wanted nothing for himself. He had no interest in anything except the war, to which all his energies, his health, his fortune, and, as it appeared in due time, his life were sacrificed.

Among all the innumerable colonels in Ottawa, only Ralston was "The Colonel" and that nickname described his unique place in the nation's life. The pale and haggard man with the massive chin, the limitless patience, the warm heart, and the devout belief in God, was the custodian of the Canadian soldier's faith in the Government and the nation's personal guarantee that the war would be fought and won. As such he was essential to King, and King knew it.

So far Ralston had trusted King. A man of simple and direct mind, he had withdrawn his former doubts and accepted at face value the promise that conscription would be used "if necessary." That satisfied him until, in the middle of the debate on Bill 80, he learned to his amazement that if it were passed, King then proposed to come back to Parliament again before imposing conscription.

To Ralston that course was unthinkable. So far as he was concerned, the passage of Bill 80 meant that the Government could and must impose conscription, when necessary, with no further delay, no second debate, and no reference to Parliament. The test of King's sincerity, of the Government's good faith, of its pledge to the nation was its willingness to conscript men for overseas service without a moment's hesitation if those men were needed. Now King apparently was wobbling again. It dawned on Ralston at last that Bill 80 might be only a façade to cover King's real refusal of conscription under any conditions.

Confronted by Ralston, King insisted that he would never invoke conscription without the specific consent of Parliament. Ralston at once wrote his resignation. This was more than King could face. He sought a compromise and found it in a formula under which the Government would impose conscription by order-in-council and then ask Parliament only for a vote of confidence. There would be no second conscription debate, King agreed, but he refused absolutely to send conscripted men overseas without making sure that Parliament was behind him. If the Cabinet rejected this final offer, he would resign and the conscriptionist Ministers could name his successor then and there.

In an emergency which might well break the Government, the Liberal Party, and the nation's war effort, the conscriptionist Ministers appealed to the revered oracle of Winnipeg. Dafoe replied that it would be folly to take chances merely to make good some parliamentary procedure. "If," he wrote to a friend at that time, "there must be division, let it be between parties, not between races."

Thus convinced, and believing that conscription was not yet needed, Ralston reluctantly agreed to King's compromise and the French Canadian Ministers accepted it because, as King warned them, the alternative was a conscriptionist national government under Ralston, or perhaps McNaughton. The Crisis, first stage, passed quietly in the Cabinet.

From that day forward, the spark of distrust in Ralston's mind could never be extinguished. It was the spark of ultimate conflagration.

King did not suspect that then. He thought The Crisis had passed for good because he did not understand Ralston. King's subtle mind could master anything complicated. It could never penetrate the armor of Ralston's simplicity.

The Cabinet breach averted, King at last was ready to bring Bill 80 to a vote in Parliament. On July 7, it was carried on second reading by 158 to 54. The Conservatives supported the Government, but 45 Quebec Liberals bolted and were joined by two Quebec independents and 6 C.C.F. members, who would not conscript men without conscripting wealth.

King had broken with a majority of the Quebec members for the first time. The break was not as serious as it looked in Hansard. The French Canadians had voted against conscription. They had not voted against the Government. They could not, for they had nowhere else to go. Now that the immediate issue was settled and their position made clear to their people, they returned to the fold. Many of them, however, were convinced, despite King's assurances, that the imposition of conscription was certain eventually.

Bill 80 had been approved in principle. Its enemies continued a ferocious guerrilla war against it in committee. The local politics of Quebec rang with inflammatory speeches; Godbout assured his people that King had no intention of using conscription; in Ontario the crusade for a national government marched on to the drum beat of the *Globe and Mail.*

Assuming, quite wrongly, that he had detached many of the Quebec Liberals from King, Cardin delivered his last blow on June 11.

The diminutive figure, the waxen face, the dainty hands, the superb clothes, and the silken voice seemed to express among the rougher Anglo-Saxons of the House all the natural elegance and finer sensibility of the French race. After Lapointe's departure there was no orator in politics to match Cardin in delicacy of phrase and gesture. Behind the silk he was sheer granite in his ambition, and the granite had hardened, the vanity expanded as his illness deepened and his time drained out. If he was to succeed Lapointe and Laurier as the father of French Canada, it was now or never.

He began, this master of English, by apologizing for his imperfect language and went on in sculptured phrases to make every Anglo-Saxon feel like a crude stonemason.

This, he said, with a sure sense of his people's memory, was simply 1917 over again though, on the Government's own statement, there was no need for conscription. With a twist of his hand, more eloquent than words, he warned the House, and through it the people of Quebec, that Bill 80 meant conscription, if not now then a little later. Most French Canadian members believed he was right. So did many Anglo-Saxons. King watched his former colleague intently and even to himself denied this warning.

If conscription was not necessary, said Cardin, with a slight rise in his silken voice, "Why in the name of God authorize it?" A good question and he knew the answer as well as King. Conscription was being authorized to satisfy the national majority.

After arguing that the plebiscite was nothing of the sort, King was now interpreting it as a vote for conscription, said Cardin. Another point for King to answer. If, said Cardin, conscription was not needed and yet was being enforced, then the Government had deceived the people in asking them to vote "yes" under false pretenses. This point, as Cardin thought, was unanswerable in Quebec. His next was still more penetrating.

Why, he asked, had the Government given its pledge against conscription? The pledge had been meaningless in English-speaking Canada, which did not ask for it. As everyone knew, it had been given solely to satisfy Quebec and maintain racial unity. And in the plebiscite the French Canadians, to whom alone the pledge had been given, had refused to surrender it. On the contrary, they had insisted on retaining it.

King fidgeted in his seat. Strand by strand the man of silk was weaving a cocoon to strangle the Government in Quebec.

Fortunately for King, there was a man in the House that day who could cut through these strands of argument. For the present, St. Laurent listened and said nothing. He was not yet ready, either in the politics of Quebec or in his own mind.

Now, in a few disarming sentences, Cardin stated the historic dilemma of Canada and the deepest instincts of his race as perhaps they had never been stated in Parliament. Mr. Speaker Glen, he remarked, was of British descent like most of the other members. They were proud of their race, and rightly. In this pride they instantly responded to the call of overseas war, to the appeal of the British flag out of their inherited instincts and memories, but, said Cardin, "I have to reason in my mind. . . . It is the result of thinking, the result of reasoning. With you it is the impulse of the heart. It cannot be the same with me. It would be against nature."

Against nature. There was the dilemma. In struggling with it, any Canadian Government was struggling with nature itself.

Through Cardin the French nature spoke from its depths and those depths were deeper than most Anglo-Saxons could understand. Deep as the memory of a people who knew no land but Canada and recognized no history outside it. Deep as the graves of countless French Canadians in this ancestral earth, precious as the life of their posterity in all time to come. Here in this frail, waxen man Parliament saw the old pull of Canadian geography incarnate. Unable to feel the other pull of a longer history overseas as his Anglo-Saxon compatriots felt it, he had brought these opposing tensions to the breaking point.

Quebec, said Cardin, had long been left alone in poverty. If it were poor it had at least the assurance that it would never be forced to fight outside Canada. In this bargain the French Canadians had made perpetual concessions to the national majority, but there came a time when the final concession would mean the betrayal of the race. The time had now come. "I do not want to pass that limit."

So far as Cardin could make it pay, Canada was now paying the price of conquest on that September dawn long ago.

He and his people had accepted conquest and outlived it. For them the enforcement of conscription meant simply that the conqueror, after a hundred and eighty-three years, was reviving the conquest. Conscription for them was not a military measure. It was not a matter of practical politics. It was something infinitely more important and repugnant—the assertion of the Anglo-Saxon's right to maintain the conquest and coerce the conquered. It was the ultimate and intolerable symbol of the Anglo-Saxon superiority. As such it would never be accepted.

Most of the House may not have understood an argument which had no practical logic. King understood it because he knew that men do not live by logic but by symbols, by memories, and by myths. Knowing that, he agreed with Cardin. Yet he, too, must live by the same laws, and the racial majority on which he lived demanded the symbol of conscription as strongly as Quebec refused it. Cardin, therefore, must be answered. At the same time, English-speaking Canada must be satisfied.

For Quebec King repeated again and again his assurance that Bill 80 did not necessarily mean conscription. For the rest of the country he laid down, as if it had been his original intention, the compromise formula of a vote of confidence, which he had persuaded Ralston to accept at the last minute. As he delivered this pronouncement, King nodded reassuringly to Macdonald, the most skeptical of his colleagues, and Macdonald nodded back. By these nods the bargain was sealed.

It did not satisfy either Cardin and his friends, the C.C.F. or the Conservatives.

Cardin returned to the fight on July 22, his silken gloves removed. Parliament, he said, was dominated by the wirepulling of a small group serving its own interests and bettering its own position under the cover of the war.

Coldwell, who had opposed even an overseas expedition in 1939, again proposed to kill Bill 80 because, failing to conscript wealth, it did not go far enough in total war. The C.C.F. motion, and another from the Quebec members calling for a referendum before conscription was imposed, were declared out of order.

Hanson condemned King's plan to secure a vote of confidence if he imposed conscription as just another wriggle to avoid final action.

King listened patiently to Hanson, insisted that he be given more than his allotted time to finish his speech, and then crushed him.

Faced with this kind of political warfare, said King, attacked by an Opposition which was trying to destroy the Government and was undermining the faith of Canada's friends abroad, clearly he must have a vote of confidence if he ever imposed conscription.

Hanson had said he had no confidence in King. When King offered him the chance to vote no-confidence, he scorned the offer. The Opposition had the right to throw the Government out if it could, but in time of war it had no right to undermine the Government by partisan sniping unless it could provide an alternative. It had no right to destroy the leader of the Government unless it could suggest another.

King looked around the House. Where was another leader to be found? There was no answer to that. Once again the whale seemed stranded.

The great debate ended in a disagreeable one-man filibuster by Pouliot, who, twisting and sputtering with rage, upbraided Ralston as the archconspirator, his generals as "mummies tied up in red tape." After Cardin's appeal to history, Pouliot's gibbering appeal to mere prejudice was a pitiful anticlimax.

Conscription, without limitation, became the law of Canada. The first stage of The Crisis was over.

King mistook the first stage for the last. If he underestimated the drain on manpower sure to make conscription finally unavoidable, up to now he had succeeded brilliantly, beyond all reasonable expectations. He had put complete conscription on the statute books, appeased English-speaking Canada, healed the breach in his Cabinet, held Ralston on one side, St. Laurent on the other, and miraculously survived a break with the Quebec members.

How deeply had he wounded the French Canadian people? Who spoke for them—Cardin or St. Laurent? It was too early to tell. With no intention of imposing conscription, King did not have to face that question yet. He never expected to face it. He could safely ignore Hanson, Coldwell, and Pouliot, and the loss of Cardin, a more formidable man, must be accepted. What King failed to observe in the summer of 1942 was the stone face of Ralston. And what Cardin and the anticonscriptionists overlooked in their fury was a Quebec which, as represented by St. Laurent, understood affairs far better than anyone yet imagined.

So, by calculation and miscalculation, by mixture of patriotism and politics, by clash of enduring historic forces and brief human persons, the second stage of The Crisis already was prepared.

Cardin had begun to push it forward with a plan of his own to force King's retirement and replace him with Howe in a Howe-Cardin administration, a new version of the traditional two-headed partnership first invented by Baldwin. Hearing of this, as he heard everything, King scoffed. He respected Howe as a genius in administration but as for political leadership Howe "hasn't even the patience to conduct an interview—how could he run a party?" The Howe movement (its intended principal having no part or interest in it) came to nothing.

Fully occupied on the tightrope of conscription, King had little time for the side issue of the Hong Kong debacle, by which Drew was now making his mark as a future party leader.

As this book cannot begin to tell the story of the military war, it must suffice to say that Chief Justice Sir Lyman Duff was appointed as a Royal Commissioner to consider whether the Government had mismanaged the Hong Kong expedition and, by failing to supply them with equipment, had left the gallant troops helpless before the Japanese hordes. The Duff report largely rejected the charge of incompetent management, though blaming the Quartermaster General's branch of the Defence Department for lack of energy in moving certain vehicles to Hong Kong. Duff called the Canadian expedition "well trained" and "well provided with equipment . . . an expedition of which Canada can and should be proud."

Drew alleged that the Government had refused Duff "very important information" and "blood-curdling facts." The Government replied that Drew had prejudiced recruiting and broken the Defense of Canada Regulations. When the legal proceedings against Drew were withdrawn, he wrote to King that Duff's findings were "directly contrary to the evidence as a whole" and that it would be fraud to deny the people the real facts. King refused to table Drew's letter because, he said, it contained secret information involving the British Government.

After two days of angry debate, the Conservative motion of censure was defeated by 130 votes to 34. The Government had suffered by the public suspicion that Drew might well be right, in part anyway. This did no harm to Drew's career as Conservative leader in Ontario. He had begun his own march toward Ottawa.

Another worry which King was compelled to endure in silence arose out of his Government's diplomatic relations with the Pétain regime of Vichy. To most Canadians the association with Vichy appeared humiliating and dishonest. King was attacked by the Conservative Party for a cynical attempt to placate the neutralists and Vichy supporters of Quebec.

He could not tell Parliament that Cordell Hull had implored him to keep his representative at Vichy so that the United States might do the same in preparation for its landing in French North Africa. As Hull warned Lord Halifax on April 25, if Canada rebuffed Pétain the United States could not remain alone in Vichy against the protests of its own people.

Halifax agreed. King, with lips sealed by the need of military security, maintained his formal recognition of Vichy and listened helplessly while his critics in Parliament and in the press accused him of profiting politically from the ruin of France. The role of middleman between Washington and London provided its secret tribulations along with its public plaudits.

Behind all the struggles of politics, the nation's military struggle went forward more successfully than the puzzled Canadian people had yet realized. Howe's industries were producing massively. Power's air-training scheme was supplying airmen far beyond its original targets. Macdonald's Navy of 50,000 men was carrying its full share of the Atlantic Battle. Ralston's Army, of five divisions in England, was becoming, in McNaughton's phrase, a dagger aimed at Berlin. Ilsley, his health almost broken by an insupportable burden of detail, by his excessive conscience, and by his distrust of King, was somehow saving the overladen national economy from an inflationary collapse. The landing fields of the Northwest air route were built as Canada's contribution to the defense of Alaska, the Americans meanwhile completing the prodigy of the Alaska highway.

King escaped briefly from his troubles in Ottawa to tell the American Federation of Labor at Toronto that the war must produce a new order in the world and, in Canada, a "national minimum" of full employment, adequate nutrition and housing, social insurance against unemployment, accident, death of the breadwinner, ill health, and old age. In December he informed the Pilgrims of the United States at New York that Canada now had 600,000 men on active service and that "the new order must be a world order . . . governed by a universal rule of law . . . based on human rights and not on the rights of property, privilege or position."

Brave words, but the Allies had yet to face the real fighting of the war and King a sudden reversal of fortune. The year ahead was to be one of his worst so far. Still worse were to follow.

Meanwhile, the Conservative Party, after its repeated defeats under Meighen, Bennett, and Manion, after watching Meighen's final elimination in York South, was preparing to rebuild itself on a new geographical base.

By its attitude to conscription it had lost any hope of re-entering Quebec in the visible future and was confined almost entirely to Ontario. If it was to recover, if indeed it was to survive, it must find wider ground.

Meighen had been meditating a Conservative drive into the West and as a former westerner he thought he saw in John Bracken, Premier of Manitoba, the perfect agent of this strategy.

Bracken—a professor of agriculture who had entered politics by accident, had fully mastered his new trade in provincial government, looked every inch a statesman with his fine mane of iron-gray hair and sharply carved outdoor face, but was hopelessly ignorant of national affairs—had been approached long before York South to accept the Conservative Party leadership but had refused.

This was hardly surprising since his coalition Government had always lived on the support of the Manitoba Liberal organization and he was regarded as a Liberal who still called himself a Progressive for purposes of convenience only. How Meighen hoped to convert a low-tariff Liberal Progressive into a high-tariff Conservative was not clear. King at least regarded the project as absurd. Nevertheless, Meighen persisted. Bracken could learn federal politics and while learning could deliver the prairie vote. As always, Meighen, who knew everything else, knew nothing of the voters.

Himself eliminated from politics, he half persuaded Bracken to take his place. When the Conservative convention met in Winnipeg in mid-December, Bracken was still in a harrowing state of uncertainty. On the one hand, as a patriot with sons fighting in the war, he was moved by Meighen's plea that his duty was to revive the Conservative Party as the essential instrument of victory. On the other, his record was Liberal in everything but name.

Murdoch MacPherson and John Diefenbaker, of Saskatchewan, and Harry Stevens and Howard Green, of Vancouver, were already candidates for the leadership. Half an hour before nominations were to close, Bracken, hard pressed by Meighen, still could not make up his mind. Agreeing at last, he rushed from his home to the convention hall and strode breathless upon the platform with a scant minute to spare.

He would accept the leadership provided the Party, as a sign of its conversion to a western and reform policy, would add the word "Progressive" to its name. The convention agreed and accepted Bracken, provided he cut loose from his past, became a Conservative, and delivered the West.

The decision was close and lacked enthusiasm. Perhaps half the Party distrusted a former Liberal, regarding Bracken as one of King's castoffs. His selection was Meighen's strategy and Meighen, even in defeat, was still the idol of his Party, an elder statesman who could do no wrong, even though he could not win an election.

Thus the Progressive Conservative Party, with a confused platform combining its ancient principles and some of Bracken's agrarian heresies, with a leader who knew nothing of federal politics and less of Conservatism, with a deep internal split barely disguised by the pumped-up ardor of the convention, hopefully began another trek toward yet another disaster.

In Ottawa, King heard the news and relaxed in the certainty that Meighen had once more delivered Canada into his hands. In Winnipeg, Bracken, by refusing to enter Parliament because he feared King and his own inexperience, assured that delivery. Another victime had been added to the long roll of Conservative immolation.

As King knew, the attempt to square the circle by placing a western, low-tariff Liberal at the head of a Conservative Party based on the protectionist areas of Ontario could not work. Meighen's final mistake was now consummated. Within a few months Meighen knew that himself. King for his part must have known that even he did not deserve such help from his enemies.

35

Back to Politics

IN THE YEAR 1943 THE WORLD TIDE CHANGED AND THE ENGULFMENT of Hitler began. By a bitter paradox the first intimation of military victory brought King and his Party within clear sight of political defeat. Before the year was out, the Canadian Government had reached the nadir of its fortunes.

King saw no advance sign of this sudden descent. On the contrary he felt that the hump of war, politically speaking, was past, though he knew that the worst military battles were still ahead. After the Cabinet crisis of the previous summer, the conscription issue was quiescent. The Canadian war effort had neared its peak and was going well. Meighen was out of the way.

Bracken, the new Conservative leader, was dismissed by King as harmless and rather pathetic. King told this writer on February 5 that Bracken was a "nice fellow" but would be a total failure. This was assured already by Bracken's refusal to enter the House, where his duty lay. How, asked King, did Bracken expect to impress the Canadian people when he spent his time like a political organizer attending country fairs, curling matches, and milking contests?

Being afraid to face Parliament, Bracken could not hope to face an election successfully. The Conservative Party, said King, would have been wiser to choose Gordon Graydon or Murdoch MacPherson. Almost anyone would be better than Bracken.

Actually, King affirmed, Bracken was in the wrong Party anyway. He had always been a Liberal, whatever he called himself, and would be gobbled up by the Tories, whom he vainly expected to convert to Progressive policies.

After Bracken's elevation at Winnipeg, King had written him a letter of gentle regret at his apostasy and saying that he had intended for some time to invite him into the Liberal Cabinet. This was rubbing Bracken's nose in Toryism and King chuckled maliciously at the thought of it.

Of course, he admitted, the Government, like all war governments, was suffering somewhat from public discontent. It would come back as strong as ever. "I only wish," he exclaimed, "I were twenty years younger for the next fight!"

Turning to the war program, he insisted that it had been kept in balance from the start. No, he added, that was not correct. The Army was far too big. "I said from the first day of war we should concentrate on the Navy, the Air Force and industry. Ralston, a very sincere man, insisted on a big Army and he got it against my judgment. Now we must take some men out of the Army and put them into industry. The present situation is ridiculous."

He would have preferred to break up the overseas Army and use it in separate contingents where it was needed. McNaughton was determined to keep it intact, organized as a complete and self-contained force. There might be a change in that policy. (Such a change was only a few months off.)

. Looking back on the record as a whole, King was well satisfied. "I was never," he said, "so right about anything in my life as when I refused before the war to make any commitments and refused to answer when I was asked what we would do if Britain went to war, and said that Parliament would decide. That brought the country into the war united.

"Yes, and I was absolutely right in the conscription plebiscite. What would have happened if I had refused to get a release from our promise not to conscript men for overseas service? I would never have been forgiven. The most difficult time was when I told the Cabinet we will go back to Parliament for approval if we conscript boys for overseas. What, they said, go back to Parliament? Yes, I said, go back to Parliament. But I knew we'd never go back to Parliament because we won't have to. There'll be plenty of boys, more than we need, without conscription. When the public sees the next budget there'll be no more demand for a bigger war effort."

He laughed again—too soon.

The most serious problem in the country, he went on, was inflation. "You know," he remarked with another chuckle, "I said to Roosevelt last time we met, how do you expect to go on spending all these billions out of deficits? The President said, well, Mackenzie, my family has held French securities since before the Revolution and they're still paying interest; why can't we do the same?"

At this revelation of Roosevelt's economic adolescence, King raised his hands in a gesture of friendly despair. It was hard, he confessed, to see what would come out of this dizzy sort of financing.

King looked well that day, better than he had ever looked to his

Y

interviewer. His eyes were bright, his cheeks full of color. His secret, he said, was never to work to the point of being tired. Whenever he felt tired he quit working. He always went to bed at ten o'clock and slept soundly. Still, at sixty-eight he couldn't maintain his old pace.

His working methods had preserved his health through three years and a half of war but they had been hard on his colleagues.

Since he had taken to rising late, arriving at his office about noon, and calling the Cabinet into session soon afterward, the other Ministers, who had been up early and worked all morning, usually missed any chance of a proper lunch and managed only to bolt a sandwich in the cafeteria before the House met. If the War Committee finished its business early and saw a chance for a decent meal, King would often insist on dealing with other business until nearly three o'clock. How his colleagues lived and ate was not his affair. Like Clemenceau, he was making war. His own health, key to the entire war effort, had first priority. He never neglected it for a single moment.

About this time he told a young Member of Parliament, recently converted to religion, that he depended absolutely on prayer. He felt himself to be a humble instrument of the Divine Will in the affairs of men. Over and over again in his speeches he was inspired to say just the right thing, which came to him suddenly, without previous preparation. Without this Force constantly in him he could not possibly have borne his burden.

Thus he moved comfortably through the parliamentary session of 1943. It developed no issues to disturb the Government and showed that King was beginning to think about the postwar world. On July 9 he announced his theory of a "functional" allocation of power among the nations in an international organization. Power in the organization, he said, could not be divided equally among all nations, because their actual power differed, but representation in the various works of the organization "should be determined on a functional basis, which will admit to full membership those countries, large or small, which have the greatest contribution to make to the particular object in question."

That was to say, if a nation like Canada could make a special contribution to any project it should be given the opportunity at the highest level, though it could not exercise the same authority in some other field.

The functional principle was applied to the United Nations from its beginning.

In the foreign-policy debate of July, King's long-vanquished enemy, the "single voice," appeared again briefly. When Howard

Green, of Vancouver, a respected Conservative of the old school, proposed that "the British family of nations should speak with one voice in foreign affairs," King allowed his new parliamentary assistant, Brooke Claxton, to demolish in argument a theory which he had himself demolished in fact at the 1923 Imperial Conference.

On the strength of his speech, Claxton—a young man with a look of owlish wisdom, a tough mind, and an almost unbelievable energy —was evidently a newcomer to watch. King was watching him and already using him for much more practical affairs than the single voice, on which he had no more time to waste. He had not quite heard the end of the single voice. A more formidable statesman than Green was preparing to revive it, with unhappy results.

From the speeches of King and Claxton, at least the skeleton of a postwar foreign policy could be glimpsed. It was fleshless but its bare bones included: victory in the war; friendship with Britain and the United States; support for their efforts to establish, with Russia and China, an international organization to maintain peace; full Canadian commitments to this organization; expansion of world trade; and maximum production at home. If most of this was vague aspiration, one item of the policy was clear and firm—Canada was finished with isolationism forever.

The same debate brought from King his first cautious gesture toward Newfoundland. When Noseworthy, Meighen's victorious opponent in York South, urged that Newfoundland be persuaded into Confederation as a vital sphere of Canadian defense, King replied that if the Newfoundland people decided in favor of union "beyond all possibility of misunderstanding, Canada would give most sympathetic consideration to the proposal."

The light of welcome was set burning publicly. Privately, King was determined to add the tenth province to Confederation if he could. He must move slowly lest he alarm the brittle and divided Newfoundlanders.

Noseworthy had feared that they might decide to join the United States, whose troops were stationed among them. King's unspoken thoughts went much further than that. He believed that the island inevitably must fall into one of the American nations or the other, that if it fell into the United States and Canada were thus hemmed in on its Atlantic coast, the results would be disastrous.

After such a spiritual defeat, after finding its Atlantic gateway in the possession of a foreign power, he feared that Confederation itself would be endangered in the long run. A Canadian nation which could not assert its own Manifest Destiny in its own area of vital interest against the original American version of that doctrine

might not be permanently viable. One essential item in the agenda
of his own Manifest Destiny, though he had never talked of it
before, was the extension of Canada to what he considered its natural
boundaries. He must do it in his own way, by persuasion. He would
not be hurried. In the end, he succeeded where all his predecessors,
from Macdonald onward, had failed or never tried to succeed.

When McNaughton's Army had been broken up in the spring and
a division assigned to the Italian campaign, King awaited the landing in Sicily with strained nerves. The Canadians were to reach
Sicily on July 10. For King it was the worst day of the war.

After the Canadians' years of garrison duty in England, while
other armies fought in the field, an impatient nation must be told at
the earliest possible moment that its boys were in the line at last.
King asked the British War Office to make sure that the presence of
the Canadians in Sicily was announced with the first news of the
Allied landing. He got no satisfaction in London. The War Office
proposed to announce merely that British units accompanied Eisenhower's Americans.

Furious at this stupidity, King telephoned Roosevelt and told him
that he could not face the Canadian people if they were affronted
by the proposed British communiqué. This, he said, was a matter of
political life and death to his Government. Would Roosevelt order
his generals to mention the Canadians in the first despatches? Roosevelt promised to cable instructions to this effect immediately.

By long experience King knew that orders of that sort might be
mislaid or ignored by some bungling staff officer. He lay awake all
night, his second sleepless night of the war, wondering if the world
would hear on the morrow of the Canadians' landing. Early in the
morning, his suspense was relieved and he fell asleep at once. Roosevelt's orders had got through and had been obeyed. The Canadian
nation knew that its Army was in action.

In August, King welcomed Roosevelt and Churchill to their first
Quebec conference. Its deliberations—apart from a useful discussion
between British and Canadian staff officers—were confined to the
two senior partners. The junior was torn between envy of their
power and relief that he did not have to face their responsibilities.
They kept him well informed on the war (being far too optimistic)
and Churchill almost cried as he thanked King for the aid without
which Britain could not have survived.

While the major Allies planned their grand strategy, King had
time and quiet to consider his own political troubles, now mounting.
He also enjoyed the satisfaction of announcing by radio that Canadian troops had joined with the Americans in occupying Kiska.

Their battle line now stretched from the Pacific to the Mediterranean.

Roosevelt visited Ottawa on August 25 and in a public speech did
his best to bolster up the sagging prestige of his host. Of King he
said that the Quebec conference had been happy to welcome "that
wise and good and gallant gentleman, the Prime Minister of
Canada. . . . My old friend, your course and mine have run so
closely and affectionately during these many long years that this
meeting adds another link to the chain." As Roosevelt was more
popular in Canada than King could ever be, his praise was valuable
to a politician who, at the moment, needed all the help he could get.

On September 8, King hurried to the radio to announce that Italy
had surrendered and that the Canadians had been among the first
Allied soldiers to land there. Two days later, on the fourth anniversary of the nation's entry into the war, he was on the air again to
praise the incredible achievements of the Canadian people, to explain
the revolution in the national economy, but to warn that the hardest
fighting had yet to come.

Canada had amazed its friends and itself by the work of those
four years. In retrospect, they were the largest years of accomplishment in its history. Achievements in battle and industry, however,
did not necessarily mean votes for the Government which had managed them.

Since the spring, the Government's political strength had deterior-
ated in inverse ratio to the increasing strength of the nation.

By midsummer, the Government's popular support, as gauged by
the Gallup poll, had sunk to a new low. In the 1940 election it had
held 55 per cent of the popular vote. Now, according to Gallup, it
held 35 per cent. The Conservatives had stood stationary with 31
per cent. The C.C.F. had risen from 8 to 21.

At the grim spectacle of the chart which showed the curves of
the three parties approaching one another, and the Liberals still in
decline, many of King's lieutenants were alarmed and incredulous.
Alarm turned to panic when the Conservatives won the Ontario election, the C.C.F. made heavy gains, and five days later the Federal
Government lost four by-elections.

By all visible signs no Canadian party could hope for a majority
in an early election. The C.C.F. believed it would win 70 or 80 seats
and might be the largest group in the next Parliament. Coldwell was
ready, if necessary, to form a government and, challenged in Parliament, to appeal to the country for a working majority. The Bloc
Populaire Canadien, a brief splinter which represented the old
isolationist rebellion against the Liberal Party in Quebec, expected

50 French Canadian seats. The Conservatives and Liberals would split about equally in a general stalemate, paralyzing the war effort.

So spoke the Gallup figures and many of King's advisers. He did not believe them. The figures might be accurate at the moment but they ignored the decisive factor which figures could not measure— the proven ability of King to turn defeat into victory when he got around to it. He was getting around to it.

Some exasperated Cabinet Ministers proposed a general election right away, not because it could be won but because a Government apparently opposed by a majority of the public could not hope to fight, much less win, a war. King had planned an election in 1944. He had no intention of throwing it away now by default. Amid the counsels of despair he remained serenely confident that he could rally the people behind his Government again. It would be, as he realized, a formidable undertaking and it must be started immediately. The next six months were vital.

What had happened to the Government's great majority of 1940? How could it be recovered?

Among the ablest politicians to ask himself these questions was the young lawyer and former regimental sergeant-major Brooke Claxton. He had many qualities, not the least of them a sense of political pressures and a talent of party organization. By now he had become a kind of junior Minister of Politics and head of a secret brain trust whose assignment was to plan the next general election campaign.

Claxton and his friends—all obscure figures, the Cabinet being too busy for such work—concluded that the public was incensed against the Government, first, because of the slow progress of the military war; second, because the irritations of wartime taxes, wage controls, and regulations of all sorts touched every phase of daily life; third, because the nation had been given no clear hope of a better future after all its sacrifice had produced victory.

The nation's public strains were easy compared to the secret strains of its Government. Ralston's Army, Macdonald's Navy, Power's Air Force, Howe's industries, and Gardiner's farmers were engaged in a wild scramble for manpower. The price ceiling was cracking under almost intolerable strain, and below it the wage freeze had started to thaw. Donald Gordon faced his Waterloo, waiting, like Wellington, for night or Blücher, and wondering if his thin red line would hold until victory. It was, as Ilsley knew best, the thin red line of deficits in the budget of a nation trying to consume more than it produced. In the low countries of that time Ilsley felt like the Dutch boy with his finger in the dike. Beside him Gardiner whispered that the whole West would be lost to the Party unless the farmers were allowed higher prices. Above all, the swelling Army of some 70,000 men, conscripted for home defense and now contemptuously called "Zombies," could no longer be justified.

As the brain trust saw it, all these physical strains must continue and probably would increase until the war ended. Perhaps they could be eased, in the public mind at least, by the promise of a richer postwar life for everyone. This promise the brain trust, in constant consultation with King, proceeded to elaborate in a many-sided diagram.

Earlier in the year, King had been laying down some broad objectives like work for everybody and a higher living standard when the cost of the war had passed. Now the brain trust handed him a detailed program for his next election and for the good society of the future. King liked it all except for the one item of family allowances, at which he balked.

The aging radical was ready to go a long way and saw at last the chance to complete the Welfare State of his dreams. The notion, however, that the Government should give money every month to the parents of all children in the land struck him as ridiculous. No Parliament, he said, would ever consider such prodigality. His Scottish instincts were appalled.

Yet family allowances had powerful support, not merely from politicians, who had to win an election, but from nonelected economists. The idea had originated in an investigation of substandard wages in some industries. Since the Government could not afford any general wage increase lest it break the price ceiling, it was urged by some of its advisers to compensate the very poor with allowances from the treasury.

As this plan was studied further, it appeared impossible in practice to draw a line between the man earning, say, $25 a week and the man earning $26. To grant allowances to one class and refuse them to another hardly better off would produce endless friction and political damage to the Government when it tried to make these delicate distinctions. Then why not allowances for everybody?

The Bank of Canada and the Finance Department answered eagerly in the affirmative, not for political but for much larger and longer reasons. All their thinking was conditioned by the great depression and by a total miscalculation of the postwar climate, from which they expected another depression to arise. They had all become Keynesians in varying degrees, accepted the general theory of compensatory spending, and believed that the state must ward off an industrial collapse by a vast transfer of income to assure an adequate public purchasing power. Family allowances provided one large channel for that transfer and they were thus supported by some of the hardest-boiled economists in the business, less for humanitarian than for purely economic reasons.

Combined with the humanitarians and the politicians, the economists were strong enough to sell their plan to the Government. Still King rejected it until, by sheer accident, he encountered one night the brilliant son of a soldier who had been killed in the first war.

This youth had been brought up and educated on his father's pension. In talking with him King exclaimed aloud at the discovery that the war pension differed only in amount and not in principle from the proposed children's allowances. The war pension had saved a whole family from destitution and produced a remarkable young Canadian, who would go far. These facts were obvious when you came to think of them but King had not thought of them. Now, in a typical moment of intuition, he saw a sudden light. As usual, he made his decision on the spot and then retired to find reasons for it.

When he emerged the following day, he was ready to claim family allowances for his own and to prove their soundness economically. The brain trust had won a notable victory not by argument, economic theory, or figures but by King's sentimental moment with the son of a dead Canadian soldier. Most Canadians imagine to this day that King based his decisions on facts. None of importance was ever based on anything more than an instantaneous conviction, supported with facts afterward.

Children's allowances were the most dramatic feature of the new Liberal platform and the most effective bait for votes in the next election but they were only one item in the omnibus plan which the brain trust now produced out of its summer's deliberations. At its September conference in Ottawa, the Liberal Federation was presented with the completed work. Its series of resolutions, all approved by King in advance, became the chart of the Welfare State and of King's lifelong dream.

Today these reforms are commonplace, the accepted methods of the social system. In 1943 they were breathtaking in their radicalism. Under normal conditions they would have required years of public education and political conflict. A nation whose mind was concentrated on the war approved them with little debate and no significant opposition.

Briefly, the new chart proposed children's allowances; housing schemes and other public works financed by the state; floor prices for farmers and fishermen; labor-management councils in industry to facilitate collective bargaining; labor representation on governmental boards and agencies; health insurance; universal old-age pensions; the extermination of monopolies in restraint of trade; the expansion of unrestricted international trade; generous pensions and employment opportunities for war veterans, later called the Veterans' Charter; full employment, a rising standard of living, and minimum nutritional standards for all. Unemployment insurance having been enacted already, the Welfare State could hardly think of anything more to guarantee.

The seeds planted in 1933 had now produced a teeming harvest. King stood where he had always wished to stand, to the left of the Conservatives, a little to the right of the Socialists, on the upward road to the more abundant life. Keynes had taken possession of the Canadian economy.

As always, the large decisions were taken with the least fuss. Perhaps the largest social decision ever made in Canada was a state guarantee of full employment by the use of the Government's fiscal powers—a decision from which there could be no retreat, around which all the politics of the future would center, and the results of which have yet to be tested in bad times. This historic turning point was marked by an obscure signpost. Few Canadians bothered to read it and still fewer understood when they had read it.

"Financial considerations," said the Liberal Federation, "have not been permitted to limit the national war effort. . . . The National Liberal Federation believes that the use of public finance and the national credit to promote the welfare and prosperity of the country in peacetime will be limited only by the measure of agreement attained by the Canadian people on national objectives, and by the united will to achieve them. . . . These objectives cannot be achieved on pre-war levels of national production, national income and national revenue. Fiscal policy should be designed to promote rather than to retard the expansion of national production and national income."

In nationalizing the Bank of Canada King had created the engine to produce this peaceful revolution (for it was nothing less) without realizing the power of his creation. Now the engine was to advance under full steam and Keynes would be the invisible figure in the driver's seat. The use of the money system "in terms of public need" had been a cliché in 1933. Just ten years later it was firm government policy.

The state, in short, had guaranteed a job to anyone who wished to work, at least subsistence to those who could not work, a richer life for the nation as a whole.

King thus had completed his own revolution of the Liberal Party and was about to build a dream into law. Had he bitten off more than he could chew? He had no doubts about that.

His speech to the Liberal Federation was the first battle cry of the election planned for the following year. After concentrating almost exclusively on the war, King was back in politics, none too soon.

He reminded the nation, with suitable modesty, that he had led his Party longer than any contemporary statesman in the world; he believed he had the confidence of the country or he would resign at once; he was certain that no other party nor any combination of parties enjoyed "a comparable degree of confidence"; and if he were to announce an immediate election "there would be throughout Canada, not rejoicing but consternation."

The Gallup polls, the Ontario election, and the by-elections he construed as the results of the Government's virtues, not its defects. The Government had abandoned political organizations and all thought of party politics after 1940, while the Conservatives and Socialists had been busy with nothing else.

The official Opposition had ceased even "the pretence of co-operation with the Government in its war effort," had introduced in York South "a conscription issue which would have split this country from one end to another and vastly impaired Canada's war effort." That issue had been avoided by Meighen's defeat, the 1942 plebiscite, and the fact that the available ships could not begin to carry all the eager volunteers overseas.

For the first time, King turned his attention to Bracken, who had yet to feel the crushing power applied to his predecessors. Bracken's duty, King said, was in Parliament. He was acting only as a party organizer instead of co-operating in the war effort. The C.C.F. was no better. Its members had favored a "stay-at-home" policy in 1939, and now, while promising co-operation in the war, "their actions fail to measure up to their words." Pretending to be Labor's only friend, the C.C.F. was quietly sabotaging the price ceiling, Labor's real protection.

Finally, the new Quebec isolationist rump, called the Bloc Populaire Canadien, opposed the war outright and was the only Canadian party "whose platform and policies are contained in the single word 'non.'"

All this political conspiracy against a Government interested solely in winning the war had multiplied parties, groups, and factions in a fashion to remind Canada of unhappy France and should be a "terrible warning" of a "national peril." These attempts to split the nation and destroy its Government had created "an intolerable situation which cannot be allowed to continue." If it did continue, the

Government would appeal to the country and King was certain of the result.

The Liberal politicians hearing that speech rejoiced to find that the old master's hand was as deft as ever. King once again had turned the defensive into the attack by indicting the opposition parties for damaging Canada's war effort and the prospects of victory. He had threatened the nation with an election which it did not want in wartime. He had ordered his own Party back into the battle of politics. He had given it a new program so comprehensive and radical as to cut the ground from under any other party. He had used the reverses of 1943, like those of 1930, to turn the tide when it was flowing hardest against him.

The tide carried certain unpleasant shapes not observed in his Party. All it saw in 1943 was a leader who might win one more election. It must be his last. In the measurement of King's physical powers, the hour was later than he or his friends supposed.

36

The Glory and the Dream

MANY STRANGE FIGURES HAD CROSSED THE INWARD AND OUTWARD life of King and in their passage largely shaped it. His mother in the first place, then the memory of his grandfather, then the noble Laurier, and Laurier's successor, Lapointe—all these to be counted as his friends, mentors, and idols, who nourished him and offered no threat to his own ambitions. The enemies he had removed one by one—Meighen, Bennett, Manion, Hepburn, and other lesser obstacles now forgotten, to which dismal roll of casualties he was soon to add Bracken. Even friends like Crerar, Dunning, Gardiner, Gouin, and lately Cardin he had quietly sidetracked before they could endanger him.

At the end of 1943, the latest of these brief distractions appeared from an unexpected quarter.

General McNaughton had long been critical of Ralston and the Canadian military command in Ottawa. For the most part he had been allowed to go his own way in building his compact Canadian overseas Army, the dagger aimed at the heart of Berlin. On the insistence of his Government he had seen that Army broken up with the dispatch of a division to the Mediterranean and, on attempting to visit it there, had quarreled openly with Field Marshal Montgomery, who threatened to arrest him if he set foot on the soil of Sicily, though this fit of temper on Montgomery's part was never put in writing.

The Imperial General Staff already had complained to Ralston about McNaughton, Ralston had stood loyally behind his General, and was finally told that McNaughton, though an able organizer and a master of military technique, was unfitted, at least physically, to command an army in the invasion of Europe. The disagreeable duty of dismissing McNaughton was left to Ralston.

After a sleepless night, Ralston told McNaughton the truth.

McNaughton accepted it with a soldier's dignity. He was tired and ill from his labors and his health could be given as the public reason for his retirement. Shortly afterward, in a bitter cable to King, he protested his treatment by Ralston, whom he seemed to hold responsible for his eclipse, as if Ralston had been anything but his much-enduring friend.

For the Government this was a ticklish business. McNaughton was at that time the most respected Canadian. His legend and magic were above politics and no politician would willingly question them. Nevertheless, when McNaughton's cable was shown to the Cabinet War Committee, the civilians proved too strong for the soldier.

As the French Canadian Ministers remarked, the Government might suffer incalculable damage in the politics of Quebec if it became known that a Canadian general had been dismissed on orders of the British War Office. That damage must be accepted. There could be only one Government and no doubt of the civilian control over the military. Ralston had dismissed McNaughton on the Government's full authority. Ralston must be supported without further question. King agreed while seeing farther ahead than his colleagues. To him McNaughton was more than a soldier. He was, perhaps, the only Canadian who, if he entered politics, might threaten the Government. McNaughton was a man to be watched, feared, and conciliated.

When McNaughton returned to Canada early in 1944 and told the newspapers, contrary to the official announcement of his resignation, that he was in good health, the public was puzzled and alarmed. The Conservatives in Parliament demanded an explanation. After King had showed them the secret record, proving that McNaughton had been dismissed on the recommendation of the War Office, they said no more.

For the next six months McNaughton was forgotten in the gathering fury of the European war and The Crisis at home. In due time he would reappear, cast up by the volcano of the conscription issue, and, having served his purposes, would join the other notable monuments of lava now marking King's long march. Among them all, from Meighen onward, McNaughton was fated to be the most remarkable and tragic.

Meanwhile, on January 24, another unhappy arrival in Canada felt King's lethal contact.

Lord Halifax, British ambassador to Washington, advocated in Toronto the Titan Theory already pronounced in the "explosive" speech of Field Marshal Smuts. Since the postwar world was to be dominated by a few superpowers, said Halifax, the Commonwealth must be one of the Titans with "a common foreign policy, expressed not by a single voice but by the unison of many."

While the common voice was thus rejected in words, King saw in the Halifax speech the old ghost exorcised in 1923. This, apparently, was a new démarche by the Empire consolidators of London. Where consolidation had failed after the first war, it might succeed after the second.

The voice of Canadian nationalism was instantly raised in full cry against Halifax, who unwittingly had touched the mainsprings of the nation's life. It was more than nationalism. Canadian liberalism— using the word without party connotation to cover most of the nation—saw in the Titan Theory not only another attempt to consolidate the Commonwealth with a single voice but a return to naked power politics in world affairs, when the free peoples everywhere had been told that they were fighting for a new world order under the rule of law.

The ferocious debate set off by Halifax was useful in clarifying the Canadian mind on the future and there could be no doubt of its judgment. Even the confused mind of Bracken rejected the Titan Theory in favor of King's concept of the Commonwealth as a community of autonomous states within the larger community of a brave new world. King obviously had the great majority of Canadians behind him when he flatly repudiated both Smuts and Halifax, and denounced the concept of a power balance maintained by the Titans. In it, he said, "lurks the idea of inevitable rivalry between the great powers."

This theory would simply mean that Canada must accept a common foreign policy in the Commonwealth and "apart from all questions as to how that common policy is to be reached, or enforced, such a conception runs counter to the establishment of effective world security, and therefore is opposed to the true interest of the Commonwealth itself. . . . Our commitments on these great issues must be part of a general scheme, whether they be on a world basis or regional in nature."

By a tortuous path, the statesman who had construed the League of Nations as a mere purveyor of sweetness and light had finally accepted Dafoe's alternative of a world authority equipped with power and ready to use it in the maintenance of peace. In his twenty-five years of struggle and defeat, Dafoe and his friends evidently had succeeded. At least they and events had converted King and turned an isolationist into an internationalist, who more and more resembled a Canadian Woodrow Wilson. Dafoe unhappily was not present to witness this conversion and the vindication of his own lifework. He was dead but his dream of the future had become the practical politics and the firm policy of Canada, supported by all political parties.

It was a springtime of dreams. The free world and its Russian ally were now assured of victory. Already they were planning the United Nations. Mankind looked forward to an era of democracy and permanent peace. It would take the world several years to detect Russia's true policy, to accept the stern fact that it was still far short of its vision, that for all its victories and its speeches it was the same old world which had blundered into the war and emerged with only a redistribution of power and a change of labels. King was to see the truth within twelve months and end his days in profoundest pessimism. At the moment he was incandescent with the light of the great dream.

He uttered it, in perhaps his greatest speech, before the British Parliament on May 11: "The glory and the dream—are they not being realized at this very hour?"

The glory and the dream. Such was the civilians' marching song as they followed from a safe distance the march of the soldiers, now about to cross the Channel and liberate Europe. A brief glory and a dream beyond mankind's reach.

King's London speech established him, if he needed any further public recognition, as an elder statesman of the Commonwealth in the company of Churchill and Smuts.

As they walked up the aisle of Parliament together Churchill, not having seen King's manuscript in advance, appealed to his "Dear Friend," in an anxious whisper, not to say anything against the British Preference, which had always conflicted with King's theories of unrestricted trade. King listened to the appeal and read his speech without change.

It was another flat repudiation of the Titan Theory in probably the most striking paragraph King had ever written: "Like the nations of which it is composed, the British Commonwealth has within itself a spirit which is not exclusive, but the opposite of exclusive. Therein lies its strength. That spirit expresses itself in co-operation. Therein lies the secret of its unity. Co-operation is capable of indefinite expansion. Therein lies the hope of the future."

A Commonwealth of free nations, pursuing their own ways and their own policies, yet constantly seeking by consultation and cooperation a path parallel to one another and to the broader march of the world's democracy—that was King's interpretation of the glory and the dream.

It contained, besides the stuff of dreams, a solid recipe for prosperity perhaps not pleasing to Churchill, the old Liberal free trader, since he had become the leader of a Conservative Party devoted to the Preference system of trade concentrated in Commonwealth and Empire. "Now," said King in a blunt passage, "is surely the time for the world to realize that, just as no nation of itself can ensure its own safety, so no nation or group of nations can in isolation ensure its own prosperity." The world, in short, must be made one both economically and politically—no Titans of politics or of trade.

If this was not what a protectionist British Government wished to hear, on the side of either politics or economics, it was exactly what the world and Canada demanded in the springtime of the glory and the dream. The London conference of Commonwealth leaders, in its brief communiqué, apparently agreed with King that the unity of the Commonwealth nations must grow in strength by consultation and co-operation but must do nothing which, in King's words, might appear to their own people "as an attempt to limit their freedom of decision or, to peoples outside the Commonwealth, as an attempt to establish a separate bloc."

The Titan Theory was thereby rejected, or, at any rate, laid aside. In 1923, King, the apprentice statesman, had needed all his courage to resist the centralizers of London. Now, when he was the leader of a nation powerful in its own right, events had made his views the commonplace of Commonwealth policy and, on a wider scale, the apparent objectives of all the Allies. History seemed to be moving forward, the dream a reality. Its motion unhappily was circular. Few saw that in the electric spring of 1944 as the Russians rolled westward to meet their friends in the heart of Europe and Stalin appeared to proclaim the spirit of a democracy slightly postponed.

King's judgment even of immediate circumstances was distorted during his English visit by no less a personage than Field Marshal Montgomery, and with appalling results.

Sipping tea at a secret hideout beside the Channel, where the European invasion was soon to be launched, King was taken fully into Montgomery's confidence. Montgomery himself had sought this curious interview. Though always skeptical of politicians, he seemed to trust King and had a message for him.

The removal of McNaughton had greatly relieved Montgomery's mind, but he wanted King to understand that if Lieutenant General H. D. G. Crerar, McNaughton's successor, did not succeed in the European invasion, he, too, would have to go. This, as Montgomery foresaw (being himself a politician of talent), would be a second pill of bitterness for King and Canada to swallow. They deserved advance notice of it.

King's reaction surprised Montgomery. He had expected the politician to resist another political embarrassment at the hands of the military. Instead, King agreed at once that if Crerar failed in Europe he would be replaced. King hoped that this would be unnecessary and that, if Crerar failed, another Canadian commander might be found. He was willing to leave these affairs to Montgomery's discretion.

This part of the secret conversation turned out to be irrelevant. Crerar did not fail and the problem foreseen by Montgomery did not arise. Before the teacups were empty, however, Montgomery, quite unwittingly, had planted in King's mind the chemicals of an almost fatal explosion.

The Overlord expedition, Montgomery said, should last only about three months (and perhaps would have ended in that time if Montgomery had been given by Eisenhower the chance to carry through his plans). The Canadians would suffer heavy casualties in the first phase of the invasion and then would be withdrawn, reorganized, and rested. King was left with the impression that the war would be won before the year's end and that the Canadian Army would face no serious reinforcement problem.

Montgomery actually warned him that large reinforcements would be needed under the best of conditions. King replied that this presented no serious difficulty because ample replacements were available. A little puzzled by this assurance, Montgomery concluded that King knew his own business.

In any case King left Montgomery finally assured that Canada could complete the war without overseas conscription or any revival of The Crisis. On the strength of the timetable outlined over the teacups, King decided to call an election late in the year or early in 1945 to catch the electorate before the first warming glow of victory had cooled.

After reviewing Canadian troops on the South Coast (where he was kept far distant from the parade so that the soldiers would not recognize and boo him as before), King arrived in Canada to find its mood much improved.

The Canadian people had been proud of his London speech, his recognition among the great, and the increased national stature which he seemed to represent. Parliament was quiescent, the Conservatives finding no reason to quarrel with the Government's foreign policy, Bracken still acting as a party organizer instead of seeking election, the C.C.F. clearly slipping. The Government had emerged from the nadir of 1943 and was climbing upward again. The Liberal brain trust had recovered from its spell of jitters.

z

When Parliament approved the Liberal Federation's program of the previous autumn, King was satisfied that he could win the next election not long hence without extending himself. The legislation now enacted was the second huge installment of the Welfare State first launched in 1935. It offered a larger package of reform than most Canadians bothered to consider and it involved future costs which they have hardly grasped, even today.

The package contained, among other things: generous provisions for war veterans; an Industrial Development Bank to finance new industries; a state-supported housing scheme; a system of credits for farm improvements; floor prices for agricultural products and fish; credits to finance exports; a promise of universal old-age pensions and health insurance if the provinces would agree to them (the pensions being inaugurated eight years later and health insurance indefinitely postponed); a system of family allowances, to begin in mid-summer 1945, more generous than any in the world. At the last minute King insisted on adding a traditional Liberal policy by abolishing all tariffs on farm machinery.

Never in its history had Canada undertaken at one bite such a gigantic budget of state intervention, whose implications are the practical politics of the present day. That was not the end of it. Behind all the state services thus promised stood the Bank of Canada, with an engine of money expected to keep the economy always in balance and the nation always prosperous.

Whether King was the architect of the Welfare State, or merely the agile tool of historic forces that would have built it without him, will always be disputed. By 1944 the fact remained that the Welfare State existed, on paper anyway, pretty close to the model laid down in *Industry and Humanity*. It had arrived perhaps earlier than he had expected and its arrival had marked him as Canada's most successful reformer.

In all this, there was a central flaw. King, or events, had been building for a world which did not exist and was not likely to exist for a long time. The powers of evil, against which his youthful fervor had rebelled, were still stronger than he and most other statesmen imagined. Soon they would drain the energies of the new society away from the pursuit of happiness into the mere pursuit of safety.

Apart from that, while the machinery of welfare had been constructed by law, while Canadian Liberalism had reversed its course under King and become almost unrecognizable by historic standards, no one could be sure how the new society would work under test, and the test had yet to be faced.

In the springtime of the glory and the dream, few Canadians

understood the current assumptions and still fewer questioned them. Another shape, much more disturbing, was overlooked by King and his enemies—the stubborn, immovable shape of The Crisis. It had always been there from the first days of the war. It had been by-passed two years before. After the long march it seemed now to be far in the rear. Actually, politics, always a circular process, was about to stumble blindly and shatter itself on this forgotten obstruction.

37

The Crisis, Second Phase

I N AUGUST, AN INTERESTING MILITARY SIGNAL FROM LONDON CROSSED
Ralston's desk. That systematic man read and initialed it but did
not show it to the Cabinet.

Had the Cabinet read the signal it would have been no wiser.
Ralston's officers in England informed him merely that a shortage in
the Army reinforcement pool would be made up within two weeks.
If Ralston had known then what he discovered later, he would have
recognized this reassurance as clear warning of trouble. It was the
first unnoted trickle of a cataract.

No wonder Ralston failed to grasp its meaning. His Army was
winning its largest battles of the war. His staff had told him and
was still telling him that no reinforcement problem existed. All
casualties would be replaced from the volunteer force now in training. The military experts had miscalculated the rate of casualties
and the reinforcements available to replace them but Ralston had no
means of guessing that in Ottawa. Hence the signal failed to disturb
him.

Under the same comfortable impression, King went to Quebec in
mid-September to attend the Churchill-Roosevelt conference in a
state of high optimism. He found the Americans apparently anxious
to finish the Pacific war almost exclusively as their own show, and he
was delighted to hear that they wanted few if any Canadian forces.
Canada offered only about 10,000 men and a small air force. This
was all, or more than all, that the Americans needed.

With the Japanese commitments thus limited, with the European
war scheduled to end by Christmas, with no sign of a reinforcement
problem, King addressed the Quebec Reform Club, his eye on a
forthcoming election. It was a speech he would regret.

Lapointe had gone but King would carry on his work of protecting the interests of French Canada. That promise was harmless and sincere enough. In the next breath King was carried by his new optimism right off the deep end. He reminded Quebec that he had refused to enforce overseas conscription and declared that he would never enforce it. This in the midst of the war's heaviest battles, which already were failing to go according to Montgomery's schedule.

Ralston heard of King's speech and instantly protested. By this time he had new reason for protest. He had heard the first disturbing rumors from his overseas Army. King mollified Ralston by saying that he had merely reiterated the policy laid down in 1942, that in speaking of conscription he had mainly the Japanese war in mind. The 1942 policy still stood—not necessarily conscription but conscription if necessary.

Perhaps Ralston should have been wiser and more cynical. Still trusting King, he was satisfied with this explanation. He took it as a confession that King had gone further than he intended in his speech and would not repeat the mistake. In any case, Ralston had no time to worry about King or the election. He was worried by something much larger.

The famous signal of August had given only the smallest inkling of a reinforcement shortage and it was denied by the assurances of the General Staff in Canada. Yet the ugly rumors continued and found their way into the press. Presently there was something more than rumor. On September 18, Major Conn Smythe, M.C., the hockey magnate, who had come home, wounded, from the war, told the newspapers that the reinforcements now joining the Canadian Army in Europe were "green, inexperienced and poorly trained" and that, as a result, casualties were unnecessarily high.

The Smythe interview angered Canada, disturbed King, and staggered Ralston. Were the real facts being suppressed by the Army command overseas or the Staff at home? Ralston decided to find out for himself at first hand. When he flew to Europe, the final act of The Crisis, still hidden from its actors, was under way.

In Italy Ralston was asked by the officer in charge of reinforcements if he wanted the official version or the truth. Shocked at this opening question, Ralston replied that he wanted the truth. He was told that the shortage of reinforcements was desperate. The figures proved it. After studying them he flew to the northern front and found the same answer at the Canadian headquarters there.

In Brussels he learned that men wounded two and three times were being sent back into the line. The Canadians were to be used in clearing the west bank of the Rhine, where they would certainly face still heavier casualties, far beyond replenishment by the available reinforcements.

As an old soldier himself, Ralston was dumfounded. As a Minister who had been misled, he was outraged. As a man long overworked and now self-accused of letting his Army down, he was sick with anger and anxiety.

As Brigadier R. S. Malone recalls in his book of war recollections, *Missing from the Record*, Ralston dined at an army mess that night in a state of agitation too obvious to be concealed. He ate little, uttered hardly a word during the meal, and as soon as it was over took Malone to his trailer. Beside a coal-oil stove, the two friends shivering in their topcoats, Ralston announced a decision certain to shatter the Canadian Government and nation. He said he had already cabled King outlining the Army's true situation and asking for an immediate Cabinet meeting. If the Cabinet would not agree to overseas conscription and thus provide the Army with reinforcements, he would resign.

He was sure, however, that this would not be necessary. King had promised conscription "if necessary." It was now necessary beyond all dispute. King would keep his word.

How had the real state of the Army been kept so long from its responsible Minister? The rate of casualties had been higher than the Army command had expected but this fact alone, as Ralston now realized, did not explain the sudden shortage of reinforcements or the Army's failure to inform him.

There was no time now to pursue these inquiries. Later on, Ralston sent a trusted military man secretly to London to study the Army reports and see when and how they had gone wrong. The facts, it was thought, would be needed to meet Conservative criticism in the next election. Those facts were never unearthed. Ralston and the Government had been led, blindfolded, into the most dangerous emergency in the nation's history.

Ralston prepared to fly home, bringing The Crisis with him. Even in these hours of harassment he still found time to visit a wounded soldier whose mother had complained that her boy had gone into the line without proper training. No detail was too small for The Colonel's attention. That quality, because it wasted his time and energy, was his only weakness as an administrator. His problem now was no longer administrative but political. He must be tested as a statesman.

Ralston landed at Rockcliffe airport on October 18 and was met by some of his colleagues. In the evening he gave King a rough outline of the facts as discovered in Europe.

From that night onward, The Crisis spun hour by hour to its climax. A record of the next month reads almost like the stage directions of a plan somewhat too fanciful even for fiction, with a fictional ending beyond belief.

As summarized below, the record is unofficial, unauthorized, and, by the nature of the events involved, can never be completely documented by anyone. Probably there are a few pertinent documents as well as King's diary. The documents cannot tell the story because it was contained mainly in unrecorded conversations. The diary will tell it from King's viewpoint only.

What follows represents the recollections of seven major participants, three of whom have since died, among them King himself, who provided the most vital passages. Actually, much of this queer business is on the public record of Parliament—the principle of Cabinet secrecy thrown to the winds—in such fragmentary and confusing fashion that few have bothered to put it together.

One word of caution should be offered to the reader before the writer attempts to place in chronological order a huge mass of disjointed facts, casual discussions, and hurried encounters: Many of the facts were never written down by anyone, some witnesses forget certain incidents, and others disagree in their recollections. But for the first time, so far as the writer is aware, the story as it emerges from the collective evidence, after several years of inquiry, can be told in some detail, with confidence in its accuracy.

October 19:

Ralston reported to the War Committee of the Cabinet his findings in Europe. Immediate reinforcements were needed, he said, and could be secured only by the full use of conscription to send the Zombies overseas. The shortage was bad enough now and would be worse after the great battles already pending.

King listened in silence. At Ralston's first words he saw that all the calculations of his tea party with Montgomery had somehow gone awry. He understood little of war on the military side, he distrusted the military mind, but he knew a political catastrophe when he saw it. And this clearly had, for him, his Government, and the nation, the makings of a catastrophe larger than any since Confederation. As usual, instead of meeting it head-on, he attempted to divert it.

As soon as Ralston finished his report King solemnly warned the Cabinet that conscription would split the country irreparably for a generation at least. In any case, he said, conscription was not practical, even from the immediate military standpoint. Before it could be invoked, Parliament must be called, probably an election would result from Parliament's division, action on reinforcements would be delayed for at least two months and might then be too late.

This statement amazed Ralston. As he had feared but never quite believed, King was slipping out of the bargain made in 1942. Without losing his temper, Ralston reminded King of the promise that if conscription proved necessary it would be imposed instantly by order-in-council, without a debate in Parliament. Conscription could be applied in two days at most.

St. Laurent (who now had become, as the accepted leader of his people, the fulcrum of The Crisis in Quebec as Ralston was in English-speaking Canada) at once expressed strong sympathy with Ralston's views. He saw the need of reinforcements. But it was late in the day, he said, to change the Government's policy. While King had promised conscription "if necessary," St. Laurent had taken this to mean "if necessary to win the war," whereas Ralston seemed to interpret it as meaning "if necessary to reinforce the Army at its existing full strength." It was a quarrel of misunderstanding.

King quickly agreed that St. Laurent had interpreted his original promise correctly. By his definition, conscription still was not "necessary."

King was quibbling with words. The facts were now laid before the Cabinet in a top-secret memorandum from Lieutenant-General Kenneth Stuart, Chief of the General Staff. Ralston's interpretation of King's promise might be reinterpreted to suit King's convenience. The facts of Stuart's memorandum were unbelievable but could not be denied.

In this primary document of The Crisis, Stuart admitted that his earlier estimates of the Army's need for reinforcements had been wrongly put together in England. In addition to this technical error, the General Staff had been faced with heavier infantry casualties than it had expected. Moreover, an early end of the war, on which the Staff's planning had been based, no longer could be assumed. Fighting, casualties, and the need of reinforcements might stretch into 1945. Thus, while other troops were being remustered into infantry formations, to which the whole problem was confined, it appeared that reinforcements would be short by some 15,000 men at the year's end. Reluctantly, Stuart asked the Cabinet to send the Zombies overseas—15,000 immediately and from then on reinforcements of 5,300 a month.

The Stuart memorandum was couched in the clipped, factual language of military protocol. It filled less than two typewritten pages. As its writer doubtless knew, it contained enough explosive power to demolish the Government.

Reading it, King felt betrayed by the military mind. Had he not been assured by Montgomery of a quick victory? Had he not been assured by the Canadian General Staff as late as August that it could find all the men it needed without conscription? Now, without a word of warning, he was handed an ultimatum, and probably would be handed Ralston's resignation also if he did not capitulate. The Government might fly apart on the eve of an election, taking with it the nation's unity and the work of his own lifetime.

Stuart was called in person before the War Committee and asked to explain his volte-face. He reiterated the conclusions of his memorandum—miscalculation of figures, unexpectedly heavy casualties, Allied reverses, prolonged war. The Cabinet heard him and adjourned without agreement. Ralston was determined on conscription. King was just as firmly opposed to it. Within the Cabinet two clear sides were taking shape for a showdown.

October 20–23:

The War Committee continued a desultory discussion of reinforcement figures while both sides stalled for time before approaching a decision. The lines were pretty clearly drawn by now.

On one side stood King, St. Laurent, Power, Gardiner, Ian Mackenzie, and some lesser members, who intended to reject Ralston's ultimatum even if he resigned. They were confident, so far, that the Government could survive his resignation. They had grossly underestimated both Ralston's strength in the Government and the strength of his policy in the country.

The other party within the Cabinet was far more formidable and determined than even King suspected. When he was told by a trusted friend that he might face not only Ralston's resignation but the loss of half a dozen key Ministers he dismissed the warning as absurd.

Besides Ralston the conscriptionists now numbered Crerar, Macdonald, Ilsley, and Gibson. Howe had remained neutral, though the conscriptionists counted on him in the showdown. There would be others. The hard core of the rebellion, Ralston, Crerar, and Macdonald, were as anxious as King to avoid a breakup. These were not amateur adventurers seeking anything for themselves. They had nothing to gain and knew as well as King what conscription would involve. Like him, they were inclined to overestimate and were horrified by the prospect of a racial disruption of Canada.

Nevertheless, they agreed that, if necessary, the risk of disruption must be taken, only after every possible chance of compromise and agreement had been exhausted.

With excessive confidence in Laurier House and a hardening unity among the conscriptionists, The Crisis, still unknown to the Canadian people, dragged through a restless and indecisive week end.

October 24:

The argument now moved from the War Committee into the full Cabinet. Still overconfident, King asked the opinion of each Minister in turn.

The Quebec members, St. Laurent, Power, Michaud, Fournier, and Bertrand, all rejected Ralston's recommendation. So did Gardiner (with his usual vehemence), Mackenzie, and General LaFleche. Humphrey Mitchell, the burly Minister of Labor, who professed to understand manpower problems, insisted that vigorous voluntary recruiting would make conscription unnecessary. Claxton seemed to agree. J. A. MacKinnon, a mild and well-loved gentleman from Edmonton, who hated trouble, thought it was too late to change the existing policy.

The conscriptionist group was smaller in numbers but powerful in influence.

Crerar, the only Minister who had sat in the conscriptionist Cabinet of the first war, said conscription was necessary now to get men and to prevent a revulsion of public opinion against the Government.

Ilsley was prepared to take the final step if reinforcements could not be obtained otherwise.

Macdonald, while equally determined, still hoped for a compromise which would apply conscription without smashing the Government and the country.

Gibson, the young Ontario Minister, was perfectly clear in his mind. He was for conscription.

Howe, obviously to be counted in the conscription camp in the final decision, said rather pathetically that it was tragic to find a purely political crisis threatening to spoil a magnificent national war record. As his colleages understood his rather confusing statement, he did not care particularly whether there was to be conscription or not, so long as the war was won and so long as the Government could stand together. With conscription or without it, he urged, the Government must not split. A decision one way or the other there must be. He admitted, however, that he would hardly dare to show his face in his own part of the country if the Government refused to send the Zombies overseas.

The meeting of October 24 settled nothing but it showed King that The Crisis was a much bigger thing than he had guessed. It was, indeed, the biggest thing in his career and perhaps the biggest danger since Confederation. He was haunted by the memories of

1917. He foresaw a nation riven by a racial wedge, the war program disintegrating, the Liberal Party wrecked by the very issue on
which he had rebuilt it after Laurier's defeat. For him tragedy was
compounded with irony in the ultimate nightmare.

Still, he managed to sleep soundly enough through it all, never
lost his temper, his outward composure, or his courtesy to the men
who, as he thought, were bent on ruining him and Canada.

He believed he could effect a compromise and keep Ralston, or
at least Ralston's friends, in the Government—provided he could
gain time. Deliberately, therefore, this master of Fabian tactics involved the Cabinet in an interminable argument on the details of
the Army's needs, the real state of reinforcements available in
Canada, and every technical point he could raise. He asked his
friends to keep talking in the hope that an accommodation of some
sort would somehow emerge.

At all cost, a decision must be postponed. To this end the fertile
mind of Claxton was given full scope in the invention of various
interesting and futile devices, while Mackenzie hurried between
the two factions, called meetings in his apartment, wrote notes to
colleagues, and, by a constant flood of correspondence and conversation, tried manfully to disguise the intractable disagreement
which his side refused to face.

October 25:

The Cabinet wearily retraced all the ground of the previous meeting, reargued Stuart's figures, and, under King's skillful steering,
remained long short of a decision.

October 26:

The War Committee met at four in the afternoon and received
from the General Staff some figures apparently offering an instant
escape from The Crisis. There were 120,000 soldiers in Canada, in
various stages of training, who had volunteered to fight anywhere,
and 90,000 more in Britain.

King and his side clutched eagerly at this calculation, for it
seemed to deny Ralston's need of conscription. With over 200,000
volunteers available, what reason to change the present policy when
only 15,000 reinforcements were presently required? For a moment
the anticonscriptionists happily concluded that there was no Crisis,
except in Ralston's mind. Only for a moment.

The over-all figures, as Ralston quietly informed his colleagues,
were misleading. Certainly plenty of men had volunteered to serve
overseas but most of them were physically unfit for service or had
not been trained as infantry.

To King this statement was incomprehensible. Over 200,000 soldiers and still not 15,000 ready for battle? This must be another mistake in the General Staff's calculations. No, said Ralston, the latest figures unquestionably were accurate. Even the urgent reinforcements could not be squeezed out of the volunteer stream. They could be found only among the Zombies.

King and his side remained incredulous. Ralston's latest figures must be checked impartially. At King's suggestion, Power and Macdonald were instructed to meet the experts of the General Staff and cross-question them that same night.

As the Cabinet broke up again, the anticonscriptionists confident that a way out had been discovered and the Ralston group standing firm on its figures, King confided to his intimates that there were larger factors in The Crisis than he cared to discuss openly. If he were to be driven from public life, he said, Roosevelt would be gravely embarrassed, since Roosevelt counted upon him to bring Canada into a postwar world-security organization and to influence the Commonwealth in the same direction.

The conscriptionists, King intimated, were playing with more dangerous international fire than they realized. Having dropped this warning, which, as he knew, would quickly percolate through the entire Cabinet, King retired early to bed while Power and Macdonald questioned the Army experts until the early hours of the next morning.

Both men knew this meeting to be vital. If they could persuade the Army to find 15,000 physically fit men in the Canadian volunteer force, The Crisis would be over before dawn. Like Ralston, the Army replied that no such reinforcements could possibly be raised. Of the 120,000 volunteers in Canada, many were not infantrymen and only infantrymen were needed. Many more, fit for home defense, could not pass the physical tests for battle.

The discussion continued for five hours, the experts refusing to yield, Power and Macdonald arguing that the necessary reinforcements surely could be raised, if necessary by a slight down-grading of physical standards among a few of them. When the meeting broke up and the exhausted participants went wearily to their homes, they were as far apart as ever.

October 27:

The War Committee listened to reports from both sides on the abortive meeting of the previous night. They settled nothing but provided at least some new points of argument and, as King wanted, another chance of delay.

October 28 to 31:

As the War Committee continued to meet daily, King's friends

began to propose a series of ingenious compromises and diversions.

At one point, King said he should perhaps consult Churchill, or
even Roosevelt. Next day he concluded that, after all, such a move
might be unwise. The mention of these two illustrious names had
served his purpose. He was using them as silent witnesses to the
danger of splitting Canada and damaging the Allied cause.

Frequently he repeated that he would never, never use conscription. If it was to be applied, some other Prime Minister could apply
it. With equal emphasis he insisted that reinforcements must be
obtained by voluntary means and he had no doubt they could be
obtained. By now the conscriptionists listened to these repetitions
as to a gramophone record. If they had listened more carefully they
might have detected more than sound. A plan was forming vaguely
in King's mind.

In the meantime, with King's encouragement, Claxton presented
an elaborate plan under which the Zombies would draw lots to
decide who would go overseas. No one was much impressed with
this proposal and variants of it. On the jutting stone chin of Ralston
all compromises seemed to founder.

For sheer improbability, the next scene in the unfolding drama
of the Cabinet chamber had no parallel in that place. King looked
around the table and asked each of the leading Ministers one by
one if he could form a government. Ralston refused, remarking icily
to King that "I assume you are only asking out of curiosity?" King
then turned to Macdonald, who also rejected the invitation. Ilsley
was not impressed. Crerar had no ambitions and neither had Howe,
who insisted again that there must be a policy for or against conscription.

None of his Ministers took King's question seriously. He must
have known their answers in advance. Why did he conduct this
solemn poll? Doubtless to demonstrate that he himself was the only
possible Prime Minister, the indispensable man. No one, not even
his strongest critics, had doubted it. All these men wanted King to
remain, the Government to live, The Crisis to be peaceably solved.
They differed only on conscription.

This kind of strain—a Cabinet on the verge of dissolution, an Army
in urgent need of reinforcements, a European campaign going badly,
a public uneasy at the first news of The Crisis in Ottawa—could not
be endured much longer. The breaking point must be only a few
days off.

The Cabinet debate had become only a kind of ritual, a daily
routine. Behind it the real debate was conducted in Ministers'

offices, in their homes, and on the telephone. No such debate had
ever shaken Ottawa before. There had been broken Cabinets. There
had been resignations, dismissals, and rebellions. There had been
betrayals, throat-cuttings, and Nests of Traitors. This Crisis differed
from all others not only because it struck far deeper into the stuff
of Canada, not only because it threatened a more deadly wound,
but because the element of personal ambition was almost entirely
absent.

The leaders of both sides were personally as close as ever. They
had no secrets from one another, continued to meet as before, and
together calculated the chances of their victory or defeat.

King's supporters, for example, fine-combed the roll of Liberal
members in Parliament and concluded that the Government could
survive in the Commons on a nonconscription policy by some
twenty-five votes. This estimate was freely discussed with the conscriptionists and they were inclined to agree with it. Power, knowing
more about the Commons than anyone, believed that a united anticonscription Government could carry both Parliament and nation
but a split Government would be defeated. Or, if it scraped through
Parliament with a small parliamentary majority, it would not be
viable. It might exist briefly but could not govern.

Mackenzie and some of the junior Ministers refused to abandon
hope of forming a new anticonscription Government. If Ralston and
his friends resigned, they could be replaced. Such outside figures as
Hepburn, McGeer, and Arthur Slaght, all critics of King, could be
imported to give the Government a new appearance of strength in
the country.

King listened and said little. He had begun at last to fear that
he might not survive the loss of half a dozen of his most respected
lieutenants. Ralston, Macdonald, and Ilsley would carry the Maritimes with them. Howe would split the Party in Ontario. Crerar
represented a large opinion on the prairies, which even Gardiner's
personal power and political organization might not outweigh. Mackenzie represented British Columbia but it would certainly repudiate
him.

King's strategy was to hold the rebels one way or another or, if he
could do no better, to split them from Ralston. The loss of Ralston
would be exceedingly grave. If he went out alone, that shock could
be endured. The trick was to destroy Ralston singly if that became
necessary. So far King dared not attempt it.

Observing the calm face of the first man who had ever seriously
threatened him from within his Cabinets, King seethed with a secret
sense of betrayal. He had not been betrayed by Ralston who, as he

knew, was incapable of betrayal, but by events, mostly by the blunders of the military men. It was insufferable that his Government should perish, that he should lead his Party back to the very ruin from which he had rescued it after the conscription schism of the first war, above all that his own career should be shipwrecked, not on a firm rock of principle but on a synthetic and false issue.

To King The Crisis was utterly synthetic and demonstrably false. On the one hand, he could not believe that with 120,000 soldiers available in Canada, less than a tenth of this number were fit for overseas infantry service. On the other, the Army could get plenty of volunteers from among the Zombies if it wanted to get them, if its officers would make a real attempt at recruiting, as obviously they were not doing.

The military experts, not he, had brought the Government to this pass. "Why blame me for the mess?" he cried out to one of his friends. The mess was the product of the General Staff. It had misled him and the Government by an unforgivable mistake in simple arithmetic. He had always suspected that the generals were overexpanding their Army, but when he asked them they invariably replied that they could carry through their plans without conscription. Now, because they had botched their job, they expected the Government to rescue them at the price of its own suicide.

King had been assured by no less an authority than Montgomery himself only five months before, and by Churchill a year earlier, that the war should be over by the year's end. If this schedule was maintained there would be no further need for large Canadian reinforcements. Now it appeared that the schedule had broken down.

The military facts were not clear to King yet. As he learned later, Montgomery had quarreled with Eisenhower on the strategy of the European campaign, had presented a plan for a concentrated knockout blow, had been refused the necessary American troops, and now saw victory postponed indefinitely while the Americans advanced on all sectors at once. For such strategy, which in any case was outside the range of his knowledge, King found no time. He had his own battle to fight and, to him, it was the battle for the inner safety of Canada.

A cruel, unnatural, and unnecessary battle which the military mind could not be expected to comprehend. It might know its own job, but once it crossed the line between military strategy and statesmanship, it was lost. It could not grasp what King had long known, what had been burned into his memory by the ruin of Laurier in 1917—that the issues now breaking his own Cabinet went far beyond military planning, were infinitely more important to Canada than 15,000 troops (who could make little difference in the war anyway), and were likely to break the nation.

King had finally reached the point where he knew that he must hold Cabinet and nation together, with or without conscription. He was still sure he could succeed without it if Ralston would give him the chance. That was the first question to be answered. If Ralston refused to be reasonable, he must go. So much, but no more—no plan for replacing Ralston, no method of holding Ralston's friends— was clear in King's mind when the Cabinet broke up after another worthless meeting on the night of October 30.

In the chemistry now threatening to explode the Government, the three basic elements could be distinguished. Each of them was a human being, a passing accident of politics, but each portrayed and temporarily controlled a separate portion of the perpetual conflict in the organic nature of the Canadian species.

On one side of the argument, Ralston represented the best qualities of English-speaking Canada. He was not an imperialist. He had no traces of colonialism in him, nor that "butler mind" of Dafoe's famous phrase. The Colonel was Canadian to the core. He wanted Canada to be a great nation in its own right, not a satellite of Britain or any other outside power. He saw everything of value in Canadian life imperiled by the war and, because he was so Canadian, he wanted his country to fight its own war to the limit of its resources.

To him the reinforcement of the Army was the test of Canada's integrity, of its worthiness to be a nation. He was no hater of the French Canadians. He understood their feelings as well as any Anglo-Saxon can understand them. He was willing to go a long way to satisfy them, had gone a long way already, had doubtfully accepted the compromise of 1942, withdrawn his resignation, relied on King's word, and worked within the limits of the Government's policy.

Now that the final test had arrived, he believed that if Canada failed it, all the Canadian people, Anglo-Saxon and French alike, would reap the harvest of national failure in the long run, and that, in the short run, the nation would be more seriously split by failure than by a bold decision. The nation could be split by Quebec's refusal to accept conscription. It would just as certainly be split, and more deeply, if the majority was finally compelled to accept the veto of a minority. The majority would end by hating the minority, which would then suffer far more from its victory than from an apparent defeat.

In short, the reinforcement of the Canadian Army, a few thousand men, could make little difference to the outcome of the war. The refusal of reinforcements would humiliate and scar the nation, damage Quebec, and sow dissension for at least a generation to come.

The Colonel, with all his abilities, was at bottom a very simple man. He believed in the simplicities of right and wrong, prayed daily before his God, and was guided by what he conceived to be the answer to his prayer. For him there could be no doubt where right lay in this argument and he was incapable, by his very nature, of defrauding it.

As Ralston represented the pull of history, which sucks the Anglo-Saxon back to his origins overseas, Power represented the pull of geography, which holds the French Canadian to his own land. In this ancient struggle, the case of Power was the most improbable and accidental element. Perhaps better than any other figure concerned in it, he revealed the nature of The Crisis. It was not military but human.

Power had no French blood, had learned the French·language only after long study, was himself a wounded veteran of the first war, now awaited news of his son, a prisoner of the Japanese in Hong Kong, and yet he, more than any other member of the Government, was determined never to accept conscription.

As this most agile political mind of his generation read the political riddle, English-speaking Canada, busy as usual with its daily business, would forgive and forget Quebec's refusal to vote the final measure of military war. The French Canadians, not so practical and far more emotional, would never forget or forgive their coercion by the majority. Conscription would convert Canada into a second Ireland. And as the Liberal Party would no longer hold Quebec, as Quebec would have no trusted interpreter in Ottawa, it would insulate itself from Canadian life. It would be represented in Parliament by a racial bloc wallowing in grievances and hating Confederation.

Besides, as one of the three Defence Ministers, Power believed with King that it was ridiculous to say that 15,000 fit men could not be secured among the available volunteers. Was the nation to be mutilated in a mere statistical dispute?

In their personal as in their public lives, Ralston and Power illustrated the Canadian nature. Its elements, always divided, somehow could get along together. Throughout The Crisis Ralston was admired by no one more than by Power. These two old soldiers might fight on the opposite sides of a political argument. They were united by the ties of affection and memory which nothing could break. In the end, Power alone would go with Ralston into the wilderness, for

A A

opposite reasons of policy but for the same reasons of honor and
friendship.

The third element appeared in St. Laurent. He was the catalyst
of this chemistry, inserted in it, as if by design, to avert the explosion. He alone possessed the blood of both races and alone could
feel their contrary instincts. In him the ancient conflict achieved a
private synthesis, toward which the nation has always groped and
is still groping. This fact of itself made him the decisive element in
The Crisis and potentially the most powerful Canadian when it had
passed.

Until now, St. Laurent had taken little part in the wrangles of
the Cabinet and less in the ceaseless conversations outside it. As
King knew, however, St. Laurent's position was vital. King might
be able to hold Quebec, or part of it, if conscription were finally
invoked, provided St. Laurent agreed. If St. Laurent followed the
instincts of his French blood, if like Laurier he preferred the fatherhood of his people to public office, if he refused conscription under
any conditions, then conscription could only mean the retreat of
Quebec into isolation again, for a long and bitter time to come.

St. Laurent was only half French, he had no personal ambition
except to retire at the war's end, and, still knowing little of politics,
was not thinking of The Crisis with his blood but with the coolest
head in the country. What was the practical course? What would do
the most good and the least harm?

St. Laurent was ready to settle The Crisis on any workable compromise, regardless of personal consequences and of strict logic. In
his private crisis this most typical of all Canadians turned instinctively to the middle course which is Canada's destiny. And more
than anything else, St. Laurent's willingness to compromise would
save Canada from rupture.

These, then, were the two elements of explosion and the third
element of peaceful combination. It was for King, the master chem-
ist, to put them together.

October 31:

King could not delay much longer. By Tuesday of this terrible
week he knew that the next twenty-four hours must produce reconciliation or explosion.

All the facts of the conflict in Cabinet and nation were now sharpened to a narrow and alarming focus.

Ralston evidently would not yield. If thwarted further, he would
take his friends with him and disrupt the Government. St. Laurent
might compromise on conscription but King still was determined
never to enforce it.

Unfortunately for both sides, and especially for King at this turning point, Power fell seriously ill and was carried to hospital for an
emergency operation. The only anticonscriptionist Minister who had
full liaison with the Ralston group was removed from the scene,
could offer no advice, and could not even be told what was happening in the Cabinet during the decisive days of The Crisis.

The newspaper readers at last had learned that something very
big was under way. Quebec was angry, with a cold and threatening
anger, at the prospect of betrayal. The rest of the country, bewildered and doubtful, evidently was massing behind Ralston.

Without any decision one way or the other, these strains were
tearing Canada apart. They could not be tolerated for another day.
After all these weeks of bootless contention there must be a decision
tomorrow. But what decision? What possible safety valve to ease the
pressure? King had no answer. He knew only that he would never
accept conscription and if necessary would break with Ralston,
taking his chance on the results.

As King stood alone in his dingy office on the morning of October
31 and, looking across the Ottawa, Champlain's river, felt beneath
his feet the supreme watershed of Canadian history, a strange accident occurred. A messenger, arriving hurriedly at the Prime Minister's door, brought a sealed envelope, addressed in the handwriting
of Mackenzie. That prolific inventor of extraordinary remedies had
conceived his largest invention and rushed it to his leader in a scribbled note. The obvious solution, Mackenzie wrote, was to dismiss
Ralston and call in McNaughton as Minister of Defence on a no-
conscription policy.

It took King less than a minute to grasp the possibilities of this
diversion.

McNaughton was a fighting soldier, beloved of the Army, the very
image of Canada in arms. The people trusted him as a man above
politics, whose word against conscription would be accepted. Mc-
Naughton was known to believe in the voluntary method, yet no one
would say, as it might be said of King, that he was letting down the
Army, for it was his creation and his darling. Besides, he had a score
to settle with Ralston and this was his chance.

As an extra dividend on the transaction, the capture of McNaughton would rob the Conservative Party of the only figure who could
possibly revive it.

This, then, was the hour and McNaughton the man.

King telephoned him and arranged an interview for that evening
at Laurier House. The tall, soldierly figure, with the handsome,
grizzled face, the melancholy, brooding eye—a passionate man who

hid his passion under a bluff exterior, a man who might be wrong but never doubted that he was right—reached Laurier House after dinner, his arrival unknown to anyone save King.

At the same hour, the real powers of the Conservative Party were still discussing ways and means of making McNaughton their leader in place of Bracken, on a policy of conscription. They had approached McNaughton months ago, and even if he had been non-committal they were confident he would agree in the end. How could they imagine that their hero even now was in King's pocket?

While they talked and schemed, while the Cabinet waited innocently for another day of evasion and delay, while the news editors of the morning papers read again the endless speculation and repetition from their Ottawa correspondents, while the nation went quietly to its bed, two men sat before a fireplace in a third-story room, beside the lighted picture of an aged woman, and there they sealed their bargain. McNaughton would get the reinforcement without conscription.

King thought it the best night's work he had ever done. In some ways it was the worst. The bargain would destroy the public career of McNaughton. It would come within an inch of destroying King. Yet, incredibly enough, though neither could foresee where the bargain led in retreat and humiliation, it would avert the explosion.

38

The Executioner

NOVEMBER 1:
The morning after the interview at Laurier House was quiet in Ottawa. No whisper of the two men's secret had·leaked out. McNaughton was nowhere visible on Parliament Hill. King was in his office, apparently at work as usual. His Ministers went about their departmental business without suspicion and then to their luncheons in the Rideau Club and the Chateau. They were seated at table among casual friends, studiously avoiding any talk of The Crisis, when they received their first intimation of the overnight change.

Crerar had encountered Howe by accident in the Club and a few random words passed between them. Howe—that paradoxical man who could always decide any practical question on the instant but had wavered for weeks over a political decision in his view utterly impractical—had grasped the meaning of The Crisis at last. He said he intended to vote for conscription. If any further weight were needed, Howe's adherence to the conscriptionist wing of the Cabinet tipped the balance. King could not face the kind of mass resignations now impending.

As he was eating his lunch, Crerar was called to the telephone. The voice on the wire was King's, with an unusual note of strain in it. The Prime Minister said he had devised a solution of The Crisis. He would bring his plan to Cabinet that afternoon and he hoped that Crerar could support it. Crerar knew better than to ask a further explanation. He said he would consider King's recommendation on its merits. Meanwhile, he agreed to say nothing to anyone.

As Crerar returned to the dining room, he asked himself what King had in mind. The latest turn of events was the last thing he could have guessed. He knew, however, that King was working through him, the most determined ally of Ralston, to undermine the conscriptionist revolt. He would wait and see. The son of the prairie soil, who had nothing further to lose or gain in politics, would not be easily shaken. Or so he thought then.

Claxton was lunching with some trusted newspapermen in a Chateau bedroom. At King's request he was still busily contriving those endless compromises and diversions that would keep the Cabinet arguing, might somehow conciliate it, and at least would postpone a decision. In the middle of the meal the telephone rang. Claxton answered it and went suddenly white. In that small room his companions could not fail to hear and recognize the voice of King. His words were few and rapid. A new complication had arisen, a new remedy had been devised, and Claxton need not continue his efforts at conciliation.

With a puzzled look, Claxton hung up the receiver. What had happened? Like Crerar, he could not imagine. He was young then in politics and had been in the Cabinet only a fortnight but was destined for rapid advancement. He was a soldier like Ralston and, like Power, was a born politician, able to reckon The Crisis in terms of political adjustment. He trusted King as the only man who could adjust it.

With a few such preliminary warnings by telephone, when it was too late for the news to spread, King was preparing his intimates for the shock of the afternoon. It was essential to his strategy that Ralston should have no warning. He had none.

In midafternoon the Cabinet met as usual. On King's placid face at the head of the table no inkling of the previous night's bargain could be read. To all appearances this was to be another day of fruitless bickering. This dingy room, fronting on the river, had witnessed remarkable events, noble, tragic, and comic. It had heard many Canadian voices, from Macdonald's onward. But it had contained no personage remotely like King. It was about to witness an event unparalleled in daring, unspeakable in brutality, incredible in consequence. Of which only King and McNaughton knew the secret. A few others had been told that something was under way, no more. The plan behind the placid face could have been conceived by no one except King and, if known, could hardly have been believed.

When Ralston began to speak in his quiet tone, King listened with every appearance of interest and respect. The hand which held the invisible razor already was twitching.

The time had come, said Ralston, for the Cabinet to accept or reject his recommendation. These were chilling words. They were followed immediately by a last offer of compromise. Ralston would agree to a final attempt at voluntary recruitment from among the

Zombies. Once again the anticonscriptionists saw The Crisis dissolving after the black night. Ralston's next words showed that this dawn was false. He would agree to a recruiting campaign only for a brief, fixed period, say two or three weeks, and only if he were guaranteed that, in the event of failure, conscription would then be applied immediately.

King listened with respect, knowing all the words to be irrelevant. He was acting the transcendent role of a long theatrical career. The play had now become a solemn travesty. The aging actor who had played many parts—Heep, Hampden, and Galahad among them—had donned, with disarming look, the robes of Lord High Executioner. After this there would be only one more part to play. The actor had not foreseen it, nor the anticlimax which must follow this hour of triumph.

Ralston observed no weapon in King's hand. He saw only a small, pale man, tapping the table, as always, with the stub of a pencil. He thought he was among friends and colleagues and he was offering generous terms, more generous than the condition of his Army justified. While he did not believe that voluntary recruitment would succeed, he was willing to try it if thereby The Crisis could be solved and if he could be sure, here and now, that he would have his reinforcements by one means or another. They must be sent to Europe early in January, he explained, he must order troopships immediately if they were to be ready in time, and he must know now, today, that the ships would be filled.

This was Ralston's ultimatum. The Crisis had been reduced to a single question: not whether voluntary recruiting should be attempted, for all were agreed on that, but whether there was to be a fixed time limit on it. Ralston's offer was reasonable, far more reasonable than most of his friends had expected, and it strained both his patience and the plans of the Army to the limit.

In a desultory exchange of questions Ralston repeated that two or three weeks were all he could possibly spare if the Army was to be reinforced. Some Ministers thought the period too short. The conscriptionists feared it might be too long.

King continued to listen in silence, knowing that the period was neither too long nor too short but quite immaterial because he would not accept conscription under any conditions. Since he could get the soldiers otherwise, he would agree to no time limit, no restriction, no concession to Ralston, no bargain of any sort. At that moment, on the strength of quite another bargain, he was in his own mind the master of the Cabinet, the nation, and The Crisis.

The argument on the single point of the time limit proceeded in a fragmentary and halfhearted fashion. After an hour of this play acting, King looked around the table and judged that his moment had come.

Still in the matter-of-fact tone of a man who discussed a purely routine affair, he remarked that some two years before Colonel Ralston had submitted his resignation. At this the dullest mind in the room could guess that a blow of some sort was about to fall. The conscriptionists exchanged quick glances. Ralston sat motionless in his chair, regarding King with a steady eye. His expression did not change.

In the sudden silence following his first observation, King added that in view of Ralston's present attitude there appeared to be no chance of agreement in the Cabinet. For this reason he had decided to accept the resignation submitted by Ralston in 1942. Ralston's place would be taken by General McNaughton, who was confident of securing voluntary reinforcements.

That was all. The execution of Ralston had been performed in less than a minute. With a few crisp sentences, without a change of voice, King had struck down the idol of the Army, the most respected member of the Government, and, though few could realize it then, the most powerful man in Canada.

Would that man use his undoubted power? There was King's gamble, the most reckless of his life. The next moment would decide everything for him, for his Government, and for the nation.

As King waited through that endless fraction of time, Ralston rose slowly from his chair. Would he accept this dismissal, a stroke of ruthlessness without precedent in this room of many strange acts, or would he rebel and carry half the Cabinet with him? In their anger and pain Ralston's friends watched his face. It still showed no change. When he spoke, the voice also was unchanged.

He said he would send a formal resignation to the Prime Minister tomorrow.

The conscriptionists, the men who loved Ralston and some who loathed King, were stunned and uncertain. Should they go with their friend? Should they remain and condone his destruction? They had no time to think. Ralston calmly thanked King and the Cabinet for their co-operation, picked up his papers, and walked around the table, shaking the hand of each man as he passed. When he reached King no word passed between them. The two shook hands and Ralston strode briskly from the room.

As the door closed, King, a little flustered at last, remarked that he deeply regretted this unfortunate occasion.

Unfortunate indeed, but not for Ralston.

He had been tossed aside like a sucked orange. Without even the courtesy of advance notice, his leader had dismissed him before the whole Cabinet and no voice had been raised in his defense. His career was finished forever.

So it appeared as the door closed behind The Colonel. In fact, the man who had left the Cabinet chamber seemingly ruined held the future in his hand. King, the Government, and the Liberal Party were his oranges to be squeezed at will. The pinnacle of his career and the nadir of King's still lay ahead.

The Cabinet was too dazed to reckon such possibilities. King for his part considered the great gamble won. Ralston had gone alone. The Cabinet was intact after a mere change in personalities. The thing had been ridiculously easy.

It was not half so easy as King then supposed. He had failed to see that no one, not even McNaughton, could replace The Colonel in Parliament or country. King assumed that the magic of McNaughton's name would get the volunteers overnight. So did McNaughton. Unhappily for both, and fatally for McNaughton, each of the partners in the bargain of Laurier House overestimated the power and the magic of the other. Their partnership, not twenty-four hours old, already was bankrupt.

39

The Terrible Secret

AFTER DISMISSING RALSTON AND APPOINTING MC NAUGHTON, KING left the Cabinet chamber satisfied that The Crisis was over. Ralston went home to write his resignation and prepare a speech for Parliament. With that speech he could defeat King, McNaughton, and the Government, if he chose. By one word of invitation he could take all his friends out of the Cabinet and command the support of a large group, perhaps a majority of English-speaking Liberals in Parliament. The whole Conservative Party was eager to follow him if he chose to form a conscriptionist coalition government.

No private member of Parliament had ever occupied a comparable position of power before. Would he use it to revenge himself on King and McNaughton, to enforce his conscription policy, and to make himself Prime Minister? Ralston had no such intention. His only interest was to assure sufficient reinforcements for the Army, whether McNaughton obtained them by voluntary methods or by conscription. He would wait and see.

King realized Ralston's power of destruction but was hopeful it would never be used. He had gauged Ralston's course accurately. Ralston, as King knew, had no personal ambition and would give McNaughton every chance to make good the voluntary enlistment campaign. As King had no doubt of McNaughton's ability to find the necessary volunteers, the problem, apparently, had been solved, or soon would be.

With equal accuracy King had gauged the course of The Colonel's friends. Crerar, Macdonald, Ilsley, and other conscriptionist Ministers had been too flabbergasted by the afternoon's events to utter a word of protest at Ralston's dismissal. Their first impulse had been to leave the Cabinet with him. Then, without a moment to confer, they reached the simultaneous decision to remain and see The Crisis through. There would be plenty of time to resign and join Ralston if McNaughton failed and King still refused to invoke conscription.

As soon as the Cabinet adjourned they asked Ralston's advice. He told them emphatically to hang on. The Crisis, he said, was far from settled. In its solution they could be far more useful in the Cabinet than outside it. Their duty, said Ralston, was to watch McNaughton's attempt to rally the volunteers, to assist him if they could, and, if he failed, to make sure that conscription followed. Ralston felt sure, as did the others, that McNaughton would fail but all agreed that night to give him every opportunity to succeed.

As Ralston's closest friends, Crerar and Macdonald became his watchdogs within the Cabinet. They both took care, in view of the uncertain future, to put their understanding of the existing circumstances in letters to King as a clear warning that they expected him to make good his pledge of "conscription if necessary" and that they would leave him if he refused.

Macdonald asked King for a definition of "necessity." He wished to know, he said, how long McNaughton would have to secure reinforcements by the voluntary method. From King Macdonald never received a clarifying reply. No time limit had been set upon McNaughton's recruiting efforts.

Macdonald and the other conscriptionists decided to wait for two or three weeks. All of them were enraged at the treatment of Ralston and even King must have known, on second thought, that by treating Ralston with ordinary good manners he could have avoided adding personal rancor to a situation difficult enough without it. The conscriptionists suppressed their feelings in public, continued to follow Ralston's advice, and co-operated with McNaughton. There was a time limit on their patience.

The magic of McNaughton's name and legend was now on trial. While the overseas Army was staggered to find that its spiritual father apparently had let it down by opposing conscription, the officers of the Army in Canada promised to redouble their recruiting efforts among the Zombies.

On November 8, King spoke to the nation by radio, urged the Zombies to volunteer, and announced that Parliament would meet on November 22. Always in a time of trouble he wanted Parliament beside him as the mechanism of conciliation and compromise. When the members were at home they remained out of his reach. Assembled in Ottawa, and confronted with stern decisions, they could be influenced and, through them, the country could be reassured. King needed Parliament to build up support for his Government and his policies. He was still confident that McNaughton would get the volunteers before Parliament met.

His confidence was shaken when McNaughton faced a public meeting at Arnprior and was greeted with derision. A second speech in Ottawa went no better. The magic was not working as King had expected. Had he overestimated McNaughton's power? The first doubt now entered King's mind.

There was none in McNaughton's. He believed his own legend. If his officers would waive their prejudices and go to work, the Zombies could be persuaded to volunteer.

Actually, no significant number volunteered. The recruiting campaign had only hardened the old resistance. Most of the Zombies said that if the Government wanted them it should come and get them. Whether they were to be used in Canada or overseas, they would stand together instead of splitting themselves into two groups, the volunteers and the conscripts. Between November 1 and 18 McNaughton secured only 549 recruits. Before then the Cabinet conscriptionists saw that the game was up. McNaughton still refused to admit it.

November 13:

A meeting of the "loyalists," as King's Cabinet supporters were calling themselves, agreed that voluntary recruitment would fail. Even if it did, they had no intention of imposing conscription. The Government must meet Parliament on a no-conscription policy. Could the Government survive in Parliament on such a policy? Most of the loyalists thought so. Power doubted it and, as before, warned his colleagues that a Government which carried Parliament by a small majority on an issue so profound would not last long afterward.

The loyalists suggested to King that he face the possibility of parliamentary defeat, see the Governor-General immediately, and make sure that if the Government fell it would be granted a dissolution and not replaced by a conscriptionist government without a general election.

King had become suddenly worried and irritable at McNaughton's obvious failure. He said he was being "undermined" and was determined to find out who were his friends and who his enemies in the Party.

When Parliament opened, he would find out. He was sure he could carry Parliament with him. There was no need to discuss dissolution. McNaughton might fail but the Government would still be master of the situation.

As an act of practical politics, King had not wavered for a moment in his refusal to adopt conscription. As a matter of abstract principle, he had often admitted to his intimates that conscription was "the fairest method of raising troops." It was fair and quite impossible in this divided country. Anyway, there was no "necessity."

November 14:

The loyalists considered at length the strategy to be followed when Parliament met eight days later. It was agreed that the Government would present a formal vote of confidence in itself to proclaim its anticonscription policy and to test its support in the House. The work of drafting the motion was turned over to Mackenzie, the expert on rules of procedure.

The position of McNaughton was more ticklish. He was not a member of the House and could not appear there to defend his recruiting campaign or justify his refusal to invoke conscription. Further discussion devised a solution—let McNaughton be appointed to the Senate, where he could speak as freely as in the Commons. King promised to consider this suggestion.

November 15:

Mackenzie continued his work on a resolution designed to commit the Government neither for nor against conscription, and to unite the Liberals of Parliament. He wrote in longhand, not trusting even a stenographer with his thoughts.

Meanwhile, Cardin, long in the wings, had edged upon the stage. Through trusted intermediaries he informed King that he was ready to enter the Cabinet, now that it was proving its good faith by opposing the conscriptionists. King would have been glad to recapture Cardin and strengthen himself in Quebec, but Cardin's re-entry at this juncture would cost too much in antagonizing most of English-speaking Canada. Cardin retired again. He would soon reappear.

The conscriptionists were satisfied that McNaughton had failed completely, that conscription must follow, and that King would never agree to it. Once the issue was raised in Parliament they would resign and join Ralston. They did not agree on the Government's prospects. Some thought it would survive, others that it would fall and be succeeded by a conscriptionist coalition under Ralston. At all events, none of them would remain with King if he refused to invoke conscription when "necessity" had been finally proved by McNaughton's failure.

November 19:

A Sunday conference between the leaders of the loyalist bloc went over the roll of Parliament and concluded that the Government could carry it by a small majority on a no-conscription policy. No one doubted that the Cabinet would split. Crerar and Macdonald at least would resign. Ilsley might be persuaded to stay. The prospects were grim but far from hopeless.

November 20:

A new cloud now appeared on the western sky. It was no bigger than a man's hand but in King's mind it grew, during the next forty-eight hours, into the shape of a cyclone. General G. R. Pearkes, V.C., commander of the 6th Division of drafted men, called an unprecedented press conference to give his officers the opportunity of discussing their difficulties with the public. Thus instructed to tell the truth about the recruitment problem, the officers declared that they could not persuade any substantial number of their men to volunteer for overseas service. The Zombies, they said, would not volunteer, though they would go overseas willingly, even eagerly, if they were ordered there.

General Pearkes added that his officers "have never been in revolt but, on the contrary, have loyally supported the Government policy of producing the reinforcements for overseas."

The newspaper reports of the press conference astounded King. Evidently Pearkes, a highly respected officer, had undertaken in defiance of all military tradition to put pressure on the Government and to discredit the voluntary recruiting system in public. At first, King thought this merely intolerable. As he brooded over the incident, it appeared worse than that. Was military discipline among the high officers breaking down? Two days later King would receive the answer to that question.

At a meeting of the loyalists in Laurier House the cheerful humor of the previous day had turned to general gloom. All the latest reports were black. The recruits were not coming in. Parliament would open in two days. The Party was more deeply divided than King had foreseen, the nation more restive, the conscriptionists more determined. The plans of November 1 had gone awry. In retrospect, the dismissal of Ralston on that day seemed of doubtful wisdom. The Crisis, which McNaughton's magic was expected to solve, evidently was returning with increased fury.

For the first time since the constitutional debate of 1926, King looked into the abyss.

The position of McNaughton was the unsettled question of urgent strategy. How could he appeal to Parliament? The suggestion of a Senatorship for him was revived briefly. McNaughton, the meeting learned, did not want it. He insisted on the chance to face the Commons. How could this be arranged when McNaughton was not a member?

It occurred to the conference that perhaps the House might meet in committee to hear him as a kind of witness. That unsatisfactory makeshift might serve if nothing better offered. Questioned further, McNaughton agreed to take a seat in the Senate for a few weeks if necessary, though he was determined to seek election to the Commons. In any case, he asked for a secret session of Parliament to hear him because his address, now in preparation, must give some information valuable to the enemy.

At this point a great parliamentary career seemed open to him, despite his recruiting problems. A vain hope, possible only to a vain, courageous, and able man.

Later that same day, McNaughton met a smaller group of the loyalists at Mackenzie's apartment. In the drama now rushing to a denouement still unforeseen by any of its actors, the secret conference on the afternoon of November 20 was a decisive act. From it the remaining acts flowed.

A new and disturbing factor had been introduced. One of the Ministers noted that the commanders of the military districts throughout Canada had met in Ottawa the previous week and seemed to agree that voluntary recruiting was bound to fail. Some of them, it was said, had told McNaughton frankly that they could not persuade the Zombies to volunteer.

McNaughton was asked outright if that was true. Did he still think there was a chance of his campaign succeeding? And he was reminded that everything depended on his answer—the Government's policy, perhaps its existence, the career of every man in Mackenzie's parlor.

In the light of what was to follow, McNaughton's answer explains much and disguises more.

McNaughton replied that he had every confidence in his military officers, mostly men whom he had chosen and who had served with him overseas. The officers of the Army could be trusted.

That statement was accepted at the moment. It should be noted well. Within forty-eight hours McNaughton would have a very different report to make and, in making it, would alter everything.

On November 20, while his friends conferred in Mackenzie's apartment, what secret calculations were forming in King's mind behind the stubborn refusal to accept conscription or to admit that his present policy might fail? Was he meditating already the somersault and transformation to be executed two days hence? There was as yet no sign of it, no hint of any change, no mention of the Army's loyalty. That, too, must be noted. As of November 20, King stood against conscription, expected McNaughton to deliver the recruits if he had more time, and believed the Government could carry Parliament.

At the Cabinet meeting later in the day, King appeared more firm than ever. When Crerar, Macdonald, Mulock, and Gibson demanded a deadline on voluntary recruiting—Ralston's original request for which he had been dismissed—and suggested December 1, King still objected. The French Canadian Ministers flatly opposed any deadline. McNaughton, to the conscriptionists' surprise, appeared willing to accept it. He was sure he would get the reinforcements before long.

The Cabinet, on going over his latest figures, saw that they were not nearly as satisfactory as it had hoped. In truth they were hopeless. McNaughton might be confident. Some of his friends were doubtful. The conscriptionists had no doubt. They were certain now that the voluntary method had been given fair trial and had failed beyond all question. Within two days that failure would have to be admitted to the high court of Parliament.

After the Cabinet meeting, King conferred privately with McNaughton, St. Laurent, and Gardiner—another meeting to be noted on this frantic day, when events moved by the hour, almost by the minute, toward their curious culmination.

The leading anticonscription Ministers told King flatly on this occasion that they would not serve in a Cabinet which enforced conscription. King faced his inevitable choice of evils. If he failed to impose conscription, Crerar, Macdonald, Ilsley, Howe, Gibson, and Mulock, perhaps others, would resign. Up to then King had only half believed this threat. Now he saw it was true. On the other hand, if he imposed conscription, he would lose not only all his Quebec Ministers but Gardiner, McNaughton, and perhaps others from the English-speaking provinces.

If this must be the choice, King evidently had made it. He would still reject conscription. Or so it seemed to his friends. In retrospect, even they cannot be sure. Had the great change in King actually begun? There was no intimation of it at this meeting.

He talked of calling an election and going to the country on his present policy. His only objection to such a test was that it would delay the whole recruiting issue for three months, and in that period the need for reinforcements might prove desperate, depending on the battles of Europe.

On second thought, the conference saw a way out of this dilemma. The Government would go to the country still pledged to impose conscription "if necessary." It would promise to send the Zombies overseas by compulsion if they were really needed. Thus the nation would be assured that there would be no delay in reinforcing the

Army, since conscription, if necessary, could be applied before the election.

The day of November 20 ended with three facts apparently clear: McNaughton believed he would finally get the recruits without conscription; the loyalty of the Army commanders, their determination to carry through the voluntary recruiting campaign, could not be doubted; and King was set against conscription.

All these three assumptions, the whole basis of Government policy, would not last two more days.

November 21:

The first suspicion of that fact emerged at the daily Cabinet meeting.

A new and moody King sat disconsolately at the head of the table. Overnight he had sunk into a state of depression never seen in Cabinet before. What was behind it? More than his colleagues knew then or know now, more perhaps than history will ever discover. The deepest mystery of Canadian politics had begun.

King opened the meeting by remarking, rather listlessly, that he thought he should resign. By now his Ministers were so physically exhausted, so punch-drunk with continual shock, that nothing could surprise them. They greeted King's announcement in silence.

As the Cabinet despairingly avoided the final break, the discussion drifted aimlessly away from the only point of importance.

Some of King's friends suggested that if he intended to resign he should first tell the Liberal caucus his plans.

As he had done so often before, Howe demanded that the Cabinet decide for or against conscription—"for God's sake, let us make up our minds!" King was not ready to make up his mind. Its present contents might have startled even his shockproof colleagues.

Macdonald, his long patience quite worn out, said he would certainly resign if McNaughton did not get the recruits without further delay. Unless the recruits were secured, he added, the Government would be defeated on its present policy.

There followed a long, digressive argument about the procedure to be followed in Parliament next day—as if procedure mattered now when the Government had no agreed policy and seemed likely to explode before nightfall.

How was McNaughton to be brought before the House of Commons to present his defense? Perhaps the House would agree to a new rule and allow McNaughton to address it from the neutral ground of the clerk's table. Arthur Beauchesne, clerk of the House and undisputed arbiter of its rules, was questioned on the telephone. He said the House could hear McNaughton if it so decided.

So much was settled, nothing else. What was the Government to

BB

say to Parliament? Agreement on that, the only vital point, was still
impossible. At least the Cabinet could decide on its agenda, of procedure. It might be so arranged as to avoid a decision for another
day.

When King said he proposed to table Ralston's letter of resignation and then adjourn the House so that all members would have a
night to think the correspondence over, no one in the room saw any
particular significance in this suggestion. In retrospect, it seems evident that King was still fighting for time. Either he had next day's
adventure already planned or he hoped that something would turn
up. That question, like the rest of the increasing mystery, may never
be answered.

In any case, it was agreed that the House would meet for a few
minutes the next day, and, on the day following, would hear a statement from McNaughton. He would say what he could say in public
and ask for a secret session in order to give further military details.
McNaughton's speech—and this fact is important to remember in the
subsequent chronology—already was prepared.

The Cabinet recessed with nothing except procedure settled. King
then discussed the proposed schedule with Graydon, the Conservative House leader, and Coldwell, of the C.C.F.

At this strange conference Coldwell accepted the Government's
arrangements. Graydon, though good-natured as always, rejected
them. He said his Party wished to go on with the debate before
hearing McNaughton. King assured him that the Government
planned to submit a motion of confidence and allow a full discussion
at the proper time. Finally, Graydon was persuaded to submit the
Government's plan to his caucus.

Graydon's objection was an unexpected obstacle. If he persisted,
the whole schedule would be upset. King and his intimates were
forced again to consider the possibility of circumventing the Conservatives by appointing McNaughton to the Senate.

It was essential to place McNaughton's statement on the record,
to prove that his recruiting campaign was succeeding, before the
Opposition attack began. The Government counted heavily on Mc-
Naughton's prestige to strengthen its hand and rally the wavering
Liberal members. His presence in the Senate would transfer the
whole debate to that chamber and most of the Commons would
flock there to hear him, leaving the Conservatives without a quorum
to press their attack in the Commons. This stratagem looked
attractive.

As King and his friends debated it and King remarked at last that
he could not carry on if half a dozen of his conscriptionist colleagues

resigned, his telephone rang. It was Graydon to announce that his Party would agree to hear McNaughton as soon as the House opened. One obstacle had been removed. McNaughton's statement could reach Parliament and country in advance of the conscriptionist attack. This still left unsettled the vital question. What policy would King submit to Parliament?

After more inconclusive talk, King at last suggested that he would ask the House for a vote of confidence on a startling new proposition: McNaughton would be given a short period to test out the voluntary system thoroughly. If at the end of that period reinforcements were not sufficient, King would retire and allow some other Liberal to form a government. His successor would not be bound by King's pledge to submit his policy to Parliament and could send the Zombies overseas by simple order-in-council.

How long, King was asked, would McNaughton have to succeed or fail? King suggested two weeks.

The anticonscription Ministers announced that they would retire with King, if it came to the breaking point. The meaning of this announcement was plain—a Liberal conscriptionist Government would follow King's resignation and doubtless it would immediately coalesce with the Conservatives. The Liberal Party would be smashed again as in 1917, Quebec would be driven into isolation, and the races of Canada would be split for another generation.

That was King's threat. It was intended to go home on both sides and, if possible, drive them together on the lip of the catastrophe. He pointed to the catastrophe, he made the threat, but did he mean it? Probably we shall never know, for the next day's events were to make the threat irrelevant. Did King already know those events in advance? That is the unsolved heart of the mystery.

The immediate reaction of the Cabinet to King's ultimatum was surprising.

Crerar seemed willing to accept King's policy, for it offered the chance of reconciliation even at this late hour and it assured the conscripted reinforcements in the end.

Howe repeated that he would support conscription or the voluntary system, as the Cabinet decided. There must be a clear decision now and the House must be informed of it next day. The pragmatist and man of practical affairs, accustomed to getting things done, was disgusted by these weeks of hairsplitting.

Gardiner, who had been as much opposed as King to conscription, suddenly amazed the Cabinet by proposing a new compromise. If the voluntary system failed, he said, the Government should conscript 8,000 Zombies. Then, if still more reinforcements were required, another force of 8,000 would be sent overseas, but after that there would be no third call-up. Conscription would end with 16,000.

This notion, hatched in the most prolific political incubator of its time, was ingenious, but the French Canadian Ministers promptly rejected it. They said it would be quite unfair to send the Zombies overseas and not call up the young men now coming of draft age, or the workers who were being released from the shrinking war factories.

Claxton produced a still more complex formula. A monthly quota of reinforcements would be set for the nation as a whole, and a proportionate quota for each military district. If the Zombies failed to volunteer in sufficient numbers, the deficiency would be made up by conscription of those needed to fill the district quotas. This suggestion received little support and was dropped.

Macdonald brought the discussion out of these abstractions by telling the Cabinet bluntly that McNaughton could not get the men. If the obvious method of conscription were still evaded, Macdonald would have to resign, probably that day. Ilsley, Mulock, and Crerar seemed to take the same view.

Once more, with a look of infinite weariness, King said that after the strain of the last two weeks he could not carry on when some of his major colleagues like Ilsley were leaving him. However, he added hastily, he appreciated Ilsley's point of view.

The meeting broke up without agreement less than twenty-four hours before Parliament would compel a decision one way or the other.

To understand the events of the next day it is necessary to note that on November 21 McNaughton was still assuring his colleagues that the voluntary recruiting drive would succeed. He mentioned no sign of trouble in the Army.

Thus, with a Government on the verge of dissolution, a Prime Minister ready to resign (or so he said) after the destruction of his quarter-century of work, a Liberal Party apparently back to its schism of 1917, the Conservative Party eager to return to power under Ralston in a conscriptionist coalition, Ralston still silent with the future in his hands, a Quebec angry with the racial anger of betrayal, English-speaking Canada determined not to accept the domination of a minority, and Parliament ready to erupt on the morrow, the night of November 21, 1944, passed into the dawn of the weirdest day in Ottawa's memory.

November 22:

King arose at Laurier House in the full knowledge that before another night his career would be remade or broken forever. With complete sincerity he believed that if he failed, the nation would be broken also. Whether, in the early hours of that morning, he already had decided on his great somersault, history doubtless will never know.

While King either meditated his coup or, as he told the story, awaited the climax which he still did not foresee, his Ministers were preparing for the debacle due that afternoon.

Power was ready to resign quietly and save King embarrassment. If he and other Quebec Ministers left the Government, King would be free to adopt conscription on the Gardiner formula or some variant of it and that might satisfy the national majority. It would mean, of course, the loss of French Canada to the Liberal Party. In any case, Power would not accept conscription.

St. Laurent did not believe for a moment that King would accept conscription by the Gardiner formula or otherwise. Then came the first clear intimation of St. Laurent's dimensions and the factor which might yet save the Government. He told his friends he would be ready to accept a measure of conscription if the voluntary system were given a further brief, fair trial and if, at the same time, King announced that its failure would be followed by the dispatch of the Zombies overseas.

This was a vital change in St. Laurent's immediate position and could alter the balance of the Cabinet. It represented no change, however, in St. Laurent's original thinking. He had refused to pledge himself to the electors against conscription under any circumstances and had warned them candidly that it might be unavoidable. He wished to make sure, by a last trial of the voluntary method, that it could not provide the troops which he was determined to secure.

In the judgment of the Quebec Ministers, St. Laurent's acceptance of conscription, if proved necessary, might save King for the moment. It would not save Quebec for the Liberal Party. Even St. Laurent, they thought, could not hold his people on such a policy or prevent the dreaded racial rupture. The Quebec Ministers were wrong.

Power's position, as the arguments of that day showed, was quite different from St. Laurent's. Power had always opposed conscription, considered it unnecessary, and felt himself fully pledged to his electors against it. If conscription was adopted, St. Laurent could accept it with honor as Power could not. It appeared, therefore, that each of these two men might soon have to walk his own path in separation.

Many secret and hurried conferences were held on that electric morning. Mackenzie, still believing that King would never adopt conscription, had drafted another of his paper Cabinets. Besides

McGeer, Slaght, and Hepburn, he now included William Fraser among those who would replace the conscriptionist Ministers after their resignations. No one was much impressed by this latest installment of *ad hoc* remedy, even when Mackenzie argued that, at worst, in the event of parliamentary defeat, the Liberals could form a fighting Opposition.

Mackenzie and the others were wasting their time. All the arguments, maneuvers, and wrigglings of the last fortnight had become meaningless. A telephone call to King's office had changed the nation's history in the space of a few seconds. The great coup was under way.

According to King's account, McNaughton telephoned him about noon and, in a voice hoarse with shock, exclaimed: "I have terrible news for you, Chief! What I must tell you will come as a body blow."

The military commanders of Canada, said McNaughton, no longer would accept the responsibility of directing the Army unless conscription were applied immediately.

A body blow. Perhaps a death sentence on the Government. So thought McNaughton. How could he suppose that King would turn the death sentence into a last-minute reprieve?

Even King (according to his own version) could see no hope of survival. He hung up the telephone knowing, as he said, that he no longer faced a political crisis, or even a racial schism, but the disintegration of the Army, a military uprising which might seize the civil power, a state of national anarchy, nothing less.

So twenty-five years of his own work, the work of all his predecessors, the whole structure of the Canadian nation laboriously built through the centuries, and now the victorious achievements of the war, were imperiled by a mad and irresponsible insurrection. At the thought of it King was struck dumb.

The secret was too terrible for communication to the Cabinet. Only St. Laurent could be told, for now St. Laurent had become the key to everything. Standing together, King and St. Laurent might still fend off anarchy—provided St. Laurent would accept conscription, to which anarchy was now the certain alternative.

Called to King's office and told McNaughton's news, St. Laurent replied bluntly that the military must be resisted. Otherwise, he said, Canada was reduced to the status of some South American banana republic where the officer class could alter governments at will. The Cabinet must fight the uprising.

"Fight?" King retorted. "Fight with what? Our bare hands?"

The calm man from Quebec was incredulous. Civil government threatened by a military putsch? It was impossible. Yes, said King, but true. There could be no doubt about it. He had McNaughton's word. And if the Army now seized actual control of the Government, St. Laurent must ask himself whether the civil power could ever recover. There was only one possible thing to do, said King—the Government, by yielding to the demand for conscription, could maintain its outward direction of events and, when The Crisis passed, could master them again.

As St. Laurent listened in silence, King felt himself reeling, with his secret, on the lip of bottomless chasm and black night. Whether St. Laurent believed King, only St. Laurent knows. Whether King believed himself, forced himself to believe, or was acting a part unbelievable and grotesque, only King knew.

Or perhaps King himself never knew, for he could believe anything he wished to believe, and at this moment complete belief in his intended course was essential. We have only King's own version of this strange meeting, the version which he repeated with rising passion and conviction until his death. So stands the only known record.

St. Laurent may have believed King and shared his alarm. He may have thought that King and McNaughton were exaggerating the danger, unconsciously or deliberately, to force conscription on the Cabinet. Exaggerated or not, the danger was serious enough. In the few minutes granted him, St. Laurent must have realized that if he opposed conscription further there might or might not be military disintegration, as King feared, but in either case the Government, the Party, and the nation would fly apart before the day was out.

St. Laurent may reveal in due time his thoughts on that noon of November 22, 1944. All we know yet is that he was ready for conscription and always had been, if it could be proved necessary, and only wished the issue settled on its merits. Now it was to be settled by pressure and panic.

Nevertheless, the need of conscription had been finally proved beyond doubt—McNaughton could not get volunteers and the Prime Minister expected national anarchy. St. Laurent was left with no option. The man who knew little of politics saw that the historic forces then in play had become irresistible. He consented to immediate conscription.

In that consent he had saved the Government, the Party, and perhaps the nation. He had made himself the nation's future master. In human measurement he had proved himself a much larger man than King.

King had acted, in Cardin's phrase, from the heart, by the compelling instinct of the Anglo-Saxon, had yielded to the call of history, had moved with the majority of his own race, and had accepted the easier political alternative; whereas St. Laurent had acted from the head, by reason, against the instincts of his race, and against all his political interests. For something larger than Quebec he had taken the harder alternative and risked his whole career without a minute's hesitation. Thereby, without knowing it, he had prepared himself, his race, and the whole nation for yet another crisis and another enemy now six years off.

Never before, except perhaps on that September dawn of 1759, when Montcalm faced Wolfe on the river bluff, had two men so held the fortunes of Canada in their hands. King and St. Laurent parted, only half aware of their power and with no assurance that it would outlast the day. By agreement, neither of them repeated McNaughton's secret.

When Parliament opened that afternoon King went solemnly through the empty motion of tabling Ralston's resignation, remarking that this was one of the most painful experiences of his life and paying a generous tribute to his former colleague.

Graydon, now leading the Opposition as Bracken's *locum tenens*, demanded debate on a "high plane," condemned all partisan maneuver, and formally moved for the imposition of total conscription.

King was ready for him. Mr. Speaker Glen ruled that the motion required forty-eight hours' notice. He would not permit an appeal from his ruling. At King's suggestion, the House agreed to hear McNaughton next day and adjourned at 4:30.

Nothing stood at that hour as it seemed to stand. Every posture was false. The Cabinet ostensibly opposed conscription. The conscriptionist Ministers planned to resign before next morning. Ralston watched in silence—a spectator or tomorrow's Prime Minister? The Conservatives crouched for the long-awaited pounce on a victim who was no longer there. King and St. Laurent had kept their secret.

The Liberal caucus met immediately after the House adjourned. As usual, King was late in arriving. Meanwhile, in the caucus chamber, only St. Laurent knew what lay ahead (though King had hinted discreetly to Macdonald, the most implacable of his opponents, that the situation had changed and Macdonald, therefore, should do nothing prematurely).

Unaware of any such change, Crerar, the elder statesman around whom the rebellion was centering, rose to address the caucus. He never uttered the words that would have proclaimed the conscriptionists' mass resignation. He was cut short by King, who entered the room at that moment and quietly asked the caucus to adjourn while he discussed "important new developments" with the Cabinet.

What had happened? The Ministers and the private members looked at one another blankly. They could read nothing in the stolid face of King. It was no time to question or argue. The caucus broke up in a buzz of rumor and speculation. King left without another word. The conscriptionist Ministers met and agreed to resign that night.

The Cabinet had been summoned to meet at eight o'clock with the clear impression that King would reject conscription, face the mass resignations, and survive or fall in Parliament next day.

Power, just out of hospital and ignorant of the day's secret events, was summoned to King's office at a quarter to eight.

The Prime Minister was in a state of extreme agitation. He looked hard at Power and opened the conversation jerkily. "Chubby," he said, "I don't know what I would do without you!" Power listened, suspecting already that King would have to do without him.

Hurriedly, and in shaky sentences (for he had only a few minutes before the Cabinet met), King explained that he had heard from McNaughton that day. McNaughton had told him that the game was up, he could not get the reinforcements, there was nothing for it but conscription.

There was no word of any military uprising, not a hint of the day's real secret. Could it not be shared even with Power, from whom no secrets had ever been withheld? Or did King know that Power would refuse to believe it? Here again the King version encounters only silence and mystery. If that version is true, if the danger of military uprising was indeed a fact and not a figment contrived for King's purposes, why was it not told to Power at this critical moment when Power's support was vital to King, when Power might be persuaded in the nick of time to support conscription? Of that the King version tells us nothing.

With no means of knowing what was in the other's mind, Power listened to King's plans. The Cabinet, said King, would be asked that night to conscript 16,000 draftees of the home defense army and send them overseas. This, however, was not conscription. It was merely a method of securing reinforcements in an emergency. The voluntary method would remain, probably based on Claxton's formula of district quotas.

Would Power accept this compromise? That was King's immediate anxiety. He had St. Laurent's consent. If Power consented also, Quebec, or a good part of it, might yet agree. King watched Power across the table and awaited his answer.

In the hardest moment of his life, Power did not waver. He said he would resign without any word of complaint against King. The other Quebec Ministers, under St. Laurent's influence, doubtless would support the conscription formula.

King could not bring himself to part with his old friend. In a broken voice, almost with tears, he pleaded with Power to reconsider. Power shook his head. Surely, King persisted, Power understood that the question no longer was the personal future of any man or party, that King's own survival had become unimportant. There was only one question—whether government itself could survive in Canada. Lacking any alternative, only the Liberal Party could hope to govern, presumably with King at its head, but how could it continue if men like Power abandoned it?

Again Power refused. In a last entreaty, almost comic in its desperation, King suggested that Power could oppose conscription and still remain in the Government. It was a wild stab in the dark and would look only absurd in tomorrow's daylight. Aghast at such constitutional nonsense, Power merely repeated that he would resign in the morning and left King alone in his office with his untold secret.

After these weeks of anguish, the Cabinet meeting was a strange anticlimax. As the Ministers waited to hear from King, McNaughton said quietly that he had received a disappointing report from his staff officers. They had concluded that the voluntary system could not supply the reinforcements urgently required. Without offering further argument or any excuse for his volte-face, he recommended that 16,000 of the home Army be made subject to immediate conscription.

King said that with reluctance he supported McNaughton's recommendation.

St. Laurent nodded his approval. For a moment the Cabinet was silent. What could be said? The conscriptionists knew that they had won, that the magic of McNaughton had failed, that Ralston had beaten King. The Quebec Ministers knew that further protest was bootless. They must accept, follow St. Laurent, or retire. Only Power was ready to retire but he said nothing. The formal decision to impose conscription, to reverse the whole course of King's policy and lifework, to concede that the conscriptionists were right and Ralston victorious was made with hardly a word of debate. No debate was needed. The actual decision had been made by King and St. Laurent that morning.

The Crisis, then, was finished? Not quite finished. Ralston could still smash the Party. Quebec might repudiate its leaders. Parliament might rebel. But the primary choice, which King had resisted from

1917 until this hour, had been approved, the Rubicon crossed, and the explosion escaped, for the moment anyway.

With relief at this escape, the Cabinet discussed until midnight the wording of the order-in-council by which the Government would take power to conscript 16,000 draftees if, under this threat, they still refused to volunteer for overseas service.

The conscriptionists saw that this was not to be total conscription. It applied to a limited number of men only. At least the fiction of the voluntary system would remain. These reservations they considered of little importance when the principle of conscription had been established. Obviously, if more than 16,000 men were needed, they would be drafted without delay.

The Quebec Ministers knew that, too. St. Laurent's only suggestion was that the Government's decision must be conveyed to the Party caucus before the news reached Parliament. It would be terribly hard for the French Canadian members to accept a policy of which they had been given no notice, especially when they expected just the opposite. In decency they should be entitled to a private explanation of this sudden change. The Cabinet agreed to meet the caucus next morning.

All this talk, and what may be regarded as the most extraordinary if not the most important Cabinet decision since Confederation, had passed without a whisper of anger from the defeated faction or a gesture of triumph from the victors. At such a time it was useless to strike attitudes. The thing was too big for words or gestures. The Cabinet system had worked, as it is supposed to work, by agreement and, at all costs, with solidarity despite its disagreement.

As the Ministers rose from their chairs, worn out by a month of uninterrupted misery, Power remarked that he would not be coming here again and might as well say farewell now. He repeated briefly what he had told King earlier.

He still believed conscription unnecessary. He could support it only in the event of a catastrophe in the war and none had occurred. On the contrary, the Allies were rushing on to victory and the Canadians could easily be reinforced on a voluntary basis if they were allowed even a brief pause in their present battles.

In any case, Power could never condone the Cabinet's action in granting conscription to McNaughton when it had refused the same recommendation from Ralston. Of all these men, none loved Ralston better than Power, who had broken with him. By that friendship, apart from anything else, Power now broke with McNaughton in loyalty to his friend. And in all this strange personal crisis within The Crisis of the nation, nothing was so strange as the spectacle of an Irish Canadian entering the wilderness alone as the representative of the French Canadian race.

Most of the Ministers were not surprised at Power's announcement. They had expected nothing else from him. But Gardiner spluttered in sudden anger. If anyone was to leave the Government on the conscription issue, Gardiner would leave, too. He had always opposed conscription since Laurier's time and he had not understood that this present policy was conscription. It was only a compromise, accepted in the interests of unanimity. If there was no unanimity he proposed to resign.

King intervened to say that he hoped the decision had been unanimous. Power indicated that he would not change his mind. As the meeting broke up, Gardiner also seemed determined to leave. King knew he could dissuade Gardiner. He did not despair of dissuading Power.

The Cabinet went home to bed, Power to write his resignation, and a great Canadian soldier, now a sadder and a wiser man, locked himself up with his experts to rewrite in opposite terms the speech against conscription already prepared for tomorrow's session of Parliament. McNaughton also was worn out by his first failure in the art of politics, which he did not understand. Toward dawn he sought a few hours' sleep before his next ordeal. His experts finished the task of turning his speech inside out by 5 A.M. and they in turn went home, exhausted.

Out of the events of November 22 two question arise.

First, had King won his greatest victory or suffered his worst defeat?

By all public appearances he had retreated under fire, swallowed his pride and his record, yielded to Ralston, and done what, up to that very day, he had sworn never to do.

King rejected this conclusion then and rejected it with increasing vehemence until his death. Nothing enraged him so much as the accepted theory that Ralston had defeated him. In his own judgment he had won a triumph unequaled by any Canadian statesman. He had succeeded where Borden had failed in persuading the responsible leaders of Quebec to accept conscription. He had saved the Liberal Party and Quebec from the isolation into which Laurier had plunged them. Under almost unbearable pressure he had kept intact the structure rebuilt in 1919. And he had kept the nation intact.

Or so he hoped that night when he knew that Party, Parliament, and nation might yet dissolve.

Second, had there been any danger of a military uprising, even of a few officers' resignations? Had McNaughton reason to believe that his Army command was disintegrating? Had he received actual threats and, if so, were they real threats from men of importance? Or had King seized on some minor discontent in the Army, exaggerated it into the threat of anarchy, convinced St. Laurent of this danger, and thus forced conscription on the Cabinet because he knew that anything less would produce the deluge?

In short, was King's decision based on a cold-blooded calculation of the political forces in play, had he realized that he could not maintain a no-conscription policy, had he invented the military coup and forced McNaughton to recommend conscription, or had Canada stood, in November, 1944, in the shadow of chaos?

King's answers to these questions in his old age were unequivocal, emphatic, and angry. He said he had positive information showing that the Army command was about to break down. The plot also involved prominent political personages whom he would not name. He had the record, however, and would print it in his autobiography for the world to judge. Then the world would see that in the face of national cataclysm he had done the only thing he could do—not because reinforcements were lacking, not because conscription was needed, not because he had been wrong in his former judgment, but solely because he, and he alone, was called upon to save the nation.

While all this, no doubt, is set down in King's private records, they cannot answer the most fascinating riddle in Canadian history. For King may have misconstrued as a dangerous conspiracy the mere mutterings of some Army officers, the prospects of a few resignations. With complete sincerity, or his habitual self-deception, he could easily have built this evidence into a formidable brief for the defense.

Those close to King are split into two groups, the believers and the disbelievers. The believers so far have produced no concrete evidence to support King's conclusion. They have not named a single officer who was about to resign. They are not sure how much King knew, or thought he knew.

But they argue, and powerfully, that the whole atmosphere of the Army, as indicated by the Pearkes' press conference, was charged with eruption. Only a few more days, perhaps hours, of resistance to conscription would have uncorked the volcano. And, they say, only a few resignations at the top would have been necessary to start the full lava flow of disaster.

The situation, in fact, was getting completely out of control by November 22 when King heard of it and, in his most heroic act, extinguished the fatal spark.

Perhaps the best evidence in King's brief is the attitude of St. Laurent. He was not a man to see ghosts. He was the last man of all to be terrified by threats. Yet King evidently convinced him, if not that a general conspiracy was hatching, at least that the nation was in danger.

On the other hand, so far as this writer can discover, few if any of King's other colleagues credited McNaughton's secret. They believed then and believe now that while the Army command certainly was restive and dissatisfied, it had no intention of adventuring into politics, no thought of defying the Government, no plan of general resignations.

The disbelievers, or some of them, are ready to agree that King may have convinced himself of these dangers, since he could convince himself of anything at will, but they think it was an act of will in pursuance of a deep-laid strategy. King, in this view, had reached the end of his no-conscription policy. To pursue it would ruin his Government and Party and, as he believed, the nation.

His problem, then, was to sell the opposite policy to French Canada and that problem centered in St. Laurent. There was no use trying to persuade St. Laurent or Quebec to accept conscription on its merits, especially when King himself still did not believe in it. Even the prospect of a Party smash would not be enough to overcome French Canada's objections. Some much larger argument, some supreme emergency and nothing less, could shake St. Laurent and the other Quebec leaders.

When King heard the first whisper of trouble in the Army—so this version goes—he seized it in a clutch of desperation and used it as only he could use it, with an actor's transcendent art. If this were not so, how explain King's silence to Power a few hours after the secret burst upon him and a few minutes before the Cabinet decided on conscription? Here was the one trump in King's deck which might have outbid Power's objections. It was never played. Nor did King mention his discovery to other colleagues until long afterward, when most of them dismissed it with a shrug of disbelief. Again, why had McNaughton heard nothing of trouble in the Army before midmorning, November 22? Why had he told his colleagues, the day before, that he could get the needed volunteers?

The believers are unmoved by this argument. They say that of course the conscriptionist Ministers disbelieved King because they wished to believe that they and they alone had defeated him. They would not share their victory with the restless Army. As for the Army itself, some of the leading figures like General Stuart are dead. Most of the higher officers were overseas throughout The Crisis. This writer, after diligent inquiries, can discover no home-service officer who had heard anything of King's nightmare.

If resignations were pending, they were well hidden. If the whole affair was indeed a figment of King's imagination, placed there by McNaughton, it served its purpose. Without it, real or unreal, The Crisis probably would have lurched into incalculable confusion far more destructive than the ruin of King.

Possibly of all living men only McNaughton knows the truth. Having sealed his papers in the Archives, he has kept his honorable vow of silence, accepted the humiliation which was to follow the shift of November 22, 1944, and gone on placidly to other fields of public service.

Was he persuaded, ordered, or tricked by King, or was he compelled by the facts into recommending conscription on one day after opposing it the day before? That is the hard core of the riddle. Some time, perhaps, McNaughton or his papers will answer it.

On November 23 he had more urgent things to consider. In the last act of The Crisis he was to replace King as the chief actor.

40

The Colonel and the General

NOVEMBER 23:

The news of the Cabinet's decision leaked soon after midnight and was published in the morning papers. The Liberal caucus was not surprised, therefore, when King informed it of the conscription order-in-council to be tabled in Parliament that afternoon. Some of the French Canadian members, counting to the last on his old pledge, could hardly believe what they considered an outright betrayal.

They said little at the caucus. What was there to say? They knew they were beaten. At least they could refuse to vote for that defeat. How many of them would leave the Party?

King tried to make his new policy appear as the unanimous decision of the Cabinet, but Power intervened, without heat, to point out that he had resigned. King replied rather clumsily that he had not yet received the resignation and implied that it might yet be withdrawn. It was too late for that now.

Power and the French Canadian members were not King's chief concern. Ralston had become the real point of danger. If he bolted he could take with him a large part of the Liberal conscriptionist wing and the entire Conservative Party as well. Would Ralston bolt?

When the House met, The Colonel sat impassively in his place as a private member though he was more powerful momentarily than the Prime Minister. Having dismissed him, King counted on his patriotism to save the Government. In that swirling climate, nothing was certain. Events and men changed from hour to hour.

As calmly as if he were filing some bit of routine information, King tabled P.C. 8891, the order-in-council which reversed his lifelong policy. It gave the Minister of Defence power to draft 16,000 men of the home army immediately and the Government power to make other drafts within its discretion.

"Surrender!" cried the jubilant Hanson. Yes, surrender. Even in perpetual defeat, the Conservatives seemed to have won. They had won conscription, but it was not enough.

Victory required the expulsion of King and the elevation of Ralston in a Liberal-Conservative coalition. For that consummation the Opposition benches panted almost audibly. Graydon gave immediate notice of his strategy. He would move a want-of-confidence motion and propose the formation of a new government under a leadership known to favor total conscription.

King had prepared for the attack with his own motion, diabolical in its simplicity and appeal to everyone. It said merely that "This House will aid the Government in its policy of maintaining a vigorous war effort." Who could vote against such a proposition? Unhappily for King, the struggle now opening was not as simple as that.

Its first stage found McNaughton in a posture such as Parliament, in all its history, had never seen before. The General, whose word had been law to the entire Army, the people's hero who seemed to express the very soul of a nation at war, the one essential man who had been called in to rescue the Government, now appeared in the center aisle of the House, not even as a member entitled to sit there but as a witness only, almost as a prisoner on trial.

In truth he was on trial, and his trial of many months was only beginning. No upset of fortune like this had ever occurred in Canadian life. On one day McNaughton had appeared to be the most potent man in Canada, overshadowing Prime Minister and Government. On the next, scarce fifteen hours later, he stood in the witness box to confess that he had been all wrong, that his policy had collapsed, that Ralston, his enemy, had been right.

The great soldier had witnessed the defeat of other men in battle. He bore his own with soldierly courage and by no word or gesture indicated the secret, shared alone with King and St. Laurent, by which the defeat could be explained and excused.

He had reached this pass because he had involved himself in a profession he did not understand, in forces he had misjudged, in human passions he could not control. And he had failed. Yet even his retreat could be turned to account. Both races trusted his honor. If he said conscription was necessary after he had opposed it so long, Quebec might accept the necessity. He had retreated, but standing on his new line, the General was still a formidable power in defense even if he had lost the power of attack.

He had never sat in the House before. In his inexperience of politics, rules of order, and the devious processes of Parliament, he was, indeed, a sitting duck for the guns of the Opposition. The master of artillery had laughed at the physical explosives of two wars. Now he was undergoing his first baptism of a deadlier fire, aimed at that inner pride which had given him a lifetime of success and then this sudden failure.

A cruel spectacle and unique—the lank, grizzled General, face worn and body depleted by days of ceaseless labor and nights without sleep; the Opposition which had wanted him as its leader until a fortnight ago and was now determined to discredit him; The Colonel facing the General whom he had dismissed and who, in turn, had replaced him; the tiny civilian in his overnight descent, still proposing to dominate the soldiers. Up to now, The Crisis had been an abstract issue of national policy. In this struggle between three men it had become a human play-within-a-play bound to end in tragedy for one of them. McNaughton was not yet aware that he had been chosen for the distinction of human sacrifice.

On the table before him lay the second statement which his experts had been rewriting, in complete denial of the first, until five o'clock that morning. Considering that it contradicted everything that McNaughton had intended to say, and everything he had believed until the previous day, it was an effective statement.

That it was somewhat confused in places was no wonder, after its hasty origin, but it had the virtue of simple wording. The national hero and his ghost writers knew that this was no time for heroics.

McNaughton began by saying that he had always preferred the voluntary system because it built the best armies. He had hoped that it could be continued until the end of the war and confessed that he was disappointed with the results of his recruiting campaign.

Then came the first point of confusion. The district Army commanders, he said, had told him frankly that they had not much hope of securing the necessary volunteers. The Cabinet Ministers who listened to him now remembered that he had given them no reason to believe that the commanders were hopeless from the beginning—quite the contrary.

Still more confusing was McNaughton's next statement—the Government did not intend to apply general conscription. Voluntary recruitment would contine "to the limit" and conscription would be used only to make good any deficits in reinforcements where the voluntary method failed.

What was the meaning of all this? Had Canada embarked on real conscription or not? And if only partial conscription was intended, would the necessary recruits be obtained? A bewildered House waited as The Colonel rose to question the General.

The Colonel was by profession one of Canada's greatest lawyers. A lesser man than McNaughton would have writhed under this cross-examination, as cold, penetrating, and destructive as it was quiet and courteous.

Two antagonists who had split the Government and might yet split the nation were locked in final grip, mind to mind.

The exchanges between cross-examiner and witness, between The Colonel and the General under his thumb, were long, detailed, and so technical that the House could hardly understand them. They related to reinforcement pools, rate of casualties, medical examinations, and complex sets of figures. McNaughton answered promptly, incisively, and patiently, but the strain showed when he pleaded that he was not skilled in debate. Ralston, with his first faint trace of animus, remarked that the witness seemed very "apt" in hiding his thoughts and in making a desperate situation appear far better than it was.

Out of this labored testimony came at last the real intent of the Government's new policy. It proposed to secure 16,000 extra overseas recruits in addition to all the usual movement of volunteers. These 16,000 would be given the chance to volunteer but if they refused they would be conscripted. Pressed to the final admission, McNaughton agreed with Ralston that without the 16,000 the Army would be "going into the red, quite deep."

That, of course, confirmed in a single sentence Ralston's own report to the Cabinet, which had rejected it as unsound. Yet McNaughton added a moment later that if the Zombies would volunteer in sufficient numbers, now that conscription was the alternative, then the nation might escape conscription altogether and, if so, McNaughton would be the "most thankful man in this room."

All this puzzled the House anew. Was there to be conscription or not? All that worried Ralston was whether there would be enough reinforcements or not. What worried King, as Ralston concluded, was whether the cross-examiner would be satisfied on that point or, being dissatisfied, would attempt to pull down the Government.

For the rest of that grim afternoon McNaughton patiently answered the barbed questions of the Conservatives. Led by Graydon, Green, and Diefenbaker, they tried to prove out of the General's mouth that the Government had long mismanaged reinforcements and that the new policy would not succeed any better. The pinpricks dragged from the witness his only word of bitterness and complaint. The voluntary recruiting appeal, he said, could have succeeded if it had been given reasonable support. Instead, in his efforts "we got the opposite." Was he referring to the Conservative conscriptionist propaganda or to the secret palace rising in the Army? On that point, at the edge of full revelation, he said no more.

After two hours of cross-examination, the House still was not sure whether it had secured real conscription. Ralston intervened again to wonder if any of the Zombies actually were going overseas. McNaughton replied that "absolutely" they would go and gave his word that the Army would never lack reinforcements.

His ordeal now took a darker turn. The aged Neill, of Comox-Alberni, an independent whose stolid sarcasms had withered many opponents in the past, reared his gaunt figure to say what others thought but did not care to say: McNaughton by his own statement did not believe in conscription. Therefore he disbelieved in his own policy. And therefore, in honor, he should resign.

This thrust went deep. King rushed in to defend his General before the wound could be opened further. He alone would decide, said King, who should resign from his Cabinet, and he pleaded, rather pathetically, for mercy on a great Canadian soldier who had never faced Parliament before, who had been up until five o'clock that morning, and surely, in decency, deserved "due consideration." Neill withdrew nothing. McNaughton sat in the witness box, alone with his thoughts, bearing himself like a soldier, in a battle of words outside a soldier's training or experience.

The evening debate, which Graydon had proposed to keep on a "high plane," descended to interjections, angry clamor, calls for order, and mere wrangling. Out of it rose the voice of Karl Homuth in hoarse shout to charge that McNaughton was not telling the truth. In a passion of protest and outrage, King demanded a withdrawal and got it.

This affair assuredly was not going as he had expected. The Opposition was demolishing the General, and Ralston had yet to be heard from. Was the whole flimsy architecture of compromise to fall to pieces within twenty-four hours of erection? Was the strategy of retreat to lead into rout?

King's distress could be disguised no longer as he suddenly cried out that he, like his General, was exhausted by weeks of strain and could not attempt to speak without a week end of rest. Glaring across the House, he hurled a final threat at the Opposition: "What alternative government have they to put in office if I resign this post within the next two weeks?"

That threat did not disturb the Opposition, for it was determined to force King's resignation. King knew that but he was trying to rally any Liberals who might waver at the last moment.

The risk was still grave. Until he knew Ralston's verdict, King lived in his private Gethsemane. He had endured moments of this sort in the stifling summer nights of 1926, but then a purely constitutional crisis involved only his Party and his own career. This process of slow crucifixion involved, as he thought, the lives of countless Canadian boys and the whole future of a people. In it even the career of the great egoist must have appeared unimportant. Worst of all, his lips were sealed. He could not tell his secret. He could not truly explain anything.

There was no sympathy in the Opposition, either for King or for his General who, until a few days ago, had been the Conservatives' hope and idol. Civilian and soldier must be destroyed together.

To King's threat of resignation Hanson retorted brutally that the Prime Minister was not indispensable. King had brought all his troubles on himself and would be well out of the way. And McNaughton, though a great soldier, had put himself in "an impossible position." Even the nation's hero, his legend and his magic, were no longer sacred.

Was nothing sacred? King leaped up again to demand consideration for a Government which, outside this debate, had a war to manage, and he added that he would not allow himself or his colleagues to be "broken down physically" by the "absolutely unreasonable" behavior of Parliament.

He was greeted with derision even as he warned the House that it was dealing with the largest crisis in the nation's life.

No man was sacred at the end of that appalling day. At least, by the hour of adjournment, Ralston had made no move to pull the plug on the Government.

November 24:

As McNaughton submitted himself to a second day of misery, the French Canadian defection began. Pouliot and La Croix, independents who had supported the Government, crossed the floor. Of themselves, they were of no account. How many more would follow them? King realized that this was only the beginning.

McNaughton obviously had been shocked to read his own statements of the previous day in the morning press and hastened to apologize for the confusion he had left in the mind of the House. He had meant, he said, that he hoped the Zombies would volunteer, and if they did not they would certainly be conscripted. The Government's policy was quite clear—it would conscript all the men it needed.

The Opposition was no more satisfied than before. Hanson still argued that the Government had no real policy and in the ensuing brawl called Mackenzie a "flannelmouth," later reduced, in the true Pickwickian sense, to "bluffer."

Coldwell appeared for the first time to charge that McNaughton was compelling men to volunteer by threatening them with conscription.

Homuth and Mitchell, the Labour Minister, conducted a private brawl of their own, Homuth hoarsely denying that on the previous night he had told an honorable member to go to hell. Again in the Pickwickian sense, he had used only the harmless expression, "Where in hell were you in the last war?" Mr. Speaker remarked that he did not think "the tone of debate is being raised." The nerves of the House were breaking.

Ralston rescued it from this childish bickering with another series of polite questions addressed to McNaughton. He was given full answers and also a tribute from the General for his magnificent administration of the Army. As the House rose for the week end, Ralston still had made no move against the Government. He had plenty of time yet.

That night King made his last attempt to hold Power in the Cabinet. At a poignant meeting in Laurier House he pleaded despairingly with his old friend to withdraw the written resignation. The pleas added nothing to Power's knowledge and did not change his mind, but in retrospect they appear highly significant.

Three unanswerable facts, said King, had compelled him to adopt conscription: The military commanders were restless and could not be counted upon to carry out an effective voluntary recruiting campaign; the whole Liberal press in English-speaking Canada was abandoning the Party; and King could not face the loss of six or seven of his colleagues. Even to Power, his confidant of twenty-five years, King gave no hint of a military uprising. Was he still unwilling to trust Power with his secret? Or did he know—which certainly was true—that Power would not believe it? Again the mystery. When Power left Laurier House his resignation remained in King's hands.

November 27:

As the House reopened on Monday, King's first act was to table the resignation, a document as honest as it was painful. Power said he could not accept a conscription policy which was unnecessary and would "not save one single Canadian casualty." He had parted

with Ralston because the number of recruits needed was comparatively so small, the means to remedy the situation without undue
strain on the soldiers at the front was so readily available, and the
end of the war so imminent that "we were not justified in pro-
voking a national scission."

Then Power denounced King's treatment of Ralston: "I cannot
accept now from a new Minister, General McNaughton, a recommendation which I reluctantly felt obliged to reject when made
by an old comrade and tried associate, Layton Ralston." This human
equation the most ignorant Canadian could understand—King had
fired Ralston and allowed another man to enforce Ralston's policy.
In human terms, there was no answer to that indictment.

Power had made his case and did not propose to exploit it. In
a brief and restrained speech he said he parted with King "in sorrow, not in anger." The whole reinforcement problem, he believed,
could be solved if the Army overseas were given reasonable periods
of rest and a slight reduction of casualty rates. "Neither victory nor
honor" required it to be in action every day, or in every battle. For
himself, Power stood by the Government's policy of last Wednesday
morning, which had been reversed on Wednesday night. "I could
not change my mature consideration in a matter of minutes." Nor
could he repudiate his promise to his electors. Conscription could be
justified and Power would support it if the nation was in danger
of defeat but "we have no right to tear this country asunder" when
victory already was at hand.

Here, surely, was one of the strangest facets of this whole weird
business. A man of Irish descent, with no drop of French blood in
his veins, was speaking for French Canada more powerfully—to the
point of ending his Cabinet career—than its own sons. In Power's
judgment, "millions of good Canadians are now hating and reviling
one another, reason has given away to hysteria, cleavage between
classes and races has been driven deeper and deeper and, most
tragic of all, faith in public men is being weakened."

When Power concluded darkly that for some time to come it
might be impossible for men of similar principles to join in common
action "across the Ottawa River," he evidently foresaw the Canadian
calamity.

Strangest of all, the Irish Canadian who spoke for Quebec, the
master of politics who had never misgauged an election, had misgauged the Quebec mind and underestimated the unity of Canada.
It seemed to be breaking, but was not.

Power's speech had given King another bad moment. He was glad
now to end his long hours on the defensive and launch his own

attack. It was an attack not from strength but from weakness. On one side, he had seen the first desertions of a French Canadian revolt. On the other, he had yet to hear from Ralston. In McNaughton he had to carry a former asset now turned into a huge liability. On behalf of his Cabinet he had to justify a humiliating midnight somersault.

Not since 1926 had he been in a corner like this, but at his first words the experienced politician could see that his hand had lost nothing of its cunning. He attempted at once to turn Power's resignation, a weapon aimed at him, against his Conservative enemies. Power, he said, had resigned for one reason, Ralston for the opposite reason. Did that not show of itself the difficulty of King's position in the gravest issue ever faced by a Canadian Prime Minister? Did it not prove the necessity of compromise, conciliation, and agreement between the two Canadian factions?

It was a moment for a great speech. Unfortunately, after a good introduction, King slipped by his old habit into masses of quotations to exonerate his record, which the House knew and the country was tired of hearing. Emerging at last from this thick underbrush, he began to grasp the attention of his listeners.

There was "nothing personal," he said, between him and Ralston (as if a colleague could be dismissed in Cabinet without warning, impersonally). They had disagreed only on policy. King had been willing to retire if Ralston or anyone else could have formed a government. King could have won an election, but would the distraction of an election campaign, the most divisive on record, have helped the soldiers overseas?

Turning from defense to attack, he declared that his own no-conscription policy would have succeeded but for the organized conscription campaign of the Conservatives. They must bear the responsibility for what happened to the nation in the future as a result of these events.

Throughout the speech, any listener could see that King, though compelled to invoke conscription, did not believe in it. Indeed, at one puzzling point, he said his policy was not "all-out conscription." It was only a method of getting quick reinforcements. No one but St. Laurent and McNaughton knew what lay behind these confusions. Not once in nearly three hours of explanation did King hint at what he was to give later on as the real reason for his reversal. The closest he came to his secret was to say that if Parliament could not unite that day "we shall have to face the possibility of anarchy while our men are fighting overseas."

No such word, he reminded the House, had been used by a Prime

Minister since the deadlock of the Ontario-Quebec Parliament before Confederation. Anarchy? The House heard the word in amazement. Yes, anarchy, said King. It was possible "that the pillars of the temple of our Canadian life might be drawn out from under and the structure come down, bringing disaster on the whole nation."

The House would have understood that sinister sentence if it had known what King knew, or imagined.

The members were not greatly alarmed by these horrendous warnings but they understood King's next threat: If he were forced out, he would not go to the country. He would resign and someone else could form a government (a clear intimation to the French Canadians that they had better accept him lest they find themselves under an anti-French Prime Minister).

Also speaking to Quebec, he said that any conceivable government would enforce conscription. The only question was whether it would be enforced by his Government or another, a new government, inexperienced, perhaps unattainable, composed of elements which, after destroying him, could not themselves combine in office.

Appealing to the House to rise above mere emotion, he shouted emotionally that Parliament would be "no use to our fighting men if we destroy their country which they are defending!"

If he resigned, who was to follow him? Perhaps Bracken, King suggested. But Bracken was not in Parliament and even to mention his name was to ridicule the obvious impotence of his Party, to prove that it could provide no alternative to the present Government.

The Conservatives were the least of King's concerns now. His concern was the Liberal Party. He looked down the ranks of his followers and spoke directly to them.

He was quite prepared, he said, to let any one of them form a government and "no man in the world would be more relieved to be free of responsibility at a time like this . . . at the age I have reached." However, if no one else could form a government it was the duty of everyone in the House to support the existing Government in fighting the war.

His next words were addressed to English-speaking Canada. Let it remember, he said, that the French Canadians had made Canada possible by saving it from two American invasions. Let it remember that he had never "appeased" Quebec but had sought only the unity of the nation on a basis of fair treatment.

Finally, he addressed Quebec directly. Let it remember Lapointe's warning that no government could survive if it refused to obey the will of the majority—in other words, King had resisted conscription as long as he could and no one could resist it further.

The speech begun so effectively and then lost in a morass of
quotations had been gathering momentum and strength in the last
hour. By half past six, in a lather of perspiration and a passion of
rectitude, King concluded by rededicating himself to his mission of
national unity. His final words reached a peak he would never
reach again:

"My friends can desert me, they can remove their confidence from
me, they can withdraw the trust they have placed in my hands but
never shall I deviate from that line of policy. Whatever may be the
consequence, whether loss of prestige, loss of popularity or loss of
power I feel that I am in the right and I know that a time will come
when every man will render me full justice on that score."

In the presence of the two military figures who had lately overshadowed him, King by this speech converted The Crisis into a
trial of his own integrity. He was at once The Crisis and the solution
of it. It was again King or Chaos.

Had he removed the issue from Ralston and McNaughton and
concentrated it on himself only out of vanity? He was far too realistic for that. He knew and he had now proved to Parliament, if any
proof was needed, that only he could possibly manage a government
without a national calamity which might not be anarchy but was
too dreadful to contemplate. Even Ralston could not do that, against
the hatred of Quebec.

Thus, at the very moment of his humiliation, his reversal, and his
apparent defeat, King was winning a kind of paradoxical victory by
compelling Parliament and nation to accept him because they could
find no substitute.

In the evening, Graydon attacked the new policy as no more than
partial conscription, since there was no guarantee of any recruits
beyond the first 16,000, at least not without another political convulsion. Anyway, said Graydon (and with literal truth), neither
King nor McNaughton believed in the new policy. Were such men
fit to enforce it? Accordingly, Graydon moved the Conservative
motion declaring that the Government had not assured adequate
reinforcements by requiring all draftees to serve anywhere.

Coldwell followed and, with unconscious irony, called the Government's policy inadequate—this from a Party which had objected
to any overseas expedition. He proposed to make all the home-
defense force available for overseas reinforcement. He quickly
added that if the Government were unsatisfactory, the Conservatives were worse. That remark was all that counted with King. He
still had the support of the C.C.F., carefully nursed since Woodsworth's days in 1921.

November 28:

At a secret session, lasting until eleven at night, the House questioned McNaughton further. It secured more detailed knowledge of the Army's true position overseas but nothing significant concerning the Government's policy.

November 29:

This day's session presented three interesting exhibits. The first was Lacombe, the Quebec isolationist, announcing that under King Canada had reverted to colonialism. The second was Fred Rose, a Communist spy, who would soon be jailed as the agent of a foreign power, and who now spoke earnestly for the people of Quebec, for national unity, and for the Government's policy. The third was Ralston.

When The Colonel got to his feet at the evening session, the House knew that it witnessed the last act of The Crisis. By denouncing the reinforcement policy as inadequate he could extinguish the Government within the hour. By crooking a finger he could pull his friends out of the Cabinet. With one word he could end King's career and McNaughton's. If King actually had tortured a dark victory out of apparent defeat, Ralston could still snatch it from him.

Would Ralston say that word? Would he crook his finger? King was sure by now that he would not. He may not have understood Ralston but he had adequate sources of information. Parliament and nation, however, had no means of knowing what Ralston would do on the night of November 29.

Ralston's manner was dispassionate, his style factual, his tone neutral as he recited the history of The Crisis from the beginning. It was only when he turned to King's part in it that Ralston permitted himself a faint hint of his contempt for his former leader. He said that when King had asked his colleagues if any of them could form an alternative government, the Prime Minister had not been "in genuine search for a successor," and had no intention of resigning anyway. Squirming a little, King interjected heatedly to deny that statement. It was obvious that the House believed Ralston.

The Colonel's next attack, the more biting because it was so legalistic and factual, arose out of the exchange of five letters between himself and King. In one of them, King had laid down the extraordinary dictum that if dissatisfied Cabinet Ministers who proposed new policies were not prepared to move into the Prime Minister's chair and enforce them, then they had no right to leave the Cabinet. With a lawyer's logic, Ralston swept that doctrine aside as ridiculous. Must all men entering a Cabinet, he asked, accept a permanent marriage until parted by death, defeat, or promotion to the Prime Ministership? King squirmed again, no doubt realizing that in his letter to Ralston his pen had betrayed him.

After dismissing these absurdities, Ralston came down to the hard fact that he had resigned simply because he wished to make good the pledge of 1942 while King had attempted to repudiate it and half the Cabinet still did not understand it. Finally, with his usual candor, Ralston confessed: "I know my own weaknesses. One of them is that I am not flexible enough. I was born that way. I am too old to change. I have not any ambition but to be a good Canadian and I know my place is not on the dizzy heights of leadership. . . . I neither felt nor feel any duty to take on responsibility for which I am convinced I am not suited."

These words ended The Crisis.

Ralston did not propose to unseat King. The panting Conservatives were cheated of their chance of a coalition. The Government was safe.

Safe, but perhaps damaged by Ralston's quick addendum. King, he said, had given a false impression of the reinforcement shortage. It was not weeks off. It was immediate and urgent. The new policy, though a reversal, was a "half-hearted, piecemeal method" which Ralston would have accepted in office, if he could not have secured total conscription of the home army, but only under protest. He would accept it now, under protest, and only on the understanding that if more than 16,000 conscripted men were needed they would be drafted without further debate.

King eagerly confirmed that understanding.

Ralston concluded by examining his own conscience in public. If he voted for the Conservative want-of-confidence motion and it carried, the Government would be dislodged, an election probably would follow, and in the confusion the reinforcements would be delayed. Since he was not interested in politics and wished solely to find reinforcements for his Army, Ralston could not vote for such delay (even, as he might have added, but he did not, if it would certainly elevate him to power).

Therefore, condemning its attempt to avoid its pledges, and dissatisfied with its policy, Ralston would support the Government.

With this warning, Ralston ended a career unique in Canadian politics—the man who had power in his grasp and refused to close his hand either in ambition or revenge. Nothing became that career better than his taking leave of it. Nothing could ever rob him of his place in history as the builder of Canada's greatest Army in its greatest war. His work was done and it had cost him his life. Broken by the pressure of the war years, he would not long survive the victory. He had made his own unsurpassed contribution to it.

In disappointment and ill-concealed anger, the Conservatives turned on Ralston, who had dashed their last hopes. Hanson pointed across the House at Ralston's massive jaw and said it should indicate determination, and yet its owner was not ready to carry through his real policy of total conscription. Ralston seemed to agree with King that the disappearance of this Government would be a catastrophe. It would be, said Hanson, nothing of the sort. A better government could be found immediately when King went.

If he had ever held it, King had no present intention of going. When the House rose that night he was in the clear.

There remained only eight more days of debate, uttered purely for the record. A dozen French Canadian Liberals protested the Government's policy and managed to secure the support of W. A. Tucker, the Saskatchewan Liberal (himself a veteran of the first war), in a motion declaring against conscription. All this had been expected. The only question was how large the Quebec desertion would be. When St. Laurent broke his silence at last, it was clear that he could save a substantial part of the French Canadian vote.

Like Lapointe in 1939, St. Laurent now faced his own hour of trial. It was easy for him because he had made up his mind from the beginning that he would support conscription if it were needed. "I came here," he said, "to do a war job. I feel I must go on." If the Army required reinforcements and conscription were essential to get them, he would take the consequences in Quebec. He would stand or fall with King. As Lapointe's successor he appealed to the logic of that great man. The minority must accept the rule of the majority under the democracy for which the war was being fought.

In a speech lasting some five minutes, St. Laurent had established his own place in Canadian history and the foundations of a unique career. He was the first French Canadian leader to accept the conscription policy rejected by Laurier. He was the only man who could carry Quebec finally out of isolation and build a durable internationalist policy in Canada.

No one could be sure that night that Quebec would follow him. And for St. Laurent himself the future career now opening was unexpected, unplanned, and unwelcome. He thought he was finished with politics and going home.

On December 7, the criticisms, the replies, and the whole anatomy of The Crisis had been piled on the record and the House was ready to vote. When the division bells rang at last, the Quebec anticonscription motion was defeated by 168 votes to 43. Only the French

Canadian members had voted for it, but they had detached two-thirds of the Quebec bloc from the Government—for the moment only.

The Conservative motion demanding total conscription fell by 170 to 44. Only the Conservatives supported it.

King's main motion of confidence provided a chance for a last dispirited chewing over of the conscription issue, with Cardin leading the attack on the Government in preparation for a new independent party in Quebec. No one was interested in further talk since nothing was left to talk about. Without excitement the House passed King's confidence motion by 143 to 70. On this vote the Conservatives were joined by 32 French Canadians, each group opposing the Government for opposite reasons.

It was a brief junction. The French Canadians had no intention of dislodging King to establish a more conscriptionist government. Now that the essential issue had been settled, they were ready to keep him in office.

41

The Last Fight

KING'S EMERGENCY OPERATION OF NOVEMBER 22 MAY HAVE SAVED the nation, as he believed. In the view of many political physicians, it had killed the Government. By the first months of 1945, that prognosis looked alarmingly accurate.

A large part of the Liberal Party in Quebec had bolted on the conscription policy. To many English-speaking Canadians, on the other hand, that policy was a cowardly compromise, a deathbed repentance, wrung from those who still did not believe in it. Historically, in any case, a government which survives a long war may expect its own defeat at the moment of military victory, as Churchill would soon find. What was to be said for a Government which had been in office since 1921 with a brief interregnum, which already had won five national elections, which had broken publicly on the fundamental issue of race, had retreated under fire, and reversed its most important policy?

The largest miracle in political history and nothing less could possibly give King another term of power.

He began at once to undertake that miracle. His first attempt was disastrous and seemed to assure final disaster in a general election.

To bring McNaughton into the House of Commons, the Government opened the Ontario Seat of Grey North. King had hoped that the Conservatives would not oppose the nation's military hero, even thought he had been pretty badly damaged by The Crisis. Hearing that Bracken proposed to fight the by-election (without daring to enter Parliament himself), King was furious and threatened to call a general election forthwith. Since the Government obviously was not ready for a general election, he abandoned his threat and confidently awaited McNaughton's victory.

This was Bracken's great chance. He had made a pitiful start, he had skulked outside Parliament, but if he could defeat the Minister of Defence he could say that the nation had repudiated the Government and the real author of its reluctant conscription policy. Bracken, therefore, threw all the power of his Party and all the accumulated grievances of the nation into the Grey North campaign. In his eagerness he went too far and assured his own ruin.

Never before had the technique of smear proved so unprofitable.

On the advice of some of his misguided Toronto friends, Bracken announced in Grey North that many of the newly drafted soldiers had been marched upon the troopships and had promptly thrown their rifles overboard—a final proof that the Government had mismanaged the whole reinforcement problem.

The fact was that one soldier, of unsound mind, had tossed his equipment into the sea. The fact could not catch up to the slander. In a few days it was exaggerated into a national sensation, was taken up by Senator Wheeler in the United States, and presently carried around the world. The fame of the Canadian Army, the good name of Canada, and the pride of all Canadians were butchered to make the Roman holiday of Grey North.

Bracken won his by-election at the cost of losing any small chance of office he might have. He did not suspect that on the heady night of February 5, 1945, when the Grey North ballots were counted, and a Conservative returned. Nor did King. Neither of them realized how deeply the slander of the Canadian Army had hurt the Canadian people. At the moment, the by-election seemed to announce the Government's certain defeat at the general polls.

King's miracle had got off to a dismal start. McNaughton had suffered his second reverse in three months and mercifully had only one more to endure. He attributed his defeat to the "forces of Tory reaction" and, having long been regarded by the Conservatives as one of their own, vowed that he would dedicate his life to King and the Liberal Party.

Still Minister of Defence, he could not put foot in the House of Commons when it met again for the last session of the nineteenth Parliament. His brief experience there as a witness had been sheer misery. He would never have to face it again.

In one of his happiest choices, King named Douglas Abbott as McNaughton's parliamentary assistant and representative in the House. This put the Government's defense into competent hands and made the reputation of Abbott overnight.

The fledgling statesman with his lighthearted manner and tough mind had yet to become the familiar figure in horn-rimmed spectacles beloved of the cartoonists. He was an unknown young lawyer from Montreal, a veteran of the first war, a genial back-bencher apparently outstripped by his fellow townsman and friend, Claxton. Assigned to defend McNaughton, he quickly showed the qualities out of which Prime Ministers are fashioned.

As the Opposition, cheered by its victory in Grey North, would be sure to concentrate all its energies on the Defence Department and the mismanagement of recruitment, Abbott decided on a strategy which King would never have accepted, had he known in advance. King was not told and even McNaughton was given little notice of Abbott's speech.

Instead of waiting for the Conservative charges and answering them, Abbott tried to foresee and forestall them. For the most part, he supposed, the Conservatives would denounce the Government because large numbers of drafted men had deserted to escape overseas service, and because the management of the draft had been clumsy, to say the best of it. Abbott therefore admitted many of these allegations. He cited every possible fact damaging to the Government before the Conservatives could say a word. Point by point he took their speeches out of their mouths.

When they attacked at last, there was little more to be said. Wherever they went, Abbott had been there first. As Abbott's speech began, King was alarmed by his candid admission of mistakes but he soon saw the wisdom of it and was delighted. He marked Abbott for rapid promotion.

Since the beginning of The Crisis the Conservatives had been hopelessly outmaneuvered in Parliament. They had hoped to exploit the Government's humiliation, the breach with its Quebec followers, and the debacle of Grey North, but they were never given the chance.

At the opening of the new session King had effectively throttled the intended inquest before the Opposition could begin it. One of his followers was allowed to make the usual opening address on the throne speech and another, instead of speaking, blandly moved the adjournment of the debate. The Government then hurried on with its sessional business. Too late, the Conservatives discovered that they could not revive the general debate or exploit the aftermath of The Crisis.

They supposed, however (as who would not?), that the Government was finished anyway and would last only until an election, which must come within months. Bracken was wise enough not to count on a Conservative majority but he hoped for a stalemate and a coalition, the form of government he had known in Manitoba.

Coldwell seemed to imagine that the C.C.F. was still at the high peak of popularity reached during the Liberal nadir of 1943. He hoped to win the largest group in the next Parliament, if necessary to form a minority Socialist government, and then to seek a decisive mandate in another election.

The interest of all politicians had been transferred from the House to the constituencies. The nineteenth Parliament, perhaps the most illustrious since Confederation, was ending in peace.

As the last hour of its legal term drew near, King was assailed by one of his fits of superstition. Only one Parliament, so far as he remembered, had ever been allowed to die in session. All others had been properly prorogued and dissolved before their legal end. And it occurred to him that after letting Parliament die, the Conservative regime of the last century had begun to fall to pieces. It would be unlucky to repeat this procedure.

On a sudden impulse King moved across the House, sat down beside Graydon, and suggested that he agree to an immediate prorogation, a decent burial. Graydon consented, the House was formally prorogued, and the Cabinet immediately met to approve a parliamentary dissolution. The nineteenth Parliament was dissolved a few minutes before its life ran out.

The spring ended the happy triumvirate of Roosevelt, Churchill, and King. Roosevelt's sudden death came to King as a deep personal grief. He said little of it, beyond the proper formal tribute, but he did not rest until, a few months later in England, he was able to communicate with his dead friend through a spiritualistic medium.

After attending Roosevelt's funeral at Hyde Park and fixing the date of the Canadian election for June 11, King set out for San Francisco, taking Graydon and Coldwell, to attend the founding conference of the United Nations. The conference had a chilling effect on him.

Ever since the days of *Industry and Humanity* he had preached the rule of law in world affairs. Throughout the war, with increasing ardor, he had acclaimed the new order which must follow and justify the victory. In moments of euphoria he had actually believed that the age of anarchy and naked power politics, condemned in his own book, was nearing its close. With victory, the world's great age might open.

He went to San Francisco, therefore, divided between two emotions. He was pessimistic about his own political prospects, as well he might be. He was optimistic about the prospects of humanity.

The first days of the conference suddenly disillusioned him. The spectacle of Molotov scoring his barren points of debate and quibble; of the Americans forcing the democracies to accept as a companion in peace the Argentine Government which had been their actual enemy in the war; of the first head-on collision between the United States and Russia; of the little nations ignored, except in public, by the Big Five (which, in fact, meant the Big Two); of power politics as naked as they had ever been at Vienna or Versailles—all this convinced King within a week that the United Nations simply would not work.

It might be worth establishing as a forum of discussion and to perform certain international chores. It might grow gradually into something better. In the foreseeable future it could not hope to keep the peace. If there were to be peace it would be maintained by some new balance of power in which, as usual, Canada's position would be difficult.

None of these doubts was ever allowed to appear in King's speeches or his manner. He went through all the appropriate motions. He was glad to be credited with inventing the shadowy concept of the Middle Powers, Canada being their most promising member. In secret he had already written off the conference as a failure.

The world was not ready for *Industry and Humanity*. Written in the innocence of his youth, that dream book now appeared naïve and sophomoric before the threatening posture of the world's new giants. King's final phase of pessimism had begun.

His fellow delegates supposed that in the privacy of his hotel suite he was studying the United Nations Charter, now being so painfully drafted by numberless committees and assorted experts from the ends of the earth, under the secretarial supervision of Mr. Alger Hiss. Graydon and Coldwell might work on the Charter. King was writing election speeches.

The spring interlude of San Francisco gave King leisure and quiet to contemplate the nature of the political miracle which he must complete by June 11. It also brought him a mixture of good and bad news.

The collapse of Germany already had made the whole reinforcement issue irrelevant. Draftees were no longer needed. The war had lasted longer than the generals had expected but now had ended ahead of the revised schedule. Now that it was too late, King could tell Ralston and the others that he had been right from the start. Conscription, he concluded, had never been required. The nation, the Government, and the Party had been strained unnecessarily. King would die with the full conviction that The Crisis had been phony from the beginning.

No use to argue about that now. If the Government's position had been greatly relieved by the peace in Europe, if the public was in a better frame of mind, if in these months of world-wide rejoicing it might recognize that King had been the chief architect of Canada's noble part in the victory, yet the Party was in evident chaos and, as King said, reeking with disloyalty to him. It was very hard for anyone to see, in those sunny days of San Francisco, how the Government could hope to be re-elected.

The immediate trouble seemed to center in Quebec. After his first breach with King, Cardin had been ready in 1944 to rejoin the Government. Then The Crisis had infuriated him a second time. The man of wax, knowing that death was near but determined on his last stroke of glory and revenge, had started to organize his own independent party. It was privately calling itself the Cardinists. Its purpose was to protect Quebec's rights from Conservatism and Liberalism, since they could not be trusted after the conscription betrayal. Cardin's own purpose was to replace St. Laurent as the leader of the French Canadian race. His party would enter Parliament as a separate bloc and contract a loose marriage of convenience with the Liberal rump, which Cardin expected to emerge from English-speaking Canada.

He had selected Howe (who had no thought of co-operating with him) as the leader of a new coalition.

King knew all these moves in detail. He also knew that Howe was loyal to him and, in any case, was completely unsuited to lead a government, being, as he had said before, too impatient even to listen to a deputation. More serious than the Cardinists was a parallel Liberal revolt growing up in Quebec around Power.

It now appeared that Power had greatly overestimated the explosion expected to follow the conscription policy. As he had written in his resignation, he expected the unity of Canada to be devastated without hope of racial reconciliation for years to come. Instead, to his amazement and to King's, Quebec had accepted conscription quietly, thanks mainly to St. Laurent.

The Crisis had marked an organic change in the dual Canadian nature—slow, quiet, but fundamental. National unity, which had seemed in peril a few months before, was a stronger growth than most statesmen yet suspected. The French Canadian mind, as represented by St. Laurent, had grown and matured silently in the night. It was still growing.

Power and his friends had underestimated this growth and St. Laurent's influence. They could not foresee certain other factors calculated to drive Quebec back to King. They had no intention of joining Cardin in a purely racial movement but they began to throw together a makeshift combination of anticonscriptionist Liberals. In Power's most celebrated phrase, this amorphous and stillborn party advocated "Not necessarily Mackenzie King but Mackenzie King if necessary." That was a cruel thrust. King forgave it and tried to lure Power back into the Cabinet. Power refused. King also tried to see Cardin. He was coldly rebuffed.

To secure the support of Power or Cardin, or both, King was ready to pay any reasonable price. None was required.

For two reasons the twin revolts of Quebec soon dissolved. The collapse of the war in Europe ended any prospect of further recruitment in that theater and any need to oppose King's conscription policy. At the same time the continuing war against Japan might involve increasing Canadian forces if it lasted long, as the Allied command feared. The practical people of Quebec knew that if King remained in office there would be no conscription for the Pacific struggle, and if King disappeared, a Conservative or coalition government might impose a new draft.

Thus peace in Europe and war in the Pacific combined to destroy the Quebec revolt. Had Japan surrendered with Germany, things would have turned out differently. In that event, according to the judgment of men like Power, Quebec would have rejected the official Liberal Party and a period of political confusion in Ottawa would have followed.

As it was, the Liberal members of the last Parliament, who had intended to run as Cardinists, or with Power as Liberal Independents, returned one by one to the fold, still denouncing conscription but ready to forgive and forget.

When King reached Quebec City in his nation-wide tour and went to bed in the Chateau Frontenac, his first caller was Power, who intended to introduce him to a public meeting that night. King's secretaries told Power that their chief was asleep and must not be disturbed. Hearing his old friend's voice, King leaped from his bed and appeared (a notable sight) in a suit of long flannel underwear. Thus garbed, he embraced Power and ended the quarrel with Quebec.

In some ways King's campaign of 1945 was the most remarkable of his life—remarkable for the obstacles to be overcome, for the sudden healing of the Quebec schism, for the vigor of a Prime Minister nearly seventy-one years old, and, most of all, for the humor of the public.

As King left the San Francisco conference and began his last speaking tour of Canada, the public regarded him with an equal content of hostility, wonderment, and gratitude.

He had reached the zenith of his power as an international statesman. He had survived a conscription issue which had wrecked the
Liberal and Conservative Parties in turn. He had led the nation
through its greatest war in a fashion which the public had thought
quite impossible for a man of his peaceful instincts. He had proved
the most durable politician in Canadian history. He was no longer
only a party leader but a historic figure, the Great Man of Canada,
so recognized the world over.

The people did not love him, some did not even respect him, but
a majority reluctantly accepted him as essential and inevitable. The
career first imagined by a schoolboy in the shadow of his grandfather's ghost had gone exactly according to plan and in the year
1945 was complete. The grandfather had been vindicated, the
mother's hopes fulfilled, the son's wildest ambitions gratified. The
homemade colossus, his whole so much larger than the sum of his
parts, bestrode his era, unchallengeable.

Most of the Canadian people had not seen King in the last five
years. They found him greatly altered. The soft and boyish look had
gone. In its place the huge audiences of his meetings beheld an old,
gray, and grizzled man, his face lined with the labors of twenty-six
years of party leadership. Old and tired as he was, and nearing his
end, he seemed to possess a new sparkle, a sense of humor (it had
always been there but kept under disguise), and a look of confidence
which his immediate circumstances hardly justified. This was to be
his final campaign, as he told the public. He would never run for
office again. Most Canadians were seeing his face for the last time.
And most of them, as it turned out, had concluded that, likable or
not, he was still the indispensable institution of government.

Moreover, he was running on a platform fitting the times. The
Canadian people, like people everywhere, looked for that richer
society surely earned by their victory in the war. King was offering
it to them in the huge program of reform inaugurated in 1944 and
now about to produce its crowning achievement of family allowances at midsummer.

He had talked of reform for a quarter of a century and, more than
any statesman before him, he had delivered it. This was especially
important at a moment when the economists and the public alike had
completely misjudged the economic prospects. Expert and layman
both expected a deflationary depression to follow the war. King was
taking steps to arrest or modify it. The public judged that he was the
best man to meet the new crisis, as he had met the old.

King's preparations for the expected postwar letdown were more
detailed and drastic than the public yet understood. In the final rush

of victory the nation had hardly noticed a document which Howe had tabled without fanfare in Parliament. It was called a White Paper on postwar policy. In fact, it was the final chart of the economic revolution launched in 1933. It represented the total victory of Keynes over historic Canadian Liberalism.

In the White Paper, for the first time, the Government accepted the whole theory of the cyclical budget, compensatory spending to cure depression, the use of the state's financial power to supplement the market mechanism and maintain full employment. The New Deal no longer was an alien theory from London, via Washington, to be scorned in Ottawa. It was the fixed and unalterable policy of the Canadian nation, accepted by all political parties and by a public which had hardly begun to grasp it. And King, who certainly had not understood what he was saying in 1933, when he demanded the management of money "in terms of public need," was now committed to it, not by political speeches, or even by the pretentious White Paper, but by the facts of politics.

The results could not be foreseen and were barely considered by the Canadian people when the White Paper slipped unnoticed into Parliament and was instantly forgotten. The brain trust had written that economic Magna Carta, some members of the Government may have read it, Howe assuredly had not realized its full implications, King was busy with more urgent business, but the economy of Canada, hitherto based at least in theory on the open market, with Adam Smith as its guardian, was now based on massive state interventions, according to the doctrine of Keynes.

All the vague aspirations counted with the voters of 1945 far less than the known character of King and the depressing contrast between him and any possible alternative. That contrast was the deciding factor of the election.

As King had foreseen, Bracken's mistake in staying out of Parliament could not be overcome. Bracken had lost his only chance of impressing himself and his policies on the public. The ball of politics had been taken away from him. Now the Conservatives' captive Liberal offered no clear policy, was floundering in issues which he did not understand, and finally floundered into a Quebec strategy which could only assure his downfall.

In Quebec, of course, no Conservative could hope to be elected. The Party's recent conscriptionist policy had prolonged indefinitely its divorce from French Canada decreed in 1917 and actually begun with the execution of Louis Riel. The effects of this separation on Canadian life were deplorable. The effects on Bracken were ruinous.

He attempted, in his desperation—or others attempted for him—

the old technique of a secret agreement with the extreme French Canadian nationalists who were more opposed to Conservative policy than the Liberals. Such a liaison had succeeded briefly in 1911 and in 1930. It required a skill lacking in Bracken. He resorted to the clumsy trick of accepting the support of various "independents" and when he refused to name them, lest the Conservative label spoil their small chance of election, the maneuver became a farce. It did not help him in Quebec. It gravely damaged him everywhere else. King had to make only an oblique and lofty mention of this unnatural combination—speaking more in sorrow than in anger—to turn it against its authors.

Coldwell had hoped that this election would make the C.C.F. a truly national party and give it at least a powerful group in Parliament. He, like so many others, had underestimated King's power of recovery and exaggerated the public discontent. This was not the nineteen-thirties, when a famished nation grasped at any chance of relief. It was a time of high prosperity, full employment, and victory —no climate for Socialism. Anyway, King offered all the reform that a reasonable man could ask. He had placed himself exactly where he wished to be, to the right of the C.C.F. and to the left of the Conservatives.

Few voters noted that King went through the entire campaign with hardly a reference to the Pacific war, still the largest current fact in the world. He knew what he was doing. Though his advisers repeatedly insisted that he could not ignore the struggle against Japan (expected to last another year, with huge casualties), King refused to discuss it. At last he told his friends impatiently that something beyond their knowledge was about to happen and would alter the whole world situation. In due time they would understand. Meanwhile they must not press him further.

King's secret was the atomic bomb. Necessarily, he had long known, in a general way, that Canada was working on this project with the United States. Howe had indicated to the Cabinet that a superweapon of some sort was in prospect. Even Howe did not know and was careful not to learn the details. They were confined to the private safe of Dean C. J. Mackenzie, chairman of the National Research Council.

That great public servant knew all there was to know. He had suffered months of secret torture in the fear that the Germans would launch the bomb first and win the war as late as 1944.

Mackenzie told King nothing, but King had his own sources of information in Washington. He knew from Roosevelt that the bomb was almost ready and, before the election, understood that it would be dropped on Japan during the summer. He could not say in public that the Pacific war was no longer a Canadian problem. Even the small proposed contribution to the American assault on Japan would not be needed.

After the first bomb expunged Hiroshima on August 6, King triumphantly recalled his silence in the election campaign. His advisers admitted that, as usual, he had been right.

By election day, June 11, the defeat of Bracken and the failure of the C.C.F.'s brave hopes were assured. In his final election King won 125 seats, Bracken 67, and Coldwell only 28. Still more gratifying to King as a final vindication, he received a plurality of votes from the overseas soldiers whom he was accused of betraying. McNaughton, however, had been defeated and the unhappy partnership of Laurier House was finally dissolved.

The miracle of a Government surviving both the war and The Crisis had been duly performed. It was to be King's last. The road in front of him ran downhill.

So far, however, there was no outward warning of that physical decline soon to begin. Now that the last threat against him had been removed, King enjoyed his job more than ever.

When, for example, the Pacific war appeared to be closing, he hurried happily to the Canadian Broadcasting Corporation's studio in the Chateau Laurier and waited through most of the day to deliver a victory broadcast. As the news of the Japanese surrender still did not arrive, he finally made a record of his address and left it at the studio with strict instructions that it should not be broadcast until the surrender was officially announced.

While he went for an evening walk at Kingsmere, a premature report of peace came over the news wires and King's speech was placed immediately on the air. A few minutes later the news was denied. His secretaries hardly dared to tell King that he had rejoiced too soon, but instead of blaming others for his mistake he accepted full blame himself. He was growing mellow in his old age.

Next day he told his Cabinet colleagues sheepishly that he "had made history" since their last meeting.

He could afford mistakes of this sort and the pursuit of publicity no longer was necessary to him. There were no more votes or prizes to win.

42

The Wrong World

THE WORLD ENTERING THE PHONY PEACE IN THE AUTUMN OF 1945 was the same world which had entered the phony war just six years earlier. The cardinal mistake of Liberals everywhere was to suppose that the world had changed. The more it had seemed to change, the more it was the same. Youth could not be expected to understand that. King understood it because he was old, tired, and increasingly skeptical of this world as he approached the next.

Of the western statesmen who had managed the war, he was perhaps the first to feel the disillusionment of the peace. At San Francisco he had privately written off the United Nations, in its present form, as quite incapable of preventing another war. Within a year he was telling his friends that the United Nations was "an impossible organization," a "façade for the Great Powers," that the Russians also were "impossible" and sooner or later must be arrested in their expansion, though the consequences would be dangerous.

The world, he saw, was still governed by that naked pursuit of power from which he had fled between the wars. In this last phase of his life he perceived the fatal lacuna in his youthful philosophy. It had contrived ingenious methods of conciliation but had never faced the dilemma of human affairs when conciliation fails and force takes its place.

It was a dilemma common to most Liberals the world over and it was peculiarly the dilemma of King. He had been raised in the nineteenth century. He had been nourished on the very essence of that century's Liberalism. By birth, education, and environment he had absorbed, until it was the whole grain of his nature, the theory of mankind's inevitable progress by a divine evolutionary process. Like all nineteenth-century Liberals, he had been horrified by the reversal of that process in the two wars of the twentieth. And like them, he had misjudged the course of world events by overestimating man-

410

kind's rate of progress, by exaggerating its virtues and minimizing its faults, by supposing that a rational world was much closer than it possibly could be.

Up to about 1945 he regarded wars as aberrations from the comfortable norm accepted in his nineteenth-century youth. He hoped that, after the second war, he would see a world order under law and he had proclaimed it again and again in his public speeches.

Even when the phase of disillusionment began with the onset of his old age and bodily decline, the old hopes still struggled in his mind with the new pessimism. He was desperately torn between the two poles of his thinking. Hence the bitter paradox of this last phase, the public devotion to the new world order which, in the other half of his mind, he had discounted; the speeches going far beyond the collective security of the United Nations to advocate actual world government and the private admission that the world had returned to old-fashioned and outright power politics.

The world was not what the nineteenth century had expected, what the early twentieth had planned, or what all good Liberals had been trained to believe in. The postwar world of the Atlantic Charter, of Dumbarton Oaks, of San Francisco, and of countless earnest declarations was intended to be a world of internationalism and, in that respect at least, a Liberal world. Whereas the clearest fact when the war ended was the eruption of nationalism in a series of explosions throughout Asia, Africa, the Near East, and wherever men had not yet felt the impact of Liberalism.

Under its various party labels, Liberalism had been preparing for a new world which had yet to be born and could not be born so long as the great reaction of Communism gripped its heartland. King had been preaching all his life a dream as yet beyond man's grasp.

In his disenchantment he saw that he would never live to see a different sort of world this side of the grave, he was therefore increasingly concerned with the invisible world on the other side, and if he still continued to preach the new order in public his preachments had become hardly more than a habitual posture or, at best, a far-distant hope for others to realize.

In short, his era was dying. The character formed in the nineteenth century could dominate the first half of the twentieth in Canada. It could not be fitted to the second half when the world of his youth was certifiably dead. King was getting old.

While the spectacle of the world at large after the second great bloodletting flatly denied the Liberal's hope, within Canada King could see the sure imprint of his work. If not by him, then under his leadership, the whole society of Canada had been changed almost beyond recognition—changed so quietly and subtly that few Canadians paused to note the transformation.

To begin with, the successive sedimentary deposits of social reform begun by King in his first days and constantly increased ever since had now become the foundation of the Welfare State. Under the program of 1944 the Welfare State was still growing. Its growth might be condemned, retarded, or distorted, but it could not be retraced.

Secondly, the power balance of society had been drastically shifted by the emergence of Canada as a rich industrial and increasingly urban nation; by the resulting emergence of big business and of big labor unions as a major estate of the realm; by a reversal in the position of the farmers who had once united against protectionism but had managed to secure a new protection for themselves through state guarantees, bulk sales, and floor prices; by a deliberate redistribution of income from the rich to the poor; and by the tax collector's assault on the middle class.

The social system surrounding King at the end of the war no longer could be called Capitalism by any former definition. If it fell far short of the ideal society of *Industry and Humanity*, it certainly was not the society in which the book had been written.

The state had taken over from the market the real management of the system (of that the closed Winnipeg wheat market was a vivid symbol). The state had guaranteed to keep the economy prosperous, fully employed, and constantly expanding, mainly through the engine of money, now under the Government's hand in the Bank of Canada. The state was the largest buyer of goods, its budget the largest single gear in the economy, and its taxes took about a third of the national income. Indirectly it influenced and sometimes decided the level of wages, as its fiscal policies (after the repeal of direct controls) largely determined the level of prices.

In a vague, imperfect, and groping fashion, the state had become, as the public's representative, that third partner in industry advocated by King. And the appetite of this third partner was growing all the time.

Neither King nor any other single man could claim to have produced this silent Canadian revolution. It was the local version of a world revolution. But King had presided at the piecemeal liquidation of the old society, he had been the midwife of the new, and he had managed these deep changes, so far as government could manage them, with so little public fuss that their depth would not be understood until after his departure.

Thirdly, in reflection of the economic and social metamorphosis, the political balance of Canada also had shifted drastically and this shift was largely King's own work. He had made Canada almost a one-party nation with three splinters of opposition.

The Conservative Party was hived in Ontario, was indefinitely excluded from Quebec after the conscription struggle, was lacking in any clear policy, could not offer an alternative to the Government, and could hardly call itself a national party. Meighen, Bennett, Manion, and Bracken had ruined the Conservative Party but they needed King's help, which had been freely given. His contribution to that work had made the Liberal Party the most powerful in Canadian history, had crushed all others in its juggernaut march down the center of the road, had left no room for competition on either side.

On the other edge of the road, the C.C.F. had suffered from the same causes. It had doomed itself as a national party by building on too narrow a class base and on a doctrinaire policy unacceptable in Canada. Whatever hope of national success it had possessed in the first place King had quietly removed by swerving far enough to the Left to expropriate anything of use in its doctrines.

Nevertheless, the C.C.F., even by 1945, could rightly claim to be one of the most effective political movements ever bred in Canada. It had insinuated a large part of its theory into King's new Liberalism. Many of the reforms that had been heretical in its early days were now not only commonplace but were represented as the life-long principles of the Government.

King's new intimacy with Coldwell was not accident or whim. It was part of the larger process at work within Liberalism. When King cultivated a receptive Coldwell, called him the man of the future, and sometimes remarked that Socialism of some vague, indefinable sort was inevitable, he doubtless was playing games with the C.C.F., but there was a good deal of conviction in it. Coldwell at least was deeply impressed by these private communications. Who knew what Socialism meant? By the standards of original Capitalism, King must have appeared to Coldwell as the most successful Socialist in Canada.

In part, his present position was the product of his own radicalism, in part the mere maneuver of politics. He had operated since the depression on the assumption that his real danger was on the Left, that the Right was historically finished. Therefore, he had moved leftward. He had engulfed the radicalism of the C.C.F., or those parts of it which he considered practical, and had worried little (apart from the conscription struggle) about the Conservatives or their western splinter, calling itself Social Credit.

King had brought a new Liberal Party through the war. Its gravity had shifted with that of the society it governed. It still rested on its eastern pillar, the conservatism of Quebec, Liberal in partisan politics by the accident of Riel and two conscription crises. It had strengthened its hold on the Maritimes and Ontario. Its other historic pillar of prairie agrarianism, the old western low-tariff bloc, which had always balanced the protectionism of urban Quebec and Ontario, was shattered. The prairies had split between Liberalism, Socialism, and Social Credit and thereby dissolved their former direct power in the Party and in Parliament.

Divided outwardly in politics, the farmers of the West had quietly united with those everywhere else outside party lines in a kind of nameless party of their own, headed by Gardiner, who still called himself a free trader in principle and was the archpriest of protectionism in practice. For the old doctrine of low tariffs he had substituted the principle of farm prices guaranteed by the state. The old war on high tariffs, high freight rates, and metropolitan finance had been largely replaced by the proposition that if the farmer must accept these evils then he must be compensated by the consumer through prices and by the taxpayer through agricultural subsidies.

Thus, for unexampled power the Liberal Party paid the price of confusion, contradiction, and sheer expediency. For the most part it operated not on principles but on pressures, like most successful governments in America. It had buried its first saint, Adam Smith, and established Keynes in his place. It was not a party in the old sense but a congeries of separate groups in coalition. Men like Gardiner as the spokesman of agriculture, Howe as the representative of industry, Mitchell as the delegate of labor, St. Laurent as the leader of Quebec, possessed almost autonomous and sovereign power within the Party and could apply, when necessary, a veto on government policy by Calhoun's ancient Law of the Concurrent Majority.

In another political system each of these men would have led his own party, making and breaking coalitions with others in the French fashion. By the genius of the Canadian system, and under an unequaled manager like King, the conflicts between the rival groups calling themselves Liberals could be reconciled within the Party. The nation's politics were thereby saved from continual derangement. If they moved repeatedly from Left to Right, or Right to Left, advanced and retreated to advance again, they maintained the semblance of order and, in general, provided competent government.

This form of tacit coalition and secret struggle within the bosom of a national party had always been the method of the Canadian party system. King had not invented the method but he had brought it to final efficiency by the end of the war. And the proof that this was a formidable task and an extraordinary achievement could be found in all the other parties. None of them had been able to find his equal or to imitate his success.

An even larger change had been grafted into the system. Necessarily in a Welfare State, basically managed by government, the non-political expert had assumed great though anonymous powers. He had often dominated government policy during the war, and consolidated himself in the peace. More and more, Canada, like other nations, was governed by a vast and proliferating bureaucracy. It had no superior, in point of ability and patriotism, anywhere.

Finally, as a result of this concentration of power in the executive and its technicians, and of the Opposition's temporary collapse, the institution of Parliament had suffered grievous damage. In part this could be blamed on King, who had gathered power into his own hands during the war, at the expense of Parliament. In the main, it was the reflection of a changed society. The people had asked government to deliver certain results and must give government proportionate authority.

In any case, King's elevation was accompanied by the eclipse of Parliament. Whether that eclipse was temporary or permanent is still not clear.

With a new society, a changed Party, and a tamed Parliament, King faced the postwar era of 1945 and soon found all his immediate calculations sadly askew, for he had listened to the economists.

Perhaps at no time in history had these trained experts in all nations so completely bungled their own business.

· On their advice, every democratic government in the world prepared for a quick depression, falling prices, and unemployment. In Washington, President Truman feverishly sought to ward off the collapse definitely fixed by his Secretary of Commerce, Henry Wallace, for the following spring. Wages must be raised, taxes lowered, purchasing power increased, according to the Keynesian theory, to counteract a deflation.

The same general policy of easy money was planned in Ottawa, but fortunately did not go far.

When, as the economists did not foresee, the expected deflation turned into a great inflation, it was greatly worsened by the American Government's inflationary policy. Gasoline had been deliberately poured on the fire under the impression that it was a frost. America, operating on Keynesian principles, had mistaken an upward cycle for the opposite. In its first test of economic judgment the state-managed society fell flat on its face.

This was only the beginning of the price rise. In Canada, as elsewhere, the ingredients of inflation had been smuggled into the money system during the war. Unable to pay its bills out of taxes, the state had created a huge new supply of money out of thin air, through the mechanism of the central Bank. A dam of tissue paper, in the form of direct price controls, had been installed to contain this rising reservoir of potential purchasing power. Whenever its owner chose to convert it into goods, the dam must break and the inundation of all fixed savings must follow in the upsurge of prices and the engulfment of the dollar.

This did not occur immediately. The cost of living in 1946 was only 23 per cent above its prewar figure and rose slowly for two more years. But the dam already was breaking.

Even more serious was the collapse of the North Atlantic Triangle, that old reliable system of trade by which Canada always sold more than it bought in Europe and used its surplus earnings to pay for a deficit in trade with the United States. The postwar world of 1945 was rushing toward the dollar crisis and Canada, apparently prosperous, toward bankruptcy.

In the meantime, however, despite all these mistakes of economic calculation (and who could hope to be right when the world economy had cracked from top to bottom?), Canada came miraculously through the period of reconversion under Howe's general direction. This was perhaps more remarkable than the wartime mobilization. The nation was richer, more flexible, and better managed than it had supposed.

The immediate postwar honeymoon was brief. For all his success so far, King now faced as daunting problems as ever. They were far graver than he had yet dreamed and too big for an old man who had begun to crack up. Though for some time he could go through the motions of leadership, could coast on the momentum of a lifetime, could not be challenged, for there was no one to challenge him, he moved on the downgrade with increasing velocity. There was important work to finish, but for all except ceremonial purposes the greatest career in Canadian politics was closing.

43

The Dwindling Days

OF ALL THE MEN WHO HAD TOUCHED KING'S DESTINY, THE LAST WAS
the most unlikely. His name was Igor Gouzenko. As a personage he was unimportant, a mousy cipher clerk in the Ottawa
embassy of the Russian Government. As the first clear warning of a
new contest in world power, he was, for the moment, the most interesting man alive. Few men affected King so profoundly.

On September 5, 1945, Gouzenko decided to break with Soviet
Russia. The mouse had turned on the lion.

That evening Gouzenko stole a bundle of incriminating documents from the embassy and took them to the offices of the Ottawa
Journal. He intended to prove that a network of Russian spies,
centered in Ottawa, had long been stealing and buying the most
precious military secrets of Britain, the United States, and Canada.
The mouse was as brave as the lion. If he failed to convince the
Canadian Government, Gouzenko knew he would be murdered by
his employers.

At the last moment, according to his own story, Gouzenko's heart
failed him and he did not dare to enter the *Journal's* office. When
he returned home his wife encouraged him to try again. This time
he managed to see an assistant editor, who advised him to tell his
story to the Royal Canadian Mounted Police. Instead, he tried to
see St. Laurent, but by then it was midnight and the Minister of
Justice had left his office.

Next morning, Gouzenko, his wife, and child appeared at St.
Laurent's office. They waited two hours and then were told that the
Minister would not receive them. The family went back in despair
to the *Journal,* where Gouzenko was urged again to see the R.C.M.P.
Finally he found his way to the office of the Ottawa Crown prose-
cutor. A secretary listened to his story and referred him to the police.

Apparently the Government did not wish to hear anything unpleasant about its Russian ally. Gouzenko could not alert Canada and now faced swift execution by the agents of Russia. He was wise enough not to return to his own home and that saved his life. While he and his family sought refuge with some kindly neighbors, four men from the Russian embassy broke into his apartment, undoubtedly intending to kidnap and execute him. The city police, already warned by Gouzenko's host, were there first. The Russians claimed diplomatic immunity and were allowed to go free.

On the following morning, Gouzenko was taken at last to the Mounted Police. His story was recorded and given immediately to the Justice Department. It reached King just before he was ready to open the first session of the new Parliament.

King kept the House of Commons waiting while he listened with increasing horror and disbelief to the report of his officials. His first impulse was to dismiss Gouzenko as a lunatic, the Russian documents as forgeries. Canada, he said, must do nothing which would arouse the antagonism of the Russian Government.

With comic desperation he suggested that Gouzenko go back quietly to the Russian embassy—to certain murder. At least Gouzenko should be shadowed for a few days to make sure that he was sane. It was unthinkable, King kept repeating, that the Canadian Government should involve itself in a diplomatic quarrel with Russia.

After this outburst, it took King only a few minutes to see that there was no easy way out of an incident bound to shake the politics of the world. He was appalled to find himself entangled in a spider web of intrigue like something out of a cheap detective story. At the center of that web, as he knew, lay the atomic bomb.

This business was bigger than Gouzenko, bigger than King, bigger than Canada. The little man from the Russian embassy had pricked the first tiny chink through the Russian wall and what King glimpsed through it confirmed all his suspicions. A poor cipher clerk had revealed a world conspiracy. Thus, as King observed, the greatest dictators are always at the mercy of some forgotten underling.

It was no time for such meditations. The House was waiting for the Prime Minister. He left Gouzenko and his documents in charge of St. Laurent and opened Parliament.

As soon as the business of the session was well under way, King paid a "courtesy call" on President Truman and told him Gouzenko's story. From Washington he hurried to London, ostensibly to discuss postwar problems with the British Government. At Chequers he conveyed the dreadful secret to Prime Minister Attlee. King even thought of going on to Moscow to confront Stalin but abandoned this project because, at this point, he could not prove anything.

Meanwhile, the secret-service agencies of the American, British, and Canadian Governments were quietly concentrated on the Ottawa spy ring. Much against his will and with violence to his Liberal principles, King agreed to a secret order-in-council which established a secret royal commission of inquiry, composed of Justices Robert Tachereau and R. L. Kellock, of the Canadian Supreme Court. Their brilliant counsel, E. K. Williams, K.C., of Winnipeg, managed the work of detection so skillfully that hardly more than a half-dozen officials knew why he had come to Ottawa. When his massive evidence was examined by Tachereau and Kellock, the police secretly investigated twenty-six persons, held them incommunicado without counsel or bail, questioned them at length, and prepared to charge thirteen of them in the courts.

To King this was a repulsive business, indefensible in theory. It was secret arrest and, in effect, secret trial, since the commission's verdict of guilt was bound to affect the verdict of the trial juries. In time of peace nothing of the sort had ever been attempted in Canada. Every Liberal instinct in King was revolted. For weeks he chafed while the royal commission continued its inquiry, and later he admitted to a friend that these proceedings were so outrageous that, had he been leading the parliamentary Opposition, he would have used them to destroy the Government.

Once embarked on the inquiry, however, he could not escape it. The thing must go on to its conclusion, whatever the results to the Government, to the principles of civil rights, and to international politics.

He had hoped that the secret inquiry would last only a few days. The commission began to examine the suspects on February 13, 1946, and its first report did not reach King until March 2. Not a word of all this had yet reached the world. King had compelling reasons for silence. His police did not wish to give advance warning to the confederates of those already arrested. The first hopeful conference of the Big Four foreign ministers had opened in Moscow in December and if the story were released then, King would be accused of trying to divide the victorious Allies.

Between the attacks of his Liberal conscience, the danger of an international explosion, and the necessity for silence he was wretched.

Throughout those heavy months of autumn, winter, and early spring, St. Laurent kept his head and stored away in it some useful lessons. He, too, was shocked to find the investigation dragging so slowly, the secret inquiry violating all his lawyer's sense of justice, but in his own thinking he invoked the supreme law of the Roman lawgivers—the safety of the state. St. Laurent believed that the state itself was endangered.

When the news burst at last upon the House of Commons, when Fred Rose, one of its members, was listed among the Russian agents, when twenty persons ultimately were given public trial and when six of them were found innocent, the rest guilty, and the conspiracy fully proved, King and St. Laurent, especially St. Laurent as Minister of Justice, were condemned by some of their best friends and by defenders of civil liberties throughout the nation for their methods of inquiry.

All that was useful and salutary. It showed the strength of civil liberty in Canada. It warned all future governments against the evil of secret trial. It probably did not weaken civil liberty, as many Canadians feared, but served to strengthen it in the end.

For the present, however, St. Laurent had to bear a public indictment calculated to ruin his political career. For that he cared nothing, since he intended to retire anyway.

After he had denied that any secret orders-in-council had been passed and next day informed Parliament that he had forgotten the order appointing the royal commission, his word was accepted without question. Nevertheless, in those days of victory, as the new age was dawning and Russia was counted as a friend, the secret trial was not easily forgiven. Seven years later, with the world living on the brink of war, St. Laurent saw no reason to regret his action. He had suspected earlier than any Canadian statesman, even King, the true state of the world, and he was ready, before King, to remedy it with a new alliance of the free nations.

Whatever his misgivings in private, King faced Parliament boldly on March 18, 1946, and took full responsibility for the secret inquisition. He refused to sever diplomatic relations with Russia on the quaint assumption that the spy ring might have been "unknown" to the Russian Government. He could not believe, he said, that a man like Stalin would "countenance" these activities, and once Stalin knew the facts "we shall find that a change will come that will make a vast difference indeed."

King could not have believed that, for he had made up his mind about the Russians already. At this point in history he was not prepared to thrust Canada into the increasing quarrels of the great powers, to have his Government blamed everywhere (as it was being blamed in the Moscow press) for upsetting the shiny applecart of the brave new world.

The results of the spy revelations could not be denied. The cipher clerk had alerted democracy to its danger. His warnings would soon be confirmed by Russia's orderly engulfment of eastern Europe and most of Asia.

It was all very well for King to protest to Parliament that he loved the Russian people, that they would never approve the action of a few erring officials, and that he would spend the brief remainder of his own life promoting friendship between all the races of mankind. He knew that, as geography and history had decreed, Canada was caught inevitably like a morsel of grain under the millstones of the great powers. The honest broker between the United States and Britain possessed the secret information of both and, as the Russians thought, was a perfect listening post, a soft spot in the democratic front. King, the great conciliator, was denounced throughout the Communist empire as an enemy of peace.

The injustice of it stung him, but not deeply. His skin had been toughened by his more than seventy years of experience with mankind. The illusions of his youth remained only for ceremonial purposes. He knew by now that he would never live to see a safe world. The only question in one half of his mind, six months after victory, was whether he would live to see the third world war.

Yet in his mind's other half, this ambivalent creature continued to hope and in public he maintained the appropriate pretenses.

After his hurried trip to London, he had gone to Washington with Attlee and there signed the three-nation declaration which retained the secret of the atomic bomb, pending a workable international agreement, and guaranteed the free use of atomic discovery for peaceful purposes.

The significance of the Washington conference was little realized at the time.

Apparently, the American President had hardly begun to grasp the power placed in his hands by atomic fission and had only a vague idea of the resulting political problems. Shocked by the inadequate thinking of the American Government, King took off his coat and worked in his shirt sleeves with Lester Pearson, his reliable handy man, to draft the hasty statement announcing that the United States, Britain, and Canada had assumed custodianship of atomic secrets, actually secrets no longer, thanks to Russia's able spies.

The discussions on the Presidential yacht had an importance beyond the field of weapons. Through Attlee and King, Britain and Canada had begun (though they were still ignorant of the events ahead in Asia) to moderate American policy while committing themselves, at the same time, to American leadership in the new struggle now opening. The rather confused discussions in Truman's floating office started that sequence of events leading to the solidarity of the free world in the final tests of Asia and Europe.

When King returned to Ottawa with Attlee as his guest, he could not anticipate a chain reaction of international disaster. On the contrary, speaking with the hopeful half of his mind, he told Parliament that the world of the atomic age must devise "some form of world government, restricted, at least at the outset, to matters pertaining to the prevention of war and the maintenance of international security."

This was not as hypocritical as it might seem to his intimates. Events would quickly uphold his belief that unrestricted national sovereignty was an anachronism which must make peace impossible. In those beliefs King was quite sincere.

Speaking from the other half of his mind, King told a friend a few months later that there might well be another world war not long hence, perhaps in some twenty or thirty years, and that the United Nations, as presently constructed, could not hope to prevent it.

So far, there was no sign of the world government to assure safety. Before long, King shortened the risk of war to two or three years and at one point expected it within months.

In 1946, his energies appeared almost as good as ever. He went to London for a meeting of Commonwealth Prime Ministers and the British victory parade, returned home, and set off for Paris at midsummer for the so-called peace conference, which devised treaties for Germany's satellite states, treaties that Russia soon began to violate. In the autumn he watched the opening of the United Nations General Assembly in New York. There the doubts of San Francisco were only increased.

All his thoughts were clouded by the new nightmare of Russian Communism. While he could not admit his fears in public, they were well known among his friends and were not without their comic side. One of his servants, said King, was a Communist, probably a spy, and this man he watched with continual amusement. To draw him out, King would talk at length about the virtues of Communism, pretending a warm sympathy for Russia. What he told his servant, if it was repeated to the Russians, might seem a valuable indication of the Canadian Government's policies. Actually it was nonsense, but King enjoyed his little game of hide-and-seek.

On June 8, 1946, King's tenure of office exceeded even that of Macdonald by one day. He had been Prime Minister just two days short of nineteen years, a Canadian long-distance record. Still, it was not enough. King intended to break Walpole's record and prove himself the most durable statesman in the history of the British nations. That would not be easy. For all his apparent vigor, his constant comings and goings across the ocean, his mastery of Cabinet, Party, and Parliament, he was tiring. He cut down his working hours, spent more time at Kingsmere, and increased his consultations with the dead.

As he approached its gates, he took an intensive interest in the spirit world. All those he had ever loved, his mother, father, brother, and sister, were beyond the gates. Even his terrier, Pat, had died and in circumstances that served to increase King's psychic beliefs.

His watch had fallen from his bedside table "for no apparent reason" during the night. On picking it up in the morning, and finding that it had stopped at twenty minutes past four, he had known "as if a voice were speaking to me" that Pat would be dead before another twenty-four hours passed. The following night the faithful animal crawled from his basket and, with his last strength, reached King's bed to die there. King looked at his watch. As he had expected, the time was twenty minutes past four.

Through Helen Hughes, a British housewife and medium, King already had communicated with Laurier, Fielding, and Sir Oliver Mowat, and with his own relatives. His mother had warned him that he was working too hard and must rest or his heart would give out. A year after his death, Roosevelt told King to remain in office, and when King protested that he lacked the strength to go on, Roosevelt replied that Canada and the world could not yet spare him. Even Roosevelt soon reversed this advice and insisted that King must retire to save the remains of his strength. Roosevelt added in another message that King should watch Asia, the center of the world's danger (King thought otherwise). Finally, the lonely master even reached Pat, now happily in the care of Isabel King.

The mediums questioned by Blair Fraser, who has revealed this side of King's life, agreed that he never consulted the spirits on the affairs of government. He refused to discuss them at his frequent séances and told the mediums that he preferred to decide such matters for himself.

The two aspects of his life were entirely separate, but in his old age the spirit world had become far more important than the physical. He was convincing himself by final proof that his journey, apparently near its end, was only beginning. The real King, who had assumed so many contrary disguises, who had compromised so often in the public interest, who had suffered so much from misunderstanding, disappointment, and loneliness, would soon be free to assume his true shape. From the dingy rooms of the mediums he

could see the light still burning in his mother's window. The boy
who had traveled so far from Woodside was coming home.

In this period occurred the first of two disagreeable clashes between King and St. Laurent. Neither reflected any credit on King.

He was absent from Ottawa when Attlee announced in a cable to
the Canadian Government that India was to be granted its independence on such generous and friendly terms that it was expected
to remain with the Commonwealth. Pearson, as the operating head
of the External Affairs Department, drafted a reply to Attlee, saying
that the Canadian Government welcomed the British policy and the
freedom of India. St. Laurent, as the reponsible Minister, signed this
document.

When King saw it in Cabinet on his return, he was furious. He
remarked that Attlee's cable had been addressed to the Prime Minister of Canada and he assumed that he and no other was still Prime
Minister. Since he alone was entitled to answer his own correspondence, he took the draft reply rudely out of St. Laurent's hands and
said he would deal with it himself. And later on he added—his pique
overcoming his good sense—that he was horrified at the thought of
an Asiatic majority dominating the Commonwealth.

St. Laurent received this outrageous rebuke in a silence which
some of his colleagues misunderstood. A man of spirit, they thought,
would have resigned on the instant. St. Laurent did not resign because in the sense of strict protocol King was probably right and
should have been consulted, but mainly because St. Laurent had no
intention of remaining in politics much longer and was watching the
clock for his hour of release. He took full responsibility for the incident, though Pearson was blamed by King as its real instigator.
Pearson was used to being in trouble, his normal habitat, and refused
to be disturbed.

In a few days, recovering his good temper, King turned his charm
on St. Laurent and Pearson as a kind of tacit apology. If King thought
that he could thus bend St. Laurent or Pearson to his will, he was
wrong, as he would soon discover.

44

The Heir-Apparent

B Y 1947, THE END OF KING'S PUBLIC LIFE WAS IN SIGHT. WITHOUT him, the Liberal dynasty somehow must go on. The problem was to find the heir-apparent. King's thoughts were concentrated upon this transfer of power. As late as June he was saying that of all his colleagues St. Laurent was by far the ablest but unfortunately St. Laurent was not available for Party leadership since he had decided to return to private life and his decision could not be altered. Someone else must be found.

For some time King had been thinking of Pearson. The jack-of-all-trades, who had begun his public service as the obscure secretary of Bennett's price-spread commission, who had risen through countless international conferences to be Canadian ambassador to Washington, who had every natural talent for politics but refused to enter them, was invited to join the Cabinet. After even a brief experience there, King suggested, Pearson should have an excellent chance of capturing the Party leadership.

Pearson refused. King persisted. All King's unequaled powers of persuasion left Pearson quite unmoved. Under his youthful and cherubic look he was a tougher man than King had supposed. What King did not realize even then was that Pearson would not serve under him. Another leader might attract Pearson and that leader, contrary to King's information, was available.

The year 1947 was passing without any satisfactory preparations for the future of the dynasty. Obviously, the transfer of power could not be delayed for another year. King was finding that he could work for only three hours at a stretch. After such a spell he could not work at all the next day. His mind was as active as ever but his memory was failing. He sometimes forgot the names of those around him. In everything but title he had ceased to be Prime Minister.

No Government could function long in this fashion, without a

real head. Among the inner circle of King's counselors it was realized
that soon someone must tell him the truth and advise him to retire.
Nobody volunteered for this duty.

Despite his dwindling energies, King was quietly completing his
final work of statesmanship by joining Newfoundland to Canada.
He had laid the foundations of the tenth Canadian province during
the war by making sure that every contract relating to Newfoundland contained a clause allowing for a future change in the colony's
status. Repeatedly he had indicated Canada's willingness to receive
Newfoundland into Confederation, taking care not to press this invitation and alarm the colony's anti-Canadian elements. He never
altered his original judgment that if Newfoundland did not join
Canada it would join the United States, that ultimately Confederation itself would be endangered if its eastern gateway were en-
filaded by a foreign power.

The seeds of union thus sown, though observed by few Canadians,
had grown steadily. When the Newfoundland people finally faced
the issue and voted in favor of joining Canada, King was disappointed by the bare majority for his policy. He had promised to
consummate the union only if Newfoundland showed its will by an
unmistakable verdict at the polls. Now he wondered if he could
regard this close vote as a sufficient mandate.

After some hesitation he was persuaded by his colleagues, who
pointed out that the Newfoundland majority actually was larger
than he had ever received in any election save that of 1940. That
argument convinced him. The negotiation of a union agreement was
left to St. Laurent, but it was King who had fulfilled Macdonald's
vision of a nation embracing the northern half of the continent. If
King had done nothing else in his life, this achievement would have
placed him among Canada's chief builders. Under him Confederation was completed.

Newfoundland was not the Government's chief preoccupation in
this period of King's decline. If he was increasingly idle, events
were on the move and seemed likely to sweep Canada toward
insolvency.

By the spring of 1947, the basic unbalance of the world economy,
between dollar and sterling currency blocs, was apparent to anyone who could read figures. Unable to sell as much as they bought
in America, the European nations were using up their reserves of
dollars and gold. As they tried to cut down their North American
imports, Canada was losing its old European markets, where it had
formerly earned a large surplus of convertible cash and used it to
pay a corresponding deficit in its trade with the United States. To

cover its American deficits under the new conditions Canada also was exhausting its dollars and gold at a dangerous rate. The reliable old North Atlantic Triangle of trade, for which the whole economy of Canada had been shaped, had collapsed and would take a long time to repair, if it was capable of revival at all.

The Canadian Government put a good public face on its new crisis and laughed off the newspapers if they pointed to the obvious facts. Meditating a remedy, Abbott (who had quickly been graduated into the key portfolio of Finance) did not dare either to admit the emergency or to indicate what he intended to do about it, lest he stimulate a further flight of money from Canada or start an unnecessary purchase of American goods before he could impose import restrictions. Thus he waited through the summer with a glazed smile and falling currency reserves.

In the meantime, a mysterious incident, still cloaked in embarrassed official silence, had begun. The low-tariff elements in the Government had concluded that Canada must sell more to the United States if it was to continue buying there in the current volume, and that, to sell more, it must get American tariffs down. King approved this general objective, which he had advocated all his life and for which he and Laurier's Government had been defeated in the Reciprocity election of 1911.

Accordingly, a secret mission of experts was dispatched to Washington to negotiate a new tariff deal. It seemed to make surprising progress. American officials, having coaxed Roosevelt out of his early protectionist policies into Cordell Hull's program of tariff reduction, were delighted to receive these overtures from Canada. They encouraged the Canadian emissaries to believe that the Reciprocity agreement of 1911, or something very near it, could be pushed through the Congress. At least the Americans were ready to make a far-reaching tariff reduction and fight for it, though whether President Truman would go that far was never quite clear.

While this project was quietly under way, without a leak to the newspapers, a more modest public approach was made at Geneva to the whole problem of trade strangulation. It eventually produced the tariff-reducing General Agreement on Tariffs and Trade, later given the revolting name of GATT.

When King sailed for England in the autumn to attend the wedding of Princess Elizabeth, he carried an assorted baggage. There was the dollar crisis to begin with. One of his secretaries took along a shotgun, which was merely a gift for a French friend, but it gave the expedition a belligerent look. Finally, there was the famous trunk of Mrs. Gooch.

The trunk of Mrs. Gooch is not a weighty object in Canadian history, yet it had its own significance. It indicated the state of King's mind in this last active year of his life.

Mrs. Gooch had long been the superb cook of Laurier House. King, one of whose main pleasures was food, valued his cook highly. When he heard that she was traveling on the same ship with him to England on a holiday, he entertained her royally in his own cabin. When he learned on arrival in London that Mrs. Gooch had lost her trunk, he was as distracted as if he had lost a brother.

At the excited command of the Prime Minister, the whole resources of Canada House, the steamship companies, the Royal Canadian Mounted Police, and Scotland Yard were thrown into the search for the missing luggage. Even the sleuths who had uncovered the spy ring could not find Mrs. Gooch's trunk. King was in despair. If Mrs. Gooch did not recover her trunk he was convinced that she would never return to Laurier House and cook his meals. The situation was critical.

The dollar crisis, the royal wedding, and all the business of the state were forgotten as King stood unhappily on the railway platform, waiting for the train to take him to Dover, for his tour of Europe. He turned to Norman Robertson, Canadian High Commissioner to Britain, and whispered anxiously, "Robertson, as soon as you locate the trunk cable me at once!" King stepped off his train in Paris to find a cable awaiting him. The trunk had been recovered. King's spirits soared, for the moment only. Yet another crisis, still worse, was ahead of him.

On the train carrying him to Brussels, King could not find his own trunks. They had been left behind in Paris. Mrs. Gooch's problem had been solved but her employer sat disconsolately in his private car, moodily observing the Belgian scenery and remarking, as a man who looks boldly into the teeth of disaster, that he supposed he would have to greet the Belgian Government looking like a scarecrow. He added pathetically that he had no other clothes, was dressed in his oldest suit, and wore a perfectly disreputable shirt. It was no matter, he repeated glumly at intervals, and let nobody worry about him. By the time the train reached Brussels he and his entourage felt practically naked.

King went stoically to bed, muttering that he would disgrace Canada by appearing at an official luncheon, and then accepting an honorary university degree, in his present costume. While he dozed, his invaluable valet, Nicol, and one of his secretaries stole out to an establishment which rented clothes and there acquired, at weekly rates, a tail coat, striped trousers, and other accessories.

They hardly expected King, the sartorial dandy, to wear the apparel of other nameless and innumerable men. One of them recalled the occasion when he had been embarrassed by the sudden appearance of local dignitaries on his car during a prairie election tour before he could even brush his hair. On that occasion King had shaken hands with the visitors and never said as much as "hello." After they departed he explained his mortification—he had forgotten to insert his dentures. Would he now agree, in a foreign country, to wear secondhand garments of unknown origin?

The entourage waited breathless in the hall as Nicol entered the Prime Minister's room. Fifteen minutes later, to everyone's relief, King emerged, resplendent in borrowed raiment. Everything was all right, he said, a perfect fit, except that the collar of the shirt was far too tight. The imperturbable valet relieved the pressure by nicking the collar neatly with a razor blade, and King went happily about his public ceremonies. When he was finished with the rented finery he insisted that one of his secretaries wear it, because the rent had been paid for a week in advance.

King's tour of Belgium and Holland was a triumphal procession. The people saw in him the leader of their Canadian liberators. They flew what they supposed to be the Canadian flag from their windows. Village bands played "O Canada" out of tune. Groups of solemn peasants watched the tiny Canadian figure, bareheaded in the rain, bowed over the graves of his nation's soldiers. King was more deeply moved, perhaps, than ever before by the welcome from the simple folk of the countryside and by the knowledge that the men lying in the military graveyards had given their lives for a nation which had given him honor, wealth, and comfort.

He was moved, too, in another fashion, by the wedding of the Princess, whom he observed with the family pride of an adopted uncle. In his age his royalist instincts engulfed him in a tide of nostalgia and a feeling for Britain never understood by his enemies.

He had been given a handful of imitation rose leaves to throw at the bride but he thrust them into his pocket to be kept as a souvenir, together with a bunch of white heather tied, as he proudly observed, with a true lover's knot of silver cord. He had received also from King George the Order of Merit, "a rare distinction, indeed, an honor to the people of Canada." Holding the precious cross in his hand, he asked those around him, "How often shall I wear it?" He would not wear it often, nor the other medals, the C.M.G. among them, that a grateful monarch had showered upon him.

A man of his eminence needed no official honors to distinguish him but the creature of history, returning to his British origins, the Rebel's grandson who was now the intimate of the Royal Family, the statesman who had abolished titles of nobility in Canada, eagerly grasped these public rewards while there was yet time.

Ignorant of King's new triumphs, of Mrs. Gooch's trunk, and the rented clothes, the Canadian Government had its mind on more practical affairs. For months it had watched its dollars and gold ooze out in alarming hemorrhage. It was ready for surgery.

Without warning, without a hint in the press, it announced its dollar-saving policy. American imports would be restricted by regulations without the consent of Parliament—a proceeding denounced by Power, the old-time Liberal, as "budget by radio." That was only the negative side of the policy. The positive was the first installment of the Geneva Agreements, reducing tariffs among all the participants.

While Abbott insisted that his emergency import restrictions, denying the whole purpose of the tariff agreements, would be removed as soon as the dollar drain eased, few believed then that he would soon make good his promise, that within four years the Canadian dollar would be worth more than the American.

Its immediate methods seemed to be the opposite, but the Canadian Government was returning, via Geneva, to its original low-tariff policy. It intimated in its public announcements that the world's golden age was returning anew. King chimed in by radio from London to declare that he was determined to seek "real reciprocity" with the United States.

Real reciprocity! The words had a magic and familiar sound out of the past. What did they mean in the present? To the low-tariff members of the Cabinet, who had been pressing the secret negotiations in Washington, they meant that King was behind the big tariff deal, going far beyond the Geneva Agreements. They soon learned better.

As soon as King heard what the Canadian negotiators had been proposing in Washington, he canceled the whole project overnight. Some of his Ministers were bitterly disappointed. The American officials now promoting Reciprocity were baffled and angry. For here was a Prime Minister proclaiming "Real Reciprocity" from London and aborting it in Washington.

This was one of the most extraordinary acts of King's life. It appeared to contradict his whole record as a low-tariff Liberal and one of Laurier's lieutenants in the 1911 election. Yes, but it confirmed in him a much deeper force than economic theory.

As a creature of North American geography he believed in the integration of the Canadian and American economies. As a creature of British history he instinctively retreated at the critical moment from any act tending to separate Canada from Britain. As his colleagues had only begun to realize, he had become a profound royalist in his old age, and he could not bring himself to do anything which seemed, even superficially, to strike an economic blow at England.

On learning the news, one of King's disappointed colleagues remarked: "The royal wedding was pretty expensive for Canada."

This statesman and others failed to see that the dominant factor in a decision deeply affecting the whole economy of Canada and the United States was typically Canadian. It was not economic but intuitive. The Liberal economist was drawn toward freer trade. The creature of history was drawn toward Britain. Above all, the unquenchable Canadian nationalist feared, in the pinch, that anything like free trade between Canada and its huge neighbor would place the Canadian economy under American domination.

Besides, after the lesson of 1911, King concluded that Reciprocity was not practical politics and would defeat any Government attempting it. And so he turned his back on Laurier's policy for which he had gone into the wilderness thirty-six years before.

What, then, had he meant by "Real Reciprocity"? The old master of the open-ended phrase had left the usual loophole. He could say that the kind of "Real Reciprocity" he desired was not available in the United States, where the Congress would reject it. His judgment of the Congress would soon be confirmed in American tariff policy.

King had not turned, however, toward protectionism. On the contrary, tariffs were scaled down by the Geneva Agreements and their subsequently expanded versions, a vast new American market was opened to Canadian goods, and Canada climbed with almost incredible speed out of its dollar crisis to find its currency the strongest in the world. King had not done what his experts expected, or perhaps what he had originally intended, but his policy had substituted an unexampled period of Canadian prosperity for what threatened to be national bankruptcy. The nation which he had found in depression on taking office in 1921 could be left to a successor at the opening of an unparalleled boom. His economic record, whatever may be said of his record in other fields, was certainly unequaled in Canadian history.

As he well knew, there was a grave constitutional flaw in the emergency solutions of 1947. He admitted privately that the import restrictions and excise taxes imposed to stanch the dollar hemorrhage had been promulgated without the approval of Parliament on the authority of an emergency powers statute, though the Government had promised never to use it for such purposes. The validity of the whole business, he thought, was doubtful, but what else could he do? Again the supreme law was the safety of the state.

Still, if he had been leading the Opposition, he said, he would have torn to shreds any government acting in this fashion. Bracken, fortunately, was not equal to that task. Bracken, said King, would never be Prime Minister.

By the first months of 1948, King had reached the lowest point of his pessimism. He feared that war with Russia might break out within three months. In this humor he faced the Liberal Federation and tacitly confessed for the first time in public the collapse of his postwar hopes. He called Communism "the new tyranny that seeks world domination," another "wolflike menace . . . in sheep's clothing, seeking, all the while, whom it may devour." In these early stages of the cold war he went further than any other chief of state by declaring that Communism "is no less a tyranny than Naziism. It aims at world conquest."

This, from the statesman who, only some two years before, had tried to send Gouzenko back to the Russian embassy, and had publicly excused Stalin, was startling. To the public, it did not sound like King—only because the public had not suspected the change in his thinking. His confidants knew that a mood of calm despair had begun to descend upon him in his last years.

Apart from these larger dangers, he had growing problems closer to home. Not only was the dollar crisis unsolved but the inflation smuggled into the currency system during the war and hidden temporarily by price controls was coming out into the open. The public did not understand this problem then and hardly understands it today. All it knew was that prices had started to rise sharply. King sought to pacify the housewife's clamor by starting a parliamentary investigation into prices, by denouncing profiteers, and promising action against monopolists.

During these distractions, it was hoped, the inflation would run its course. Within a year prices began to level off, only to shoot up again in the great post-Korean buying panic. From the viewpoint of early 1948, not quite three years after the war, it appeared that Canada had come unharmed through the reconversion period, without dangerous inflation, the anticipated depression, or unemployment. As a result, the Government's political position looked sound.

While the Government was even sounder than it looked, it was shaken by secret troubles. The second and really alarming break between King and St. Laurent had developed. For a few hours it seemed likely to end St. Laurent's public career. In the end it established his ascendancy in the Liberal Party.

Ilsley had gone to the United Nations in New York for a rest as leader of the Canadian delegation. (Exhausted by his long labors, he fell asleep in a committee discussion on the problem of Spain, his head sank from his upraised hand, and the chairman, thinking the Canadian delegate had raised his arm, called on him to speak. Ilsley had been equipped by the experts with a written speech, but could not find it in his pocket. Still, with no knowledge of the subject, he made a good pretense of arguing Spanish affairs.)

He was not napping, however, he knew exactly what he was doing when he agreed to the appointment of a Canadian to the United Nations commission in Korea. In King's absence from Ottawa, St. Laurent, acting as Prime Minister, approved Ilsley's decision.

When King returned he was incensed again, as in the incident of India. There was more than anger in his denunciation of Ilsley's action. Already he had become obsessed with the dangers of Korea, two years before the eruption there. He told the Cabinet that, as he had learned from Truman and Ernest Bevin, Korea was the most critical spot in the world. It was unthinkable that Canada should involve itself in that area by taking a place on the Korean commission. He simply could not understand how the Government, in his absence, could have committed such a folly.

St. Laurent took full responsibility for Ilsley's action and still considered it wise. King listened but was not convinced. He was piqued with St. Laurent at the moment anyway. St. Laurent had ventured to announce in Winnipeg that he was available for the Liberal Party leadership on King's retirement. King thought he should have been told of this announcement in advance. He said nothing of it to the Cabinet. He was concerned only with the possibility of trouble in Korea. Taking the matter out of the Cabinet's hands, he sent Pearson posthaste to Washington to see Truman. Pearson's instructions were to ask that the President release Canada from the Korean commission. Truman refused. King muttered that obviously Pearson had not carried out his mission.

In this dispute St. Laurent and Ilsley stood firm. They would not agree with King that Canada should withdraw from the commission. As he insisted, Ilsley prepared to resign. A man of honor, he could do nothing else. St. Laurent said little but made it clear that he could not remain if his action in the United Nations was repudiated. Claxton, who had strongly backed St. Laurent's policy, was ready to go with the others.

On learning this, King was incredulous. He had expected no more rebellions in the last illustrious months of his reign. Ilsley had always been brittle, of course, and had never pretended to like his leader, but St. Laurent was not only King's closest colleague but the man already chosen to succeed him. What a spectacle it would be if St. Laurent resigned on the eve of his elevation, if King could not control his own official family just as he was about to leave it, if a cabinet upheaval clouded the sunset of the career which now exceeded even that of Walpole!

King capitulated. He asked St. Laurent to dinner at Laurier House and, in his most charming manner, remarked that he had not realized how keenly his colleague felt about the Korean matter. St. Laurent replied that naturally he must resign if King repealed his policy. Resignation, King protested, was unthinkable. If St. Laurent, the prospective Prime Minister, believed in the wisdom of his action, then there was nothing more to be said. King would not think of embarrassing him.

This affair, so carefully hushed up, marked a watershed in the political lives of King and St. Laurent. King no longer was the dominant power in the Government. He was too old to fight. St. Laurent, the rising man, had challenged and beaten him. He was stronger than even King had suspected and the Party could be left safely in his hands.

King never agreed, however, with the Korean policy. He was right about the danger of Korea, wrong in imagining that Canada could escape it merely by refusing to join a United Nations commission. As will be shown in the proper place, King was thinking beyond Korea. He regarded it as a whistle stop only on a longer journey toward the ultimate atomic war.

By this time he had handed foreign affairs largely over to St. Laurent. Until the end of 1946, King had refused to give up the External Affairs Department, holding that it was too important for anyone but the Prime Minister. When at last he parted with it, St. Laurent took the Department over not only in name but in fact, and with a sudden new vigor which began to alter Canada's position in international conferences.

Thus appeared the hopeful paradox of a French Canadian who, having passed the first hurdle of conscription, was making himself the strongest internationalist in Canadian history and already was quietly proposing the North Atlantic Treaty. Where King had found the United Nations an "impossible" organization, St. Laurent, with the practicality of his race and with the energy now lacking in King, saw a method of constructing a defensive system within the bounds of the Charter.

As one of the original architects of the transatlantic alliance St. Laurent first demonstrated his independent thinking and the qualities of an international statesman abler and bolder in this field than King. The old man watched him skeptically, with admiration, some misgivings, and a little secret envy.

For this work St. Laurent required Pearson, not as an official assistant but as a colleague, and he was determined, if he became Prime Minister, to take Pearson into his Cabinet. Pearson would not accept office under King. In due course he found himself unable to refuse the invitation of St. Laurent, to whom he was devoted and in whose policies he believed. The team of St. Laurent and Pearson, who would place Canada in N.A.T.O. and persuade a doubtful Cabinet into the Korean war, was taking shape.

On April 20, 1948, King broke Walpole's record of 7,619 days in official office. He had held power longer than any statesman in the English-speaking world.

The current parliamentary session was to be his last as Prime Minister, though he might attend others as a private member of the House. In taking leave of his faithful Party caucus, he made a curious apology. He had always wished, he said, to entertain the Liberal members in his own home as friends, but, as a poor man, he simply could not afford the expense. And he dropped the broad hint that he would like the Party to buy Laurier House and thus assure him enough money to support his last years. The horror of poverty, inherited from his mother and his grandfather, haunted him even now when he was almost a millionaire.

His farewell to the parliamentary Press Gallery was equally strange. He had generally avoided newspapermen and told them little. At the annual Gallery dinner of 1948 he suddenly unbosomed himself. The amazed correspondents beheld him caricaturing himself. He began by burlesquing his own speeches, with all the familiar open-ended paragraphs and complicated verbiage to be interpreted one way or the other. The old actor could afford at last to take off his mask and reveal that sense of absurdity so sedulously repressed in his working days. Very late in the play the real King was making his entrance as the old King approached his exit.

Then of a sudden the tone of burlesque was droped. King gave the correspondents his real thoughts about the future, told them candidly his dark estimate of the world's prospects, and admitted his fears of general war.

Altogether, it was an extraordinary performance, possible only in a man who had aged and mellowed, who had nothing more to hide.

The arrangements for his successorship were well advanced. With a Liberal convention called for August, St. Laurent had yielded to an irresistible destiny. His future was written in his talents. The dream of retirement, the well-filled home in Grand Allée, the ease after long labor, all were abandoned. No statesman had ever felt less personal ambition. No Canadian ever had been more clearly marked for eminence.

It is hard to realize now, when his position in the Party is as unchallengeable as King's had been, that St. Laurent made a lamentable beginning in the contest for the Liberal leadership. So far he had confined himself entirely to the business of government. As a first experiment in practical politics he used the Quebec provincial election of 1948 to try out his platform appeal. He appeared to have none. His speeches were legalistic, impeccable, and worthless in a political campaign. The sweeping victory of Duplessis over the Quebec Liberals looked almost like a repudiation of St. Laurent. His friends wondered if they were backing the right man.

King had no such doubts. He knew that in federal politics Quebec would support one of its own sons, while in English-speaking Canada St. Laurent would yet make his mark. King had never given a wiser opinion.

In the spring of 1948, however, it was by no means certain that St. Laurent would carry the Liberal convention. Gardiner was confident that he would achieve the ambition he had held from the beginning of his career and nourished in the successful feud with Dunning. Howe was the senior member of the Government and already a legendary figure. On the other hand, the Party might desire a young man, durable for a long time ahead, and it had such candidates as Abbott, Claxton, Martin, and Stuart Garson. Finally, Power was determined to run, not because he had any chance of victory, but because he intended to get certain things off his chest even though his friends told him that if he remained silent he could be sure of any reward within the Government's gift.

King had made up his mind to hand the dynasty on to St. Laurent. He was certainly a little jealous of his successor. He would have been jealous of any successor. Still, he knew that St. Laurent was by far the best man available and believed that his succession would assure the least possible decline from the leadership of the last three decades. He set to work, therefore, to assure St. Laurent's control of the convention.

The work was done silently and with all King's subtlety. In public he never indicated his choice by word or gesture. In private he pulled the strings.

It was easy to persuade Howe, Abbott, and Claxton to allow their names to go before the convention if necessary, and then to withdraw in St. Laurent's favor. All of them wanted St. Laurent. Howe was tired, talked of quitting politics, and knew his limitations.

Abbott and Claxton had plenty of time later on. Martin was more difficult, was surrounded by a claque which provided much noise and few votes, but he, too, could be induced not to run in the face of obvious defeat.

Gardiner was the sticking point. He could not be convinced and must be defeated. King had never liked him anyway, and had often been angry with him, especially as he found Gardiner too strong to be dislodged, as indeed he was—a kind of sovereign power in loose diplomatic relations with the Canadian Government. Gardiner's political talents were undeniable, his personal power untamable and ferocious, his influence in the Government and Party so great that he had even forced the famous British wheat deal on a Prime Minister who had never believed in it. Gardiner was an invaluable lieutenant, but, said King, only a man of deep culture could ever hope to be Prime Minister of Canada and in that respect Gardiner did not qualify. As Liberal leader he was "impossible."

Since Ilsley was out of politics and back in the law, there remained only Angus Macdonald, whose friends regarded him as the most eminent contemporary philosopher of politics. Macdonald, however, had been comfortably reinstalled in the premiership of Nova Scotia and was happy there. In any case, his record on conscription disqualified him at once. He could never hold Quebec for his Party.

When the convention met on August 5, King had it well in hand. The frail little figure acknowledging the sudden outburst of cheers from the same auditorium where he had received the leadership exactly twenty-nine years before was not the man he had been then. He was old, he was within two years of death, he had broken Walpole's record, he was tired, and his work was done. If he could leave it in St. Laurent's hands he would be content.

Between August, 1919, and August, 1948, King had traveled far on his circuitous journey back to this platform. He had stood upon it as a young and untried man, aspiring to fill the shoes of Laurier and to lead a broken Party. He had far exceeded the accomplishments of his predecessor, mended the Party, and dominated the nation longer than any other man. All this achievement, all the tributes now paid by his grateful followers, all his fame throughout the world had sprung from his first speech here. For as he always said, his decision to welcome the conscriptionist Liberals back to the Party, his opening words as Liberal leader, had been the beginning of his success. Now all was finished, according to plan. All the old familiar faces of friend and enemy were gone and with them the world of his youth. He looked dimly upon a horde of young strangers among whom the young rebel had become an old conservative. It was a new and alien age. He did not belong to it.

The tears poured from the old man's eyes—tears of satisfaction, of gratitude and regret. Apart from a few last ceremonies, this was the end of politics for him. Without the craft which had filled it for forty years the craftsman's life stretched ahead barren and solitary. It did not stretch as far as he then supposed.

He had come to the convention determined to remain publicly neutral between the aspirants. He would not even cast a ballot. When Gardiner delivered his unhappy speech, proclaiming himself the "spark plug" of the Party, the man who knew how to win elections, King was so disgusted that he seized a ballot and prepared to vote for St. Laurent.

His protégé, at the moment, was scrawling a few notes on the back of an envelope. As St. Laurent rose to speak, the convention and the nation suddenly beheld the real man, long hidden behind the dry lawyer. He made just such a homely, unaffected speech as King desired and could never make.

The really great speech of the convention came from Power. King must have listened to it with a strange mixture of memories and emotions. Power had entered the convention not to win it but to warn it. The child of the Commons was outraged by the decline of Parliament, the elevation of the executive, the growth of the bureaucracy, the violence done to Liberal principles during and after the war. His friends still vainly tried to silence him. Power was determined to have one last word.

All the feelings of a Liberal who saw Liberalism endangered suddenly exploded in his speech, the best he had ever made. Power knew that it would have no effect on the contest for Party leadership. The man who had discovered St. Laurent in the first place was defeated in advance by his discovery. That suited Power well. Like King, he was glad to leave the Party in St. Laurent's hands. Power hoped, however, that the Party would remember his warning, that Liberalism must return to its original principles, its old respect for Parliament, after the aberration of the war years. Privately, King said he agreed with Power's view.

From the beginning there was no doubt about the convention's choice. St. Laurent could have won without King's backing. After Howe, Abbott, Claxton, Martin, Lionel Chevrier, and Garson withdrew and the ballots were counted, St. Laurent had 848 (including King's), Gardiner 323, and Power 56.

The King era was over. The era of St. Laurent had opened. As the convention hall emptied, a tired little man walked out the door alone.

45

The Pilgrim's Return

KING HAD RESIGNED AS LEADER OF THE LIBERAL PARTY BUT NOT AS
Prime Minister. He could hardly bear to surrender the sweet
sense of power, his food and drink for so long, to admit that
the boyhood dream was ended, to share his glory with any other
man—as if a few more days of barren ceremony could add a cubit to
his stature or stretch the shrinking substance of his life.

St. Laurent was kept for three more months in the painful position
of Party leadership and responsibility, without the power to control
the Government which the convention had put in his keeping, while
King went on his farewell tour to France and Britain.

The new leader's career thus got off to an unfortunate start when
he needed every possible day of office to prepare himself for his first
election. He suffered this humiliation with such patience that some
Liberal politicians wondered if he could establish his mastery, could
prove that he was not King's shadow, before the polls opened. Those
fears were unfounded. Once sworn in as Prime Minister, St. Laurent
showed that he would be his own man, as King had always been.

King's last voyage was pathetic in the childish grasp of empty
honors, public demonstrations, and worthless banquet applause. In
London he proposed to attend a conference of Commonwealth leaders, though clearly it was the business of the Prime Minister-
designate. The proceedings had not opened when King's unfitness to
represent Canada was cruelly demonstrated.

Returning to the Dorchester Hotel one evening, he told the newspaper correspondents that he would have no news for them, as he
was going to see a "friend." That friend was Lord Moran, the famous
physician, who realized immediately that King was critically ill with
a heart condition and dangerous complications. The doctors called
in consultation were alarmed but decided not to alarm King unduly.
He was put to bed and told that he could do no more business.

If he could not go to the Commonwealth conference, the conference could come to him. This it did. Churchill, Attlee, Nehru, Liaquat Ali Khan, and other Commonwealth statesmen sat by King's bed and listened to his opinions. Sometimes, with the stub of a pencil, he set down his views in minute handwriting and circulated them among his colleagues.

The business before the conference was important and historic, since it involved India's continued adherence to the Commonwealth. In a moment of irritation two years before, King had reprimanded St. Laurent for welcoming India's independence, had feared the domination of the Commonwealth by an Asiatic majority. Now his good sense reasserted itself in a final work of conciliation.

He believed afterward that by his friendly influence on the British Government and on Nehru he had contributed substantially to the happy solution of a Commonwealth constitutional problem—the paradox of a Republic recognizing the symbol of the Throne—insoluble in any other organization.

King's visitors were not all politicians. One day a quiet man in a bowler hat walked unnoticed through the hotel lobby and entered the invalid's room. The King of Canada had come to call on his Prime Minister. As they sipped tea together they must have suspected that it would be their last meeting—a melancholy occasion for both. In the official relationship of the last ten years a shy and curious sort of friendship had grown up between them and must soon end. Perhaps King guessed, as his sovereign left the room, that he would never see his young friend again. He could not guess that George had little longer to live than he.

Another visitor was the actress, Gracie Fields, whom he agreed to receive only on condition that her husband accompany her.

In a life of almost unbroken health King had felt the first touch of death. He was looking beyond it with hope and anxiety. The newspaper reporters haunting the hotel lobby in the necessary death watch of their trade did not observe two plainly dressed women enter by a side door to be hastily smuggled into King's room. Their names, Geraldine Cummins and Beatrice Gibbes, would have meant nothing to the press. They were King's favorite mediums, through whom he had long talked to the dead. He was now seeking a last communication with the other world before his arrival there. As his health mended, that event was briefly postponed.

St. Laurent had been summoned from Ottawa to represent Canada at the conference which he should have attended in the first place. He was now Prime Minister in fact.

The Prime Minister in name arranged his passage to Canada and managed at the last moment to leave his bed, to dress, and to walk to his limousine, clutching for support the arm of Norman Robertson. He waved his hand gaily to the crowd as the car moved off and cried, "God bless you all!" It was his farewell to England.

On reaching Canada, King was annoyed to find that the newspapers had quoted him as saying, on shipboard, that he regarded himself as "the watchdog of the Commonwealth." He said he had used no such expression. Said or not, it was a true report of his feelings. The rebel of the new land was ending as the passionate and sentimental friend of the old.

On November 15, King at last resigned and, by his own choice, vanished almost entirely from public view. His constituents of Glengarry, to whom he said a fleeting good-by, the House of Commons, which he attended occasionally as a private member, were shocked at his appearance. The mark of dissolution was on his haggard face and shrunken figure.

At Kingsmere, however, he seemed to revive. His thoughts were fixed on a book wherein he would give his full story to the world. He planned his autobiography in three volumes, with ten volumes of documents, he hired assistants, appointed Norman Roberston, Fred McGregor, John Pickersgill, and Dr. Kaye Lamb as literary executors, could not decide whether to publish or burn his diary, and never reached more than the outer fringes of his records. He thought he had enough time left to complete the book, but those around him knew that he would not start it. Even in good health he would have stretched the work out interminably, providing a history as heavy as it would be valuable. The old man whose heart was running down had neither health nor time.

Though his mind was as keen as ever—except that he often forgot the names of those around him—he had lost the physical and mental energy for work. Always a diffuse and laborious writer, he could not hope even to organize, much less distill his mountain of material. So the days and months passed with futile notes, synopses, and chapter headings.

Still, he never gave up hope, he continued to fumble through his documents and repelled visitors who would waste his time. In other moods he was hungry for companionship, for the gossip of current politics, and talk of battles long ago. Some old colleagues like St. Laurent were scrupulous in showing their interest in him and paying frequent calls at Kingsmere. They understood what an unhappy period of readjustment he now faced after his lifetime of activity, accomplishment, and admiration—a process particularly painful for King because he had no family and no deep friendships to cushion this change.

There were many others whose careers King had molded, some-

times out of mud, who had licked his boots so long as he could help
them and now ignored him. He was suffering the penalty of his
greatness. The physical decline thus was accompanied by a sudden
intellectual deflation, the last price which eminence pays to time.

A loneliness sometimes driving him from Kingsmere to meet an
obscure companion of happier days for a quiet talk about mutual
recollections must of itself have contributed largely to the pessimism
now heavy upon him. The historic fact, once removed from the flow
of history, can hardly hope to be a contented human being. King,
like Thoreau, was living through one world at a time. He expected
a better world but he clung to the last shreds of the world he knew.

As they slipped through his fingers, Canada's most eminent son
also became its most solitary. The solitude was intensified by the
knowledge that Canadians as a whole had not yet understood the
measure of his work. No modern Canadian had accomplished so
much. None had received so little public thanks. That was the inevitable result of his nature, his methods, and his inner detachment
from life when he seemed most involved in it. Alone, he had achieved
what he set out to achieve. Alone such a man must end.

As Sir Charles Tupper was once told by a drunken interloper whom
the defeated Conservative leader threatened to pull out of his bed,
"Ex-Prime Ministers ain't got any pull!" King had no wish to dominate St. Laurent. He would have enjoyed an occasional gesture of dependence. There was none. With full respect for King, with a delicate
sense of obligation and continual evidences of his concern for the old
man's welfare, St. Laurent was going his own way (thus confirming
King's judgment of him) and already had changed the whole climate
of government, to the immense relief of the Cabinet and its advisers.
St. Laurent's singlehanded and overwhelming electoral victory in
1949 publicly buried the King era.

The sense of property burned into King by the childhood privations of his mother had constantly increased his holdings of good
Gatineau land, had made him almost a millionaire, despite his fear
of poverty, and had never deserted him. On February 28, 1950, when
he made his massive and meticulous will, he found that he had a
surprising supply of goods to bestow on his heirs.

The will was one of the most revealing documents King had ever
written.

It reveals on the one hand the grasping side of his nature. He had
somehow accumulated, on the small wages of a public servant and
large gifts from friends like Peter Larkin and John D. Rockefeller,
Jr., an estate worth almost a million dollars.

It also reveals the opposite and generous side, which prompted him to give Laurier House and Kingsmere to the nation (the former as a center of study, the latter as a summer residence for future Prime Ministers), to use most of the residue to support these shrines, and to establish a series of scholarships for Canadian students.

King had received much from Canada. He was giving back virtually everything he owned, asking for himself only "a piece of rough Canadian granite" beside his parents in Toronto, with nothing but his name carved upon it, and a memorial table to his grandfather in Dundee. He added a typically ponderous and sentimental message to posterity: "It has always seemed to me that the highest joy in life is to be found in some form of public service; that instead of the State being indebted to one who gives of his time and means to the country's affairs and to the betterment of human conditions, the obligation is the other way round; where the opportunity of public service is given, one cannot be too grateful to the source whence it arises."

The will, like other memorials, was designed, in benefiting the nation and repaying the testator's debt, to make sure that his name and works should never be forgotten. Laurier House and Kingsmere would remind every visitor of their former owner. The Canadian students who won his scholarships would be encouraged to imitate his life.

If there was personal vanity in the will, that towering egoism which he had concealed so well in life, there was also a high sense of public obligation. He had taken large sums of money from powerful men like Larkin and Rockefeller ($100,000 from the latter on the day he left office), but he had spent little of it on himself and even his worst enemy would not suggest that these gifts had ever influenced his public policies. The grandson of the half-starved Rebel had merely assured himself a decent state of comfort, helpful to his work. The obligation, between him and the nation, he said, was on his side. Perhaps, in his own words, it was "the other way round."

After making his will, King seldom left Kingsmere. He was lonely and for the first time may have realized that for all his troops of apparent friends he was friendless, in the deepest meaning of the word, by his own choice. It was too late to alter that choice now. Anyway, though lonely, he wished to be alone with his unborn book, his memories, his intimations of immortality, and his fame. Until the end, news of him seldom appeared in the press. Canada seemed to forget its greatest son. Only a few neighbors of Kingsmere realized that the old man strolling slowly along the country lane in his cap and rough Scottish tweeds had bestrode the state only yesterday.

Those few he received found him cheerful, interested in the world's news, eager for gossip, and candid in his opinions. Not since his entry into politics had he been free as now to speak as he pleased, without any thought of its effect on his fortunes. When he could say exactly what he thought he appeared to have abandoned some of his youthful illusions only to return instinctively to others. He had learned, as all old men must, that a society cannot be quickly reformed. He had come a long way from *Industry and Humanity*. In international affairs he was not far from his original position after his brief adventure into a visionary world order under law.

Thus he told a former associate, in the summer of 1950, that the outbreak of the Korean war had confirmed and justified his opposition to Canada's involvement in the Korean commission. (This, of course, was absurd, as King must have known, for Canada would have been engaged in the Korean war whether it had joined the commission or not.)

He added quickly that while the present war was bad enough, Korea was not the real danger point. The Russians, he said, would make frequent trouble in Korea and elsewhere, but these were diversions only. The real prize of the world struggle was the oil of the Middle East and the Russians intended to have it.

Watch the Middle East, he repeated, his finger raised in a gesture of warning. If the Russians struck there, the third world war would follow. He had sometimes expected it before now and he still half expected it sooner or later.

Within himself he was content, for he had nothing to lose, his work was done, and his second life assured. The affairs of humanity in this life he regarded with a steady and unruffled pessimism. Humanity was not ready for the glory and the dream.

Although he feared Canada's involvement in war, it is an oversimplification of his mind to say that he ended an isolationist. He was an isolationist in his age as in his youth, if that word implies only an attempt to escape international dangers. He was not an isolationist if the word implies any real hope of escape. Unlike many of his colleagues, and a large part of the Canadian people, he had always known that there could be no final escape. He had understood better than they what war must cost, he had put off commitments to the last possible moment, he had been willing to go to the utmost lengths of appeasement, but he ended in pessimism precisely because he saw at last that his philosophy of conciliation would fail at some point, that force in the end would rule until humanity itself was changed. In time it might change. Not in his time.

It must not be supposed from this that he had reached final conclusions. He had only lost the sure conclusions of his younger days.

The greatest mistake of his contemporaries was to imagine that he was always clear-headed, cold, calculating, and realistic. In large affairs he usually lived in a mist of uncertainty, not because he was ignorant of them but because he knew too much and often saw possibilities hidden from those around him.

So he ended his days. His unequaled accumulation of facts had persuaded him that in the business of this world there were no reliable facts. His long experience had taught him that experience is no sure guide. His religion, as confirmed by psychic communication, had proved that this world was of relative unimportance, that all the essentials lay beyond it.

In another corner of his many-chambered mind he still enjoyed this world as a safe spectator, whom trouble could no longer touch. Walking across his billowing meadows, he would pause frequently for breath and, leaning on his heavy cane, would utter the opinions of the accepted Canadian oracle on passing events.

It was quite wrong, he said, to suppose that he had resigned for reasons of health (though such reasons were apparent enough in his worn face). He had left office while in full possession of his powers and in control of his Party so that he could play his part in choosing his successor and then have ample time to finish his book.

He was watching St. Laurent with interest and thought the new leader was doing well. Three weeks before the 1949 election, King said, he had made up his mind that the Government would win a large majority. He had been so sure of the result that, on election night, he had not even bothered to turn on the radio and hear the returns until just before bedtime. They had not surprised him.

He was not in the least jealous of St. Laurent. He regarded the election, indeed, as a final endorsement of his own record, since nine-tenths of the Liberal Party's platform had been of his own contriving. If St. Laurent had done well, and he had done extraordinarily well, the Liberal victory had been overwhelming, thanks mainly to the performance of Drew.

Without vindictiveness and considering the matter from a detached, philosophic viewpoint, King went on to assert that no one could successfully carry a provincial feud into federal politics. Drew's feud with him was only the latest proof of that law. Hepburn had destroyed himself in the same way. Aberhart had conducted a feud in Alberta and had never become a national figure. Duplessis had succeeded in Quebec but, living on his feud with Ottawa, could never exercise any power outside his own province. Even Mowat, in trying to defeat Macdonald by invoking provincial policies long followed in Ontario, had failed. In similar fashion Drew had fatally

limited his appeal to a small sector on the Right while Coldwell had
carved out an insignificant territory on the Left. Both of them had
abandoned the broad central highway of politics to the Liberals.

Suddenly King exclaimed that St. Laurent had been fortunate in
appointing Pearson to his Cabinet. King himself had tried for years
to entice Pearson into politics and, as he admitted ruefully, had
failed—a brilliant young man, that, and now the only possible successor to St. Laurent as Liberal leader.

Pausing again in his stroll and panting a little, King insisted that
it was absurd to regard the C.C.F. and the Social Credit movement
as national parties any longer. If he were still Prime Minister he
would advise the Speaker of the House of Commons not to recognize
these two splinters as having the privileges and recognition of parties
in Parliament.

If Drew were ever called to power, King remarked with distaste,
one of his first acts would be to restore titles of nobility in Canada.
The thought of it was intolerable.

King repeated that St. Laurent had done well but suggested that
the new Prime Minister ruled with too loose a rein in Cabinet. Soon
St. Laurent would find that a Prime Minister cannot be merely the
first among equals. He must assert the authority residing in his office.
(King's fears on this score were ungrounded but it was then too
early to judge his successor, who would soon have as much authority
in Cabinet, of a different sort, as King had ever exercised.)

The ruthlessness of his battles in politics still clung to him. Mellowed though he was, he could show no mercy to his enemies. They
might be conciliated in bad times as he had conciliated the Progressives and the Socialists only to absorb or destroy them. Now that
he had left the Liberal Party in full possession of the road, with
narrow footpaths for the other groups on either side, it was no time
for mercy or even generosity. Full forgiveness was denied even to
occasional offenders within his own Party. He had made sure that
no such honors as membership in the British Privy Council had gone
to men like Macdonald and Power, who had crossed him.

He had been fortunate, he confessed, in his political opposition.
Meighen and Bennett had both ruined themselves by their own
bitterness. Asked if Meighen were not a great man, King replied that
Meighen had "a precise mind, trained as a mathematician." That was
as far as the triumphant tortoise would go in praise of the forgotten
hare. He said he did not intend, however, to criticize his opponents
in his autobiography. He would state their position on public issues
as clearly and fairly as his own and leave the facts to justify him.

At another pause on the path, he wondered aloud why Canada

was the only Commonwealth country with a Liberal Government or even a strong Liberal Party. In Britain, he thought, Liberalism had declined to its present state because it had forgotten John Bright's remark to Gladstone that "the Liberal Party must always be friendly to its rebels."

That advice King had always followed. His entire success had sprung from his first great decision, in the convention of 1919, to forget the conscription split within the Party, to welcome the conscriptionist Liberals home, to refuse to punish anyone for honest beliefs. Whatever he had been able to accomplish had been possible only through the instrument of a united Party.

In reviving the Liberal Party he felt he had not served merely its interests but the nation's. If the Liberal Party had not been revived after the schism of the first war, what would have been left of Canadian politics? A solid Tory Party on the one hand and on the other a farmers' splinter, a labor group, and a Quebec rump—in short, political chaos, ineffective government, and a weak nation.

Yes, looking back on it all, his plan had worked out well, incredibly well. For he had started his career with nothing solid under his feet but a French Canadian anticonscriptionist fragment, with the conscriptionist Liberals outlawed and hated by their former friends, and with a farmers' party sweeping the West in revolt against Liberalism.

Until these sores were healed, nothing could be accomplished. The wisest thing he had ever done was to reject the advice of those die-hard Laurier Liberals who wanted him to keep the conscriptionist rebels outside his door in punishment for their apostasy. Until their return the great advance could not begin.

Yes, the wisest thing he had ever done, the most useful to Canada. Thoughtless people railed against political parties, yet only through them could democracy possibly function, could the parliamentary system work. He was proud to consider himself a party politician. If he had been anything else he would have been nothing.

Of what was he most proud? Why, of course, he was most proud not of any detailed accomplishment but of the understanding and co-operation he had produced among the diverse Canadian races, of which his successful management of the 1944 conscription issue had been the supreme triumph. And once more, as he had done with all his trusted visitors, he reiterated his version of that incident, the threatened military uprising, the danger of anarchy, the salvation of the state. The full story, with names and facts, could not be told now. It would be told in his book.

Thinking back farther, King said his method of leadership could be summarized in a conscious effort to anticipate reform and thus to deprive leftist radicalism of its sting. In this he thought he had succeeded.

When the talk turned to his personal life, he volunteered the statement that he had never married solely because, in supporting his parents and other relatives for so long, he could not afford marriage. When at last he was financially comfortable it was too late to marry. There was no other reason for his bachelorhood.

In the last few days he had made a depressing discovery. Among the litter of old papers he had come across a bundle of his mother's letters which he had never read before. In them she had discussed her household penury, her daily pinching to put him through college. In a wave of gratitude he had realized for the first time the sacrifices made for him by both his parents.

Looking across the folds of the hills, with eyes moist, King began to talk of his mother's birth in exile and disgrace. At one time his grandmother had written to a friend that there was no food in the house and she didn't know how she could manage with an extra mouth to feed. Those, said King, were things a man thought of at the end of his life. They explained much. (They really explained everything in a man whose whole life had been a vindication of his mother, his family, and himself.)

He walked on a few yards and halted again to wonder what he would do with his diaries. At first he had decided to burn them. Now he thought of editing them and fixing a date, after his death, when they could be published. They must be withheld for some time, as they would embarrass many living people. His papers, he admitted, were full of embarrassment for others—letters from various people who had written foolish things, requests for jobs from the most surprising applicants, and so on. As far as he himself was concerned, any letter he had ever written on any matter of public business could be published immediately. He had nothing to hide.

After another pause, he suddenly referred, as he always did, to one of those petty annoyances more irritating than any major problem of government. Apropos of nothing, he said the newspapers had committed an outrageous falsehood in reporting that Ralston had refused to shake hands with him on the celebrated day of the resignation. Of course Ralston had shaken hands with him. He knew, he added darkly, where the popular and mischievous version had come from. It still rankled.

He kept returning to his book. He needed two years to finish it and he thought he would have them. The doctors had tried to put him in hospital but he would not go. He would spend the summer at

Kingsmere and enter hospital in the autumn. (He still did not know how ill he was and stubbornly refused to obey the orders of his medical men, some of the ablest in Canada. Had he accepted their advice he might have gained his two years.)

So the old man in baggy Scottish tweeds walked slowly across his broad acres until he reached the knoll where the square of ruins stood. Now, in the deliberately broken stone walls and in the tiny figure of their architect, the true picture of King, his achievements, his failures, and his hopes could be discerned.

The ruins were of no consequence to anyone else but they told the story of the architect better than any book could tell it. These walls bounded and defined the Canadian paradox in King and in his people. By their synthetic antiquity they revealed a radical in politics who, in life's essentials, was a conservative, a prophet who preached the future but was anchored in the past, a nationalist pulled by the geography of Canada yet never free of history's tug across the sea, a worldling who had built his own monument to be remembered in this world, while all his hope lay in another.

How unbelievable, considering their origins, the works of the man now appeared, the old and dying man who bent over his cane and surveyed the long, tortuous road leading back to this place. Under his management, if not by his hand, the whole society of Canada had been transformed almost beyond recognition, two races had survived their ultimate racial crisis, isolationism had ended, the Commonwealth had grown into a league of independent, sovereign states, and Canada, for the first time, had become truly a nation, the most fortunate in the world.

Like these ruins, his life had been built of the most unlikely materials. As he had gathered broken stones from anywhere and somehow put them together in the semblance of order, so he had combined his second-rate talents into a first-rate achievement, the whole being immeasurably greater than its parts. And as the ruins were made of assorted and contradictory stuff, so was his life the accurate image of a diverse, divided, and groping people.

At the end, after all his plans had been completed, the whole design worked out in minute detail, the little boy's dream fulfilled like a fairy story, yet, as in these ruins, the emptiness remained. Standing on the knoll above the broad gleam of the river, contemplating his barren monument and the durable works of statecraft beyond it, he must have realized, too late, how much he had missed of ordinary men's rewards, the unspoken, private joys of fireside and family, a mate's companionship, and the abiding support of children. He had won everything he sought but it was not enough. Only

G G

another world, where he could start afresh, offered the essential satisfactions lost in his hurried and ravenous passage.

Deep within him, and now legible on an old man's wistful face, there dwelt, for all his triumphs, an inborn sense of inadequacy, humility, fear, and sin. He had done many secret kindnesses and great public works, greater than any Canadian before him by any possible measurement, but often at the expense of companions shouldered aside in his march, of meanness, smallness, and cruelty. Those shadows lengthened in the twilight.

Nevertheless, all things considered, who of all men in his time could have done better? He need not depend on this pitiful heap of stones for his monument. His monument was a nation. And by a final paradox the nation had never understood him as in the deepest sense he had never understood it—a nation still groping in its youth for what it knew not, a leader groping in his age for unknowable immortality.

The mystery of that combination between leader and people was unsolved. The grass surged up around the ruins and around his work. The ruins, like his life, would fall and be overgrown and forgotten in the new era. The broad and gleaming river would endure, moving silently in the night, and the land of Canada to the rim of its three oceans, and the life of its people. For King—beyond the ruins, beyond the uttermost boundaries of the nation and the earth—lay something still larger, the life everlasting.

Strange land, strange people, and strange pilgrim, their adventure together was finished.

On the night of July 22, 1950, the doctors watching beside the antique brass bed in the upstairs room of the farmhouse knew that the end was near. It came quite peacefully at eighteen minutes to ten. William Lyon Mackenzie King had completed one pilgrimage to begin, as he believed, a second.

The crowds of Parliament Hill filed past his bier and watched his last procession in a peculiar silence. They did not weep, for they had never loved this man. They were respectful, they glimpsed King's greatness even if they had seen in life only his self-made caricature, but they were puzzled because King reflected them, as in a true glass, and the Canadian people did not understand themselves.

In the crowd a little boy asked his mother who the dead man was. She tried to tell the child that King had been the Prime Minister, that he had made Canada a better place for all little boys. And suddenly she turned away in tears, unable to answer her son or explain her own feelings. The mystery of King and Canada remained, unanswerable.

Postscript

S̲ince this book was set in type and prepared for publication the largest question asked in it has been answered—and in such an extraordinary fashion that a postscript is required at the last moment.

The reader has seen that the supreme crisis of King's life occurred on November 22, 1944, when he suddenly enforced a policy of overseas conscription after resisting it all his life, and declaring, even on the previous day, that he would never accept it. His public explanation for this about-face was that the campaign for voluntary overseas recruits, among men drafted for home defence service, had failed. His private explanation to his friends was that his minister of defence, General McNaughton, had suddenly discovered plans for some sort of uprising among the army commanders, who insisted on total conscription.

As this book indicates, the writer was sceptical of King's explanation, even his private explanation. I was never able to discover, until after this book was set in type, the slightest evidence of any trouble in the high army command. And King's former colleagues for the most part agreed that he had imagined such trouble to justify a sudden shift in policy necessitated by purely political reasons.

Recently, however, the full facts came to light and they show that King's action was not based on imaginary but on real and desperate trouble.

When McNaughton met his military advisers on the morning of November 22 he still believed that he could secure sufficient reinforcements for his overseas army from volunteers among the home-defence draftees. He was staggered when his advisers laid before him a formal memorandum stating that the voluntary recruitment drive had failed and advising him to enforce conscription immediately. If the army commanders could no longer take responsibility for the existing policy no government could hope to maintain it, even as a fiction.

But the memorandum was the lesser half of that historic interview. The larger half was verbal and never recorded. It explains everything.

Having handed their written memorandum to McNaughton, the military officials added that if their recommendation were rejected they must résign forthwith. That was the "terrible news, the body blow" which McNaughton instantly communicated to King by telephone.

Both of them saw what it meant. If the Government continued to reject overseas conscription and if the highest officials of the army within Canada resigned, then the government would be destroyed in Parliament, but that, in King's judgment, would be the smallest consequence of a national explosion.

In the ensuing confusion and bitterness he believed, rightly or wrongly, that the nation's war effort would be damaged, perhaps fatally. He could not face those resignations. On the other hand, he dared not reveal the army officials' threat, at this critical moment in the war, lest it undermine the nation's faith in the government. No government could live if Parliament and people knew that it had come within an inch of losing the confidence and forcing the resignation of its military advisers.

That is why the great secret of King's life was shared with two men only—McNaughton and St. Laurent. Neither has revealed it to this day. Rather than break a confidence and perhaps reflect on his former chief, St. Laurent has preferred to let many people imagine that he was taken in and deceived by King's imagined trouble in the army, when St. Laurent knew how real that trouble had been.

But not long ago some of the army men who attended the critical meeting with McNaughton decided that it was time to give the Canadian people all the facts. They have therefore permitted me to answer herewith the question raised in my book. Unfortunately their revelation came too late to be incorporated in the text and is appended here as an inadequate postscript to the strangest story in the political record of Canada.

Index